Publish It on the Web!

Macintosh® Version

Publish It on the Web!

Macintosh® Version

Bryan Pfaffenberger
University of Virginia
Charlottesville, Virginia

AP PROFESSIONAL

Boston San Diego New York
London Sydney Tokyo Toronto

This book is printed on acid-free paper ∞

AP PROFESSIONAL
1300 Boylston Street, Chestnut Hill, MA 02167

An imprint of ACADEMIC PRESS, INC.
A Division of HARCOURT BRACE & COMPANY

United Kingdom Edition published by
ACADEMIC PRESS LIMITED
24–28 Oval Road, London NW1 7DX

Library of Congress Cataloging-in-Publication Data
Pfaffenberger, Bryan, 1949–
Publish it on the Web! / Bryan Pfaffenberger. -- Macintosh version.
p. cm.
Includes index.
ISBN 0-12-553143-5. -- ISBN 0-12-553144-3 (CD-ROM)
1. World Wide Web (Information retrieval system) I. Title.
TK5105.888.P426 1995
005.75--dc20 95-31982
CIP

Printed in the United States of America
95 96 97 98 IP 9 8 7 6 5 4 3 2 1

Contents

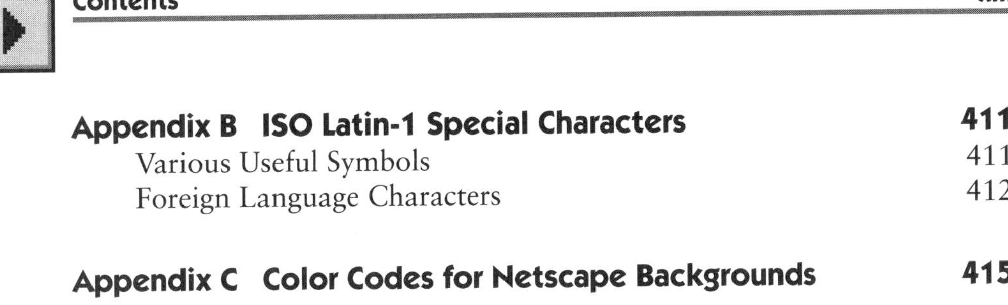

Introduction

In the space of just two short years, the World Wide Web has hit the big time. Growing far beyond its humble 1989 beginnings as an academic information system, the Web has become the medium of choice for just about everyone who wishes to make information available on the Internet.

Just how big is the Web? It's anyone's guess, but one recent estimate noted that the number of Web servers—programs capable of making documents available on the World Wide Web—is doubling every 53 days. And how many people are using the Web? Because the Web is winning out over all other means of accessing data on the Internet, the number of users out there will steadily grow until it approaches the total number of Internet users. A cautious estimate puts that number currently at 13.5 million—and it's doubling every year. According to Internet Index, everyone in the world will be hooked up to the Internet by 2004, if current growth rates continue. That's not going to happen, obviously—the growth curve will flatten when the Internet's market is saturated. Still, it's evident that the Internet, with the Web as its chosen user interface, is well on its way to becoming a mass publishing medium.

What kind of mass publishing medium is the Web going to be? One of the most amazing things about the Web is its democracy—the fact that anyone, ranging from an impoverished college student to a huge corporation, can put up a home page and publish something on the Web. This doesn't mean, of course, that a college student can gain a mass audience of millions of people. Most Web servers can handle only a few dozen simultaneous accesses, called *hits*, before overloading the systems on which they're housed. Servers designed to handle millions of hits per day are high-powered machines, beyond the means of most individuals and small businesses.

Still, the Web is one of the most revolutionary developments to have occurred in a century of communication innovations. What's so remarkable about the Web is that it's the first non-broadcast medium to reach a mass market. In a non-broadcast medium, a consumer of information can turn the tables and become the producer of information. And that's exactly what's happening on the Web. Of course, the Web isn't needed for ordinary individuals to publish information, as the existence of more than 75,000 newsletters attests. But the Web has a huge advantage over newsletters or any other do-it-yourself publishing medium: virtually zero distribution costs. Once you've obtained Internet access and equipped yourself with a reasonably powerful computer and server software, you're ready to publish on the Web and you're putting yourself in touch with an audience that's achieving significant penetration in the English-speaking world.*

Can I Publish on the Web?

Yes—anyone can publish on the Web. Here's a quick overview of your publishing options, and approximately what they'll cost you:

---

* If you're thinking of publishing in a language other than English, you should know that the Internet has a pronounced English tilt at the moment—but that's just an artifact of its birth in the United States. Already, there is significant Internet penetration in France and Germany, as attested by the rise of French- and German-language newsgroups on Usenet, a computer discussion system that's widely distributed via the Internet. Internet service availability is also picking up steam in Latin America, spearheaded by forward-looking Mexico.

- **Using a server on a computer at school or work** If the computer you're using at school or work has Internet access, it's possible you can publish on the Web for free. Just make sure that your publishing plans conform to your organization's acceptable use policies.
- **Renting space on your Internet service provider's computer** Many Internet service providers (organizations that provide Internet access) enable their customers to make their Web pages available, usually for a small monthly fee (typically $25).
- **Renting space on a Web publishing firm's computer** If your service provider doesn't enable you to publish on the Web, you can rent space from Web publishing firms—again, for as little as $25 per month. These firms can also provide assistance with Web page design.
- **Setting up your own server** Here, you obtain permanent Internet service—a costlier proposition than the dialup service you're probably using right now—and set aside a reasonably high-powered Macintosh or Power Macintosh for use as a Web server. You'll also need Web server software, which will cost you approximately $300 to $500. Soon, this option will become much less expensive than it is at present. Spreading rapidly throughout North America is digital telephone access via ISDN, which provides two high-speed (64,000 bits per second) lines for every subscription, currently averaging approximately $35 per month. This is sufficient information-carrying capacity (bandwidth) for a small- to medium-sized company or educational institution.

Make no mistake about it: It's easy and relatively inexpensive to publish on the Web, and its getting easier and cheaper all the time. If you're in business, you should know that your competition is already looking at the Web and evaluating its publishing options. The time to start thinking seriously about Web publishing is right now.

Who Should Read This Book?

This book is for anyone who wants to publish information on the World Wide Web. You don't need to have any previous experience with the Internet or the Web to understand this book. If you're already an experienced Web user, you can skip the introductory chapters and proceed to the more advanced material.

What's So Special about This Book?

If you're browsing at the bookstore, take a look at the other Web publishing and HTML books that are available. I'll bet they concentrate on the HTML code. That's fine—after all, it helps to know a little HTML even if you plan to let somebody else do all or most of the coding.

But these other books can't help you with the big picture. They're obsessed with the technical details. They don't tell you the one thing you really need to know: Considering the unique characteristics of the Web as a publishing medium, what should you publish? That's a very important question, and one that goes far beyond putting your HTML tags in the right order. As anyone who's worked in professional publishing can tell you, the first and most important step in any publishing effort is to frame your objective.

This is the first book on Web publishing that takes the Web seriously as a radically new publishing medium. Underlying this book is the philosophy that the most successful Web publications begin with a thorough understanding of the Web's technical basis, its novel characteristics as a publishing medium, and the changing demographics of the Web audience. You'll find all the HTML you'll need, to be sure. But you'll also find an approach to Web publishing that's unique among the books on this subject—and it's an approach that's designed to make you a winner in Web publishing.

There's one more thing about this book that makes it especially useful: It's designed specifically for users of Macintoshes and Power Macintoshes. In each chapter, the discussion, tips, and resources are focused squarely on the possibilities of Web publishing the Macintosh way. You'll also find a ton of useful software on the CD-ROM disc included with this book—but more about that in a minute.

How Is This Book Organized?

This book comprehensively presents all the information you'll need to embark on a serious Web publishing effort. You'll begin by fully understanding the technical basis of the Web and its unique characteristics as a publishing medium. You'll continue by planning your Web pages, using a time-proven publishing design system, and by learning enough HTML to meet your needs—and that could be very little indeed (Chapter 10 alone teaches everything you'd need to know to put together a decent Web page in short order).

Although this book isn't intended to turn you into a professional multimedia designer, it goes on to fill you in on the basics of producing sounds, graphics, and movies for your Web site. Finally, the book concludes by surveying the fast-breaking developments that will affect the Web's future—and yours, if you get involved in Web publishing.

Part I: The New Opportunities in Web Publishing

In this part of *Publish It on the Web*, you'll fully explore the technical basis of the World Wide Web and learn to grasp its radically new possibilities as a publishing medium. You'll learn how the Internet transmits information, and why it's spreading like wildfire all over the globe. You'll next explore the principles of hypertext (nonsequential writing) that provide the basic information-browsing metaphor for the Web. (In addition, you'll learn that the Web—or something very much like it—has actually been under conceptual and even technical development for almost 20 years.)

Next, you'll examine the Web protocols (standards) that make the Web workable as a worldwide information system, and you'll examine the Web's characteristics as a publishing medium (especially in contrast to broadcast media). Part I concludes with a survey of Web publishing possibilities and an examination of Web server software, which provides the technical basis for Web document distribution.

Part II: Planning Your Web

In any publishing effort, the first and most important steps are to frame your objective and know your audience. Part II begins by examining these steps in detail, and goes on to survey the possibilities for Web content design. It concludes with a useful survey of Web publishing Do's and Don'ts.

Part III: Creating Your Web

Part III delves into the nuts and bolts of HTML—but you may only need to read the first chapter, which presents everything you'll need to know to create and publish a nice-looking home page. If you'd like to learn more, Part III is rich in information—and what's more, it's tailored for the Macintosh environment. You'll learn how to exploit the incredible power of HTML Editor, the HTML publishing software that's included on this book's CD-ROM disc. You'll even learn how to implement clickable image maps, tables, forms, and multimedia, and—thanks to the cool software on this

book's CD-ROM disc—you won't have to learn how to do any computer programming to get these exciting interactive features to work.

Part IV: Producing Multimedia

This section thoroughly surveys subjects that almost all HTML books ignore: The specifics of what goes into the preparation of multimedia material for Web pages. Although Part IV can't tell you everything there is to know about preparing multimedia for the Web—each of these chapters could easily grow into a book of their own—you'll learn the basics of scanning, graphics production, sound recording, movie and animation production, and the use of Adobe Acrobat to prepare richly formatted documents for the Web. Like Part III, this part is tailored to the Macintosh environment—you'll learn how to use the top Macintosh programs for multimedia production.

Part V: Web Publishing Issues

As fast as the Web has grown, it's not surprising that some thorny issues have come along with the rapid growth. Who controls the Web's standards processes? What about copyright in an age of digital transmission? What do current technological developments mean for the Web's future as a publishing medium? These questions and more are addressed in Part V of this book.

Where Do I Start?

It depends on how much previous experience you've had with the Internet and the Web. If you're new to the Internet and the Web, start with Chapter 1. If you're a seasoned Internet vet but new to the Web, start with Chapter 2. Web-savvy readers should begin with Chapter 4, which surveys the Web's novel characteristics as a publishing medium.

If you'd just like to learn some quick HTML so you can get your page up in short order, don't miss Chapter 10—it's a great "quick start" and it may very well contain all the HTML you'll ever need. Don't miss the HTML Ultimate Cheat Sheet at the back of the book!

Special Features of This Book

As you're reading this book, you'll find the following icons, which are intended to point out helpful features:

You're sure to run into some roadblocks on your way to Web mastery. Look here for tips and strategies for overcoming common problems.

Look for the Treasure Trove icon for pointers to rich repositories of information and resources that are available on the Web—for free.

Look for the Webmaster icon for practical tips of value to anyone who's thinking about setting up a Web server.

What's on the CD-ROM Disc?

Think of this book's CD-ROM disc as a treasure house of tools and programs that you can use to build exciting Web pages. Here's a quick overview of what's included:

Icons	Hundreds of icons that you can include on your Web pages.
Buttons	Hundreds of buttons that you can use to add interactive navigation aids to your Web documents.
Rules	Hundreds of beautiful graphic rules that you can use in place of that plain old line that HTML draws across the screen.
Bullets	Hundreds of bullets to give visual appeal and zing to your lists.

Clip Art	Hundreds of public-domain clip art images that you can use to add a pictorial dimension to your Web presentations.
Backgrounds	Hundreds of background patterns that you can use to replace that boring old gray.
Programs	Included on the disc are shareware and demo versions of some of the hottest Macintosh Web publishing software available: HTML Editor (a great HTML editor that can cut down Web development time considerably), TR-WWW (an amazing program that enables you to create searchable databases of Web documents without doing any programming), NetForms and NetCloak (utterly, fabulously cool programs that enable you to set up amazing forms capabilities without any programming) and WebMap (a graphics editor that enables you to create clickable image maps—again, without requiring any programming).

A Word from the Author

Web publishing may seem overwhelming at first—there's so much to learn. But you can start small. Get going the Web way, by giving something back to this amazing network that's benefited us all so much. Surely there's something you know about that you can share—for instance, knowledge of a hobby or a place you enjoyed visiting. More seriously, maybe you've been through an experience that you'd like to share with others, such as an illness or a summer that you spent working with a social service organization. After putting your page on the Web, you'll soon find that people are starting to access it, and even to include hyperlinks to it on their own pages. Soon, you'll become aware of other people who have tried to accomplish much the same thing, and all the while your knowledge of the Web—and its amazing publishing possibilities—will grow by leaps and bounds.

If you're contemplating a Web presence for your organization, don't hesitate to get some professional assistance for your Web pages. After all, would you prepare your own advertisement for a published monthly magazine?

Unless you're a graphics and advertising genius, chances are it would look like an amateurish effort. The Web's no different.

I'd like to hear from you—tell me what you thought about this book, and please include any suggestions for material you'd like to see covered in subsequent editions. My e-mail address is bp@virginia.edu, and I try to answer every letter I receive. (If you don't get a reply right away, I might be on vacation for a week or two.) In the meantime, my best wishes for a successful publication venture on the Web!

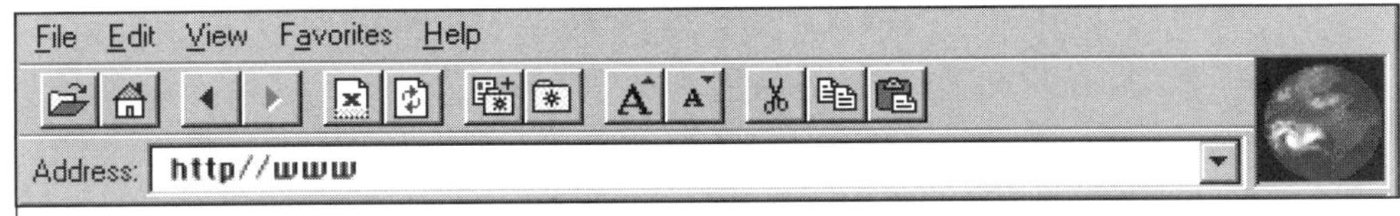

Part I

The New Opportunities in Web Publishing

Chapter 1

A Quick Introduction to the Internet

If you want to understand the Web and its possibilities for publication you'd best begin by grasping the Internet. The Internet provides the physical medium for the exchange of information on the Web. It has some characteristics that make it very much *unlike* other information-exchange networks, including other computer networks and (especially) the telephone system.

This chapter introduces the Internet, so it's good to read if you're just getting started with the Internet and the Web. Even if you're already familiar with the Internet's basic concepts, though, you should give this chapter a quick skim. The Internet can be broadly conceptualized as a publication medium, and it has many lessons to teach aspiring Webmasters. Remember, too, that the Web is based on the Internet, and many of the Web's peculiarities—again, from the publishing medium standpoint—are the peculiarities of the Internet in general.

For the Time-Challenged

- The Internet allows computers of differing makes and models to communicate and exchange data. That's one reason why it's so phenomenally popular.
- The Internet also permits one computer to control another one—for example, by telling it to find and send a file. This is called *interoperability.* Again, it doesn't matter if the two computers are of different makes and models.
- The Internet is unlike the phone system in that there's no distance-based billing. There's no cost for reaching out over long distances, beyond your monthly access fees. This encourages the formation of *translocal communities*—communities formed of people who know each other only through on-line contacts.
- Internet applications (electronic mail, mailing lists, FTP, Gopher, WAIS, Usenet, and Telnet) have shaped the way people view the Internet. Users know that they work together to build collective information pools. They are accustomed to getting valuable information and software for free or nearly so. They respect people who are considerate of others while on-line.
- Before the Web came along, the Internet was fairly difficult to use. Gopher broadened the Internet's user base by providing a user-friendly, menu-based interface to Internet resources. The Web also provides access to almost all Internet resources, but it adds multimedia and hypertext—two crucial ingredients that have fueled the Web's explosive growth.

What's the Internet?

Physically, the Internet consists of a variety of connecting media. The most basic connecting medium is a home computer linked by a telephone line and modem to an Internet service provider or an on-line service (such as CompuServe or the Microsoft Network).

Thousands of universities and corporations provide Internet access via local area networks (LANs), which connect dozens, hundreds, or even thousands of desktop computers. Spanning long distances are high-speed data communication networks of every conceivable variety, including densely packed telephone wires, microwave relay stations, fiber optical cables, and even satellites.

But just which wires or cables are used really doesn't matter. The incredible thing about the Internet is that it is more or less oblivious to the connecting media it's using—that's the reason it is so explosively, wildly, phenomenally popular!

It's the Protocols, Stupid

The Internet is the Esperanto of computers. On the Internet, any computer, of any make or brand, can "talk" with any other. Macintoshes can talk to Sun workstations. NeXT workstations can talk to PCs running Microsoft Windows.

The Internet isn't really a physical network. (Physically, it's made up of lots of different kinds of networks and individual computers, which are all linked together in just about every conceivable way.) The Internet is really a set of protocols (standards) by which dissimilar computers can exchange information.

Linked to the Internet are Macintosh users, people using Windows systems, engineers using Sun workstations, graphic artists using NeXT workstations, academics using IBM mainframe computers, and some kid using her dad's Toshiba laptop. And more!

If you've ever tried to swap disks with somebody using a different type of computer system, you'll appreciate just how cool the Internet really is. The Internet protocols (also called the TCP/IP protocols) break down the barriers between computers made by different manufacturers—barriers that in some cases were put there deliberately in an attempt to corner the computer market.

You don't really need to understand how this works—just take it on faith. When you equip your computer with Internet (TCP/IP) software, your computer suddenly knows how to package information so that it can be sent out over the Internet and be received and used by somebody with a completely different computer system.

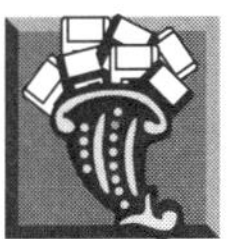

Information about the Internet
For more information on the Internet and Internet protocols, check out the well-organized Internet Protocols & Standards page at http://netlab.itd.nrl.navy.mil/Internet.html. This page includes a search engine that enables you to search for Internet-related terms.

The Magic of Interoperability

The Internet does more than merely allow various kinds of computers to talk to each other. It also allows them to *control* each other. (Scary, isn't it? Now you know why science fiction authors keep writing all those novels about computers getting together and taking over the Earth.)

One Internet computer can tell another, "Hear and obey. Send me the file named galactor.doc." If the receiving computer has been configured to respond to such requests, it coughs up the file and sends it to the requesting computer.

The ability of one Internet computer to control another, even if the other computer is made by a different manufacturer, is called *interoperability.*

Interoperability and Security

Interoperability is great, but it comes with obvious security risks. Sitting at my computer here in Virginia, I could link to your system, right on your desk—and if you hadn't configured it correctly, I could erase your entire hard disk while you watched, helpless to interfere! But that wouldn't be nice.

Kidding aside, security issues really are a problem on the Internet. That's why I'll recommend that you set aside a computer to use for Web publishing—do your important work, and carry on your business, with another machine.

There's very little risk involved in getting on the Internet and browsing the Web, unless you send personal information (such as credit card data) over an insecure link. The risks come only when you set up a server, allowing outsiders to control your computer. So for now, don't let security issues keep you from joining in the fun. Later, you'll learn how you can avoid security problems with servers, just by following a few simple rules.

Why the Internet Isn't Quite Like the Phone System

In one sense, the Internet is like a global telephone system for computers—it enables any two Internet-linked computers to establish a connection and exchange data. Right now, there are probably five to ten million computers that are directly connected to the Internet. Soon, there's going to be lots more.

Sitting here in the country in Earlysville, Virginia, I can link with computers in Taiwain, Sri Lanka, Norway, Belgium, France—and one right down the road.

Each of these computers has a unique Internet address, called an *IP address* (also called a *domain name*), that precisely and uniquely identifies the computer's location. An Internet-linked computer's IP address is like its telephone number.

But the telephone analogy is pretty misleading. For one thing, telephone call charges are based on distance billing. In theory, the longer the distance traversed by the call, the higher the fee. (In reality, it costs me more to call somebody in rural Virginia, two counties away, than it does to call my buddies in Hawaii, but that's because my regional telephone system and Genghis Khan have a lot in common.) That's not the way the Internet works. Once you pay your access fee and get on the Net, the cost of linking to a computer in Cucamonga is the same as linking to a computer in China.

Reach out and link to someone
From a marketing angle, the amazing thing about the Web is that your publications reach a national and even international audience with zero distribution costs, beyond your monthly access fees. But that doesn't mean the Web is less useful for publications with a local or regional audience, as long as there are sufficient numbers of Internet users around to make the effort worthwhile.

Internet Applications

As the Internet has developed and grown, people have found a number of different ways of using it, including electronic mail and other applications you've heard of, such as FTP and Gopher. Here's a brief overview of e-mail, FTP, Gopher, Usenet, and WAIS, in case you're not familiar with them. (The Web gets a whole chapter to itself, Chapter 3.)

Even if you are familiar with Internet applications, you might wish to read this section anyway. In keeping with this book's focus on publishing, each of these applications is examined as a *publication medium*—and as

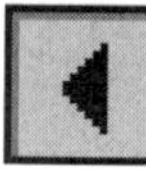

you'll see, there are some important clues about just what makes the Internet such a new and exciting medium for your publishing purposes.

Electronic Mail (E-mail) and Mailing Lists

By far the most popular Internet application is electronic mail. Because only a minimal Internet connection is needed for electronic mail, an estimated 45 million people can exchange e-mail via the Internet and associated networks.

E-mail isn't a publishing medium—you'd annoy people to no end if you bombarded their electronic mailboxes with advertisements. However, *mailing lists* employ e-mail to create a publication medium of sorts, and it's interesting (for our purposes in this book) to examine how it works.

To create a mailing list, you need a mailing list manager program, such as LISTSERV. People who subscribe to the mailing list send e-mail messages to the LISTSERV program, which makes copies of the messages and bounces them back to all the subscribers.

There are thousands of mailing lists on every conceivable subject. Many are publicly accessible, meaning that you can join them just by sending a "subscribe" message to the manager program. You can find the addresses of these programs in Internet reference books, and there are a number of online lists that are periodically posted on Usenet.

One of the most interesting things about mailing lists is that they form online communities. Even though the participants may have never physically met, they develop warm, personal relationships. More than a few of them have blossomed into Real Life friendships and, yes, romance and marriage.

Internet Communities

People using the Internet want to contribute something—they want to give something of themselves and see it added into a group product of which they can be proud. They want to *join*, too: They want to be part of a community that shares their values and interests. In later chapters, we'll see how some of the most successful Web publication ventures have made very intelligent use of these facts.

FTP

FTP is short for File Transfer Protocol, which pretty much describes what it does. Using FTP, you can exchange program or text files with anyone connected to the Internet.

You can't just browse around in anyone's computer in search of files. Normally, you need an account and a password to access someone else's computer on the Internet. But some kind souls have created *publicly accessible file archives*. This is also called "anonymous FTP," since you have to log into these computers as "anonymous" when you are using an FTP program.

What do people do with FTP? Many organizations use them to exchange information. As for anonymous FTP, it's become the de facto headquarters for the distribution of *freeware* (a copyrighted program that is made freely available for noncommercial use) and *shareware* (a program that you can preview for free, but which requires a registration fee if you want to continue using it).

The Freebie Lure

People are used to getting things for free on the Internet. The availability of more than 100,000 freebie programs has habituated your audience to getting something for nothing.

This doesn't mean that the Internet is useless for commercial enterprises, but it does mean that people browsing your Web site will expect to get some kind of freebie out of it—some useful information, maybe a file or program, or a neat graphic. As you'll see later in this book, the most successful Web publication efforts are those that provide free goodies.

Gopher

A menu-driven information system, Gopher had its origin as a campus-wide information system at the University of Minnesota, the mascot of which is—you guessed it—a gopher. It enables people to access all kinds of different information with the same easy menu-based browsing system. Those nice University of Minnesota folks made the program freely available, and what do you know? Colleges and universities everywhere used Gopher to make information available. A few private organizations did, too.

Before the Web came along, Gopher was the Latest Best Thing for accessing Internet resources, and it grew wildly. Just by browsing easy-to-use Gopher menus, you can access all kinds of Internet resources, including text documents, FTP file archives, Telnet sessions, and more. But the Web's success has choked off Gopher's growth. Still, there are lots of useful resources available in Gopher menus, mainly because people haven't had the time to put them on the Web yet.

Ease of Use + Multimedia = Phenomenal Growth

Gopher is easy to use, but its text-only interface wasn't sufficiently sexy to fuel an explosion of Internet usage. Moreover, menus are tedious, forcing information browsers into a rigid, hierarchical means of organizing information. The Web solves both problems by providing tightly integrated graphics, sounds, and videos, and by employing hypertext as the vehicle for information browsing. The next chapter presents the basic principles of hypertext and shows why hypertext provides such an appealing means of organizing Internet resources.

Usenet

Usenet is a computer-based discussion system that's widely distributed on the Internet. When you log on to Usenet, you're confronted with a list of several *thousand* topically named discussion groups, each of which contains—at any one moment in time—anywhere from a few to a few hundred messages, called *articles*. These articles are contributed by upwards of seven million Usenet users worldwide.

One of Usenet's worst problems is its own success. Every day, Usenet contributors post the equivalent of 80,000 pages of text—the days are long gone, obviously, when anyone could hope to read all or most of the newsgroups. Most people follow just one or two of them and ignore the rest—but even so, many newsgroups receive dozens or hundreds of messages per day.

Viewed as a communications medium, Usenet has remarkably low *latency* (the time that messages stick around). Due to limitations on storage space, Usenet administrators often find it necessary to delete articles after only a few days of availability. And once they're gone, they're gone forever. (A few newsgroups maintain archives of past articles, but only a few do this.)

The idea underlying Usenet is devilishly clever: The Usenet software works behind the scenes, copying and relaying the messages users contribute, so that in time every participating computer (called a *Usenet site*) has an exact copy of every message contributed to the network. The software knows how to organize these messages into topical categories, called *newsgroups*, which you can read. In addition, you can contribute your own messages to these newsgroups.

There's no formal central governing authority with the power to regulate Usenet, and as a result Usenet is much plagued by antisocial behaviors, such as *flaming* (posting angry messages filled with name-calling), *carpet-bombing* (pelting hundreds or thousands of newsgroups with advertisements that

are totally irrelevant to the newsgroup's topic), and *trolling* (posting obviously false information in the hope of making somebody appear foolish by pointing out the mistake).

As a result of this antisocial behavior, Usenet participants have developed a set of informal rules, called *netiquette*, that they feel very strongly about. Netiquette basically boils down to being very considerate of other peoples' feelings on-line.

What webmasters need to know about netiquette
Internet users do *not* like to have blatantly self-promoting material thrown in their faces. This makes them *very* angry. The Web is less of a problem here, since blatantly self-promoting document titles aren't thrown in the faces of thousands of unwilling readers. Even so, you'd be well advised to soft-pedal the promotion. Many, if not most, Usenet users believe that Usenet netiquette should be extended to the whole Internet.

Internet users respect and value people who make a special effort to be as considerate as possible of other peoples' feelings while on-line. Your Web pages should reflect the same consideration.

Telnet

Some computers cannot connect to the Internet. Among the worst offenders are IBM mainframe computers, which don't speak the same "language" that most other computers do. In addition to mainframe computers, the roster of Telnet sites includes thousands of bulletin board systems (BBSs) all over the world, and a good sprinkling of freenets (community information services). All in all, there's a lot of interesting stuff out there, as long as you're willing to forgo multimedia—Telnet is strictly text-only.

Telnet ranks far below e-mail, FTP, and Usenet in popularity, but it does have its devotees—and once again, the reason is the availability of freebie information, including the on-line catalogs of dozens of the world's leading universities.

WAIS

Short for Wide Area Information Server, WAIS is a program that indexes a collection of text documents and produces an index listing *all* the words these documents contain.

When you perform a keyword search using the WAIS search engine, the software will retrieve any document that contains the keyword for which you're looking, even if the word is used peripherally in the document.

WAIS is the least popular of all the Internet applications. And there's a very good reason. Long experience in the on-line industry proves that people just don't like searching for information using keywords. They have a lot of trouble understanding the basic search concepts—and with good reason. Done any Boolean searching lately, and how about those substrings! (Huh?)

Keyword searching isn't a mass-market technology
Keyword searches of databases will continue to be used by librarians and information professionals, as well as by power computer users who have become familiar with the basic concepts, but it's just not going to wash as a mass medium. Although keyword searches can be implemented on Web pages, and there's often a very good reason for doing so, it's not a good idea to rely upon such searches as the only way of providing information.

If the Internet Is So Great, Why Didn't It Catch on Sooner?

It was too hard to use.

FTP, Telnet, and WAIS require substantial computer smarts and at least some knowledge of how the Internet works. Internet usage started to grow much faster when Gopher became available—and there's a lesson to be learned there. Gopher doesn't only provide easy-to-use menu access to Gopher documents; it also provides a *unified* interface to other Internet resources as well, including FTP file archives, Telnet sessions, and WAIS databases.

Gopher was a move in the right direction, but it still locks you into a text-only interface. The Web gives you multimedia. It gives you access to almost all the resources of the Internet, including FTP, WAIS, Telnet, and Gopher. What's more, it gives you an easy-to-use method of browsing Web resources, based on *hypertext*. The Web is the Internet's killer application. The next two chapters explain what the Web's all about and help you to understand the Web as a publication medium.

FROM HERE

- To publish successfully on the Web, you need to fully understand the concept of hypertext. Check out the next chapter for a complete explanation, in plain simple English.
- You don't need an electrical engineering degree to publish on the Web, but it helps to understand a little about how it works. In Chapter 3, you'll find a thorough explanation of the Web's three fundamental acronyms: HTTP, URL, and HTML.

Chapter 2

Understanding Hypertext

When you publish on the Web, you're publishing in a hypertext medium. Succinctly defined, the Web is a global hypertext system that employs the Internet as its physical medium. Actually, the Web is a *hypermedia* system, one that organizes resources using hypertext but which incorporates multimedia, including graphics, movies, and sounds.

Hypertext is unfamiliar to most people; it isn't taught in high-school English classes (although it soon will be). Due to this lack of familiarity, most of the people now creating Web pages do not fully understand the basic principles of hypertext. That doesn't stop them from putting material on the Web, and sometimes very good material. Still, the most effective Web presentations show full awareness of hypertext principles.

This chapter introduces the basic principles of hypertext, which are very easy to learn. After reading it, you'll know more about the hypertext spirit

than most of the people putting up pages on the Web right now. And you'll also know why the Web has some serious deficiencies as a medium for mass publication.

For the Time-Challenged

- Hypertext is a form of nonsequential writing in which the text of a document is broken down into conceptual chunks. These chunks are then interlinked in a way that permits the reader to access the material in any way he or she pleases. Theodore Holm Nelson first envisioned hypertext in 1965.
- Some hypertexts contain just one document. Usually, they contain a welcome page (also called a home page) and a number of linked documents, called a *web*.
- A good welcome page lists the available chunks in a web, in decreasing order of importance.
- To aid browsers in navigating a web, thoughtful authors include navigation buttons.
- Hypertext systems on standalone computers are time-consuming to create and maintain. A computer network provides the ideal platform for hypertext because the responsibility of creating and maintaining it can be distributed among thousands or even millions of users.
- In a network-based hypertext system, synergy occurs as authors build on the achievements of other authors. You don't have to reinvent the wheel; you can link to documents that other authors have already contributed.
- In a network-based hypertext system, the boundaries between authors and readers break down. Readers become authors by incorporating documents that link to existing texts.
- Nelson's idea of a global hypertext system, called Xanadu, preserves intellectual property rights and grants royalties to authors who publish on the system. The Web's rapid growth vindicates Nelson's conviction that a mass market exists for a networked hypertext system. The Web's deficiencies in protecting intellectual property rights, discussed in the next chapter, also vindicate Nelson's ideas concerning the preservation of intellectual property rights in such a system.

WHAT IS HYPERTEXT?

In 1965, a computer visionary named Theodore Holm ("Ted") Nelson coined the term *hypertext* and described it as the way virtually everyone would write in the future. Nelson says it's simply *nonsequential writing*. Regarding hypertext, Nelson has this to say:

> Ordinary writing is sequential for two reasons. First, it grew out of speech and speech-making, which have to be sequential; and second, because books are not convenient to read except in a sequence. But the structures of ideas are not sequential. They tie together every which-way (Ted Nelson, *Computer Lib/Dream Machines*, rev. ed. [Redmond, Washington: Tempus Books of Microsoft Press, 1987], p. 29).

By this, Nelson doesn't mean that a hypertext is a jumble, all out of order. Rather, a hypertext consists of various *chunks* of text. To prepare a hypertext, you break down all the information you want to present into manageable chunks and then let the reader pick his or her way through the chunks.

For example, suppose you want to present some information about North Carolina's Outer Banks. In no particular order, here are some chunks that came to mind as I was thinking about this subject:

Ecology
Lighthouses
Barrier reefs
Hurricanes and Nor'easters
Vacation rental properties
Investment in vacation rental properties
Beaches
Shopping
Shipwrecks
Windsurfing
Restaurants
The Nature Conservancy
Kayaking

What interests you? (Um, I'm starving and sunburned, I think I'll check out "restaurants.") The neat thing about hypertext is that you can quickly

select the topic in which you're interested. A hypertext is organized so that you can pick your own way through the chunks, without necessarily having to follow a sequence dictated by the author. (Note: In Nelson's terminology, each chunk is called a *node*, although terms such as *page*, *card*, and *document* are used synonymously. I prefer *chunk*.)

"I can't let go of my authorial authority!"
This is the biggest problem people run into in writing hypertext effectively. Take the Outer Banks example just mentioned. I'd love to give you a big lecture about the Outer Banks' fragile ecology and the need to protect the barrier islands from overdevelopment. But maybe you're interested in shopping, or just hanging out on the beach. To create an effective Outer Banks hypertext, I've got to let go of my authorial impulse to organize all the material around a theme, like ecology. I must chunk the information and let you, the reader, decide what, if anything, you want to read. I'll put a chunk in about the ecology; it's there if you'd like to read it, but it's *up to you* whether you read it or not. Giving the reader permission to make his or her own decisions is tough for some authors.

What's a good chunk? It's up to you, but the general rule is the smaller the better. For Web presentations, an effective chunk is one screenful of text. (This rule shouldn't be taken so literally that it forbids longer pages; it's just a rule of thumb.)

The chunks of a hypertext are linked by *anchors*, which are underlined (and often shown in a distinctive color) so that you can tell them from ordinary text. (There are two synonyms for anchor: You can also say *hyperlink* or just *link*. Sorry the terminology is so confusing, but that's what happens when you let computer people run around unmuzzled.) Links are put in by people.

You can't really do hypertext in a printed book. You'd have to flip repeatedly to the page where the linked document appears—and that would be very tedious. But the computer is a natural for hypertext. It does the flipping for you. In most compter-based hypertext systems, you activate a link by pointing to it with the mouse and clicking. The computer then displays the requested page.

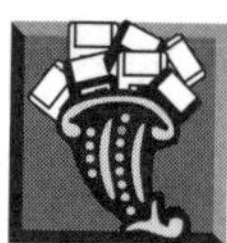

The Hypertext FAQ
The ultimate hypertext information repository is The Hypertext FAQ, accessible at

http://www.eit.com/reports/ht93/hypertext.faq.txt

Understanding Hypertext: An Example

It's hard to convey the look and feel of hypertext in a printed book like this. But let's take a stab.

A hypertext document usually begins with an overview document, called a *welcome page* or a *home page*, such as the following. Note the anchors (links):

> The term **anime** refers to an impressive Japanese tradition of cartoon animation. Based on comic books called **manga**, anime TV shows, videos, and movies attract a wide audience in Japan, where adults as well as children join in the fun. In subtitled **videotapes** and **laserdiscs**, anime is increasingly available in the United States. Try looking for titles such as Akira or Bubblegum Crisis at your **local video store**. For an example of the best in anime, look for **My Neighbor Totoro**, a wonderful children's film that the whole family will enjoy. If you'd like to know more about anime, check out this **more detailed introduction** and read the **reviews** of popular anime films.

To activate one of the anchors, you move the mouse pointer to the anchor and click. Presto! The computer displays the document you want to see.

Suppose you click "My Neighbor Totoro." Here's what you'll see:

> **My Neighbor Totoro**
>
> In this magical film, an artist's heartfelt tribute to the beauty and the customs of the traditional (but disappearing) Japanese countryside, Hayao **Miyazaki** tells the story of two children who discover a magical being, Totoro. Visible only to children, Totoro lives within the base of a gigantic, beautiful camphor tree. The older of the two children, Satsuke, calls upon Totoro's aid in finding her sister, Mei, who become lost while trying to visit her hospitalized mother. Roger Ebert, one of the thumbs in the famed Siskel & Ebert duo, says "Very few films come along that are magical for all ages and are wholesome, sane, intelligent, and entertaining. 'My Neighbor Totoro' is one of them." The film is available in an excellent English dub from **Fox Video**.

As this example illustrates, you're not tied to the author's idea of how you should read the material. You can choose your own path, just as your interests dictate.

Notice that there are additional anchors on the "My Neighbor Totoro" page: The "Miyazaki" anchor tells you more about this talented animator, while the "Fox Video" anchor tells you more about how to order this videotape.

A good hypertext system provides lots of links and cross-links and new links and who-knows-where-you'll-wind-up links. It invites exploration, adventure, play, learning. Hypertext is *fun.*

What's *Hyper* about *Hypertext?*

Some of the most useful 20th-century technologies have their origins in the work of obscure 19th-century mathematicians. Every time you use a computer, you ought to thank George Boole (1815–1864), an English mathematician who invented the binary logic that underlies today's computer designs. And every time you use the World Wide Web, you ought to thank the German mathematician Felix Christian Klein (1849–1925).

What was Klein's contribution? Working in geometry, and going against all common sense, Klein conceived a geometry of what he called "hyperbolick space" (or just *hyperspace*)—a space with many more dimensions than the four we're used to (height, width, depth, and time). In fact, hyperbolic space consists of all the possible dimensions that can be constructed mathematically—lots more than four!

Klein's conception of hyperbolic space inspired hypertext visionary Ted Nelson to ask, "What is the hyperspace of a document?" Just as Klein broke down a given area into all its possible mathematical dimensions, Nelson took a document and broke it down into all the *concepts* it contained.

The conceptual hyperspace of the preceding paragraph, for example, would include *Klein, hyperbolic space, Nelson, Klein's methods*, and *Nelson's methods*. In a hypertext system, a document is broken down into a series of documents, each focusing on one of the concepts.

Welcome to My Web

A really good hypertext system contains lots of links—the more, the merrier. The result is a collection of interlinked documents that enable you to navigate through them in dozens or even hundreds of different ways. This is called a *web*.

Figure 2.1 shows the spiderweb-like appearance of a number of documents that are connected in a web. The lines indicate what the links do in each document. Note that there are multiple pathways through the web.

Many webs begin with a welcome page that succinctly lists the available topics. For an example, take a look at the University of Virginia's welcome page (http://www.virginia.edu/), shown in Figure 2.2.

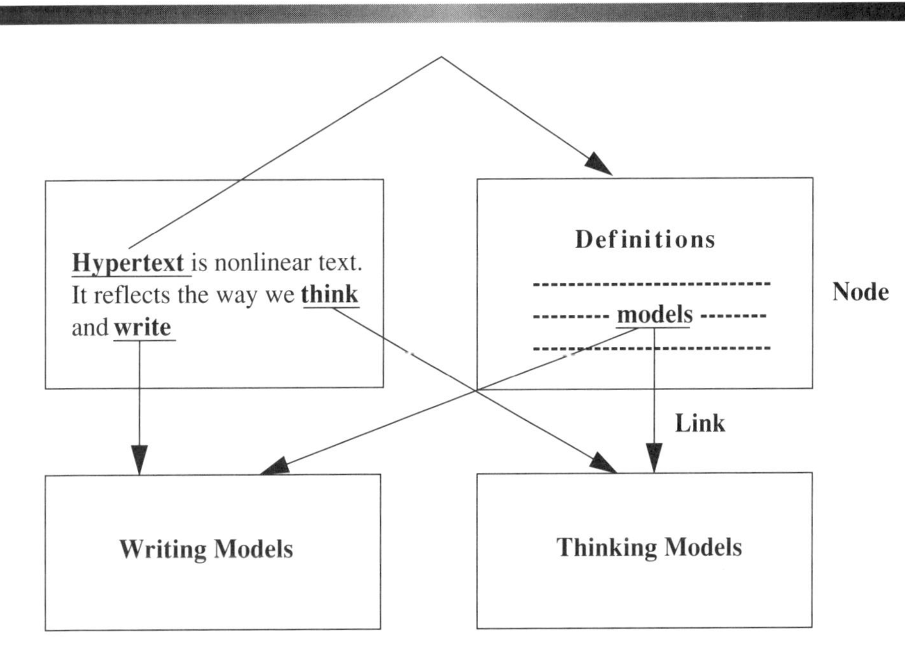

Figure 2.1 Nodes and links in a web. (From V. Balasubramaniam, "State of the Art Review on Hypermedia Issues and Applications," http://www.isg.sfu.ca/~duchier/misc/hypertext_review/index.html.)

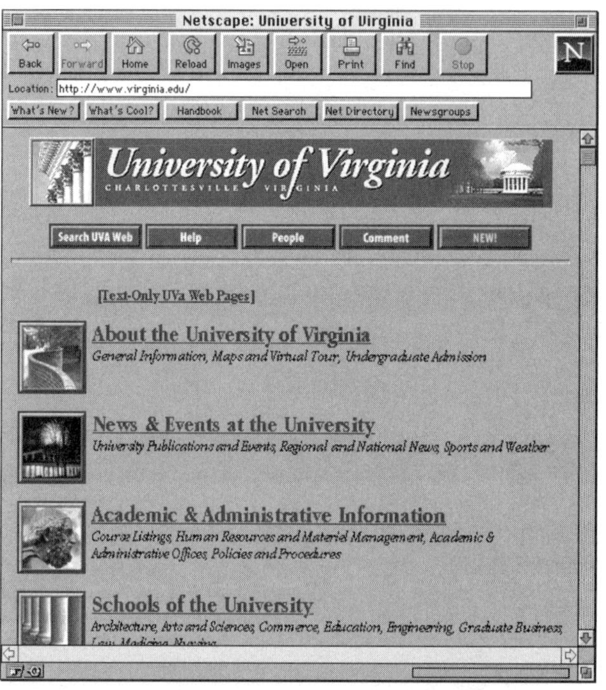

Figure 2.2 University of Virginia welcome page

Creating an Effective Welcome Page
Ask yourself, "What do the people accessing my page really want to know?" Write down the topics that you think would interest them. Then, put them *in order of decreasing importance*—the first link on the list should be the topic of greatest importance to most of your readers. Check out Figure 2.2—UVa's welcome page does a nice job of this.

Help! I'm Lost!

The wonderful thing about hypertext is that you can choose your own way of navigating through the material from dozens or even hundreds of options. That's also the bad thing about hypertext. It's easy to get lost!

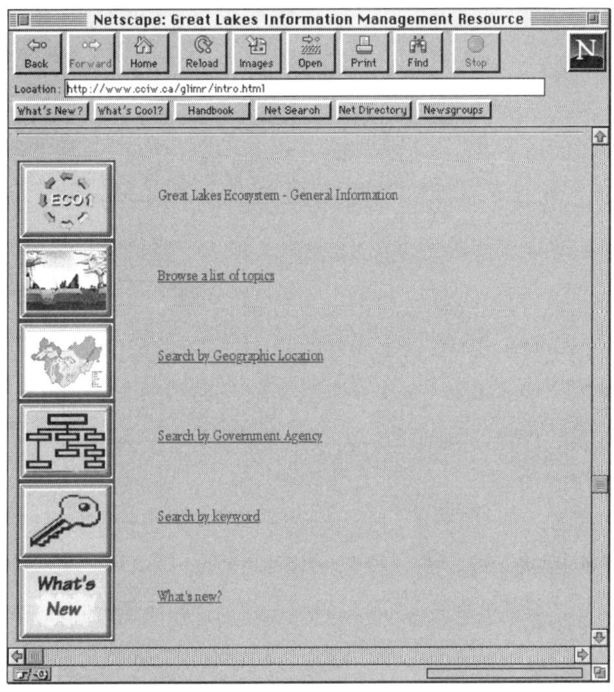

Figure 2.3 Navigation buttons

Helpful web authors include *navigation buttons*. Minimally, these buttons include a Home button, which lets you go back to the introductory (top level) document. Figure 2.3 shows the navigation buttons used in the Great Lakes Information Management Resource (http://www.cciw.ca/glimr/intro.html).

Is Hypertext Suitable for All Kinds of Documents?

Hypertext is beautifully suited to any written work in which the material can be broken down into chunks and navigated in the order that the reader prefers. Many kinds of documents are immediately and obviously suited to hypertext, including employee handbooks, catalogs, archives of technical

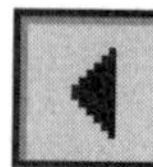

documentation, and much more. But hypertext isn't so hot for fiction, in which sequence really counts. If you found out too soon that Darth Vader is really Luke's father, it sort of spoils the fun. (That said, people are experimenting with hypertext stories that enable you to choose your own plot!)

Hypertext Fiction
Check out the following page for an introduction to the possibilities of hypertext fiction:

http://www.duke.edu/~mshumate/hyperfic.html

If this subject intrigues you, join the hypertext lit (ht lit) mailing list (http://www.eng.carleton.ca/~kmennie/ht_lit.html). To subscribe, send e-mail to subscribe@journal.biology.carleton.ca with "subscribe ht_lit" in the body of the message.

For scholars, hypertext provides a wonderful way to annotate literary texts. For a sample, check out the annotated version of Doyle's "The Adventure of the Speckled Band":

http://www.seas.upenn.edu/~dlelong/band.html

Remember, though, that a hypertext system can include ordinary, sequential documents. Here's an example of an opening page of a hypertext system containing ordinary (that is, sequential) short stories:

Short Stories

Welcome to the Short Story Page! Here you'll find short stories written by students in Green Valley University's extension writing program. There are plenty of stories with **science fiction** and **fantasy themes**, a student (and faculty) favorite. You'll also find some chilling **ghost stories**. **Local myths and legends** are favorite subjects of our students, many of whom come from families that have lived and farmed Green Valley for more than two hundred years.

If you click "ghost stories," you'll see this page:

Ghost Stories

There's something spooky about Green Valley—as you'll surely agree after reading some of these! Click on one of the titles to see and read a story.

```
Alice Bates, "Spirits of the Night"

Karen Sawyer, "Secrets of Dark Water"

Jim Tantzakis, "The Unbroken Brooch"
```

Clicking one of these anchors brings up an ordinary, sequential document.

In sum, hypertext provides a nonsequential method of navigating through all kinds of information, including types of information that can't be broken down into hypertext documents themselves.

What Is Hypermedia?

Hypermedia is more than the addition of multimedia (sounds, pictures, and movies) to hypertext documents. Far more than mere windows dressing (pardon the pun), it's the use of multimedia as an integral part of the presentation.

By this standard, there are relatively few hypermedia documents, but there are millions of hypertext documents with pretty pictures.

Figure 2.4 shows what true hypermedia looks like. It's the Virtual Frog Dissection Kit, available at http://george.lbl.gov/ITG.hm.pg.docs/dissect/dissect.html. Try it!

Toward a Global Hypertext System (Xanadu)

Nelson first advocated hypertext in 1965. And for a long time, very few people listened. As Nelson beat the hypertext drum, a few hypertext programs were developed, mostly as experiments in instructional technology (yawn). The concept gained wider notice with the mid-1980s release of HyperCard, a file card program (loosely based on hypertext principles) that was included free with every Macintosh computer.

But Nelson saw a much bigger future for hypertext. He didn't see hypertext as a program running on a single computer. Instead, he envisioned a global hypertext system, linking millions of networked computers. Nelson called this system Xanadu, using the name of a magical place described in Coleridge's mystical poem "Kubla Khan."

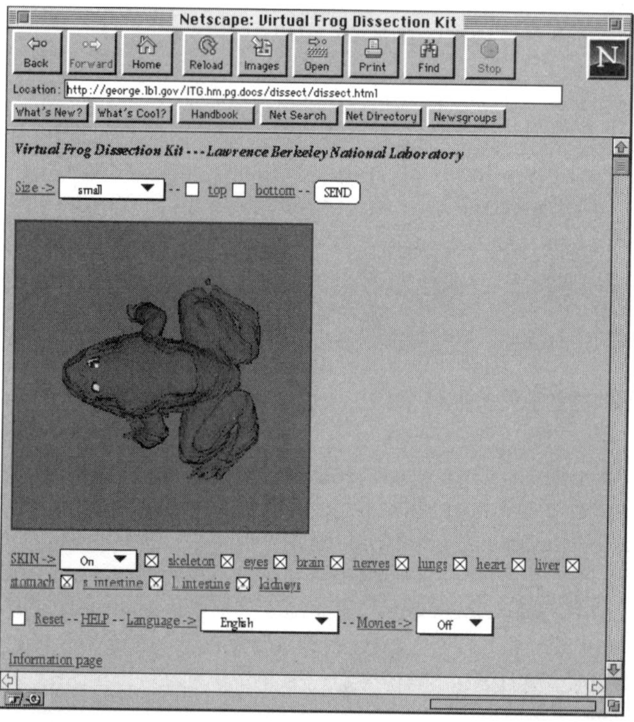

Figure 2.4 Virtual Frog Dissection Kit (http://george.lbl.gov/ITG.hm.pg.docs/dissect/dissect.html)

Nelson has received a great deal of recognition for inventing hypertext, but precious little for envisioning Xanadu. Yet, as you will see in the following paragraphs and the chapter to follow, the way the World Wide Web has developed amounts to nothing less than a total vindication of Nelson's vision. What the Web has become shows that Nelson's vision can excite the imagination of millions. And what the Web lacks shows the need for something very much like Xanadu.

A Brief History of Xanadu

Part of the reason Nelson hasn't received much recognition for Xanadu is that it doesn't exist. His book *Literary Machines*, first published in 1981, describes the features of Xanadu. As initially envisioned, Xanadu would

consist of millions of computers, all of them running Xanadu software and linked via modems to regional file servers, which would retrieve documents on request. Nelson did not foresee the Internet.

After working on various prototypes of hypertext software from the period 1960 to 1979, Nelson formed the Xanadu Operating Company, Inc., in 1983. The company was formed to implement the design of Xanadu, as specified in *Literary Machines*.

In 1988, the company was purchased by AutoDesk, publishers of computer-aided design (CAD) software. However, AutoDesk dropped the Xanadu project in 1992 after a new, cost-conscious management team took over the company.

In 1993, Nelson departed for Japan, where he continues work on Xanadu in what he claims to be a more supportive environment.

The Ultimate Xanadu Site
For (a lot) more information on Xanadu, including Nelson's latest writings and opinions, check out http://sensemedia.net/850.

Explorations in Synergy, or, Breaking Down the Author/Reader Distinction

Why did Nelson envision a global hypertext system based on a network of millions of computers? In a word, *synergy*. It's a big job to create an information-rich hypertext system all by oneself. By implementing hypertext on a computer network and encouraging many people to build on what's already there, the system can grow by leaps and bounds. That's synergy—the extra value that occurs when people cooperate instead of working alone.

Let's say you're putting together a document on the history and geography of the Eastern Shore of Virginia, an ecologically and culturally interesting place. As you browse the networked hypertext system, used by millions, you find that many other people have contributed information regarding the Eastern Shore.

Rather than duplicating their efforts, you build on it by including hyperlinks to their documents in your own work. In a networked hypertext system, everyone would be potentially both a consumer *and* a producer of information. And no document would ever exist by itself; it would be linked to, built on, summarized, and otherwise manipulated by readers who are themselves producing information on the system.

Because Xanadu breaks down the distinction between authors and readers, it is far more democratic than any previous publication medium. Authors and readers are considered to be equal. What is more, any author who places a document in Xanadu must concede to others the right to reference that document, to link to it, to comment upon it, to summarize it, and in any other way to use it as a platform for building and extending the database of Xanadu documents—or, as Nelson calls it, the *docuverse*.

Xanadu as a Publication Medium

Although Xanadu radically equalizes the balance between authors and readers, it fully preserves the notion of copyright and includes mechanisms to compensate authors for the use of their documents.

Every time a document is accessed and read by means of a hyperlink, the author would receive a royalty—only a fraction of a cent, to be sure, but fractions of a cent mount up quickly when a document is referenced thousands or millions of times. As Nelson points out, you can sell a few thousand books for $24.95 (with $1 author royalty after all the middlemen take their cut) or have many thousands of readers, maybe millions, on Xanadu, and make the same amount of money. Or more! (If authors wish, they can make their documents available for free.) And anyone who actually downloads or prints the document would have to pay a higher fee.

Advanced features of Xanadu would give authors the right to charge varying fees for different parts of a document. Suppose that Samantha writes a book-long document. She could decide that the abstract will be free, enabling readers to find out what's in her document, but that Chapter 2, which contains a sophisticated data analysis, will be charged at a higher rate than the rest of the document.

What happens when I create a document that includes linked portions from other peoples' work? Suppose, for example, I create a document in which I use Samantha's Chapter 2 instead of writing my own chapter. When people read my document, Xanadu automatically credits part of the royalties to Samantha.

The Inevitability of a Global Hypertext System

Nelson became convinced—correctly, it turns out—that the idea of a global hypertext system is so attractive, and so useful to so many people, that the development of such a system was inevitable. Writing in 1981, Nelson said:

> Forty years from now (if the human species survives) there will be hundreds of thousands of file servers—machines storing and dishing out [hypertext] materials. And there will be hundreds of millions of simultaneous users, able to read from billions of stored documents, with trillions of links among them. All of this is manifest destiny. There is no point in arguing it; either you see it or you don't. Many readers will choke and fling down [this] book, only to have the thought gnaw at them gradually until they see its inevitability.

The meteoric rise of the World Wide Web vindicates Nelson's vision. As you will see in the next chapter, the Web perfectly embodies Nelson's vision of a global hypertext system fueled by synergy, in which the distinction between authors and readers breaks down. What it also vindicates is Nelson's fully developed vision of how intellectual property rights could be protected in such a system. And as you will see in the next chapter, that's where the Web is sadly deficient.

From Here

- As an aspiring Web publisher, you need to understand that the Web has a built-in bias toward academic, nonprofit publication. You also need to understand how the Web implements Nelson's hypertext ideas within the Internet medium. The next chapter gives you the lowdown on both points.

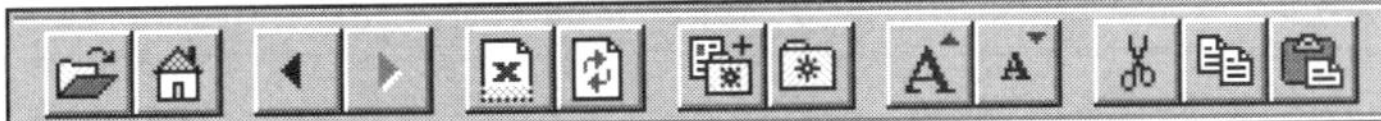

Chapter 3

Introducing the World Wide Web

"A good scientist," says physicist Freeman Dyson, "is a person with original ideas." But a good engineer "is a person with as few original ideas as possible." There is no single quotation that so compellingly sums up the engineering that went into the creation of the World Wide Web (WWW). Basically, the Web drew on four existing ideas: the Internet (Chapter 1), Ted Nelson's conception of a network-based hypertext system (Chapter 2), the idea of workstation-based client programs that interact with server programs capable of dishing out data, and the concept of a *markup language*, which enables Web users to see nicely formatted documents that don't consume a lot of network bandwidth.

This chapter shows how the marriage of these four ideas led to the two fundamental concepts of the Web: the HyperText Transport Protocol

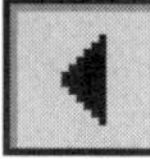

(HTTP) with its concept of Universal Resource Identifiers (URI), and the HyperText Markup Language (HTML). All of these thorny acronyms are fully introduced in this chapter, with particular attention to their implications for Web publication.

But this chapter makes another important point. Unlike Ted Nelson's Xanadu, discussed in the previous chapter, the Web includes no technical means for compensating authors for the appropriation of their intellectual property. The reason is very simple: The Web was born in an academic environment, and incorporates academic values about publication. Any would-be Web publisher needs to fully understand these values—and recognize that, as yet, there's no convenient way of charging people for information they access on the Web.

"A Culture of Distributed Computing": CERN and the Development of the Web

Not far from Geneva, Switzerland is one of Europe's leading scientific think tanks, the European Laboratory for Particle Physics. Known by the acronym of its French name (Conseil Europeen pour la Recherche Nucleaire), this lab—called CERN—is the birthplace of the World Wide Web.

Like academic think tanks elsewhere, CERN has some permanent researchers, but most of its scientists visit there on one- or two-year fellowships. These researchers, called fellows, need to keep in contact with local researchers during their visit, as well as colleagues posted at universities worldwide. And after the fellows leave, they need to keep in contact with CERN so that they can keep abreast of fast-breaking developments there.

Understanding their fellows' need for local and long-distance collaboration, the CERN computer services staff see computer networks as a communication medium as well as a means of sharing programs and data. In the early 1980s, CERN experimented with a variety of computer networks, both local area networks (LAN) and wide-area networks (WAN). When CERN staff learned of the Internet, they knew almost immediately that it held the answer to their fellows' collaboration difficulties. By 1988, CERN had established a link to the Internet and, by 1990, became the largest Internet site in Europe.

For the Time-Challenged

- The Web was born in a European think tank (CERN), where computer specialists were searching for ways to enable widely scattered physics researchers to work with reports, notes, databases, computer documentation, and computer help files. Since these researchers used a variety of different computers, the Internet seemed ideally suited. Hypertext promised to provide an easy-to-use mechanism by which these researchers could browse through and obtain the resources they needed.
- The Web is based on a client/server model. You run a program called a client on your computer. Under your direction, this program originates requests for information, which are received by server programs running on some other computer. The server program coughs up the requested data, and the client displays it. On the Web, clients are called *browsers*.
- CERN's greatest accomplishment was the HyperText Transport Protocol (HTTP), which specifies how a Web client requests information from a Web server. This is done by means of a Universal Resource Locator (URL), which precisely specifies the location of the requested information.
- So that the requested documents will look pretty on-screen, the Web development team at CERN added the HyperText Markup Language (HTML) to the emerging Web cocktail. HTML enables people using the Web to see richly formatted documents, replete with nice-looking fonts, emphasis, and text alignment, without requiring all that bulky formatting information to be conveyed over the Internet. With HTML, a Web author tags the parts of a document, such as headings, body text, and extended quotations. The Web browser reads the HTML tags and displays the document using all the font and graphics resources of the user's workstation or PC.
- The first successful graphic browser, NCSA Mosaic, was developed at another think tank, the National Center for Supercomputing Applications (NCSA). It, too, was designed for nonprofit academic use.
- Growing out of academic cultures in which it is customary to share one's work without expectation of financial gain, the Web lacks one of the key characteristics of Ted Nelson's Xanadu: The Web does not provide any convenient means to compensate copyright holders for use of their work.

CERN's early experience with the Internet provided fertile soil for the birth of the Web. Recalls Ben Segal, who was responsible for the introduction of the Internet into CERN, an "entire culture of distributed computing" had been created at CERN; everyone was thinking about ways of spreading computer resources around and creating new, computer-based means for scientific collaboration. By providing electronic mail, mailing lists, and newsgroups, the Internet came with many useful tools.

What it lacked was a user-friendly way of allowing scientists to exchange documents with each other.

Enter Tim Berners-Lee

By the late 1980s, Tim Berners-Lee, a computer specialist at CERN, had drunk deeply from the Internet wellspring; he perfectly understood its nature and possibilities. Segal recalls that Berners-Lee could connect your NeXT workstation to the Internet in a matter of minutes.

But Berners-Lee also understood hypertext. He knew of Nelson's Xanadu project and had himself written a standalone hypertext application. In a brilliant flash of inspiration, Berners-Lee saw that the Internet could provide the basis for an easy-to-use document exchange system based on hypertext principles. In 1989, Berners-Lee and his colleagues began experimenting with these ideas. In November 1990, they proposed a Web development project to CERN's directors.

The Web Proposal

The Web proposal emphasized that, first and foremost, the Web was intended to facilitate access to the types of information that CERN fellows needed. As Berners-Lee put it in the original Web proposal, "[the Web] provides a single user-interface to large classes of information (reports, notes, data-bases, computer documentation and on-line help."

It would also be easy to use. The Web's hypertext foundations would provide an extremely easy-to-use interface: to access a document, you would just point at its hyperlink and click.

In addition, it would make a wide variety of documents accessible. As Chapter 1 noted, the great thing about the Internet is its ability to ensure interoperability among computers that formerly couldn't exchange data with each other. The Web would integrate the many different kinds of hardware at CERN, enabling any two researchers to exchange documents without having to go through a tedious byte-by-byte translation process.

Like to know more about the Web's history? Check out Ben M. Segal's "A Short History of Internet Protocols at CERN" (http://wwwcn.cern.ch/pdp/ns/ben/TCPHIST.html).

Clients and Servers, or, Hey! Send Me That Document!

Berners-Lee learned another lesson from the Internet. Many of the Internet's most popular tools, such as FTP, involve two different types of programs, called *clients* and *servers*. The Web has a client/server basis.

Think of a client program as a program that works for *you*. It runs on your computer, taking full advantage of your computer's storage and processing capabilities. It also knows how to present itself (and Internet data) in a way that looks pretty on-screen.

A server program is like a robot that has been programmed to wait for information requests and then dish out the requested document. Clients know how to communicate with servers. The client says, in effect, "Hey, send me document such-and-such." The server receives the requests and says, in effect, "OK," and sends it. The client then displays the requested information on your computer screen.

On the Web, clients are called *browsers*, because they help you to browse for information.

Once Berners-Lee and his colleagues had come up with the idea of marrying the Internet, hypertext, and the client/server model, they could see how it would have to work. Take a look at a sample hypertext document (from the last chapter):

> The term **anime** refers to an impressive Japanese tradition of cartoon animation. Based on comic books called **manga**, anime TV shows, videos, and movies attract a wide audience in Japan, where adults as well as children join in the fun. In subtitled **videotapes** and **laserdiscs**, anime is increasingly available in the United States. Try looking for titles such as Akira or Bubblegum Crisis at your **local video store**. For an example of the best in anime, look for **My Neighbor Totoro**, a wonderful children's film that the whole family will enjoy. If you'd like to know more about anime, check out this **more detailed introduction** and read the **reviews** of popular anime films.

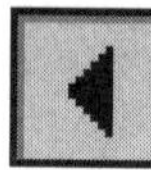

Suppose this paragraph of hypertext is being displayed by a browser, running on your computer. You want to click one of these hyperlinks and see the requested document. But the requested document isn't on your computer. It's somewhere on the Internet.

To create the Web, Berners-Lee and his colleagues saw that they needed a *protocol* that would enable a browser to send out a document request via the Internet. So they created the HyperText Transport Protocol (HTTP), the foundation of the Web.

The HyperText Transport Protocol (HTTP)

You don't really need to know much about how HTTP works, except for one thing: HTTP specifies precisely how a given resource can be located and retrieved on the Internet. (A *resource* is anything of value that you can get from another Internet computer, such as a document, a sound, a graphic, an animation, a movie, or a computer program.)

HTTP does this by specifying the form of *uniform resource identifiers*—abbreviated as URI (no relation to the guy who used to go around bending spoons with psychokinetic power). A URI is simply a series of characters (letters, numbers, or punctuation) that identifies the location of an Internet resource.

There are two kinds of URIs: Uniform Resource Locators (URLs) and Relative URLs (RELURLs).

- A URL is used to locate a resource on a computer other than the one on which the client is running.
- A RELURL is used to locate a resource on the same computer.

Let's ignore RELURLs for now; what's important here is the URL, the subject of the next section.

Uniform Resource Locators (URLs)

Basically, the Web consists of client programs that send URLs out over the Internet, and server programs that field these requests and cough up the

appropriate information (which could be a text document, a sound, a graphic, a movie, a compressed file, a program, or other things). The client program then displays the requested information, if it can.

A Uniform Resource Locator (URL) looks like this:

http://watt.seas.virginia.edu/~bp/parents.html

It has three parts:

1. **Protocol Identifier (*http://*)** This specifies what type of resource the URL accesses. Here, it's a World Wide Web document (http://). It could also be an FTP file (ftp://), a Gopher menu (gopher://), a Usenet newsgroup (news://), a Telnet session (Telnet://), and more.
2. **Domain Name (*watt.seas.virginia.edu*)** This gives the exact Internet address of the computer that houses the resource.
3. **Resource Location (/~bp/parents.html)** This specifies the resource's exact location and file name.

In sum, a URL specifies the type of resource, the location of the resource, and the name of the resource. When a Web client sends a URL to a Web server, the Web server responds by locating the resource and sending it back via the Internet.

The HyperText Markup Language (HTML)

The Web is basically a networked hypertext system that enables people to retrieve documents from the Internet. It wouldn't be much fun if the documents didn't look nice, with pretty fonts and graphics.

But there's just one problem. Documents that are formatted with fonts and graphics are *big*—too big to be transferred efficiently via the Internet. The Microsoft Word file containing this chapter, for example, consumes 39K of disk space. And the version I'm writing right now doesn't even contain any graphics—it's just fonts and formatting information. But the text-only version of the same file uses only 16K of storage—less than half!

To reduce the load on the Internet, Berners-Lee and his colleagues decided to compose Web documents using a *markup language*. Unlike a word processing program, a markup language does not attempt to specify precisely how the formatted document should appear. It just identifies the *parts* of the document.

HTML: Sorry, but you'll have to learn it
As Ted Nelson originally envisioned the global hypertext system, it would enable readers to become authors. With the Web, that's possible, but at a cost. You need a pretty good Internet connection, one that gives your computer a permanent address—and that doesn't come cheap. (More on this point in Chapter 6.) In addition, you need to learn at least some HTML. Sure, you've doubtless heard of those easy-to-use HTML editors that do all the coding for you. But here's the bad news. I haven't seen one yet that frees you from knowing at least a little HTML coding. Maybe that will change, but for now, there's some HTML in your future.

An Example

Here's the difference between a word processing program and a markup language. Suppose you're formatting a document title with a word processing program. You type it, and then format it with centering, the Galliard font (18 points), and bold. Here's how it looks:

A Heading

In a markup language, you don't choose the alignment, font, font size, or emphasis. You just use codes, called *tags*, that tell the browser that this text is a certain part of a document—here, a second-level heading. The codes look like this:

```
<H2>A Heading</H2>
```

When people read this document on the Web, their browser looks at the text, and says, "Aha! A second-level heading!" The browser then decides how to format this text. Most browsers give their users at least some control over the way given parts of the document appear. Perhaps Mark has chosen the all-business Avant Garde font, so his heading looks like this:

A Heading

But Sujitha wants something a bit on the informal side, so she chooses Gazelle, and formats the second-level heading flush left:

A Heading

Randi, meanwhile, adds zing by choosing 36-point Marker Felt Wide:

A Heading

As you can see, the good thing about a markup language is that it lets the user choose his or her own formatting preferences. That is also the bad thing about a markup language.

Fair warning: Users may choose bizarre fonts!
As a Web author, you can't control the way your document will look on-screen. You can try, but you're paddling upstream. Most browsers give users options to ignore the efforts you might make to force a certain kind of formatting, such as a background color.

The HyperText Markup Language and SGML

Berners-Lee and his colleagues didn't invent markup languages. The concept already existed, and so did the *Standard Generalized Markup Language (SGML)*, an international standard that was defined in 1986.

SGML isn't exactly a markup language. Rather, it's a metalanguage that provides the means for formally defining markup languages. With SGML, you can define a *document type definition (DTD)*. This is a formal statement of how a particular markup language identifies the parts of a document. Once the DTD has been created, you can create another program, called a *parser*, that understands this particular document type and knows how to display it on-screen.

The HyperText Markup Language (HTML) is a document type defined by SGML. And Web browsers are also parsers for HTML. Simple, isn't it?

Actually, HTML does more than enable you to add tags defining standard document types such as headings, body text, and quotations. It also lets you create hyperlinks—and hide them so that all the user sees is the underlined text. When you click on the hyperlink, the parser sends the URL out over the network.

Graphical Browsers

The National Center for Supercomputing Applications (NCSA), located at the University of Illinois, Champaign-Urbana, is the birthplace of NCSA

Mosaic, the Web's "killer application." Just as Lotus 1-2-3 was a decisive factor in creating a mass market for the IBM PC, Mosaic brought the Web to millions of people who might not otherwise have used it.

Opened in 1986, NCSA is one of four government-funded supercomputing research centers. The scientists and researchers who work at NCSA are all involved in what NCSA calls computational science, the attempt to understand natural phenomena by simulating them on high-performance computing systems.

NCSA's Software Development Group (SDG) has been working for years to create software that could enhance scientific visualization. At NCSA, they developed high-performance graphics programs that could display amazing simulations on monitors directly connected to supercomputers. But they recognized that not everyone could afford to come to NCSA. A way needed to be found to make supercomputing resources more widely available.

Enter the Web. A talented young programmer, Marc Andreessen, quickly saw that the Web provided just the distribution and access mechanisms that NCSA was looking for. The program could run animations and videos, so that a researcher in Tuscaloosa, or Tehachapi or Tonapah for that matter, could view much the same patterns that NCSA researchers were seeing. What's more, a researcher in an isolated college or university could upload some data by means of FTP, have the NCSA staff analyze it on a supercomputer, and then view the results on the Web.

Mosaic is a *graphical browser.* At the minimum, this means that the program can parse HTML documents and display them using a computer system's font resources. Graphical browsers can also display *in-line graphics*, the pictures that HTML authors often include with their documents.

Released in 1993, Mosaic took the Internet by storm. However, it quickly became apparent that NCSA got more than it bargained for with its freebie release of X Window/Motif, Macintosh, and Windows versions of the program—a support nightmare. In 1994, NCSA licensed Mosaic to a for-profit spinoff company, Spyglass, which was charged with the task of creating commercial versions of the program. Spyglass did not market these programs directly, but instead resold licensing rights to book publishers (such as O'Reilly and Associates), operating system publishers (Microsoft and IBM), and third-party software vendors (Luckmann Associates). The commercial version of the program is generically known as Enhanced NCSA Mosaic, but it's available under many different names when repackaged by licensees.

Although millions of copies of NCSA Mosaic have been distributed, the real action has shifted to a program called Netscape Navigator, published by Netscape Communications, Inc. Netscape, as the program is often called, was authored by a team led by the same Marc Andreessen who created NCSA Mosaic. Andreessen co-founded Netscape in 1994. An estimated two million copies of Netscape are in use today.

The Potlatch Factor

Along the northwest coast of what is now British Columbia, Native American peoples developed a unique culture, one that is very different from the cultures of industrialized countries. The central theme: 'Tis nobler to give than to receive. As you'll see, the Web embodies the same spirit.

To be reckoned great, a chief would hold a ceremony called the *potlatch*. The objective of this ceremony was to *give away* hundreds of barrels of fish oil and hundreds of blankets. At the end of the ceremony, his guests—shaken and humiliated by this massive display of generosity—would cart off the goodies, and the chief's name would resound throughout the land. (The chief's house was pretty empty after this, but nobody cared. After all, if you needed some fish oil or blankets, you could always go to some other chief's potlatch.)

You'd think the potlatch values aren't consistent with modern capitalism, but take a look at any university's promotion and tenure system. In universities, you gain professional advancement by publishing the results of your work in scholarly and scientific journals. These journals do *not* compensate you for publishing your work in them. In fact, some of them make you *pay* for the privilege of seeing your work appear in such distinguished company. Department chairmen and deans everywhere tell junior faculty, "If you get money for it, it doesn't count." You become famous in academia not by getting rich off your ideas, but by giving them away to low-circulation journals and publication series.

In short, wherever you find academics, there's a potlatch factor. And that's true of the Web. Growing out of two academic think tanks, the Web embodies the potlatch values of academia; it assumes that people will be more than willing to contribute documents to the Web, without the slightest expectation of remuneration.

That works fine in academic environments. Academics are (usually) pretty willing to share information and resources. It also works well for hobbyists. Hobbyists love to share information with each other and don't expect much in return, except friendship and more information.

But will the Web suffice as a mass publication medium, along the lines envisioned by Ted Nelson? Not without some additional means to recompense copyright holders for information they make available on the Web.

As developed at CERN and NCSA, the Web includes only very primitive capabilities for charging people for accessing copyrighted material. This is one of the biggest drawbacks to the Web, at present. That's why they say, "The Web is cool, but it isn't Xanadu."

"Nobody's making money on the Web!"
Don't believe it. To be sure, the Web's academic origins, especially when coupled with the broader noncommercial values of the Internet, make it very difficult to charge for the information you want to make available. But nobody said it's *impossible*. In Chapter 5, you'll see lots of ways that Web authors are using right now to make money on the Web—or to establish a presence that enables them to make money elsewhere.

From Here

- What are the defining characteristics of the Web as a publishing medium? Flip to Chapter 4 to find out.
- Given that the Web isn't Xanadu, what can you publish on the Web? See Chapter 5 for lots of examples.

Chapter 4

The Web as a Publishing Medium

If you want to publish on the Web, be forewarned: The Web isn't like any publishing medium that's ever existed. If you think it's anything like a traditional broadcast medium (such as magazines, newspapers, television, or radio), you'll fall flat on your face. Recognizing the peril, big companies are bringing in talented young Web developers to create highly interactive, engaging Web sites for their firms.

But that's not an option for most of the people reading this book—the individual entrepreneurs, owners of small businesses, freelancers, and consultants in today's economy. You'll need to make the break with conventional thinking, and do it fast, if you're going to take full advantage of the Web. To help you accomplish this is the goal of this chapter. It begins by dismissing the *broadcast model* of publishing—a model that's very misleading when

applied to the Web. It continues by considering the unique characteristics and possibilities of the Web as a publishing medium and by discussing its very real problems and limitations. As you'll find, though, the limitations are decreasing in importance with each passing month. It seems clear that the Web is destined to become one of modern society's most important media for the distribution of textual and hypermedia-based information.

Broadcast Model? Forget It

Let's start by killing off the mind-set that leads to quick, conspicuous failure in Web publishing: Thinking that the Web is anything like a broadcast medium.

In a traditional broadcast medium, a firm prepares content (such as an advertisement), selects a medium (such as radio or a magazine), and publishes the content. It's a one-way, one-to-many process, in which consumers are more or less passive consumers of the information the firm puts out.

If you're thinking this way, you're going to have a tough time understanding the Web. Let's look at some of the ways the Web departs radically from the broadcast model.

Characteristics of the Web as a Publishing Medium

In contrast to the broacast model, the highly interactive Web is well on the way to obliterating the active broadcaster versus passive consumer distinction: information consumers are becoming information producers—even to the extent of creating their own product advertising! As more and more people create information and link it to previous efforts, the richness and depth of the available information grows. No Web author has any inherent advantage over any other; all Web pages are equally accessible. Distribution costs are zero, in effect, and it doesn't really matter where you're located: Billings, Montana is just as appropriate a setting as New York City (provided you can get access to the Internet). The following sections go into these characteristics in detail.

For the Time-Challenged

- The Web can't be understood if you're thinking of it as a broadcast medium, with content providers involved in a one-way relationship with passive information consumers. Information consumers are becoming information producers, and they're even appropriating advertising!
- You don't have to prepare content exhaustively—if somebody else has already contributed something of value on a subject, you can link to it instead of reinventing the wheel.
- All the money in the world won't give you any *technical* advantage over a college student when it comes to accessing your site. To be sure, the deeper your pockets, the more non-Web publicity you can afford. Still, some of the best Web advertising is word of mouth.
- Other characteristics of the Web as a publication medium: Whether you're in New York City or Billings, Montana, you can look forward to zero distance and zero distribution costs, once you've forked over the monthly fees to your Internet service provider. And your Web publication sticks around, 24 hours a day, unless you deliberately alter it or remove it from your site.
- Disadvantages of the Web include the difficulty of creating and maintaining Web pages, low control over your documents' look, the difficulty people are going to have locating your site, the lack of audience measurement tools, and the lack of established payment mechanisms. Most of the problems are being resolved, however.

High Interactivity

In contrast to broadcast media, the Web is highly interactive. If channel selection is a measure of interactivity, the Web's millions of documents greatly exceed that of the best cable systems. What is more, many Web documents—the best ones—are designed with user interactivity in mind.

For a taste of the Web's interactivity, check out the Interactive Web Fun page of EINet Galaxy:

http://www.einet.net/galaxy/Leisure-and-Recreation/Interactive-Web-Fun.html

Information Consumers Are Becoming Information Producers

One of the most striking ways in which the Web differs from traditional broadcast media is that consumers and readers can themselves become content providers. The cost of placing a document on the Web and making it available to others is already very low in comparison to traditional broadcast media—and it's falling. In Figure 4.1, you see a classic low-budget Web production: equestrian enthusiast Karen Pautz, a journalism student at the University of Missouri–Columbia, created a home page to bring together a number of high-quality horse-related sites on the Web. Her page's name? Hay.net.

The Web is well on its way to a Xanadu-like destruction of the distinction between authors and readers. In Ted Nelson's vision of Xanadu (see Chapter 2), every reader becomes an author almost automatically, in that he or

Figure 4.1 Hay.net (http://www.missouri.edu/~jourkap/index.html)

she builds on existing documents by referencing links and adding notes, commentaries, and summaries. The Web isn't there yet—Web browsers provide only minimal facilities for annotation, and annotations aren't accessible by other Web users—but it's on its way. In Figure 4.2, you see a Web document in which hyperlinks to other documents are seamlessly embedded in the text itself, supplementing the presentation and providing branchpoints for exploration. The example is drawn from a genealogy page.

Future HTML editors will do away with the need for programming expertise, both for HTML documents and interactive forms, leading to an explosion of content provision by information consumers themselves.

If you need any more convincing that the Web radically departs from the previous distinction between information producers and information con-

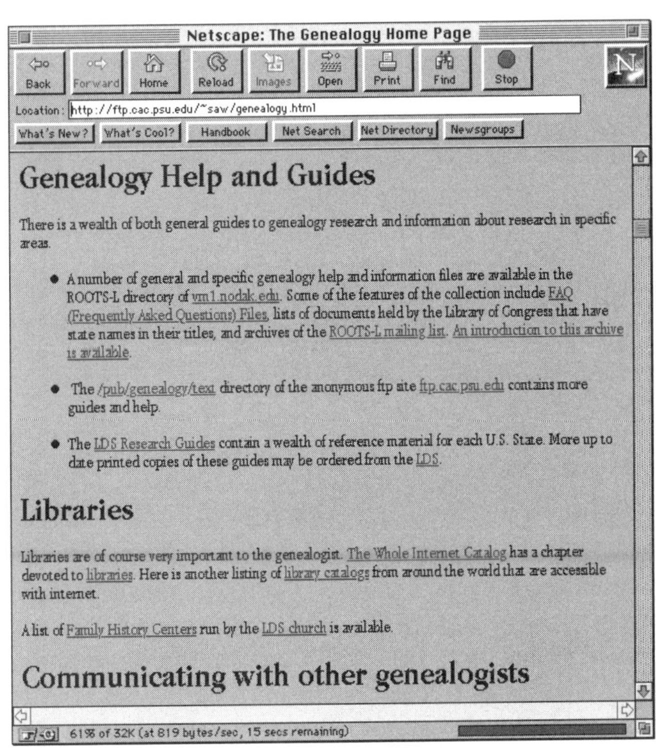

Figure 4.2 Hyperlinks seamlessly embedded in text (http://ftp.cac.psu.edu/~saw/genealogy.html)

sumers, here's something else to chew on. In traditional media, firms create advertisements for their products. You can advertise on the Web, but something else is happening too: Consumers are themselves creating Web pages that are concerned, often adoringly, with specific products, including Barbie dolls, Lego toys, and more (for an example, see Figure 4.3). Generally, they do this without asking for permission—and without receiving compensation.

Compared to the content produced by traditional advertisers, consumer "advertising" isn't necessarily the same kind of advertising that a firm would do; although most consumer advertising is done by product enthusiasts, it's likely to come with a good dose of criticism and consumer tips. The

Figure 4.3 Consumer-originated advertisement for high-performance Ford Probe exhaust system (http://www.wpi.edu/~ss/PGT/exhaust.html#Exhaust)

Ford Probe page, for example, comes with links to service bulletins, which Probe owners can use to make sure they get the warranty service to which they're entitled.

Synergy (The More the Merrier)

A traditional publishing effort is a solitary thing. It can refer to other publications, perhaps through footnotes or in-text references, but it cannot build on them. The Web, like any hypertext system, is different. In a hypertext document, you can include hyperlinks to other peoples' efforts. You don't have to reinvent the wheel by covering knowledge that's well represented elsewhere on the Web. In time, as a number of people contribute their knowledge and resources in a specific area to the Web, the value and depth of this knowledge grows and grows. The result of this process is an *information community*, consisting of as many as thousands of people worldwide who share varying levels of commitment to improving the collaborative information pool.

An example of synergy in action is the remarkable Froggy Page, which brings together an astonishing variety of Web resources related to these amphibians—songs, pictures, stories, scientific documents, famous frogs, and even recipes.

All Web Pages Are Equally Accessible (An Information Democracy?)

Let's say that an undergraduate at Virginia Tech invests two hours of time in a home page, while a major magazine publisher spends $125,000 on an extravagantly illustrated Web version of its print-based publication. Which is more accessible?

In strictly technical terms, they're equally accessible. The magazine publisher has more resources to spend on publicizing its site, but the technology doesn't give the big spender any way to make a bigger splash. Compared with virtually any other medium, this feature alone makes the Web an inherently democratic medium.

All the advertising in the world won't do you much good, moreover, if Web users perceive your site to be clueless, Web-wise. To succeed on the Web, you'll need to offer some valuable information or resources for free, you'll need to appeal to the Web user's sense of Web aesthetics (and etiquette), and you'll need to use traditional Web publicizing methods (discussed in Chapter 19).

Distance Doesn't Matter (There Are No Long-Distance Charges)

In traditional businesses, as in real estate, the old saying "location, location, location" makes very good sense. Suppose you're setting up a traditional manufacturing business in rural Montana. Good luck—although it's not impossible, you'll have to overcome extraordinary shipping and communication costs attributable to your isolated location.

But that's not true of the Web. Owing to the limitations of the current TCP/IP protocols, which were never designed to permit usage-based billing, Internet service providers offer Internet access based on a *flat pricing model*—you get so many hours of Internet access per month for a flat fee. And once you're on the Net, you can go anywhere you please. From a publisher's viewpoint, this means that you potentially have an international audience for your work.

Of the various publishing and communications media available in our society, in this respect the Web closely resembles the 800 telephone number service (except that it's international in scope, which 800 services aren't). With an 800 number, you can do business from any state in the Union; from your customers' perspective, it doesn't really matter where you're located. The Web will doubtless contribute to a number of trends that are moving people and jobs out of urban and even suburban centers, raising rural populations and straining meager rural social service resources.

With millions of people using the Internet, service providers are spending billions upgrading their long-distance transmission systems—and not surprisingly, they're talking about ways to create distance-based billing. But it's unlikely they'll succeed. Within the current Internet protocols, there is no technical basis for performing such billing. Moreover, expanding Internet usage is providing additional revenue based on the existing flat billing model. In addition, Internet users are accustomed to the flat billing model and might desert the Net in droves should distance-based billing be imposed. Industry complaints aside, most observers believe that the flat billing model will survive.

Zero Distribution Costs

Once you've placed a document on the Web, it costs you absolutely nothing to distribute it. Every time your document is accessed—this is called *hit*—a

copy of your document is conveyed via the Internet, where it is temporarily stored in the browser's local memory space.

There's one caveat to this point, though. If your Web site becomes very popular, you may find that it's necessary to upgrade your equipment to handle the load! The shareware servers designed to run on Microsoft Windows and Macintosh computers can handle, at most, a few hundred accesses per day; the most popular sites have several UNIX workstations running at high capacities.

High Latency (Documents Stick Around)

The term *latency* refers to the amount of time a message sticks around in a communication medium. Among the various Internet formats, Usenet exemplifies a medium with very low latency: To make room for the dozens of megabytes of new messages coming in daily, system administrators may set the system software to erase posts automatically every 24 hours.

In contrast to Usenet, the Web offers exceptionally high latency—the document remains available, 24 hours a day, until you deliberately remove it. And the longer you let it remain, the more chance there is that somebody else will create a link to your document. And the more people link to your document, the more hits you'll get.

The Web's high latency makes it ideal for creating organizational and corporate *memory structures*, inventories of information that grow over time and eventually constitute an indispensable resource.

Drawbacks to the Web as a Publishing Medium

Compared to the Web, traditional media are more easily accessed, more familiar from a technical standpoint, more susceptible to design control, and easier to find. And you'll have little trouble figuring out just who's reading your publication—and how to charge them for the valuable information you're distributing. In all these areas, the Web has shortcomings. The following sections elaborate these points.

Technical Barriers to Web Publication

It's pretty easy to find printers who can handle a newsletter, including design, layout, printing, and even mailing and addressing. But would-be Web publishers find several barriers in their path:

- **The relative scarcity of direct Internet connections.** In order to set up a Web site, you need an Internet connection with a permanent IP address. Just a year ago, such connections were a luxury enjoyed only by people working in universities, research centers, think tanks, Internet-savvy corporations, and government agencies. (That's one of the reasons there are so many Web pages authored by college students.) However, new Internet connectivity options, including connections with permanent IP addresses, are now becoming widely available.
- **The technical difficulty of setting up a Web server.** Until 1994, almost all of the available Web servers were UNIX programs that required considerable technical expertise to install (not to mention the fact that they ran on expensive UNIX workstations). However, easy-to-use Web servers are now available for Windows, Windows NT, and Macintosh computers.
- **The need to learn HTML.** To publish on the Web, you need to learn HTML—and that's still true, despite the arrival of a number of programs that claim to make "HTML programming" unnecessary. To be sure, these programs have reduced the drudgery involved in creating and maintaining HTML documents. But it's still necessary to understand how HTML works, and you will still have to write some HTML code manually. You can hire a Web author to write the HTML, but then you'll be dependent on him or her to maintain the document.

Is the Internet running out of IP addresses?
You may have heard of the "IP address crisis," and heard dire warnings of the "impending death of the Net." When the Internet was first designed, a 32-bit address space was thought to be sufficient. This would have been enough to handle billions of computers, but the 32-bit address was broken down into classes (called A, B, and C) to reduce the processing burden on Internet routing equipment. This reduced the number of addresses available and led, ultimately, to the

current problem. Only 128 Class A networks are permitted, but each Class A network can have millions of hosts. There can be thousands of Class B networks, and each can have thousands of hosts. There can be millions of Class C networks, but each can have no more than 254 hosts. At current rates of Internet growth, Class B network addresses—by far the most popular choice for networks seeking to link to the Internet—will be exhausted shortly. However, this crisis will be resolved soon. The Internet Engineering Task Force (IETF) has proposed a revision to the Internet Protocol that will provide a 64-bit address space while retaining compatibility with existing Internet programs and equipment. With a 64-bit address space, there will be sufficient IP addresses for every man, woman, and child on the planet, as well as every single addressable byte of storage in their computer systems. That ought to be enough!

These access barriers are becoming less significant with each passing month. Direct Internet connectivity is becoming widely available, and a new generation of "point-and-click" Web servers will enable virtually anyone to set up a Web site in short order. As for HTML, it's not terribly difficult to learn, and the years to come should see improved HTML editors.

Low Formatting Control

The HyperText Markup Language (HTML) is designed to mark up the parts of Web documents, but it's up to the *browser* to determine exactly how the documents appear on-screen. This is advantageous in one sense—document downloading proceeds quickly because the formatting information does not have to be transmitted—but very disadvantageous in that a site's author cannot control how a given document will look. For example, it's impossible with HTML to use a corporate font (such as Apple's Garamond Narrow) so that all of your firm's documents have a consistent look.

There's a way around this problem: You can construct pages out of GIF or JPEG graphics, which browsers display just the way you created them (see Figure 4.4 for a good example). Current Web technology enables you to make graphics such as these clickable; for example, when you click the "What's New" button in Figure 4.4, you activate a hyperlink that displays another document. There are several embedded hyperlinks on this page.

Figure 4.4 Controlling format through the use of full-page graphics

Graphics enable Web authors to create a consistent look and feel for a Web publication, but this comes at a price: Documents containing graphics take far longer to download than documents containing nothing but HTML and text.

Low Discoverability (Where the Heck Is That Page?)

The Web is making it possible for just about anybody to establish a presence on the Internet—just take a look at all those college students' home pages, which serve no other purpose (apparently) than to gratify egos. With approximately 5 million documents already available on the Web, will yours get lost in the shuffle?

That's a valid concern for any would-be Web publisher. A basic point about the Web is that the technology doesn't thrust your Web pages in peoples' faces—they must deliberately seek you out. And often, that's a tedious and ultimately unsuccessful enterprise.

To be sure, there are search tools available, including *subject trees* (the Web equivalent of a library's subject card catalog) and *search engines* (databases of Web documents that are automatically compiled by programs, called *spiders*, that can detect and index new Web documents). In addition, magazines such as *Internet World* and *NetGuide* report new and interesting sites monthly. Still, many people complain that it's very difficult to locate information on the Web.

Publicity: The key to an effective Web presence
It's not enough just to put your pages on the Web. Sure, they'll be discovered by spiders eventually, and you might attract a few curious surfers. If you want people to visit your site in larger numbers, though, you'll need to devote some time, energy, and possibly money to publicizing your site. See Chapter 19 for publicity strategies you can use.

Lack of Audience Measurement Tools

In traditional broadcast media, fairly precise tools exist for measuring both the size and the demographics of the audience. These tools help generate advertising revenue because publishers can describe their audience size with some precision.

On the Web, the only tool that's available for the measurement of audience size is a *hit counter*, a program that records the number of times the page is accessed. However, hit counters can't tell you whether the person accessing the site stuck around to read the material, or just surfed through en route to another destination. Worse, a hit counter simply measures how many files have been accessed—and for documents containing a large number of bitmapped graphics, the number might be as high as one or two dozen for a single Web page. *HotWired* magazine records some 600,000 "hits" per day—but estimates that only 6,000 people are accessing the site on a daily basis.

As for demographics, no tools of any kind can automatically detect and record information about what kind of people are accessing a site. However, traditional survey research methods could be adapted to investigate Web usage patterns—and that's exactly what's happening. A.C. Nielsen, the TV

ratings company, recently announced a strategic alliance with ASI Market Research and Yankelovich Partners to measure Web site usage, appeal, and impact. Called "ANYwhere Online," the alliance represents "a growing recognition that the World Wide Web and other components of the online world are fast evolving into a major new medium for advertising and commerce."

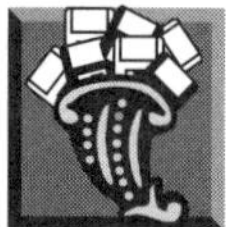

Like to learn more about Web usage tracking systems? One that's currently under development is called NetCount (http://www.digiplanet.com/DP/DP1/abtnetcount.html). NetCount's objective is to create a Web page rating system that's as accurate—and comprehensible—as the Nielsen TV ratings.

No Established Payment Mechanism

As the previous chapters have explained, Internet and Web users are accustomed to accessing free information. Still, they tell survey researchers that they'd be willing to pay for information that has obvious commercial value. The problem is, how do you collect?

Developed in an academic environment, the HTTP protocols (the standards underlying Web communication) do not include the security and other features required to sell information on-line. However, a number of Web publishers have developed interim solutions to this problem, and developments in Web security—discussed in Chapter 26—will soon make it possible for your customers to order documents on-line using Visa and MasterCharge.

One interim solution is to take advantage of the HTTP protocol's authentication standards. In brief, *authentication* is the process of ensuring that a given user, logging on to a site, is in fact the person that he or she claims to be. Most computer systems try to authenticate users by means of a *password*, a string of characters that the user types to identify himself or herself. Most browsers automatically detect the demand for a password and display an appropriate dialog box. One can therefore set up a subscription-based service in which users are charged a monthly fee that enables them to gain access to the system. To be sure, password-based authentication is far from perfect; if users are careless about safeguarding their passwords, others could gain access to your site. Still, password-based authentication is sufficient for many information-vending applications—especially those applications where the information being sold is voluminous and constantly changing, so that an occasional unauthorized access wouldn't cause serious damage.

A case in point is InfoSeek, a Web search service that permits Web users to retrieve up to ten citations for free. To retrieve more citations and take full advantage of InfoSeek's many advanced features, users must subscribe and pay a monthly fee. In return for the subscription, users receive a username and password, which must be supplied when the system is accessed.

From Here

- Given the Web's unique characteristics as a publication medium, what can you expect to publish successfully on the Web? Check out the next chapter for a variety of very successful Web publication strategies, ranging from purely voluntary efforts to successful commercial enterprises.
- How does one go about publishing on the Web? See Chapter 6 for a quick introduction.

Chapter 5

What Can You Publish on the Web?

As people have gradually understood the Web's unique characteristics as a publication medium, a number of Web publication genres have emerged. (In literature, a *genre* is a particular style or category of writing that emerges as authors try to achieve a certain purpose. As you'll see, the term applies to Web documents as well.)

So that you can fully understand the nature and the potential of the Web as a publishing medium, it's worthwhile to take a look at the Web publishing genres that have emerged thus far. You'll get lots of ideas about what seems to work—and what doesn't—in this unique publishing medium.

This chapter begins with informal Web publishing genres, stressing the efforts of individuals, hobbyists, and volunteers, and moves on to more

organized efforts, including corporate presences on the Web. By no means meant to be exhaustive, this chapter surveys some of the more prominent genres of Web publishing activity—but don't be surprised if several new ones have emerged in the year or two following this book's publication!

For the Time-Challenged

The unique characteristics of the Web make it ideal for doing the following:

- Creating a personal home page
- Sharing amateur knowledge
- Getting your message out
- Organizing political action
- Finding an audience for creative work
- Creating trailblazer pages
- Creating consumer advertising
- Creating a stupid Web trick
- Creating a 'zine
- Creating an on-line fan club
- Supporting communities
- Providing documentation
- Providing services
- Providing self-help support
- Sharing your professional knowledge
- Educating on the Web
- Creating a corporate image
- Establishing a marketing presence
- Creating advertiser-supported versions of print publications
- Creating an on-line shopping catalog
- Creating an agent

Creating a Personal Home Page

ARPAnet, the forerunner of the Internet, was meant to be used solely for technical communication and sharing data related to scientific and military research. To the surprise of the ARPAnet's planners, though, scientists and engineers using the network spent a great deal of time exchanging personal electronic mail and otherwise having fun with the technology newly available to them. The researchers were not content to use the ARPAnet solely as a professional tool; they wanted to make their personalities known to their colleagues. What was intended to be an impersonal, faceless exchange of information became social interaction.

The Web strongly encourages electronic personality sharing. Given the opportunity to share themselves with a potential audience of millions of Web surfers, many people post home pages that feature pictures of themselves and their families, descriptions of professional and hobby interests, and multimedia exhibits, both serious and light.

The best home pages aren't merely monuments to their creators. Good home pages provide useful resources and links to other Web documents. The Web is a project in community authorship, and there's no reason to re-create a resource that's available somewhere else. Make your home page convey your personality, but don't make it the networked equivalent of your vacation slide show. Make it useful to people so they'll want to return again and again. The home page of Meng Weng Wong (Figure 5.1) is a good example.

Like to see more individuals' home pages? Check out Who's Who on the Internet (http://web.city.ac.uk/citylive/pages.html). There are thousands of links here to the home pages of individuals all over the world!

Sharing Your Amateur Knowledge

Lots of Web pages exist to share hobby and avocational information with the Web community. These pages aren't authoritative resources in the same way, say, that government publications or corporate press releases are, but they're wonderful for hobbyists and casual communities of people with common interests. Usually, the people who post pages containing amateur

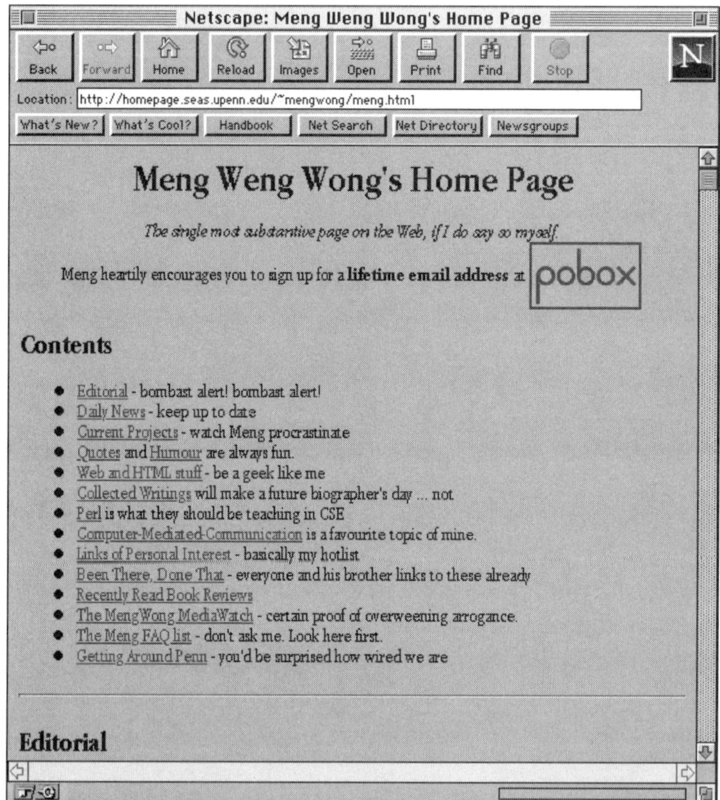

Figure 5.1 Meng Weng Wong's Home Page
http://homepage.seas.upenn.edu/~mengwong/meng.html

knowledge aren't certified authorities—how do you certify a kite expert, or an expert stamp collector, anyhow?—but they have some sort of experience that's valuable to others.

The Web lends itself to, among so many other things, swapping information among amateurs. Just as model airplane enthusiasts gather at hobby shops to exchange tips, they can gather on-line to do the same thing. The Web and the other resources the Internet provides enable practitioners of obscure hobbies, or hobbyists who are geographically far removed from others with similar interests, to participate in communities of hobbyists.

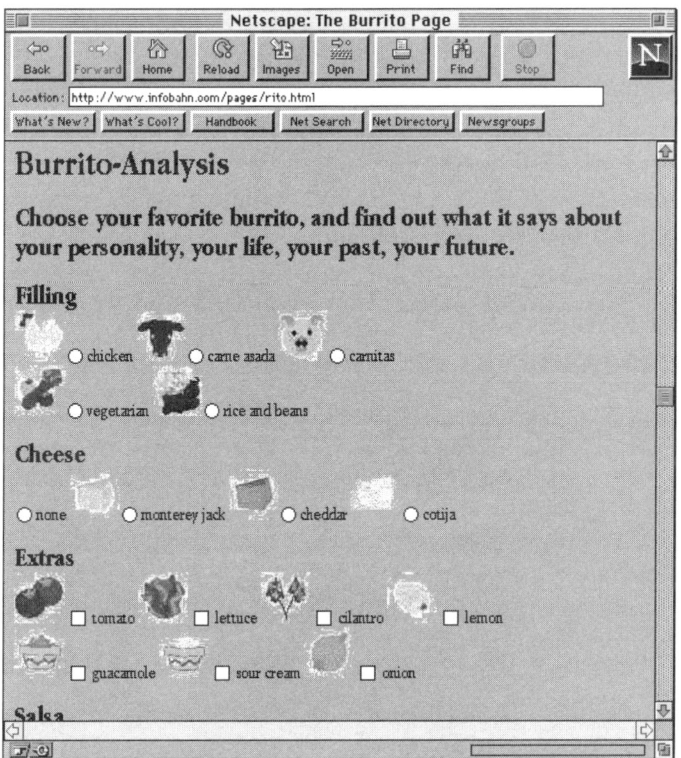

Figure 5.2 The Burrito Page
http://www.infobahn.com/pages/rito.html

The Burrito Page (Figure 5.2) covers burritos, the ever-popular Mexican dish, in depth. It's not likely you'd find burrito information anywhere but on an amateur page.

Getting Your Message Out

Give people a soapbox, and they'll think of something to say. Lots of Web sites have to do with people who, regardless of whether anyone agrees with

them or even cares, think they have been wronged. There are sites relating to whistleblowers—people who risk their jobs by exposing illegal or unethical situations in their places of work—and criminal defendants who feel they've been wrongly accused. One of the most elaborate sites of this genre is that of the Leonard Peltier Defense Committee, which has worked to free Indian-rights activist Leonard Peltier from prison since he was convicted in 1975 of killing two FBI agents. The Foundation's site (Figure 5.3) features Peltier's account of what happened the day the agents were killed, and calls for surfer support of his cause.

The Web lends itself to the genre of calling for support of a cause. Few of the traditional media of cause champions—handbills and small-press

Figure 5.3 The Leonard Peltier Defense Committee Page
http://www.unicom.net/peltier/index.html

books—can present this kind of information with the professional look of the Web, and certainly no traditional medium offers comparably broad distribution.

The Web gives a professional look and wide distribution to soapbox-type presentations. Whether it garners them any more attention from the general public remains to be seen.

Organizing Political Action

Sites that attempt to organize political activity are different from informational sites in that they try to draw viewers into the cause and get them to act. Though political action may be implicit in sites that get a message out, political action sites call for participation.

The nice thing about organizing political activity on the Web is that you can make a strong logical case for your cause. It's easy to attach supporting documents to your site, to be read at your viewers' leisure. While traditional political organization techniques rely on slogans, brief examples, and high emotional content, a Web political action site can combine those things with rational statements of position.

On the other hand, political action sites lack the charisma factor that fuels traditional political movements. It's hard to rally around a leader when he or she is represented only by a static picture, a thirty-second audio file, and perhaps a video clip. You'll have to weigh both of these characteristics when you incorporate a Web site into a political movement.

Though it's maintained by an individual, the Nature Conservancy site (Figure 5.4) is a good example of a site that promotes a political cause.

Finding an Audience for Creative Work

Once, it was very difficult to publish paintings, photographs, and short stories because there were so few venues for publication. There were magazines, but these magazines had a limited number of pages and could contain only so much material in an issue. Outlets for creative work were few, for a very uncreative reason: the limited capabilities of printing presses, paper mills, and broadcast media such as television, radio, and film.

Figure 5.4 The Nature Conservancy
http://copper.ucs.indiana.edu/~sheehan/conservancy.html

The Web, in some ways, is like a magazine with an unlimited number of pages and free global circulation. If your artwork can be recorded in computer-readable form (computers cannot handle some media, such as feature-length film or ballet, easily), you can publish it to an audience that will soon exceed one billion people.

With ease of publication often comes a decline in the quality of what is published. Just as the advent of desktop publishing software meant anybody could put together a font- and clip-art-laden document without paying a skilled printer, the rise of the Web makes it possible for anybody to publish their boring short stories or whangingly melodramatic teenage-angst poems. The best sites, such as OTIS (Figure 5.5), have some sort of selection criteria that keeps the quality of published material high.

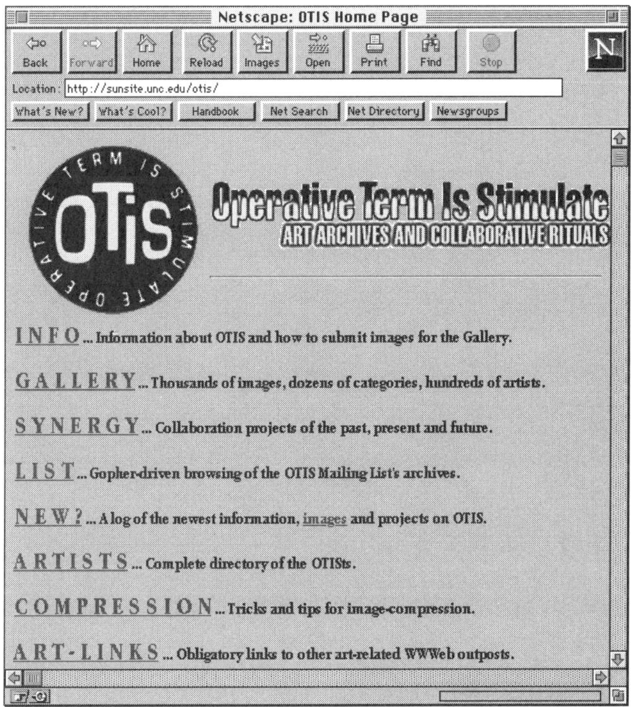

Figure 5.5 OTIS
http://sunsite.unc.edu/otis/

CREATING A TRAILBLAZER PAGE

If you've used the Web for anything other than random surfing, chances are you've developed a hotlist containing links that likely would be useful to people with interests similar to yours. In the spirit of sharing that exists on the Web, and in the interest of making things easier for you, why not publish your hotlist on a trailblazer page?

A trailblazer page is a page that contains little data itself, but has metadata in the form of links to other sites or pages that contain useful information. If you give your trailblazer page a title that describes its subject clearly, your page will appear when someone uses a search engine, such as InfoSeek

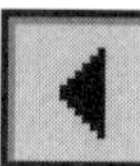

Figure 5.6 The Fox Box
http://cswww2.essex.ac.uk/Web/am/foxbox.html

or Lycos, to hunt for sites on that subject. Also, make a link to your trailblazer page from your home page, or set your browser to go to it every time you start using the Web.

Nothing says a trailblazer page has to deal with a deadly serious topic. The only requirement is that the page provide lots of links to resources that relate to a particular topic. The Fox Box (Figure 5.6) is one of the best trailblazer pages on the Web.

Creating Consumer Advertising

Advertising on the Web isn't the same as advertising in a broadcast medium. Not only do consumers reach company propaganda by different

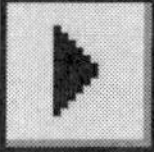

means, they can post statements about products themselves. Consumer advertising is a natural—if people really like (or really hate) a product, nothing can stop them from saying so on the Web, as long as they operate within the constraints of copyright and libel law. Consumer advertising on the Web is traditional word-of-mouth advertising taken to a higher level, since instead of being able to speak to a few people in their neighborhoods or at work, Web users can post their opinions of products for millions of people to see.

Barbie dolls, for reasons unknown, are among the products most heavily advertised by consumers on the Web. The Barbie Page (Figure 5.7) praises Barbie, in her various incarnations, to the stars—but the site has no affiliation with Mattel, Barbie's maker.

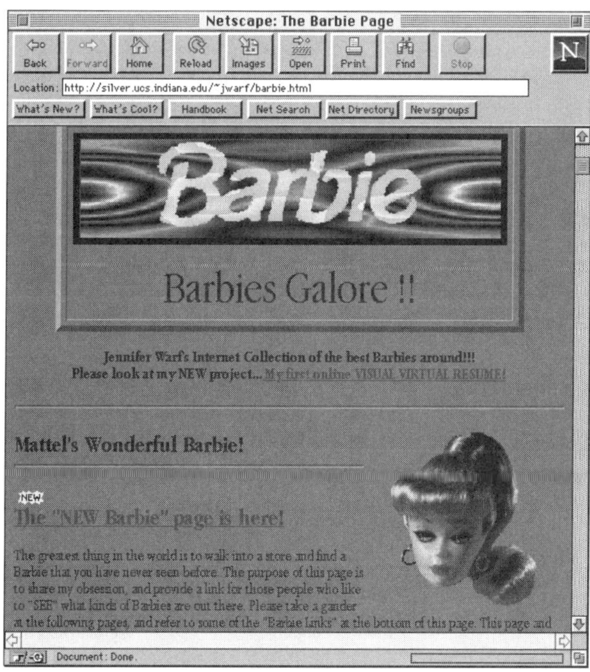

Figure 5.7 The Barbie Page
http://silvcr.ucs.indiana.edu/~jwarf/barbie.html

Creating a Stupid Web Trick

A significant portion of the Web community is composed of college students and computer programmers, which means frivolity is bound to permeate the Web. Plenty of sites exist to entertain Web users, and they often do so in a way that reflects their creator's unique—and technically impressive—skills.

Foam Bath Fish Time (Figure 5.8) is a great example. It's technology for technology's sake, since no one logs onto the Web to check the time. It's kind of cool, though, to see how the programmer used a Perl script (his first Perl effort) to combine the time of day with images of kids' bath toys. Sure it's silly, but that's the point.

Figure 5.8 Foam Bath Fish Time
http://www.northcoast.com/cgi-bin/fishtime

Creating a 'Zine

'Zines are like other outlets for creative work, except that they have a coherent theme and style unto themselves and usually change regularly, like print magazines. 'Zines combine qualities of amateur information sites with qualities of outlets for creative efforts.

Print 'zines exist, but even they, noted for their wild content and bizarre illustration, cannot match the level of weirdness of Web 'zines. Furthermore, print 'zines come out infrequently, as their often financially strapped publishers struggle to put out each issue.

The Web's free global circulation and virtually zero startup cost guarantee Web 'zine publishers an advantage over their print counterparts. The best 'zines, such as Cyberkind (Figure 5.9) are edited carefully, just like print

Figure 5.9 Cyberkind
http://sunsite.unc.edu/shannon/ckind/title.html

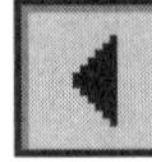

publications. Some Web 'zines are truly odd—there seems to be sort of a competition among 'zine publishers to see who can put out the strangest publication and embrace the weirdest genre of literature.

Creating an On-Line Fan Club

The trouble with being a fan of a little-loved actor or musician is that there are few people with whom to share your passion—and even fewer of them live near you. In the past you had to spend money on a small-circulation fan 'zine, or go to fan conventions and incur large travel and time costs.

Fan clubs exploded on the Web because it amplifies the good parts of clubs—access to bootleg recordings and information about performances—while reducing the effort involved. There's no longer a need to travel to real-life meetings when the exchange that occurs at such meeting happens every day on the Web. More fans can become involved in the club and a community can be maintained, not just formed and quickly dissolved as fan-club communities often are.

Pete Lambie's Bruce Springsteen Page (Figure 5.10), like others devoted to Springsteen's music, enables an on-line fan community to share information and enjoy each other's personalities without traveling.

Supporting Communities

Geographic communities, as well as virtual ones, can benefit from the information-distribution capabilities of the Web. Unlike government-access cable television or public notices in local print newspapers, which are not access-on-demand systems, the Web offers the citizens of a town or city ready access to government information whenever they need it. Tax information, city council agendas, and school data, when posted to the Web, can be had whenever citizens need them.

Community Web pages grew out of the desire of communities to provide information effectively, but also sprang from the same spirit of boosterism that inspired towns in the American midwest to build grand hotels and railroad stations in the last decades of the nineteenth century. A town with a slick, information-rich Web site has bragging rights that less-wired commu-

Figure 5.10 Pete Lambie's Bruce Springsteen Page
http://www.gla.ac.uk/~gkrx11/Bruce/

nities lack. The town of Blacksburg, Virginia, has received international attention for its Web site (Figure 5.11).

Providing Documentation

The Web, though its composition is changing, is made up largely of computer experts. Many people who use the Web write software for a living—and for fun—and some of their efforts get published as shareware or public domain software. The Web is a natural place to provide documentation (the manuals and other information that—in theory, anyway—help you use

Figure 5.11 Blacksburg Electronic Village Home Page
http://www.bev.net/

software) and support (answers to questions and solutions to problems) for software.

Documentation sites aren't just for small-time computer hobbyists, either. Microsoft has a giant archive of software that includes bug fixes and extensions for its many popular programs. Popular programming languages, such as Perl, have support sites on the Web, too (Figure 5.12).

If you want to get information out to computer users, there's no better way to do it than publication on the biggest computer network in the world.

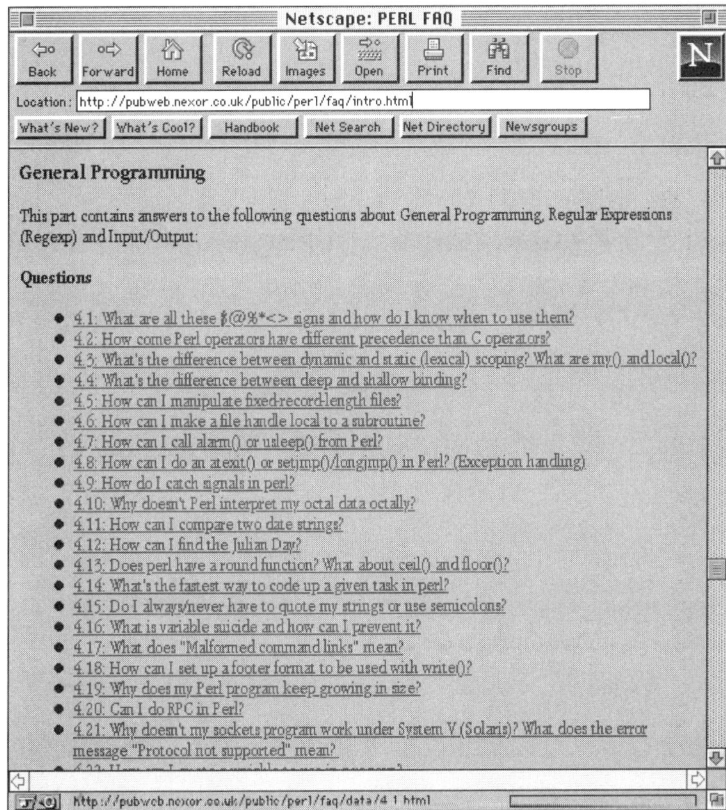

Figure 5.12 The Perl FAQ
http://pubweb.nexor.co.uk/public/perl/faq/intro.html

Providing Services

The real-time capabilities of the Web make it useful to companies that want to provide better service to their customers. Companies who have traditionally used toll-free telephone lines and dozens of attendants have turned to the Web to take some of the load off their customer service departments and give customers a sense that the company is on the leading edge of customer-service thinking.

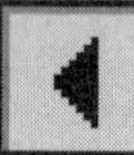

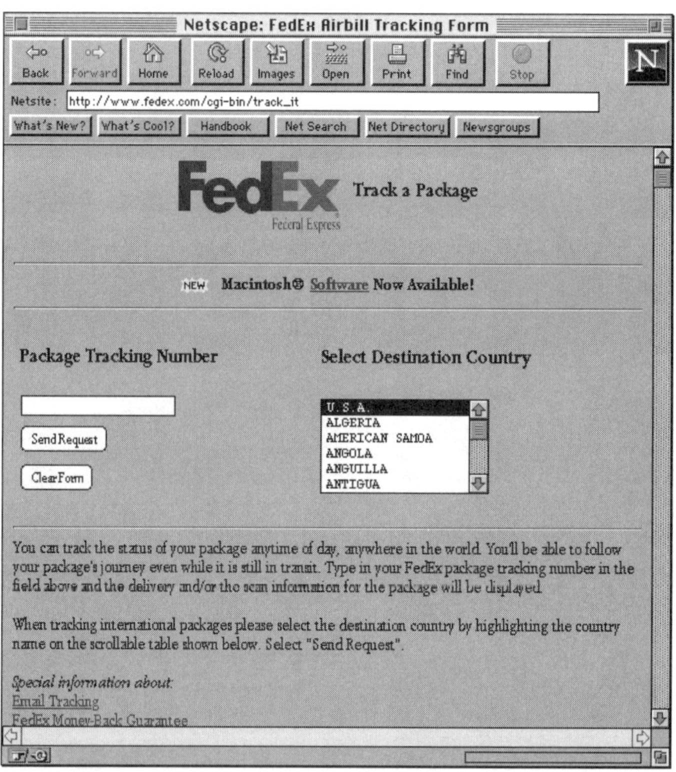

Figure 5.13 FedEx tracking
http://www.fedex.com/cgi-bin/track_it

The best service sites are no-frills deals; there's often little to them except a search engine and a very simple interface. At the Federal Express site (Figure 5.13), for example, you can enter a package tracking number and see where a package is en route to its destination.

Providing Self-Help Support

Sometimes, people are drawn together by something less frivolous than love of a band or other celebrity. Dozens of Web sites have sprung up to support people with a common experience, such as an illness or handicapping condition.

These sites have developed for the same reason as fan club sites, but perhaps the motivations are even stronger. While fans of a musician may not care enough about being a fan to travel to a convention and thus miss out on some interesting talk and good companionship, people who cannot, for medical or financial reasons, participate in a support group may miss lifesaving information or medically valuable support.

The best community support sites provide lots of data—such as vendors of special equipment or lists of doctors with particular specialties—and encourage interaction among community members. Often, such sites are affiliated with a mailing list, Usenet newsgroup, or other discussion facilitation device. The alt.support.stop-smoking Home Page (Figure 5.14) is associated with the Usenet newsgroup alt.support.stop-smoking.

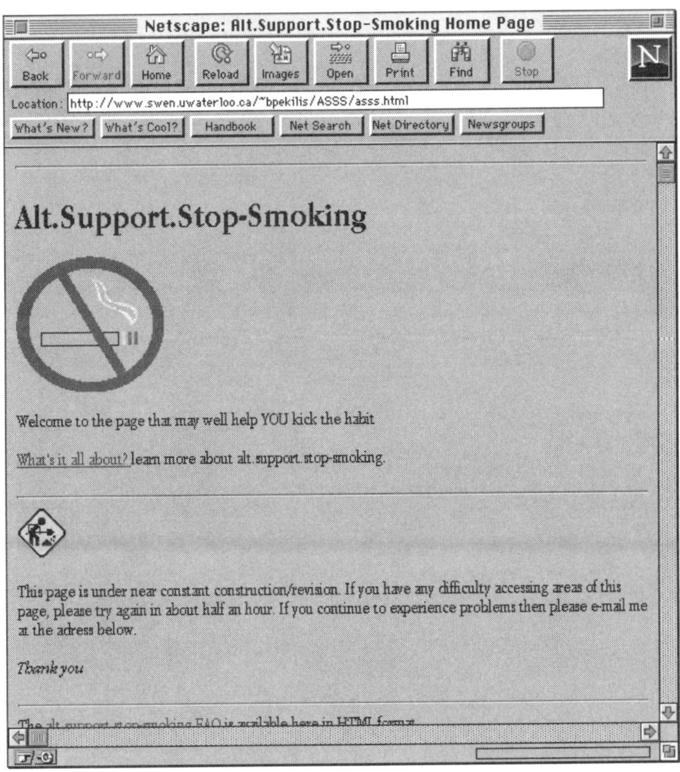

Figure 5.14 The alt.support.stop-smoking Home Page
http://www.swen.uwaterloo.ca/~bpekilis/ASSS/asss.html

Sharing Your Professional Knowledge

For now, anyway, many people who use the Web have valuable professional knowledge. The Web was created to provide a way for nuclear physicists to share information, and it came of age in academic institutions, where professors and students posted information they felt would be useful to others.

The Web, with its spirit of sharing and free access to information, encourages people to give of themselves on-line. Even if yours is an arcane discipline like chinchilla genetics (Figure 5.15), somebody may appreciate that you posted some of your knowledge to the Web.

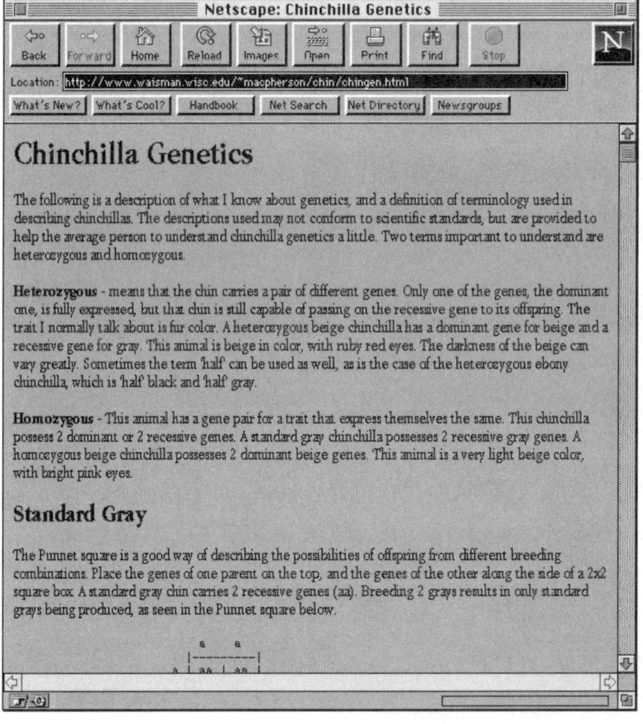

Figure 5.15 Chinchilla Genetics
http://www.waisman.wisc.edu/~macpherson/chin/chingen.html

Educating on the Web

Sharing professional information is what education is all about, so it makes sense that instructors at all levels and in all specialties have employed the Web as an instructional tool—sort of a high-tech blackboard. Since the Web is available to far more college professors and students than elementary and secondary students, most use of the Web as a teaching device is at the college and university level. Professors typically post pages containing links to sites they consider useful to their classes, and often include reference information such as syllabi and grading standards.

Professor John Unsworth of the Institute for Advanced Technology in the Humanities at the University of Virginia used a Web page (Figure 5.16) as part of his class "Engineering the Self in the Late Twentieth Century."

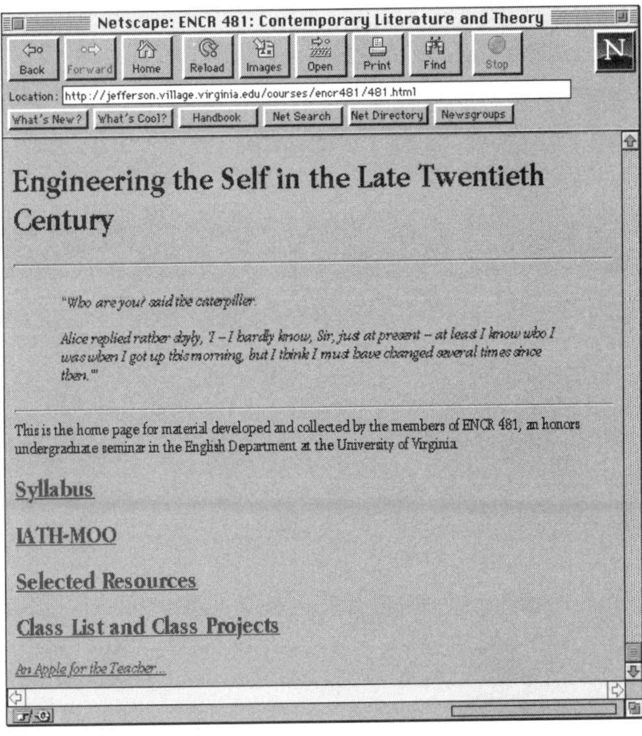

Figure 5.16 Engineering the Self in the Late Twentieth Century
http://jefferson.village.virginia.edu/courses/encr481/481.html

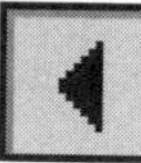

Creating a Corporate Image

The Web is still sufficiently avante garde that companies with sites are considered by many people to be technologically savvy. By investing some money in a site that doesn't try to sell a particular product but instead projects a high-tech corporate image, a company can claim to be participating in a hot new medium and show itself to be willing to embrace new technology. Sites that attempt to create a corporate image likely will soon be combined with sites that serve a marketing function by providing product information and purchase opportunities.

AT&T doesn't try to sell particular goods or services at its site (Figure 5.17), but it tries to show AT&T as a high-tech, growing company.

Figure 5.17 AT&T Home Page
http://www.att.com/

Establishing a Marketing Presence

Marketing presences appeared on the Web when corporations, particularly sellers of hardware and software, found that the Web was populated by people who had a great deal of influence over their organizations' purchasing decisions. Companies put information about their products on-line in hopes that professionals, when preparing to make purchases, would think of products they saw advertised on the Web.

Unlike AT&T's site, Sun Microsystems' site (Figure 5.18) includes lots of product information and instructions on how to order hardware and software. It's an active pitch, instead of a passive display.

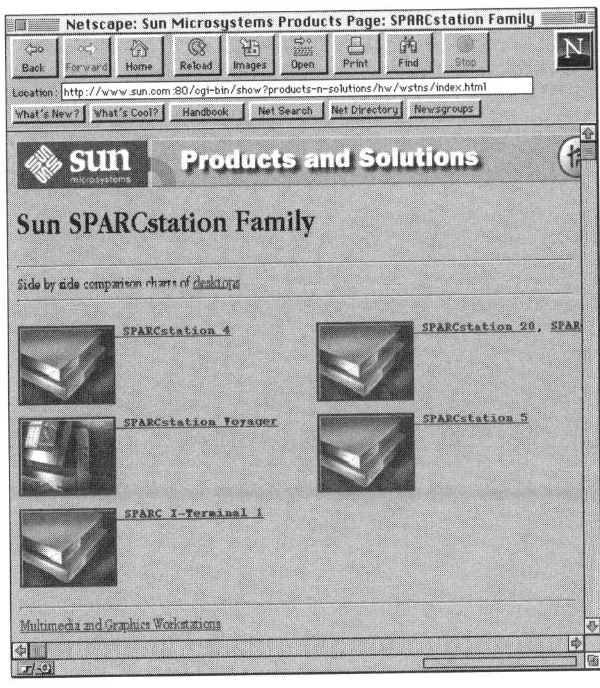

Figure 5.18 Sun Microsystems' SPARCstation Page
http://www.sun.com:80/cgi-bin/show?products-n-solutions/hw/wstns/index.html

With the forms capabilities of today's graphical browsers, it's possible to create interactive Web documents that solicit user opinion. Firms can ask for feedback on products, policies, service, and more. The result won't be scientific—the Web-browsing population has its own unique characteristics—but the information could prove of value as long as it's kept in perspective.

Creating Digital Versions of Print Publications: Advertiser-Supported

The Web has attracted lots of attention from publishers who have been successful in print publications and want to project their influence and expertise into the Web environment. Some magazines and newspapers have created better-looking and more popular Web editions than others.

Advertiser-supported Web publications exist for two reasons. First, it is (or, at least, was, before the question of accurately measuring site visits arose) fairly easy to sell advertisers on the idea of putting an ad where millions of people could see it. Second, it took some time for Web design techniques to allow the construction of subscription-based pages that allowed publishers to collect money directly from their readers.

People Magazine's on-line edition (Figure 5.19) had ads for Ford and AT&T at the bottom of its welcome page.

Creating Digital Versions of Print Publications: Subscriber-Supported

The alternative to unsupported publications ('zines, generally) and advertising-supported publications is support by means of subscription. Subscription-supported publications grew out of the needs of publishers who wanted to take advantage of the distribution potential of the Web but did not want to put out information, such as financial tables or real estate listings, that might cut into their print-edition sales and revenue stream.

Figure 5.19 *People Magazine*
http://www.pathfinder.com/@@j0fjzwAAAAAAAD8J/people/

The Money and Investing Update (Figure 5.20), an on-line publication of the *Wall Street Journal,* gives free access to some features, but restricts others to the use of people who have paid a subscription fee. The site also offers a free trial subscription to those who want to try before they buy.

Creating an On-Line Shopping Catalog

Shopping catalogs sprang up on the Web when entrepreneurs saw a way to offer products to consumers without investing a lot of money in a physical

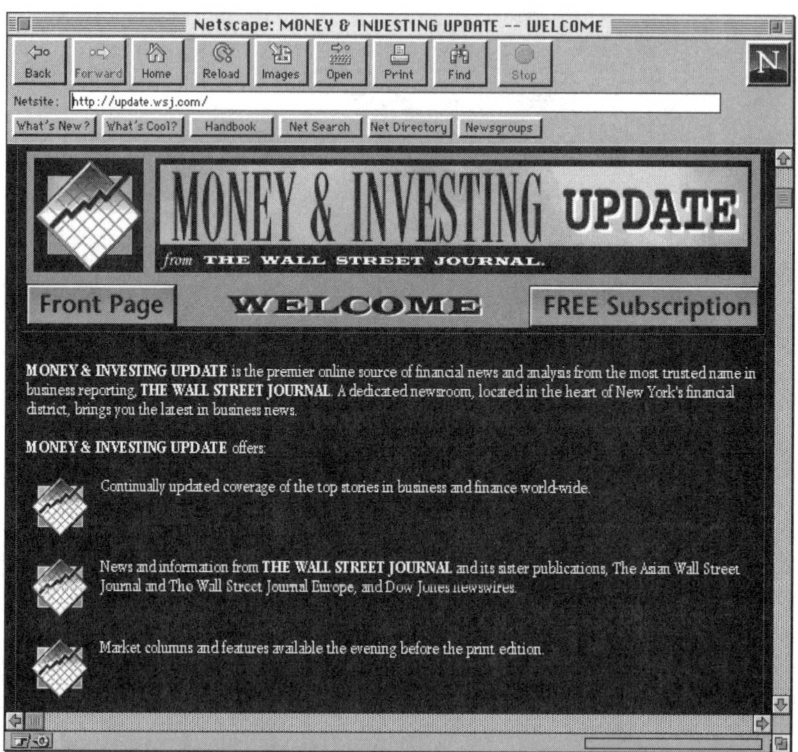

Figure 5.20 Money and Investing Update
http://update.wsj.com/

store or inventory. By creating a few pages that listed goods for sale and providing a toll-free telephone number or secure Net connection, business people could sell things and incur little cost except to cover server access and time.

Some of the most popular shopping catalogs contain listings of recorded music—records, tapes, and compact discs for sale. Sites like CDNow (Figure 5.21) have search engines that give prices and availability for thousands of recordings.

Shopping catalogs will have to adapt—in favor of the consumer—to accommodate agents.

Figure 5.21 CDNow
http://cdnow.com/from=einet/

Creating an Agent

Agents take Web commerce to a higher level. Instead of merely offering something and charging for it, agent sites include search routines that hunt for a particular item of information or product and find the best price. Agents throw a wrench into the plans of Web merchants who planned to use advertising or links to high-traffic sites such as search engines to help ensure their sites' success.

Figure 5.22 Andersen Consulting's BargainFinder Agent
http://bf.cstar.ac.com/bf/

Agents, like Andersen Consulting's BargainFinder (Figure 5.22), have two of the Web's core characteristics. They promote free access to information, in that they make the best price on a given product or item of information available to people who aren't willing to hunt for it on their own. Also, they are essentially hacks—really cool programming tricks that accomplish a task in a novel way.

From Here

- Like to know more about what it takes to publish on the Web? Check out the next chapter.
- To get started on designing your Web site, flip to Part II.

Part II

Designing Your Web

Chapter 6

Choosing a Web Server

In previous chapters, you've learned what makes the Web a distinctive publishing medium. To understand your Web publishing options fully, there's one more important chunk of information that you need to grasp: the technical basis by which Web pages are made accessible to people using Web browsers. In order to make your Web pages accessible, you'll need to place them on an Internet-connected computer that's running a *Web server*, a program that fields browsers' requests for information and doles out the requested documents.

The subject of this chapter is technical, but it doesn't require any technical expertise to read and understand. Its goal is to orient you, not to drag you through every last detail concerning Web servers. And once you've finished reading it, you'll know what you're up against when you want to make your Web pages accessible to others.

For the Time-Challenged

- Web servers receive browsers' requests for information, run scripts, ensure security, and provide statistics on access.
- You'll need to decide whether to run your own Web server or obtain space on a system where Web server software is already installed (a commercial system, or one at school or work).
- To run your own Web server, you'll need an Internet connection with a permanent IP address.
- Macintoshes can't handle very many simultaneous accesses, so Macintosh servers are a good choice only for individual hobbyists, individuals who wish to set up a light-access server on their office Macs, or small organizations with a strictly local draw.

What Web Servers Do

A Web server is a program that fields requests for information from Web browsers, runs scripts, and provides a variety of additional functions, including the vital one of ensuring the security of the host system.

Dishing Out Documents

The most important function of a Web browser is to intercept requests from Web browsers and deliver electronic copies of the requested documents—or an error message, if the requested document is not available. Such requests are made using the HTTP protocol.

Web servers are *stateless programs*. This means simply that the server software does not remember anything about previous transactions with a server. In the course of downloading a document, a server must establish a distinct connection for *each part* of a retrieved document—the text, each in-line graphic, each multimedia object. This design enables the server to field requests from dozens, or even hundreds, of browsers simultaneously.

The stateless design of Web servers ensures that many browsers can access the server simultaneously, but it also means that Web servers consume big chunks of computer system resources (memory and processing time). Just think about it—a request comes in over the network, and it's a request for a document or graphic, which are stored on disk. The document or graphic must be read from the disk and transferred to the network. That adds up to a lot of byte-crunching. You can draw one conclusion from this right now: If you're thinking about running Web server software, you'd better be prepared to set the computer aside for exclusive use as a Web server.

Don't be misled by claims that such-and-such a page has received several hundred thousand or millions of hits per day—that doesn't mean that huge numbers of people are accessing the page. To download a relatively complex document that has dozens of in-line images, the browser and server may establish dozens of completely independent connections, each of which will be recorded as a hit. There's still no reliable *technical* way to estimate how many distinct individuals are accessing a given Web site. That's why Nielsen and other media assessment firms are developing surveys and other techniques for measuring the popularity of Web sites.

Any Web server can dish out a document, but servers vary in their capacity to handle the fine points of this function. For example, CERN's HTTPD cannot send certain error messages unless a programmed script is provided. Some shareware and freeware servers do not automatically respond to a browser's request to send a document only if it has not been modified since a certain date (this is a very desirable feature; without it, the browser will download the document from the network rather than loading it from the disk cache, which is considerably faster).

Running Scripts

Web servers also provide another important function, running *scripts*. A script is a short computer program that is needed to support the interactive features of HTML, such as fill-in forms and searches.

As you will learn in Part III of this book, it's relatively easy to insert HTML tags for interactive features, such as option buttons, drop-down list boxes, and fill-in text boxes. However, these features do not *do* anything in the absence of scripts. When someone using one of your pages fills in a form and clicks the Submit button, nothing will happen unless you have provided a script that is specifically designed to deal with this action.

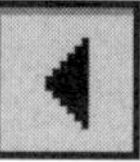

When you access a Web page that contains an interactive element, such as a fill-in form, you'll see a Submit button (or an equivalent). When you click this button, the page originates a message, which is basically a URL: It points to the exact location of the script. The server intercepts the message, locates the script, and executes it. The script performs the requested action and generates a new Web page, which is sent to the server; finally, the browser displays the new page. All scripts work this way—the browser originates a request, the server routes it to the script, the script creates a new Web page in response, and the browser displays it.

With most servers, scripts can be written in any programming language—preferably, one that's suited to the type of computer on which the server software is running. On Windows systems, for example, the scripting language of choice is Visual Basic, while Perl is the preferred choice for UNIX systems. Some servers (such as MacHTTP) require a specific language (MacHTTP requires AppleScript).

Can a nonprogrammer learn to write scripts? If you've got some time, the answer is almost certainly yes. For most computers, you can obtain scripts that are ready to use after minor modification. To be sure, you'll need to learn some of the basics of the programming language in which the script is written. If you don't have the time to write scripts, you can find programmers who can do it—but be prepared to pay a hefty price for this service, which is very much in demand.

Ensuring Security

A third vital function of Web servers is ensuring security. Web servers vary considerably in the number and quality of security options that they offer. More than any other single factor, security features distinguish commercial server software from freeware and shareware efforts.

The following lists the ways that Web server software protects the host system as well as the people accessing the host system by means of Web browsers:

- **Password authentication** The server demands a login name and password from people attempting to access the system.
- **Prohibited access** The server excludes accesses from certain IP addresses or domain names. Some servers can be set up to restrict access so that no one outside an organization, community, state, or country can log into the site.
- **File security** The server ensures that outsiders cannot access files in any directories other than those set aside for Web documents.

- **Confidentiality** The server accepts encrypted data using the S-HTTP or SSL security protocols, or both (see Chapter 26). This feature ensures that people using secure browsers (such as Netscape Navigator) can upload credit card information without fear of its being intercepted en route.

Logging

A fourth function of Web servers is to provide access statistics. Often, it's necessary to install additional software to provide these statistics, but it's well worth doing so; without statistics, you have no way of knowing how often your site is being accessed and which documents people access the most. Increasingly, this vital function is being built into server software. Here's what logging software can tell you:

- Which browsers people are using
- How often your site is accessed each day, broken down by the hour
- Which documents people are accessing the most
- How many new accesses you're receiving each day
- Which countries are accessing your site

Should You Run Your Own Server?

Anyone interested in Web publishing is faced with this question—and it shouldn't be taken lightly. Your choices boil down to the following:

- **Setting up your own server** You'll need a fast Internet connection, a Web server program, a PC or workstation that you can set aside for Web publishing, and time to configure and maintain the system.
- **Using a server at school or work** If you're attending a school or working for an organization that has a Web server, you may be able to install your presentation on the same computer (or one that's networked to this computer). Chances are that the server is running on a reasonably potent UNIX workstation or minicomputer—and what's more, there's probably somebody around who knows how to configure the server and perhaps do a little scripting, too. But you'd

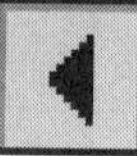

better find out what your organization's policy is with respect to acceptable uses. If your Web presentation is closely related to your organization's mission, you might be able to place it on the server—but you may be asked to create the presentation in line with your organization's established guidelines for Web design.

- **Leasing space from a commercial service provider.** Pricing and service options vary, but you should be able to find a service provider that will place your presentation on a fast UNIX workstation for a flat monthly fee. If you want the service provider's help in implementing interactive features, expect to pay hefty programmer's fees.

Web Server Connectivity Options

If you're thinking about setting up a computer system to run Web server software, you need to understand one important point: Web servers require a much better Internet connection than Web browsers do. With a Web browser, you can make do with a SLIP or PPP dialup account, in which your computer is assigned a temporary Internet address (called an *IP address*) every time you log on. However, this won't do for a Web server. In order for people to access your documents, your server needs to be located at a permanent IP address. Only in this way can people locate your documents.

Does your computer system already have a permanent IP address? Here are some things to think about:

- If your personal computer is connected to the Internet via a local area network (LAN), it probably does have a permanent IP address—ask your network administrator.
- If you connect via a dialup SLIP, CSLIP, or PPP connection, however, your computer probably doesn't have a permanent IP address. You can set up and run a server, but it won't do you any good—people won't have a permanent address where they can locate your documents. That's because most dialup connections use dynamically assigned IP addresses—your system is given a temporary IP address, and it's good for the current session. But that particular address might be assigned to someone else's computer after you log off. And consider, too, that people won't be able to access your site when you're not logged on. To make your documents available on the Web, you need a computer that's permanently connected to the Internet.

Solutions

Permanent Connection Options

If you've decided to go the do-it-yourself route, you'll need a fast and permanent Internet connection. Here's a quick overview of your options:

28.8 Kbps modem on a separate phone line If your Internet service provider offers a dialup service that assigns permanent rather than dynamic IP addresses, you can set aside a separate phone line for Web access. At 28.8 Kbps, you'd be wise to avoid Web presentations that incorporate large graphics.

56 Kbps dedicated line Most Internet service providers can make arrangements for the installation of a specially conditioned telephone line that is permanently connected to the service provider's computer. Formerly, this service was extremely expensive—on the order of $500 to $1000 per month—effectively restricting this type of access to relatively well-endowed organizations and corporations. However, 56 Kbps access costs are in free fall, especially in competitive metropolitan areas. You may be able to arrange for this type of service for $200 per month or less, but it's an attractive option only if ISDN isn't available.

64 Kbps ISDN Short for Integrated Services Digital Network, this service is finally becoming widely available in North America (it is already well established in Europe and Japan). A standard for digital telephony, ISDN is available in a variety of service configurations, the cheapest of which is called Basic Rate ISDN (BRI). A significant advantage of BRI is that it does not require the installation of expensive digital telephone wiring; a type of analog wiring known as *twisted pair* will suffice. (Most homes, schools, and offices built after 1980 have twisted pair wiring.) With BRI, the monthly service fee gets you three lines, two of which are used for phones or data (the third is reserved for control signals); you can connect your telephone and your computer with just one BRI service contract. For your money, as little as $32 per month in many areas (not including Internet access), you'll get 64 Kbps service on a noise-free digital line. One drawback: You'll need to invest in a digital telephone, a digital modem, and circuit termination equipment, which can cost as much as $600. But that's a one-time expense, and then you're set—and you'll have better service than a lot of colleges and universities do right now.

Web Servers and Operating Systems

For anyone contemplating setting up a Web server, the most important consideration isn't so much which program to buy, but which *operating system* you should run the server on. Web servers are available for Windows 3.1, Windows 95, Windows NT, OS/2, the Macintosh OS, and UNIX. The following sections detail what's at stake when you choose one operating system over another.

Windows 3.1

Still in use on millions of IBM PCs and PC compatibles worldwide, Windows 3.1 and Windows for Workgroups 3.1 can run Web server programs, but these systems are a good choice only if you're expecting relatively light loads. The reason? These 16-bit operating systems do not provide sufficient system-level support for *multithreading*, in which a program can carry out more than one task simultaneously. This translates into sharp restrictions on the number of simultaneous accesses—with most servers, you're limited to two dozen or less. That's OK for a site that receives only a few hundred hits a day, but if you're hoping for a bigger audience, look beyond Windows 3.1

Windows 95 and Windows NT

Unlike Windows 3.1, Windows 95 and Windows NT are 32-bit operating systems—that is, they take full advantage of the 32-bit architecture of Intel microprocessors (486 and Pentium). This translates into somewhat faster performance. More important, Windows 95 and Windows NT offer true multithreading, which enables a program to run many functions simultaneously. In practical terms, this means that Windows 95- and NT-based servers can handle many users simultaneously. WebSite (O'Reilly and Associates), a 32-bit version of Robert Denny's Win-HTTPD software, can handle 30 requests *per second* on a 90 MHz Pentium.

What's the difference between Windows 95 and Windows NT? Windows 95 is Microsoft's entry-level operating system. Not a true 32-bit operating system, it is designed to run existing 16-bit Windows programs. However, it also contains all the resources necessary to run 32-bit Windows programs, with advanced multithreading capabilities. Designed with excellent Internet support built in, Windows 95 is an excellent choice for a Web server platform. Windows NT is a true 32-bit operating system; it can't run 16-bit Windows 3.1 programs. Worse, its Internet support is poorly documented and requires experience to configure correctly.

OS/2 Warp

IBM's OS/2 is a true 32-bit operating system with many advanced features and excellent built-in Internet support, but its future is cloudy. Even IBM's CEO, Lou Gerstner, concedes that OS/2 will never dominate the desktop. In many respects, OS/2 Warp is an ideal Web server platform—but you'll need to consider whether OS/2 is going to be supported long enough to make your investment in an OS/2 system worthwhile.

Macintosh OS

The Macintosh operating system (OS) is a good choice for a Web server if ease of use is your primary consideration, but be forewarned: Due to limitations in the current version of the Macintosh OS, Mac servers can handle a theoretical maximum of 64 simultaneous users—and in practice, Mac servers function best when the maximum number of users is set to about a dozen or less. That's enough to handle the load for an infrequently accessed page, but it puts the Macintosh out of the running for medium-to-large-sized organizations.

On the plus side, the Mac provides an excellent environment for scripting, thanks to AppleScript, a scripting language included free with the Mac OS (Version 7.5 and later).

For Mac servers, there's really only one game in town: the shareware MacHTTP and the commercial version, WebSTAR, now marketed by O'Reilly & Associates. The following sections describe these servers and the wealth of point-and-click utilities that have been developed for them. Using these utilities, nonprogrammers can set up an impressive Web site in short order.

MacHTTP and WebSTAR The work of programmer Chuck Shotton, MacHTTP (http://www.biap.com/) is a shareware Web server that's widely in use in the Macintosh community. Available at a cost of $65 for educational institutions, or $95 for all other users (including commercial and governmental), MacHTTP is a good choice for Web hobbyists, individuals in organizations who wish to make documents available locally, and other light uses. Security is minimal, limited to password authentication and domain name restriction.

A commercial spinoff, WebSTAR (http://www.starnine.com/webstar/webstar.html), offers increased speed and can handle many more connections—up to several thousand per hour. Forthcoming versions will implement SSL and S-HTTP encryption. For both servers, easy-to-use utilities are available

for implementing forms, database searches, and clickable maps. WebSTAR is currently priced at $599 for commercial users; educational institutions pay $295.

MacHTTP and WebSTAR Utilities The widespread adoption of MacHTTP and WebSTAR as de facto server standards in the Macintosh community has led to the development of several excellent server utilities. Using these utilities, nonprogrammers can set up impressive interactive Web sites. The following describes the most frequently used utilities and provides information for obtaining them from the Internet.

- **WebMap** This utility enables nonprogrammers to define GIF and PICT files as clickable maps, in which rectangles, cicles, and polygons are defined as "hot areas" that are linked to a URL. The program supports both the CERN and NCSA imagemap formats. WebMap is a commercial program that will cost $25 on its release. For more information, access http://www.city.net/cnx/software/webmap.html.
- **Mac-ImageMap** This utility provides the script support needed to serve clickable maps with MacHTTP and WebSTAR. Conforming to the NCSA standard for clickable maps, the program enables map designers to assign URLs to rectangle, circles, elliptic regions, arbitrary polygon regions, and nearest points. Created by Lutz Weimann, a German programmer, the utility can be accessed at http://wyl.zib-berlin.de/imagemap/Mac-ImageMap.html). Currently available as freeware, the program is available in 68x00 and Power Macintosh versions.
- **WebStat** This utility takes the log output from MacHTTP and converts it into summaries based on time, domain, and files. To download a copy, access http://snodaq.phy.queensu.ca/WebStat.sit.Hqx.
- **Annotate** This utility enables people browsing your site to leave comments for you to read. To download Annotate, access http://snodaq.phy.queensu.ca/Annotate.sit.Hqx.
- **ROFM CGI** This utility enables you to provide Web access to FileMaker Pro databases. Users can query the databases using key-

words, and they receive a new HTML document in reply. To download this script, access http://rowen.astro.washington.edu/.

- **NetForms** This utility, an AppleScript package, enables people browsing your site to add new documents. The text that users enter is automatically formatted as HTML. For more information, access http://www.digimark.net/maxum/netformshome.html.
- **TR-WWW** This utility enables users to search and subsequently load documents from your site. Using fill-in forms, users can search using keywords and Boolean operators. TR-WWW can work with any Macintosh text document, including Word files, and can handle libraries up to 15 MB in size (you can create more than one 15 MB library if you wish). For more information, access http://www.monash.edu.au/informatics/tr-www.html.

Additional Mac Servers As noted previously, MacHTTP and WebSTAR are the only games in town—and here's some evidence. Directly available from Apple itself is the Apple Internet Server Solution, a CD-ROM disc that's loaded with Internet server software, including—you guessed it—WebSTAR and a number of utilities that provide interactive functionality to WebSTAR, including e-mail reply, clickable maps, and software for searching databases. For more information on the Apple Internet Server Solution, access

http://www-abs.apple.com/HomePage/Products/Internet.solution/index.html

UNIX

Versions of the UNIX operating system have been developed for just about every computer in existence. A true 32-bit operating system, UNIX provided the platform for the development of the first Web server, CERN HTTPD (and the later NCSA HTTPD). The public domain NCSA server is generally considered to be the best available, and has been ported to a variety of UNIX "flavors" (including Linux, a shareware UNIX operating system for Intel microprocessors).

UNIX Web servers set the standard for functionality and power, but at a price: Most require considerable UNIX experience to install, configure, and maintain.

From Here

- Whether you've decided to create your own Web server or take advantage of an existing Web server installation, your next task is to think about the design of your web. Check out Chapter 7 for suggestions on getting started with your Web presentation's plan.
- Even if you're planning to use an HTML editor (a program that helps you code HTML), you'll still need to learn the basics. Chapter 10 provides an easy-to-follow tutorial that teaches much of what you'll need to know to create a high-quality Web site.

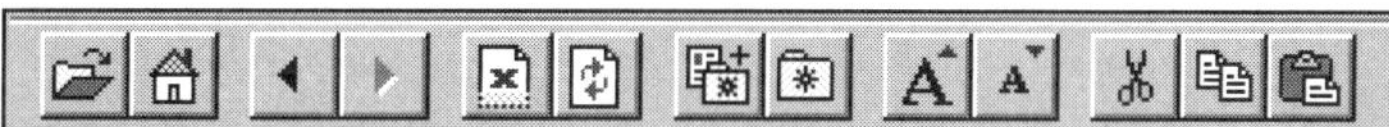

Chapter 7

Developing a Publishing Plan

You wouldn't try to build a house without a blueprint. Nor would you try to invest money without thinking about your goals, or invite a friend to dinner without first considering the menu. Most things we undertake are much more successful if we first think about what we want to accomplish and develop a plan for achieving those goals.

The Web is no different. If you want to put together a successful Web site, you have to think about the people you want to use it and how you will make them want to visit your site. What sort of things interest them? Which of their needs are served by existing Web resources? What do they consider cool—and how can you incorporate those features into your documents?

You have to consider technical factors as much as aesthetic ones. Does your audience have computer equipment to handle the MPEG video clips you want to include, or would they be more inclined to come back if you

provided stills from the video clips—which require less computing power—instead? Does your audience speak the language in which you want to write your page? How will potential visitors learn about your site in the vastness of the Web?

In this chapter, we'll examine the thought process behind preparing to publish a set of killer Web documents. With examples, the chapter will show that the thinking process that precedes actual HTML coding is the most essential part of publishing on the Web.

Framing Your Purpose

Before you begin to think about the details of your documents, you need to spend time considering what they will do. What effect do you want to have on people who visit your site? Do you want to entertain them, inform them, rally them to political action, what?

Chapter 5 provided an outline of Web publishing genres. Each of those genres lends itself to a different purpose. Chances are, the purpose you have in mind for your Web publication falls into one of these categories:

- Sharing information about yourself
- Sharing information about a hobby or avocation of yours
- Informing people about a situation
- Bringing about political or social change
- Sharing creative work
- Helping others find Web resources
- Promoting (or panning) a product you don't personally sell
- Entertaining others
- Publishing a magazine or newsletter (without financial support, or with support from advertising or subscriptions)
- Organizing an on-line community of fans or hobbyists
- Smoothing the operation of a geographic community
- Supporting a software product
- Providing customers of your business with a service

For the Time-Challenged

- Before you delve into the details of designing your site, you need to identify your audience. Everything you do in developing your site will be geared toward making that audience happy.
- Demographically, the average Web user is a white male North American with an annual income between $50,000 and $60,000 and at least one college degree. Further demographic analysis is on the Web at Georgia Tech (http://www.cc.gatech.edu/gvu/user_surveys/User_Survey_Home.html).
- Consider your audience's technical skill, reading ability, interests, concerns, and activities.
- Identify people who are *not* in your audience as well as those who are.
- Before creating your site, use the various Web search tools to discover which sites compete with yours and which sites complement yours. You can alter your plan to avoid competition (if you want), and you can build hyperlinks from your site to complementary sites.

- Supporting a community of ill or disadvantaged people
- Sharing your professional knowledge
- Educating others
- Giving your company a Web presence
- Marketing your company's products on the Web
- Selling things on the Web

Developing a Purpose Statement

When you start a business, you need a business plan. At its core, a business plan is a statement of what the proposed business will *do*—what it will sell, to whom it will sell, and how it will grow. Your Web site needs a written plan, too. You need to write a purpose statement.

Overall Topic

First, decide on an overall topic—something like baseball, big game fishing, or Lithuanian politics. Your overall topic should be something about which you're both interested and knowledgeable, since you'll have to put up with it as long as you maintain the page and people will ignore your resources if they sense you've tried to publish on a subject you don't really understand.

Let's say you're a journalist, and you decide to make news and features reporting the overall topic of your page.

Specific Objective

You need to get more specific, though, than a general statement of topic. You have to decide what your Web pages will do—what services they will provide that will make people want to visit and return to see them again. This is the point in the planning process at which you draw on your experience as a Web surfer. What have you seen that relates to your general topic, and what is lacking? Are there any sites that take on an important task but do a poor job of handling it? Trust your intuition here. You're a member of the community of people interested in your general topic, so you know what is and is not available to that community on the Web.

In the reporting example, you might conclude that there are lots of Web sites that provide news updates, and lots of Web sites that offer long feature stories. There are few sites, however, that offer critiques of on-line reportage. There's a market niche available for a site that offers weekly reviews of the on-line news media's performance and hyperlinks to the best and worst of on-line reporting.

Expected Outcomes

When you're designing your page, complete this sentence: "After reading this page, my audience will..." What do you want your site's visitors to do after reading your page? Vote a certain way? Buy your product? Laugh? Think of your company in a particular way? You need to consider your site's effect on people.

Consider Web sites you've seen that have moved you in a particular way. Which of those feelings would you like to see duplicated in the people who view your documents?

In our reporting-critique example, you would probably conclude that after visiting your Web site, your visitors would go see the coverage you rated highly and the sites you panned. You might also conclude that, upon leaving your pages, the visitor would make a mental note to return as soon as the next week's critiques were posted.

The Web Audience: Who's Out There

Unlike television audiences, which have been analyzed and studied for more than 50 years, the people who use the Web are largely a mystery. A few studies have been done, but these have been fairly small-scale affairs, and they usually involve some major skewing factor, such as attracting responses from only people in the United States or drawing a disproportionate number of people from educational institutions or government laboratories. Still, there are a few conclusions to be drawn about the composition of the Web audience.

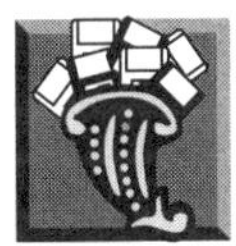

For a complete rundown of the results of one of the best Web-user surveys, point your browser to the Graphics, Visualization, and Usability Center at Georgia Tech's College of Computing:

http://www.cc.gatech.edu/gvu/user_surveys/User_Survey_Home.html

The most recent GVU Web survey was conducted in May of 1995, and this site provides extensive analysis of what that survey found and how its findings compare to those of older surveys.

It's White, It's Male, It's Wealthy, and It's Educated

The Georgia Tech survey found that the people who use the Web are predominantly white (82 percent, with no other racial group comprising more than 5 percent), male (82 percent), wealthy (median annual income between $50,000 and $60,000), and educated (almost 60 percent have a bachelor's degree or better). The survey also found that most Web users are married, have no children, and own at least one personal computer.

What do these demographics mean to you? They're good news if you're trying to sell something on the Web, as these folks have lots of income to spend and, the survey also found, considerable influence over buying decisions at their places of work. The demographics are bad news if you're trying

to appeal to poor people or racial minorities. As shown later in this section, Web demographics are changing quickly, though, and they may suit your needs better in a year.

It's Changing All the Time

The May 1995 Georgia Tech survey, compared to earlier surveys, showed significant change in the population of Web users. No longer are the people who use the Web mainly technical experts who work with computers for a living. An increasing number of Web users have little technical background, and use the Web just like an extension of their commercial information service or company network. These people are more impressed by sites that are both powerful and easy to use. They don't have time to dicker with unintuitive interfaces and obscure site organizations.

Try to consider how the Web audience will relate to your site in the future. If the Web is becoming a more representative cross-section of the world's population at large, any markets you target will have more potential participants. You'll also have to design your site to appeal to people with less technical skill.

Specifying Your Target Audience

Marketers, who are employed to figure out what new products people will pay for and to identify ways to make existing products more appealing to people, spend entire careers identifying target audiences. They need to know who consumes a particular product, and why, so the product can be made even more appealing. Whether your pages are to be business-related or not, you need to take a second to consider who will use them.

Level of Technical Ability

How technically savvy are the members of your target audience? Are they familiar with basic Web operating rules, such as how to use hyperlinks? Are they familiar with forms? Are they sufficiently trained to handle a link to a Telnet server? You have to keep the technical abilities of the members of your target audience in mind so you don't baffle them with cutting-edge features or bore (or insult!) them with excessive hand-holding.

The target audience for your reporting-critiques documents will consist of reporters and those who appreciate fine reporting. It's probably fair to say

that these people aren't afraid of computers, but probably don't use them for the sake of using computers, as more technically oriented people do. The target audience for this site will be able to use the Web with considerable skill, but won't be inclined to spend hours figuring out an unintuitive or poorly designed set of documents. They will get no thrill out of solving a technical challenge—they will consider that an unnecessary hassle.

Literacy Level

What sort of language should you use in your pages? Like so many other things, it depends on your audience. If your desired readers are high-school students, it's not a good idea to use obscure words and irregular grammar structures that would challenge a well-read adult. If, on the other hand, your desired audience is made up of automotive engineers, it's okay to use technical jargon and references to authors and studies not widely known outside the automotive industry.

Consider the lowest common denominator when you go about choosing what sort of language to use in your documents. As a reference, the news sections of most major metropolitan newspapers are written to be understood by people with eighth-grade educations. Keeping your style and diction simple makes your site less forbidding and encourages more people to use your documents.

In your example reporting site, you can probably assume that reporters and avid newspaper readers are better read than most Web users. In such a site, you shouldn't shun lofty language. In fact, people who work with words for a living and those who consume them for enjoyment will be turned off by simplistic language and basic vocabulary. A site that celebrates good writing should employ good writing itself.

What Are They Interested In?

Consider what your audience wants, then figure out a way to provide it to them. If your site is oriented around, say, the Seattle Mariners baseball team, think about whether your audience prefers to see a searchable database of statistics for every Mariners player since 1985, or a page, updated daily, with information about the team's performance this season? Since you feel you're qualified to publish information about a topic, you're probably qualified to guess at the needs of the people who will consume the information you put on your pages.

In the on-line reporting example, you might conclude that your audience is in a hurry to get the best news stories on the Web. You might also decide that if your patrons were in a real hurry, they'd turn on their radios and that they come to your Web site for a careful, well-thought-out analysis of trends in on-line reporting and essays on why you liked the stories you applauded on your site. Since these two audience desires conflict, you may have to structure your site to accommodate both...but that comes later in this chapter.

What Are Their Activities?

This is part of the process of getting a mental picture of the people who use the Web resources you post. Think about what they do. Do they raise children? Vote Libertarian? Work on farms? Drive Studebakers? Attend Unitarian church services each Sunday? What will members of your audience be doing when they're not looking at the Web resources you've posted for them?

Identifying the activities of your audience members will also help you figure out what you can do to improve their lives. If your desired audience consists mainly of Web authors, you won't impress them by including a guide to basic HTML programming in your site. You might, though, draw a good crowd by posting collections of public-domain icons and graphics for use in Web documents.

Presumably, the visitors to your reporting pages will spend at least part of their days working with newspapers—and many of them will work for papers and magazines full-time. Therefore, you might want to avoid summaries of the day's news, since it won't be news to your readers by the time they get to your page. Instead, include a good analysis of the news as it was reported on the Web that day—analysis your readers wouldn't have seen elsewhere during their daily activities.

What Are Their Concerns?

What do the people for whom you're designing your site *want?* What are they worried about, and what problems can you help them solve? Your readers may be concerned about getting good grades in high-school calculus, or about the development of the war in Bosnia. They may care about last night's hockey scores, or maybe they couldn't care less about sports. Draw on your knowledge and feelings as a member of the community you're trying to appeal to and build a site that would make your life better.

Journalists and newspaper fans are very much concerned with the future of the paper, as no one seems sure what will happen to the printed word as paper prices continue to rise and electronic publishing technology grows better all the time. Therefore, it would appeal to the audience of your proposed reporting page if you included information about the potential replacement of printed media with electronic media, and perhaps took a stand that amounted to something like, "These stories, published during the last week on the Internet, are every bit as good as stories published on paper. They represent the future of reporting."

Who Do You *Not* Care about Reaching?

Just as important as deciding who your audience *is* is deciding who they are *not*. As the cliché goes, you can't be all things to all people. You might as well draw the line at the beginning about who you're not interested in having visit your site.

Most of the time, your site's content will determine who visits and who returns. Nobody but kite hobbyists really care about kite sites, and gerbil aficionados will generally segregate themselves from the followers of Kenyan soccer. If you run a set of commercial pages, your products likely will attract mostly the sorts of people they're designed for, as only those people will know what to seek.

In your example reporting site, you probably don't care about reaching people who want a quick rundown of the latest news. Lots of sites already do that, and you'd be hard pressed to beat some of them. In this example, you decide not to be a publisher of news, but rather an analyzer of the news that other people publish. Your site won't be a briefing page; it will be a media critique page, two steps removed from actual news events.

Checking Out the Competition

Unless you're selling something and somebody else on the Web is hawking the same thing, other Web publishers aren't really your competitors. Consider other people who have documents that deal with topics similar to yours to be allies, since they take some responsibility off of your shoulders and enable you to pursue more exciting publishing topics. Still, you should hunt the Web for people with sites similar to the one you want to do so you can be sure to differentiate your site from theirs and provide hyperlinks to those sites as appropriate.

Don't Reinvent the Wheel—Link Instead

Since, barring communications problems and other technical difficulties, your viewers can't tell the difference between documents at your site and documents at a distant site, you can enhance the quality of your Web publication by linking your site to useful resources elsewhere.

Also, send electronic mail to the maintainers of related sites and encourage them to put links to your pages on their documents. Post your site's URL to relevant Usenet newsgroups and mailing lists, and soon your page will be integrated with others' Web publications.

Searching for Competitors

Use the various Web search tools to look up resources that might complement—or conflict with—your planned site. Check out all the usual suspects, as one search engine's database may list a site while the others do not. This is especially true if your documents are to deal with an obscure topic.

The search engines to visit are as follows:

- **InfoSeek (http://www.infoseek.com)** InfoSeek is a very powerful search tool—but everyone knows it. Unless you subscribe to InfoSeek's subscription-based service, odds are good you'll be unable to get through to the server. Keep trying, or try on a weekend when the site is less busy.
- **Yahoo (http:///www.yahoo.com/)** Yahoo is a subject tree—a list of sites organized by topic. Look for your general topic in the Yahoo index, then follow links to more specific listings. You may find that someone has already published on the topic you planned to cover, or that someone has a resource to which you want to link.
- **Virtual Library (http://www.w3.org/hypertext/DataSources/bySubject/Overview.html)** Like Yahoo, the Virtual Library is a subject tree with information organized by category. Virtual Library listings tend to be academically oriented, so it's not the best place to look for fan club or hobby site information, but it's a great place to search for sites dealing with more serious topics.
- **Lycos (http://lycos.cs.cmu.edu/)** One of the oldest and most respected search engines on the Web, Lycos has a great user interface

that lets you customize your search fairly extensively. It doesn't search entire documents, though—it searches just the information in the header and first paragraph of text.

- **Webcrawler (http://webcrawler.com)** Webcrawler is slow, and its database doesn't contain many URLs, but the ones it contains are listed in full-text form. If you think some data relevant to your planned site might be buried deep within somebody's document, try this search engine.

I keep trying to reach one of the search engines, but it won't respond!
Remember those old movies in which, for some reason, everybody in town wanted to place a telephone call at the same time, and there was a scene that featured the frazzled telephone operator frantically plugging patch cables into her switchboard? That, in essence, is what's going on when you can't get through to a search engine. Try again right away and you might get through, but if you wait until late at night or a weekend, you'll certainly have better luck.

If you're fortunate, there will be a trailblazer page somewhere on the Web that was put up by a person interested in your proposed field of publication. Try the search tools to hunt for the names of esteemed experts in the field, and see if they have posted resources for others to use.

Revising Your Purpose Statement

Now that you've examined the Web for competition, it may be time to alter your purpose statement. The odds are slim that you found another document that deals with your proposed topic in the detail you have in mind, but you may need to alter your plan to take advantage of someone else's resources.

Creating Your Purpose Statement

Use the form on the following page to help you summarize the decisions you make about the market for your Web publication.

Purpose Statement

Overall Topic: ______________________________

Competing Sites: ______________________________

____

Complementary Sites: ______________________________

____

Justification for This Site: ______________________________

____

Specific Goals:

1) ______________________________

2) ______________________________

3) ______________________________

4) ______________________________

5) ______________________________

Intended Audience: ______________________________

Technical Ability: ______________________________

Language Ability: ______________________________

Interests: ______________________________

Concerns: ______________________________

After visiting this site, my audience will...

From Here

- Once you've devised your purpose statement, you're on your way to crafting a successful web. In the next chapter, you'll take the next step: Selecting a web architecture.

Chapter 8

Understanding Web Architecture

As in building a house or a computer, you must decide on a basic design scheme to use. During the early years of Web construction, three basic architectures have emerged as forms for organizing information placed on the Web.

The three architectures are the *Web page*, the *Web presentation*, and the *semantic net*. These designs are described in detail later in this section. Generally, single Web pages are the simplest, Web presentations allow you to control the flow of information to the viewer, and semantic nets allow the viewer a great deal of flexibility.

It's also important to remember that you're not tied to a particular Web architecture. Just as you can deviate from the standard ranch, colonial, and A-frame plans in designing a new house, you can mix and match aspects of each Web architecture or even develop a new architecture that suits your application better than any of the others. And besides, mingled Web architectures

look much better than mingled home architectures: a semantic net goes well with a linear presentation, but Gothic buttresses don't complement Federalist columns.

The architecture you choose depends on several factors, but, as with nearly every other aspect of Web design, the nature of your audience is the most important. You'll want to pay special attention to such characteristics as their attention span, their skill in navigating among Web documents, and whether they need to be led from one topic to another or they can draw conclusions from a generally unorganized collection of data.

You'll also want to consider your goals for the site, and think about what Web architecture best suits them. If your goal is to sell a product, for instance, you may need to lead your site's visitors through a presentation one step at a time. If your goal is to provide hobbyists with references and technical information, it might be better to create a site with many small pages—and perhaps a search tool—that would enable hobbyists to quickly find the data they need and move on.

The prime issue at stake in your Web-architecture decision is the question of who is in control. In a traditional medium, such as a novel, the author is in nearly complete control. Though the reader can read the last page of the novel first, it won't make any sense and he or she will have missed the fun of seeing the story develop. That's not the case on the Web.

Web authors can design their sites so the reader has a great deal of control. By giving readers the freedom to move among many different chunks of data at will, the Web author enables them to navigate through the material in their own way and absorb it in the order they wish. Instead of having to offer the reader a more or less linear collection of thoughts and arguments, the publisher of a Web site can give the reader a three-dimensional collection of data to explore in any number of ways.

Such an approach may not be right for your data, though, and this chapter aims to help you decide among linear and nonlinear methods of presenting information. Consider single *Web pages*, multi-page *Web presentations*, and elaborate *semantic nets* as you plan your site.

A Single Web Page

The fastest and easiest way to publish on the Web is with a Web page—a single HTML document that contains information. A Web page may also contain links to distant pages, but those pages are maintained by someone else. A Web page is shown in Figure 8.1.

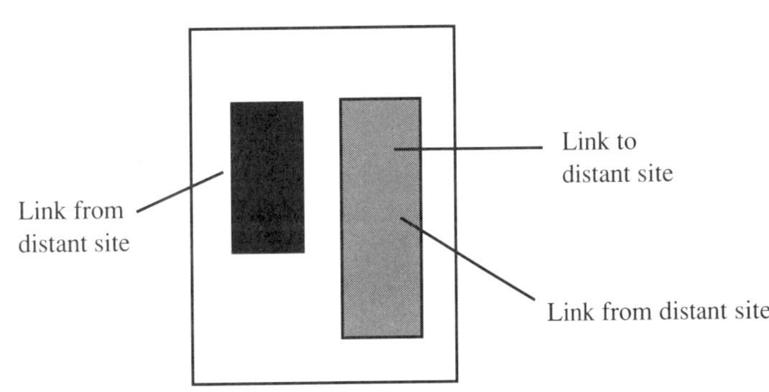

Figure 8.1 Web page architecture

For the Time-Challenged

- Web sites have architectures, just like buildings. A site's architecture is its general design, the way the information the site contains is organized.
- There are three popular Web architectures: the Web page, the Web presentation, and the semantic net.
- A Web page is just that: a single HTML document containing information. Web pages are useful when only a little bit of data is to be published and it's important that the data be viewed in a particular sequence.
- A Web presentation is a series of Web pages that must be viewed in a particular order. Web presentations are useful when a lot of data is to be published and it is important that it be viewed in a particular order. Sales pitches and logical arguments are examples of information that fit into Web presentations.
- A semantic net is composed of lots of little chunks of data, each posted to the Web on its own page. A semantic net architecture makes it easy to navigate among the pieces of data and draw conclusions from them without help from the Web author.
- You're not limited to these three architectures. You're free to combine two or more of them, or develop a new one that suits your application better than the older architectures.

Advantages

Single-page sites offer the advantage of encapsulating all the information they hold into one location on the Web—there's no need to hunt around a complex structure involving dozens of Web pages. Also, when a spider finds your page and lists it in a search engine's database, it's likely that search results will be more useful, since there won't be 15 listings for the same site in a search report. (Imagine running a Lycos search for "Cleveland, Ohio"—the subject of your site, say—and getting back listings for "Sports in Cleveland, Ohio," "Museums in Cleveland, Ohio," and "City Government in Cleveland, Ohio," all of which are pages in the same collection.)

Single Web pages are relatively easy to maintain, since there's only one HTML document to download from the Web server, modify, and upload again. You will probably want to consider a single Web page if you're planning to provide frequently updated information or to alter your page's appearance often.

Web pages also allow you to make a point in a linear fashion, as you learned to do in school. You can treat a Web page like a piece of typing paper by starting with a thesis at the top, explaining some supporting ideas, and wrapping up with a conclusion. If your site's purpose calls for making such a point, you'll probably want to use a single-page architecture.

Disadvantages

The main disadvantage of single Web pages is that they don't take advantage of the Web's unique ability to break data into small, specific chunks for readers to navigate through as they wish. If you choose to post your data in the form of a single Web page, you're tying yourself to conventions of design that were established for print media.

That's not necessarily a bad thing, as print media have been used successfully for millennia and there is a large body of knowledge about what makes a printed document look good while style rules for HTML are still being debated. You have to decide between using a new technology that might make it easier to communicate your message and using an old technology for which rules and styles have been established.

Applications

There are two popular kinds of single-page Web sites: home pages and information pages. Home pages are perhaps the oldest genre of Web publication, and by definition they're single-page documents. Even if your home page has hyperlinks to several subsidiary documents, you still point your browser to a particular URL at the beginning of a browsing session.

Information lends itself to single-page architecture when there is not a lot of it or when it's important that it be presented to the reader in a sequential way and a linear, multi-page presentation would distract from the information. Many amateur and professional information-sharing sites are of single-page design, as are many sites that are based on lists or tables of data, since organizing data on a single page enables visitors to use the search functions of their browsers to find specific information.

If your single-page design is lengthy, include a table of contents at the top and use internal hyperlinks to link each item with the appropriate section. You can do this using the NAME attribute of the <A> tag. For more information, see Chapter 13.

A Web Presentation

If you want to share more information than can easily fit on one page, but don't want to surrender control of the way that information is presented to your readers, a Web presentation may be the best way to organize your information.

A Web presentation, though it is made up of several pages, gives the viewer little flexibility in navigating through the information presented. Typically, the viewer enters the presentation through a welcome page, then proceeds one page at a time through the information, which is presented in the order the site designer wants. A viewer can get out of a Web presentation only by invoking a feature of his or her browser, such as a Hot List item or a URL from a history list.

In some Web presentation designs, viewers have options at different places in the presentation. They may opt to see information about one of several products, for example, instead of having to page through information about products that are uninteresting to them before reaching the product data they want. Typically, Web presentations include navigation aids, such as links back to the welcome page or other pages from which others branch, that help viewers quickly find the portion of the presentation that's relevant to them.

A Web presentation architecture is shown in Figure 8.2.

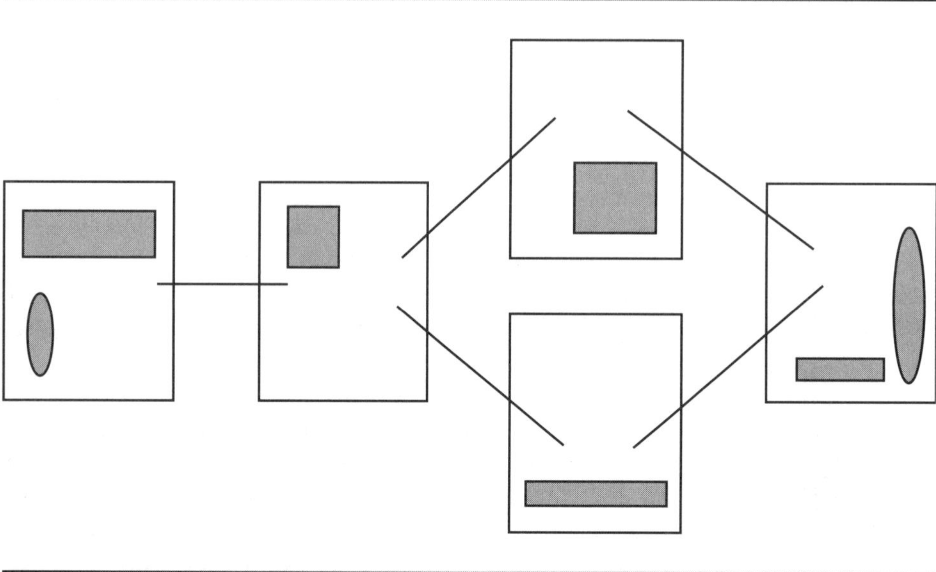

Figure 8.2 A Web presentation architecture

Advantages

The advantage of Web presentations is that they break large quantities of information into manageable chunks, but allow that information to be viewed in an orderly manner. Unlike semantic nets (described next), Web presentations keep control in the hands of the Web designer and surrender very little of it to the person viewing the pages.

Disadvantages

Web presentations are somewhat in violation of the spirit of the Web, where it is considered poor taste to restrict a person's navigation options. You must be sure that if you're going to take away a visitor's freedom of movement, you do so for a good reason and he or she goes away happy after the presentation.

Web presentations lock your site's viewers into a predetermined routine, something they may not appreciate. If your presentation moves too fast, viewers may become intimidated, while if it moves too slow, they may grow bored or conclude that you don't think highly of their intellectual abilities. Either way, they probably won't return and your site will start to earn a bad reputation among users of the Web.

Applications

Certain applications involve too much information for a single page, but do not lend themselves to the chaos of a semantic net. Those applications, which typically involve some kind of linear flow from one idea to another, are good candidates for inclusion in a Web presentation.

The steps involved in a recipe, for example, must be presented in a particular order. If the steps to the recipe won't fit easily on one page—if the recipe is for, say, a home-built aircraft—a Web presentation is an excellent option. The same idea applies to sales pitches. It wouldn't be good if the viewer of your Web site first came to the page that said "Model V: $14,439" and *then* saw the pages that explain why the Model V is such a great machine.

If you use a Web presentation architecture, be sure to include navigation buttons at the top of each page. One button should be linked to the next page, one to the previous page, and one to the page where the presentation started. Your site's viewers will appreciate being given some extra flexibility in navigation.

A Semantic Net

Semantic nets take advantage of the capabilities of hypertext authoring, but require the creator of a site to surrender navigational control to the reader.

Semantic nets require you to puree your data—you must chop your information into tiny bits and link all the bits together with hyperlinks. There should be only one idea—a paragraph of text, a graphic, or an item of some other medium—on each page. You then provide a point of entry and set the viewer free to explore the information at will. A semantic net architecture is shown in Figure 8.3.

Advantages

Semantic nets are the highest form of hypermedia, since they are freely navigable and offer almost limitless possibilities for interpretation. By organizing your information in a semantic net, you offer your site's visitors great freedom to examine and draw conclusions from data at their leisure. You're not forcing them to look at data in a particular way, and you're not demanding that they conclude certain things from it. Your site's viewers, assuming they have the brain power to absorb data presented in a random way, will appreciate the fact that you gave them free rein over the data you posted.

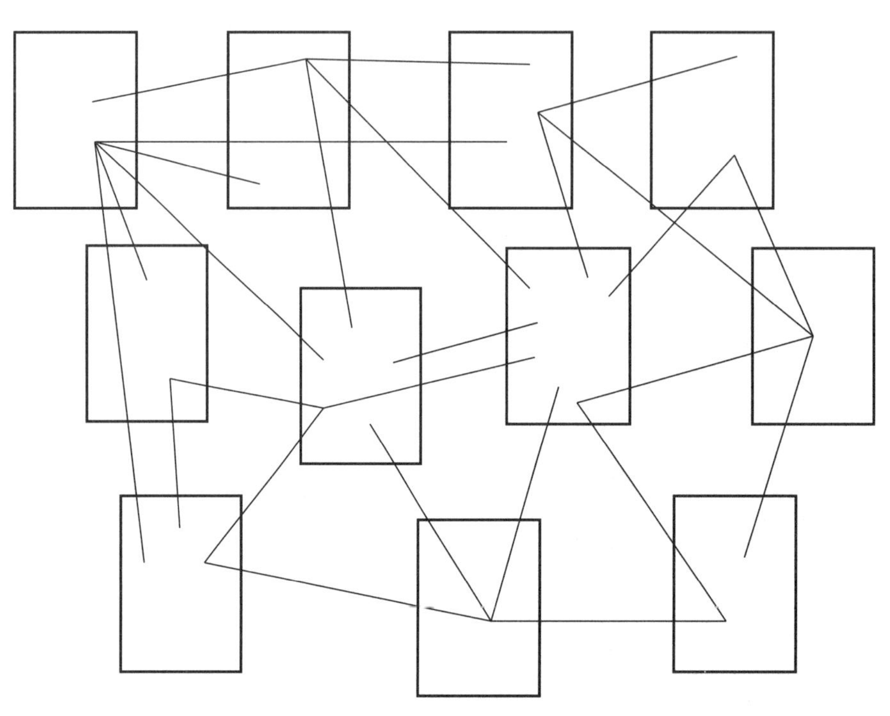

Figure 8.3 A semantic net architecture

Creating a well-done semantic net is rare, and if you succeed at it you'll probably receive considerably more attention than if you post a single page or a Web presentation. The Web community generally rewards hard work and careful design, and a good semantic net requires both.

Disadvantages

Creating a well-implemented semantic net isn't easy. You have to break your information into small pieces, then post all the pieces to the Web. Simply managing the dozens, hundreds, or thousands of HTML documents a semantic net requires is a monumental chore. Then you have to develop a powerful but user-friendly means of moving among the chunks of data, and figure out a way to keep that navigation tool up-to-date when you add new pieces of information.

Basically, ease of use for the site visitor translates into headaches for the site designer and maintainer. If you're willing to spend the time and effort to post and maintain a site based on semantic net architecture, your audience will probably love you for it. On the other hand, you'll probably spend a significant portion of your time maintaining the site and keeping it up-to-date.

Applications

Semantic nets are not suited to applications in which it's important that viewers see certain information before they see other information. You wouldn't want viewers to see the conclusion of your thesis paper before seeing your argument, and you wouldn't want to show viewers a price list before telling them why the thing you're selling is very reliable and is probably worth twice what you ask for it. In such applications, a single Web page architecture or a carefully organized presentation is probably a better bet, as there's less chance of confusing your viewers with a somewhat chaotic presentation of data.

Semantic nets are better suited to applications that involve lots of information of equal importance, such as the rosters of a football team for each of fifty years or biographies of all the middle-level executives in a company. By providing an easy way to navigate from one item of information to any of the other items of information of equal importance, you encourage visitors to your site to choose the information they want to see and ignore the information that doesn't interest them. Semantic nets give Web users a feeling of control—a concept that may be hard for those who are used to dealing with linear media, such as printed text or television, to accept.

A New Architecture

The three architectures above aren't your only options. You may choose to combine a linear presentation with long lists of reference data on single Web pages by means of hyperlinks. Or you might choose to have a semantic net with branches that lead to presentations on particular topics that require orderly presentation. Or you might conclude that none of these architectures suits your purpose, and decide to create a new organizational scheme. Go right ahead—the Web and HTML make that easy.

From Here

- You're probably ready to start coding, but hold on to your horses—and check out the next chapter ("Web Publishing Do's and Don'ts").

Chapter 9

Web Publishing Do's and Don'ts

In this chapter, you'll find brief snippets of Web wisdom and encapsulated summaries of serious Web gaffes. It's divided into the following sections: content, organization, HTML, and hypermedia.

Content Do's and Don'ts

Web users access your site for its content. Everything else is secondary to the material you publish on your Web pages. It's important that you're careful to include content of the highest possible quality before you begin to worry about how to present that material. These tips point out some

common content-selection mistakes and offer suggestions about how to avoid or correct them.

Do post information that's valuable to your target audience.

Make sure you've identified your target audience and have determined a suitable objective for your site (see Chapter 7). Then, post only information to your site that will help satisfy that audience's needs and help your site achieve its purpose. You can always make more sites—make sure each one sticks to its stated purpose.

Don't intentionally duplicate someone else's topic.

Unless you're absolutely positive you can do a significantly better job and the Web audience will benefit, don't try to enter into competition with another Web publisher. There are plenty of subjects as yet uncovered on the Web, and you'd do a greater service by concentrating your efforts on one of these areas.

Do advertise your site.

So others know it is available, publicize it everywhere you can think of. Post notices to relevant mailing lists and Usenet newsgroups, and submit your site's information at those search facilities that allow you to contribute URLs. Also send mail to whats-new@ncsa.uiuc.edu, which may get your site listed on the What's New page available from the Mosaic home page. Also post a message to the Usenet newsgroup comp.infosystems.www.announce—a newsgroup devoted to announcements of new Web resources.

Do follow rules of grammar and spelling.

You'd be careful about spelling and grammar if you were submitting a letter to a city newspaper. Doesn't a publication with a circulation approaching one billion people deserve the same attention? Many otherwise good Web pages are rendered foolish-looking by careless spelling and grammar errors. Run that spell-checker!

For the Time-Challenged

- Make sure your site deals with original material that appeals to your target audience.
- Advertise your site by filling out search engine forms and posting notices to relevant mailing lists and Usenet newsgroups.
- Observe rules of spelling and grammar in your Web documents.
- Organize your information carefully. Put all information that conveys a single idea onto one page, but don't divide your site into too many parts and commit yourself to a giant maintenance task.
- Code your documents in the HTML 3.0 version of the Netscape extensions whenever possible.
- Be considerate of those who lack graphical Web browsers.
- Make sure all links to large multimedia files are labeled as such, with a clear description of the file and a statement of the file's size.
- Use small graphical elements throughout your site. They look better than large graphics and they keep transmission time down.
- Use small transparent GIF images to make small adjustments to the position of document elements.

Organization Do's and Don'ts

Once you've carefully selected the content that is to appear on your Web site, you need to organize it so it's useful to those who visit your site. The do's and don't in this section should help you organize your information to make it easier to find, easier to use, and easier to remember.

Do provide easy-to-use navigation aids to help people find their way around your site.

It's sloppy programming to rely on the features of a Web browser to help site visitors move among your documents. Provide visitors with navigation

buttons—typically one that leads to the next page, one that leads to the previous page, and one that leads back to your site's welcome page.

Do put your navigation buttons at the *top* of each page.

It's silly to expect your pages' readers to scroll all the way to the bottom of documents before they are able to use the built-in navigation buttons. Instead, put the buttons right below the heading at the top of the page.

Don't over-chunk.

If you're arranging your information in a semantic net architecture (see Chapter 8), you need to split up your information into small pieces so that each piece of information conveys one idea and is assigned its own page. The problem with this arrangement is that it is potentially confusing—navigating among lots of little bits of data is a hassle. Unless you have a very good means of assisting your site's visitors with finding the data they want (such as a powerful search facility), don't break data into unmanageably small chunks.

Do keep your URLs reasonable.

It's likely that you have no control over the directory in which your Web publications are stored, but you do have control over the filenames you assign—and they will be as much a part of your URL as the domain and directory names. Give your files short, descriptive names; names like "Valerie_Jones_Subject_Page_022695" will not earn you the friendship of anyone who has to key in your URL manually.

Do group related information together.

If you were laying out a print newspaper, you wouldn't put sports stories right next to play reviews. The same concept holds true for Web documents—except that it's easy to group all related information on a page or group of pages and still encourage navigation among documents. Keep related information together, either on the same page or connected with hyperlinks.

Don't use hyperlinks frivolously.

It's easy to go overboard with hyperlinks because they're such a nifty way to move among pieces of information and they're so easy to create. But don't

be tempted to link every word in your document just because it relates tangentially to some point you make in another document. Using too many hyperlinks makes it easy for your readers to get distracted and leave your site before experiencing its overall effect.

Do acknowledge the value of traditional media.

Some documents, such as academic papers and traditional short stories, were designed to be read from beginning to end and don't take advantage of the hypertext medium. Particularly when you're converting old documents to HTML format for Web publication, you'll run into documents like this. Don't try to alter these documents to take advantage of hypertext, especially without the permission of the author. Instead, put these documents on pages by themselves or provide an easy means of downloading them in ASCII or PDF form.

HTML Do's and Don'ts

These hints deal with the technical aspects of publishing on the Web: coding in HTML. They're designed to teach you to avoid common HTML programming mistakes, and thereby make your code more readable, more efficient, and easier to modify and expand. Since HTML lies behind all aspects of Web publishing except audience identification and content selection, following these HTML tips should enable you to create publications that are generally better all-around.

Do code for Netscape Navigator 1.1.

There are HTML purists out there who say that coding for the "nonstandard" HTML extensions supported by Netscape 1.1 is a travesty of markup languages, but so what? The Netscape extensions are quickly gaining acceptance, Netscape Navigator is the most popular browser used on the Web, and the extensions offer you great control over the appearance of your pages. Take advantage of the power of the Netscape extensions and let the purists fume. Do note, however, that HTML 3.0 will incorporate its own version of most of the Netscape extensions—and what's more, Netscape 1.1 recognizes the HTML 3.0 variants as well as the Netscape extensions. To code for the greatest possible audience, therefore, code for Netscape 1.1—but use the HTML 3.0 versions of the Netscape extensions wherever possible.

Do include a <HEAD> section in all your HTML files.

Create a <HEAD> section and include in it lots of information about the file. Always include your name, your e-mail address, and the date the file was last revised. Head sections are useful for people who download your HTML to see how current your page is, or who want to ask you questions by e-mail.

Do consider the hapless users of text-only browsers.

Though they're shrinking in number, lots of people still browse the Web with Lynx or another character-based browser. Nothing is more annoying to these people than sites that assume they have graphics capabilities. When embedding graphics in your documents, be sure to include a descriptive word in the ALT="....." attribute of the <IMG> tag.

Do use tiny transparent GIF images as typographical tools.

As suggested by David Siegel in his HTML Tips for Graphic Designers page (http://www.best.com/~dsiegel/tips/graphics.html), you can use small transparent GIF files to adjust the horizontal and vertical spacing of text and graphical elements. You can also use little GIF images to create em dashes (—) and attractive drop capitals (characters that begin a paragraph and extend downward through several lines). It's not good HTML form, but it allows typographical control that even the Netscape extensions to HTML do not support.

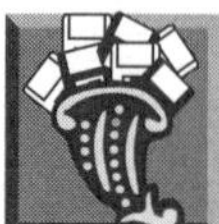

David Siegel's HTML Tips for Graphic Designers page (http://www.best.com/~dsiegel/tips/graphics.html), is an excellent resource and is well worthy of a visit. In this page, Siegel, a professional typographer, explains tricks he employs to create aesthetically sound documents with the limited tools provided by HTML.

Do give your documents descriptive titles.

Many spiders include only the titles of Web documents in their databases, so be sure to use titles—descriptive ones. "Bill's Page" is not a descriptive title; "Bill's Model T Ford Restoration Page" is.

Don't use heading tags for emphasis.

Use heading tags at the beginning of sections, not as a means of emphasizing important information. Instead, surround important information with <STRONG> tags or other tags designed to add emphasis to text.

Do use tables extensively.

Tables are useful not only for traditional purposes, such as organizing lists of labels and numbers, but also for enhancing the formatting capabilities of HTML. Consider putting all the text in your page in a table, since doing so enables you to precisely define your page's margins and even to lay out your text in multiple columns. Make the table borders invisible so they don't interfere with the rest of your layout.

Don't show table borders in most cases.

Even aside from those occasions when you use tables in a tricky way, such as for laying out text in columnar form, consider not showing the lines that make up a table. On a cramped computer monitor, the lines and borders can distract from the data a table contains, and thereby make it more difficult for you to communicate your message.

Do sign your documents in the body as well as in the head.

You wouldn't send a letter to somebody without signing your name at the bottom, and you wouldn't want your creative work to be published in a newspaper or magazine if you didn't receive credit. You should do the same with your Web publications.

At the end of a document, insert a short horizontal rule, then add some information:

- Your name
- Your e-mail address
- Your organization
- The date the document was last revised
- Any copyright information (i.e., "Copyright 1996 Bill Smith")

This information will help your site's visitors ascertain how current your information is and enable them to contact you if needed.

Do test your pages with a variety of browsers.

Some browsers are more forgiving of HTML errors than others. Netscape, for example, will forgive many errors with closing tags. Should you display a page containing such an error with Netscape, it would look OK—but another browser might skip the tag entirely. The more browsers you try, the more likely it is that you'll find your errors, if any.

Hypermedia Do's and Don'ts

One of the appealing features of the Web is its ability to handle hypermedia, such as sounds and motion pictures. This is an attraction of the Web because the feature is new—no other medium has been able to handle multimedia and hypertext easily before.

Since it is new, hypermedia is also at the root of many Web-publishing blunders. It's easy to make a hyperlink to an MPEG movie that looks great on your brand-new Pentium, but that probably won't work so well on somebody's 386-class laptop. It's very tempting to load your site up with attractive graphics, even though doing so will increase your site's download time so much as to make it unusable. These tips are here to help you avoid such foul-ups.

Don't use graphics in excess.

Most Web users are connected to the Web at 14.4 Kbps, which is great for text but barely adequate for graphics. Always think twice before including a graphic, especially a big one, in a document. Will the graphic add sufficient value to the site to offset the increased download time? Lots of little graphics, such as icons, are better than one or two giant graphics.

Do use the same graphics over and over.

It sounds boring, but using the same graphics repeatedly in a document both improves the appearance of the document and speeds up its transmission. By using the same icons and rules repeatedly, readers pick up on the signifi-

cance of different graphical elements. Also, the browser needs only to download a graphic once, then retrieve it from the cache for each subsequent use.

Do let your site's viewers know when a link leads to a sound or video file.

It's not nice to allow people to click an innocent-looking hyperlink thinking it leads to another Web page, and then have them find out that it really leads to a giant multimedia file. Label links to multimedia files as such with words or, better, with icons.

Do include preview information about multimedia files.

Until real-time viewing of video comes along, viewers of Web documents have to download an entire file before they can see it. Even small video files can take ten minutes or more to download, so be sure to let visitors to your site know what they're getting into before they begin to download. A brief description of the clip ("Man in red coat rides horse around track") and a statement of the file's size is adequate.

Do make your cool multimedia files freely available.

It's frustrating to go to a site, see a cool graphic, and not be able to download it for use in your own Web publication. New Web browsers are making it possible to download graphics even if they aren't hyperlinked to source files, but older browsers lack this capability. Be a good Web citizen and make it easy for everyone to download any public-domain graphics on your site.

Don't use obscure multimedia file formats.

No one likes to use a site in which all the graphics are in PostScript format, all the sounds are in .AIFF format, and all the movies are in .FLI format. It's a royal pain to configure all those helper applications, and if the material is available elsewhere, that's where your audience will go. Make sure your movies are MPEGs, your graphics are JPEGs or GIFs, and your sounds are in .AU or .WAV format. Your site visitors will thank you.

Part III

Creating Your Web

Chapter 10

Your First HTML Document

The easiest way to get started with publishing your information on the Web isn't by getting bogged down in the rules of HyperText Markup Language (HTML). You'll learn the details of HTML in the following chapters. Instead, the best way to learn HTML is the same as the best way to learn to dance: just try it, and know that you can't mess up too badly. In this chapter, we'll build a home page—one of the simplest and most frequently encountered type of document on the Web. You can make this page the default home page for your browser, and there it will be every time you start the program.

This chapter presents a tutorial that you can adapt to your own purposes—put in your own name, for instance, and add hyperlinks to your own favorite sites. It would be nice if you could get a friendly soul to scan a small photograph of yourself into a JPEG or GIF file (no more than 20 KB

or 25 KB in size, please), although this isn't necessary to complete the tutorial.

Here's a sweetener: After reading this chapter, you'll know a great deal of the HTML that's actually used to put pages on the Web!

A Few Basics

As with dancing, there are certain ground rules for creating documents in HTML. If you understand these basic rules, you're more than halfway to creating Web documents and you'll be able to comprehend more advanced HTML features with ease.

A few basic points to remember:

- HTML isn't a formatting language. Rather, it defines the *parts* of a document, such as titles, heading, body text, and block quotations. These parts are called *elements*.
- Just how a particular element appears on-screen—which font is used, for example—is up to the browser.
- To define an element, you use *tags*.
- Tags take the form of angle brackets surrounding letters, numbers and other information, such as <B> or <H2>.
- Tags usually come in pairs, with one tag at the beginning of text to be formatted a particular way and another at the end. For example, the expression "<B>Hey, You</B>" would make the words "Hey, You" appear in boldface type in a Web browser.
- Tags that come in pairs have a start tag (such as <H1>) and an end tag </H1>. The slash mark is used to denote the end tag. All the text within the start and end tag is to be considered part of the element that the tag defines.

That's it! Remember that all HTML is ASCII text with special tags embedded in it, and you have a conceptual framework in which to hang details about specific tags and fancy formatting techniques. Let's get started on your first HTML document, your home page.

For the Time-Challenged

- An HTML document is simply ASCII text, which you can create with a word processing program. Web browsers read HTML and transform the codes into a richly formatted document.
- Every HTML document should begin with an <HTML> tag and end with an </HTML> tag.
- The heading tags (<H1> through <H6>) enable you to establish a logical structure of headings for your document. Remember, though, that most people will feel that your <H1> tag is your document's title.
- Web browsers don't read your word processor's hard returns. To break paragraphs, you must surround the paragraph text with <P> and </P> tags.
- To center text, use the ALIGN=CENTER attribute of the <P> tag (as in <P ALIGN=CENTER>Here is the centered text</P>).
- To see how your HTML code looks, save your document and open it with a Web browser. You'll surely find mistakes—fix them, save the changes, and click the Reload or Refresh button in your browser.
- Use the <BR> tag to force a line break.
- There are two kinds of hyperlinks, one that links to an external document (<A HREF>) and one that links to a location within the same document (<A NAME>). To link to an external document, you must precisely specify the URL, as in the following example: <A HREF="http://watt.seas.virginia.edu/~bp/parents.html"> Parent's Guide to Anime </A>. It's easy to make typing mistakes when typing links, so check your work carefully.
- Use the <UL> and <LI> tags to make a bulleted (unordered) list.
- Add in-line images with the <IMG> tag, but be sure to specify the location of the graphic correctly (<IMG SRC="portrait.jpg">) and enclose the file name in quotation marks. You can use the ALIGN and WIDTH attributes to control the graphic's appearance.
- To add a rule (a line spanning the screen), use the <HR> tag—but don't overdo it.
- Always sign your document with the <ADDRESS> tag. Include your e-mail address and the date of last modification.
- To enable people to reply to your page by e-mail, use the following tag: <A HREF = "mailto:*e-mail address*">*e-mail address*</A>.

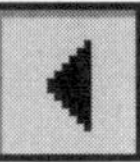

Starting Your Home Page

To create your HTML file, just use your word processing program. But be sure to save the file as plain text. Most word processors save documents to a proprietary file format, which uses lots of formatting codes that will show up as garbage in a Web browser.

Consider using the SimpleText editor that comes with your Macintosh to create your HTML file. It isn't fancy, granted, but you don't need fancy word processing capabilities to create an HTML file. And SimpleText has one huge advantage: It automatically saves files as plain text, with no formatting codes.

You can call your HTML document by any legal filename you want, but in order for Web browsers to recognize the file as one containing HTML text, you must give it a special extension. In most operating systems, the extension is .html. Microsoft Windows systems, however, allow extensions of only three characters, so on those systems the proper extension for HTML documents is .htm.

Before adding any other text or tags to your document, type

```
<HTML>
```

Then press Enter, and type

```
<HEAD>
```

Press Enter again, and type

```
</HEAD>
```

Continue by typing the following, each on its own line followed by a hard return (Enter):

```
<BODY>
</BODY>
</HTML>
```

In this and subsequent chapters, you'll see boxes such as the following whenever a new HTML element is introduced. The box sums up important information about the element. Don't worry if you don't understand all the contents of these boxes right now; you'll learn later, for example, what attributes are and how to use them. You'll also find a review of HTML in Appendix A, "The Ultimate HTML Cheat Sheet."

HTML

Purpose: Tells Web browsers that your document is in HTML.

Usage: <HTML>. . .</HTML>

Example: <HTML>Rest of document text here.</HTML>

Can Contain: <HEAD>, <BODY>

Can Be Contained By: None.

Don't Forget: Within this tag you must include the <HEAD>. . .</HEAD> and <BODY>. . . </BODY> tags.

Hot Tip: Although most browsers will figure out that an HTML document is in HTML even without these tags, it's a good idea to include them anyway for the benefit of those with less-sophisticated browsers.

BODY

Purpose: Defines the body of the HTML document (the portion that's seen in the browser's display window)

Usage: <BODY>. . .</BODY>

Example: <BODY><P>This is the text of the document.</P></BODY>

Can Contain: <ADDRESS>, <BLOCKQUOTE>, <DIR>, <DL>, <FORM>, <H1>, <H2>, <H3>, <H4>, <H5>, <H6>, <HR>, <MENU>, <OL>, <UL

Can Be Contained By: <HTML>

Don't Forget: Elements that can go into the BODY element can't go in the HEAD element, and vice versa.

Hot Tip: Although most browsers will figure out that an HTML document is in HTML even without these tags, it's a good idea to include them anyway for the benefit of those with less-sophisticated browsers

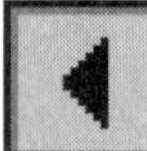

HEAD

Purpose:	Defines the head of the HTML document. The head contains the document title and certain other elements.
Usage:	<HEAD>. . .</HEAD>
Example:	<HEAD><TITLE>This is the document's title</TITLE></HEAD>
Can Contain:	<BASE>, < ISINDEX>, < LINK>, < META>, < NEXTID>
Can Be Contained By:	<HTML>
Don't Forget:	The document's title will appear on the title bar of most browsers, and may not be noticed; be sure to reiterate the document's title in an H1 element.
Hot Tip:	Virtually the only HEAD element in common use is TITLE.

What Did You Just Do?

You just set up the basic structure that every HTML document should have. It looks like this:

```
<HTML>
<HEAD>
</HEAD>
<BODY>
</BODY>
</HTML>
```

Note the following about this basic structure. First, every HTML document has two overarching sections:

- **The Head** Within the head, demarcated by <HEAD>. . .</HEAD> tags, you position the document's title and certain other information. This information does not appear within the browser's document display area. The head contains information *about* the document.
- **The Body** Within the body, you create the document. The body will be displayed within the browser's document display area. The body contains the *content* of the document.

Note also that HTML tags can be *nested* (positioned within each other). This is a little easier to see if you use tabs to indent the nested codes, as in the following example:

```
<HTML>
  <HEAD>
  </HEAD>
  <BODY>
  </BODY>
</HTML>
```

As you can see, the <HEAD>. . .</HEAD> tags and the <BODY>. . . </BODY> tags are contained (nested) within the <HTML>. . .</HTML> codes. Or to put it another way, every HTML document consists of a head and a body.

Giving Your Home Page a Title

The title of an HTML document appears only in the browser's title bar—not anywhere in the document's body. A document's title should be both descriptive of the document's contents and short enough to fit on small monitors.

<TITLE> and </TITLE> tags surround the title of an HTML document. On the line right after the one containing <HEAD>, type the following, except substitute your own name for the one given in the example:

```
<TITLE>Sue Thompson's Hotlist</TITLE>
```

The line you just entered into your document will make a Web browser show the words "Sue Thompson's Hotlist" in its title bar when it displays your page.

At this point, your file should look like this:

```
<HTML>
<HEAD>
<TITLE>Sue Thompson's Hotlist</TITLE>
</HEAD>
<BODY>
</BODY>
</HTML>
```

If the TITLE element only appears in the title bar, why bother creating it?
It's required, for one thing, and really persnickity HTML editors will balk at reading your document unless it's included. Most browsers won't panic if a TITLE element isn't included, though. Still, it's best to use it. Web spiders look for titles and attach a great deal of weight to the words contained therein. In addition, most browsers use your document's title in history lists. So be sure to use a title that really describes what's in your document. Don't say "My First Try"; say "Arizona Iguana Habitat Hotline."

TITLE

Purpose:	Displays the document's title on the browser's title bar.
Usage:	<TITLE>. . .</TITLE>
Example:	<TITLE>Arizona Iguana Habitat Hotline</TITLE>
Can Contain:	Text only.
Can Be Contained By:	<HTML >
Don't Forget:	Please don't omit the TITLE element—and be sure to make your title as descriptive as possible.
Hot Tip:	Make your title as descriptive as possible, but make it short enough so that it fits within a browser's history list window. For best results, stick to 60 characters or fewer.

Adding Headings

Documents are much easier to read when they're broken into sections. HTML is designed to accommodate as many as six different sizes of heading, which can be used to organize your document into paragraphs of decreasing importance or increasing specificity. There are six heading tags: <H1>, < H2>, < H3>, < H4>, < H5>, and <H6>. Just how these headings appear depends on which browser you're using; Figure 10.1 shows how Netscape renders the six levels of document headings.

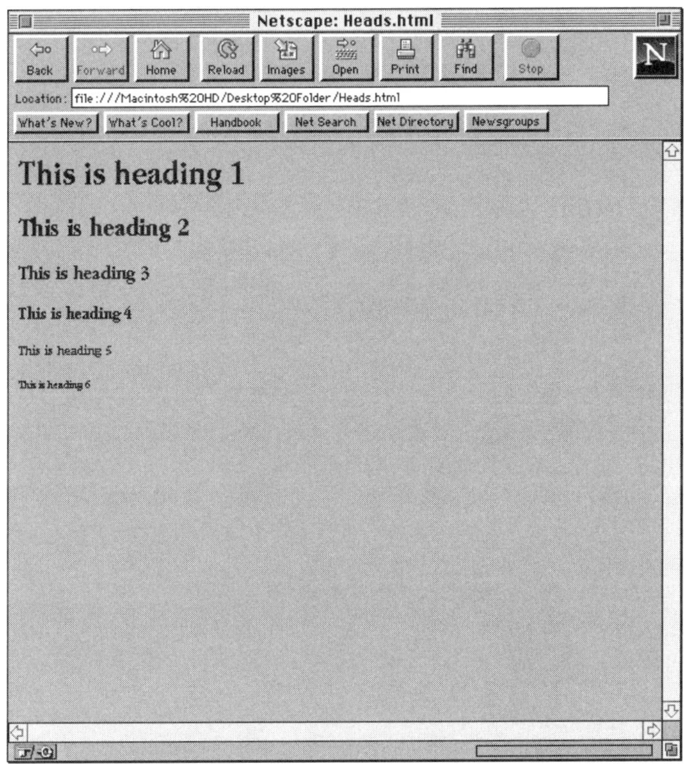

Figure 10.1 Headings rendered by Netscape Navigator

The title of your document usually appears as an H1 heading at the top of the body text. Right below the <BODY> tag, echo your document's title surrounded by <H1> tags:

```
<H1>Sue Thompson's Hotlist</H1>
```

You can use other heading tags to establish a logical order of headings and subheadings in your document. Try entering an H2 subheading now. Type:

```
<H2>Music Sites</H2>
```

The H2 heading is less dramatic than the H1 heading, and attracts less attention. You can use the various heading tags together to create an outline of information. But please don't use them out of sequence: You shouldn't stick an <H6> tag into a document that only has <H1> and <H2> tags.

Using the heading tags, you can define your document's logical structure. Try entering the following under Music Sites:

```
<H3>Grunge</H3>
<H3>Industrial</H3>
<H3>Techno-Rave</H3>
<H3>Trance</H3>
```

Start a new H2 heading as follows:

```
<H2>Movies</H2>
```

Add some H3 headings under this:

```
<H3>Classics</H3>
<H3>Horror</H3>
<H3>Science Fiction</H3>
```

At this point, your file should look like this:

```
<HTML>
<HEAD>
<TITLE>Sue Thompson's Hotlist</TITLE>
</HEAD>
<BODY>
<H1>Sue Thompson's Hotlist</H1>
<H2>Music Sites</H2>
<H3>Grunge</H3>
<H3>Industrial</H3>
<H3>Techno-Rave</H3>
<H3>Trance</H3>
<H2>Movies</H2>
<H3>Classics</H3>
<H3>Horror</H3>
<H3>Science Fiction</H3>
</BODY>
</HTML>
```

You don't have to make your document's title the same as the first heading; in fact, doing so is somewhat inefficient since you're displaying the same information twice. It may also be a good idea to use H2 or H3 as the largest heading in your document, since most browsers display H1 in very large type that takes up valuable screen real estate.

What's the difference between a title and a first-level heading (H1)?
It's where the title appears. Bear in mind that your document's title will only appear on the title bar of the browser—and it might not be very noticeable. So you'll need to use the <H1> tag, discussed below, to make your title more visible. But please, don't skip the title—Web spiders and search engines consult the title in order to build searchable databases of Web documents.

H1, H2, H3, H4, H5, H6

Purpose:	Define headings and subheadings within the document body.
Usage:	<H1>. . .</H1>
Example:	<H1>This is the "real" document title, as browsers display it</H1>
Can Contain:	<A>, <IMG>, , <EM>, <STRONG>, <CODE>, <SAMP>, <KBD>, <VAR>, <CITE>, <TT>, <B>, <I>
Can Be Contained By:	<BLOCKQUOTE>, <BODY>, <FORM>
Don't Forget:	The heading tags should be used in a logical sequence. . . in other words, don't use <H5> if you haven't used <H4>.

Adding Body Text

Most of the information included in your Web documents will be in the form of body text. Body text is the kind of text you use for paragraphs that require no special formatting. In your home page file, below the <H1> line, type something about yourself, such as the following:

```
<P>I'm a communications consultant at Tao Enter-
prises, located in Eugene, Oregon. Here are some
of my favorite sites. </P>
```

Solutions

Making Your HTML Easier to Read

Since browsers ignore the extra spaces, tabs, and hard returns you insert into your HTML documents, you might as well use these to clarify your code's structure. Here's the document we're working on right now, after inserting tabs and blank lines to clarify its structure:

```
<HTML>
  <HEAD>
    <TITLE>Sue Thompson's Hotlist</TITLE>
  </HEAD>

  <BODY>
    <H1>Sue Thompson's Hotlist</H1>
      <H2>Music Sites</H2>
        <H3>Grunge</H3>
        <H3>Industrial</H3>
        <H3>Techno-Rave</H3>
        <H3>Trance</H3>
      <H2>Movies</H2>
        <H3>Classics</H3>
        <H3>Horrow</H3>
        <H3>Science Fiction</H3>
  </BODY>
</HTML>
```

```
<P>Please let me know if you have any cool addi-
tions to the sites I've listed. My email address
is suet@fictitious.com</P>
```

The above lines, when read by a Web browser, will yield two distinct paragraphs. Though the details of formatting the paragraphs (size, typeface, color, etc.) are left up to individual browsers, it is safe to assume that text formatted as body text will have less emphasis than text formatted as any sort of header.

Note: In previous versions of HTML, you could use the <P> tag to separate paragraphs; it was not necessary to begin a paragraph with <P> and end with </P>. Most browsers will read paragraphs formatted in this (incor-

rect) way. There's still considerable controversy over this point, but to be on the safe side, you should use the <P>. . .</P> tags in pairs rather than breaking paragraphs with <P>.

I separated my paragraphs with a hard return, but the Web browser won't pick up the paragraph breaks!
That's right. As far as your Web browser is concerned, a hard return is the same as a space. If you want to set off a paragraph, you must use the <P>. . .</P> tags. Even if you press Enter to start a new word processing program's paragraph within these tags, your browser will still read all the enclosed text as a single paragraph. Try it!

The <P>. . .</P> tags are useful because HTML does not understand the significance of the ASCII carriage return character (the character generated when you press the <Enter> or <Return> key). If you don't use <P>...</P> tags, all your body text paragraphs will merge into one giant, unreadable glob of text. The <P>. . .</P> tags ensure that each paragraph of body text is neatly separated from the others.

At this point, your file should look like this (except that you're substituting your own name and areas of interest):

```
<HTML>
  <HEAD>
    <TITLE>Sue Thompson's Hotlist</TITLE>
  </HEAD>

  <BODY>
    <H1>Sue Thompson's Hotlist</H1>
      <P>I'm a communications consultant at Tao
      Enterprises, located in Eugene, Oregon. Here
      are some of my favorite sites. </P>

      <P>Please let me know if you have any cool
      additions to the sites I've listed. My email
      address is suet@fictitious.com</P>

        <H2>Music Sites</H2>
          <H3>Grunge</H3>
          <H3>Industrial</H3>
          <H3>Techno-Rave</H3>
          <H3>Trance</H3>
```

```
      <H2>Movies</H2>
        <H3>Classics</H3>
        <H3>Horror</H3>
        <H3>Science Fiction</H3>
  </BODY>
</HTML>
```

P

Purpose:	Defines a unit of text as a single paragraph.
Usage:	<P>. . . </P>
Can Contain:	<A>, <IMG>, , <EM>, <STRONG>, <CODE>, <SAMP>, <KBD>, <VAR>, <CITE>, <TT>, <B>, <I>
Can Be Contained By:	<ADDRESS>, <BLOCKQUOTE>, <BODY>, <DD>, <FORM>, <LI>
Don't Forget:	Web browsers will ignore tabs, spaces, and hard returns entered by your word processing program.
Hot Tip:	To center text, use the <P> tag with the ALIGN attribute, as in the following example: <P ALIGN = CENTER>This is the centered text </P> .

Hey! What Does It Look Like So Far?

Why not find out? Save the HTML file to disk, fire up your browser, and use the Open File command in the File menu to open the document you're creating. It should look like the one in Figure 10.2.

The browser just ignored some of my tags!
That's what happens if they're not correctly written. Check the following:

- Did you enclose each tag with angle brackets?
- Does each start tag have a matching end tag? You can't start with <H3> and end with </H4>.
- Did you type the tags correctly?

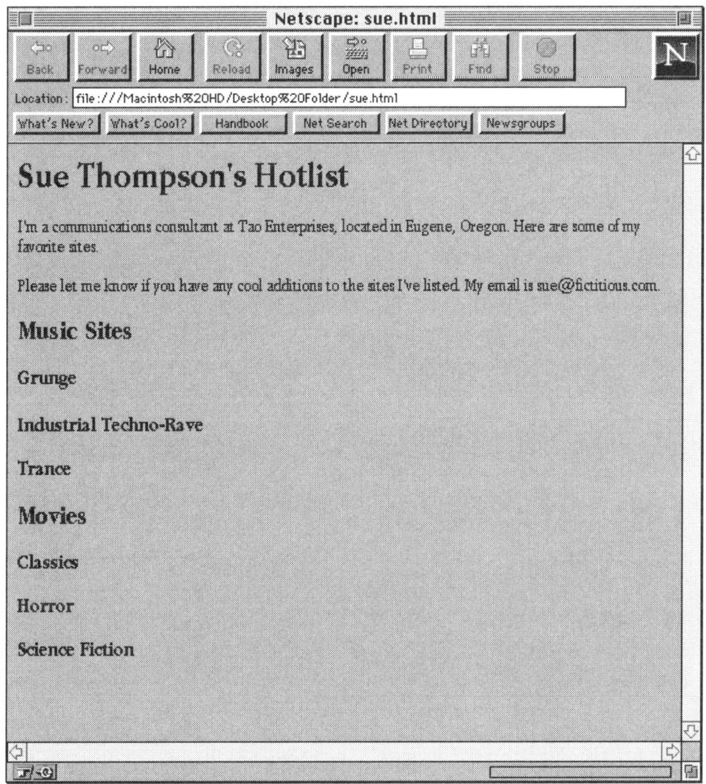

Figure 10.2 The file thus far (as displayed by Netscape Navigator)

Keep looking—you'll find the error. Correct the error, and resave the document. In your browser, click the Refresh button to load the corrected version of the file.

Character Formatting (Italics, Boldface, and Underlining)

HTML is designed to identify document elements, and it leaves the formatting up to the browser. However, some latitude is given to document designers in

the area of emphases, such as italics, boldface, and underlining. The following tags are commonly used to format character emphases:

<I>. . .</I>	The text within these tags will be italicized.
<B>. . .</B>	The text within these tags will be shown in boldface type.
<TT>. . .</TT>	The text within these tags will be shown in a monospace typewriter font, such as Courier.

Note that the <I>, <B>, and <TT> tags are considered by some HTML purists to violate the spirit of HTML—they tell the browser precisely how to format the text. However, that doesn't stop very many people from using them! If you'd like to be an HTML purist, you can use two tags that leave the formatting up to the browser:

<STRONG>. . .</STRONG>	Most browsers show this text in bold.
<EM>. . .</EM>	Most browsers show this text in italics.
<CODE>. . .</CODE>	Most browsers show this text using a monospaced font of some kind.

You can nest character formats. For example, the following tags are used to produce these formats: *I'm not an HTML expert . . . **YET!***

```
<I>I'm not an HTML expert...<B>YET!</B></I>
```

Note that you must include stop tags for both of the emphases.

B

Purpose:	Boldfaces the marked text.
Usage:	<B>. . .</B>
Example:	<B>Text to be boldfaced.</B>
Can Contain:	<A>, <IMG>, , <EM>, <STRONG>, <CODE>, <KBD>, <VAR>, <CITE>, <TT>, <I>

Can Be Contained By: <A>, <ADDRESS>, <B>, <CITE>, <CODE>, <DD>, <DT>, <EM>, <H1>, <H2>, <H3>, <H4>, <H5>, <H6>, <I>, <KBD>, <LI>, <P>, <PRE>, <SAMP>, <STRONG>, <TT>, <VAR>

Don't Forget: Not all browsers can display boldface. A text-only browser such as Lynx will display this format with underlining.

Hot Tip: Use character emphases sparingly.

CODE

Purpose: Marks text for display in a monospace font.

Usage: <CODE>. . .</CODE>

Example: <CODE>Text to be shown in monospace</CODE>

Can Contain: <A>, <IMG>, <BR>, <EM>, <STRONG>, <KBD>, <VAR>, <CITE>, <I>, <B>, <TT>

Can Be Contained By: <A>, <ADDRESS>, <B>, <CITE>, <CODE>, <DD>, <DT>, <EM>, <H1>, <H2>, <H3>, <H4>, <H5>, <H6>, <I>, <KBD>, <LI>, <P>, <PRE>, <SAMP>, <STRONG>, <TT>, <VAR>

Don't Forget: This format is a good choice if you want to display a single line of computer code, but you should use it in combination with the <PRE> tag for multiline examples.

Hot Tip: Use character emphases sparingly.

EM

Purpose: Emphasizes the marked text; most browsers display italics.

Usage: <EM>. . .</EM>

Example: <EM>Text to be emphasized.</EM>

Can Contain: <A>, <IMG>, <BR>, <STRONG>, <CODE>, <KBD>, <VAR>, <CITE>, <TT>, <I>, <B>

Can Be Contained By: <A>, <ADDRESS>, <B>, <CITE>, <CODE>, <DD>, <DT>, <EM>, <H1>, <H2>, <H3>, <H4>, <H5>, <H6>, <I>, <KBD>, <LI>, <P>, <PRE>, <SAMP>, <STRONG>, <TT>, <VAR>

Don't Forget: Not all browsers can display italics. A text-only browser such as Lynx will display this format with underlining.

Hot Tip: Use character emphases sparingly.

I

Purpose: Displays text in italics.

Usage: <I>. . .</I>

Example: <I>Italicized text</I>

Can Contain: <A>, <IMG>, <BR>, <EM>, <STRONG>, <CODE>, <KBD>, <VAR>, <CITE>, <TT>, <B>

Can Be Contained By: <A>, <ADDRESS>, <B>, <CITE>, <CODE>, <DD>, <DT>, <EM>, <H1>, <H2>, <H3>, <H4>, <H5>, <H6>, <I>, <KBD>, <LI>, <P>, <PRE>, <SAMP>, <STRONG>, <TT>, <VAR>

Don't Forget: Not all browsers can display italics. A text-only browser such as Lynx will display this format with underlining.

Hot Tip: Use character emphases sparingly.

STRONG

Purpose: Emphasizes the marked text; most browsers display bold.

Usage: <STRONG>. . .</STRONG>

Example: <STRONG>Text to be emphasized.</STRONG>

Can Contain: <A>, <IMG>, <BR>, <EM>, <CODE>, <KBD>, <VAR>, <CITE>, <TT>, <I>, <B>

Can Be Contained By: <A>, <ADDRESS>, <B>, <CITE>, <CODE>, <DD>, <DT>, <EM>, <H1>, <H2>, <H3>, <H4>, <H5>, <H6>, <I>, <KBD>, <LI>, <P>, <PRE>, <SAMP>, <STRONG>, <TT>, <VAR>

Don't Forget: Not all browsers can display boldface. A text-only browser such as Lynx will display this format with underlining.

Hot Tip: Use character emphases sparingly.

TT

Purpose: Displays text in a monospace typewriter font.

Usage: <TT>. . .</TT>

Example: <TT>Text to be shown in monospace</TT>

Can Contain: <A>, <IMG>, <BR>, <EM>, <STRONG>, <CODE>, <KBD>, <VAR>, <CITE>, <I>, <B>

Can Be Contained By: <A>, <ADDRESS>, <B>, <CITE>, <CODE>, <DD>, <DT>, <EM>, <H1>, <H2>, <H3>, <H4>, <H5>, <H6>, <I>, <KBD>, <LI>, <P>, <PRE>, <SAMP>, <STRONG>, <TT>, <VAR>

Don't Forget: This format is a good choice if you want to display a single line of computer code, but you should use it in combination with the <PRE> tag for multiline examples.

Hot Tip: Use character emphases sparingly.

BREAKING LINES

When you're working with body text, you'll find it helpful occasionally to be able to determine precisely where a line breaks. Suppose you're working with an address, such as the following:

```
If you'd like more information on Tao Enter-
prises, please contact:

Tao Enterprises
11219 19th Street NW
Eugene, OR
```

Unfortunately, your browser will format this text as follows:

```
If you'd like more information on Tao Enter-
prises, please contact:Tao Enterprises 11219 19th
Street NW Eugene, OR
```

To force the browser to start a new line just where you want it, you can use the <BR> tag, as follows:

```
If you'd like more information on Tao Enter-
prises, please contact:<BR>
<BR>
Tao Enterprises<BR>
11219 19th Street NW<BR>
Eugene, OR <BR>
```

Note that the <BR> tags should come at the *end* of the line, not at the beginning—unless you deliberately want to insert a blank line *before* the line that contains the tag.

BR

Purpose:	Forces a line break.
Usage:	 (no stop tag)
Example:	This item should end with a line break.
Can Contain:	None.
Can Be Contained By:	<A>, <ADDRESS>, <B>, <CITE>, <CODE>, <DD>, <DT>, <EM>, <H1>, <H2>, <H3>, <H4>, <H5>, <H6>, <I>, <KBD>, <LI>, <P>, <PRE>, <SAMP>, <STRONG>, <TT>, <VAR>
Don't Forget:	Browsers ignore the hard returns you enter with your word processor.
Hot Tip:	Need a blank line? Just enter on a line by itself.

Adding Hyperlinks

One of the Web's strongest appeals is its ability to handle hyperlinks, which enable people viewing your document to jump to other Web resources. Like all other special features, hyperlinks are encoded into HTML documents with tags.

The Two Types of Hyperlinks (<A HREF> and <A NAME>)

To add a hyperlink, you use the <A> tag. You can hyperlink in two ways:

1. **To another document** To create a hyperlink to another document, you use the <A HREF> form of the <A> tag.
2. **To another place in the same document** To create a hyperlink to another place within the same document, you use the <A NAME> form of the <A> tag. You'll learn more about <A NAME> in Chapter 13.

The form of an <A HREF> tag looks like this:

```
<A HREF="the URL of the site you're linking
to">The hyperlink text</A>
```

Things to Remember When Typing Hyperlinks

To type a <A HREF> tag, you need the exact URL of the document to which you are linking. Be sure to test the URL with your browser before attempting to write a hyperlink. Note that URLs are case-sensitive: you must follow the exact pattern of uppercase and lowercase letters.

Here's an example of a properly written <A HREF> tag:

```
<A HREF="http://watt.seas.virginia.edu/~bp/par-
ents.html">Parent's Guide to Anime</A>
```

It's easy to make a mistake when you're typing hyperlinks—and you'll know if you made one of the more serious ones, because you'll see the hyperlink code, not the hyperlink text itself. Be sure to check the following:

- Did you enclose the entire URL within quotation marks?
- Did you forget the equals sign?

- Did you omit the stop tag (</A>)?
- Did you omit the slash mark in the stop tag?
- Is the URL correct?
- Did you leave a space between A and HREF?
- Did you place any extraneous spaces at the beginning or end of the hyperlink text (the text that will appear in the browser)? Don't place any spaces after the start tag's trailing bracket (>) or before the end tag's beginning bracket (<). Such spaces will produce unwanted spacing errors in your document.

Adding Hyperlinks to Your Document

Let's add some sites about grunge music to the home page you're creating. Under <H3>Grunge</H3>, type the following:

```
<A HREF="http://www.vtek.chalmers.se/
~v94zinn/">The Grunge Page</A>

<A HREF="http://www.vtek.chalmers.se/~v94zinn/
Grunge.html">Some of the best GRUNGE Links</A>

<A HREF="http://www.engin.umich.edu/~galvin/
pearljam.html">The Pearl Jam Page</A>

<A HREF="http://geffen.com/hole.html">The Hole
Page</A>

<A HREF="http://www.ncsa.uiuc.edu/SDG/Software/
Mosaic/Docs/whats-new.html">New Web Sites</A>
```

Save your document and use your browser to take a look at the links you've created. It won't look very nice—you'll find out why in a moment—but for now test the hyperlinks to see that they're working. Note that some of the above sites may have folded or moved since this book was written; that is the Way of the Web.

Hey, the hyperlinks all run together!
They sure do. Unlike the heading and subheading tags you've added to your document, the <A> tags don't imply any formatting. To make your hyperlinks look nice, you'll need to include them within some text or add them to a list. In the following section, you'll learn how to add them to a list.

A HREF

Purpose:	Defines a unit of text as a hyperlink to another Web document.
Usage:	<A HREF="*Universal Resource Locator*">Text to appear in browser</A>
Example:	<A HREF="http://geffen.com/hole.html">The Hole Page</A>
Can Contain:	<IMG>, , <EM>, <STRONG>, <CODE>, <SAMP>, <KBD>, <VAR>, <CITE>, <TT>, <B>, <I>
Can Be Contained By:	<ADDRESS>, <B>, <CITE>, <CODE>, <DD>, <DT>, <EM>, <H1>, <H2>, <H3>, <H4>, <H5>, <H6>, <I>, <KBD>, <LI>, <P>, <PRE>, <SAMP>, <STRONG>, <TT>, <VAR>
Don't Forget:	You must enclose the URL within quotation marks.
Hot Tip:	Be sure to check for errors—angle brackets, extraneous spaces, mistakes in typing the URL, lack of a trailing stop tag.

Making a List

Among body elements, one of the most frequently used is the list. With HTML, you can create two kinds of lists:

- **Ordered Lists** An ordered list is a numbered list. The browser will number the items automatically.
- **Unordered Lists** An unordered list is a bulleted list. The browser will insert the bullets automatically.

In this section, you'll transform the poorly organized series of hyperlinks you just added into a nicely formatted bulleted list.

Tags Needed for an Unordered (Bulleted) List

To create an unordered (bulleted) list, you need to add two HTML tags:

1. **<UL> . . . </UL>** Place the <UL> tag at the beginning of the list, and the </UL> tag at the end.

2. <LI> . . . </LI> Place the <LI> tag at the beginning of each item you want preceded by a bullet, and close the item with </LI>.

Here's an example of a properly formatted unordered list:

```
<UL>
<LI>This is item Number 1.</LI>
<LI>This is item Number 2.</LI>
<LI>This is item Number 3.</LI>
</UL>
```

Figure 10.3 shows how the list looks when formatted by a browser.

Adding the Tags to the Hyperlink List

Here's what the hyperlink list looks like with the added tags, shown in bold. Try adding these to your home page document:

```
<UL>
<LI><A HREF="http://www.vtek.chalmers.se/
~v94zinn/">The Grunge Page</A></LI>
```

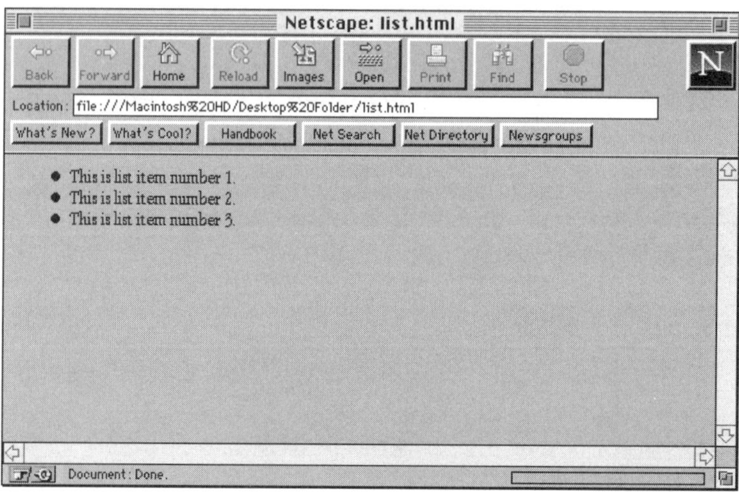

Figure 10.3 Unordered list

```
<LI><A HREF="http://www.vtek.chalmers.se/
~v94zinn/Grunge.html">Some of the best GRUNGE
Links</A></LI>

<LI><A HREF="http://www.engin.umich.edu/~galvin/
pearljam.html">The Pearl Jam Page</A></LI>

<LI><A HREF="http://geffen.com/hole.html">The
Hole Page</A></LI>

</UL>
```

It's a huge drag to type these tags!
Yup. Confusing, isn't it? That's why HTML editors have been created. For more information on editors, see Chapter 18. Bear in mind, though, that I haven't seen one yet that freed you from the need to understand what's going on in the HTML code you're writing. It's best to learn how to write HTML manually first, and then use an editor for the sake of convenience later.

For now, do everything you can to make your HTML document as readable as possible. For example, separate each of the list items with blank lines (they won't show up in the document as viewed by the browser).

UL

Purpose:	Creates an unordered (bulleted) list.
Usage:	<UL>. . .</UL>
Example:	<UL><LI>This is item no. 1</LI><LI>This is item no. 2</LI></UL>
Can Contain:	<LH>, <LI>
Can Be Contained By:	<BLOCKQUOTE>, <BODY>, <DD>, <FORM>, <LI>
Don't Forget:	Within the list, you need to demarcate each item with <LI>. . .</LI>

LI

Purpose: Demarcates an item in an unordered (bulleted) or ordered (numbered) list.

Usage: <LI>. . .</LI>

Example: <LI>This is item no. 1.</LI>

Can Contain: <A>, <B>, <BLOCKQUOTE>, <BR>, <CITE>, <CODE>, <DIR>, <DL>, <EM>, <FORM>, <I> , <IMG>, <ISINDEX>, <KBD>, <MENU>, <OL>, <P>, <PRE>, <SAMP>, <STRONG>, <TT>, <UL>, <VAR>

Can Be Contained By: <DIR>, <MENU>, <OL>, <UL>

Don't Forget: The list must begin with the <UL> or <OL> tags, and must end with the </UL> or </OL> tags.

Hot Tip: Most browsers will format the list correctly if you omit the stop tag (</LI>), but it's still good form to use it.

Use your word processor's copy and repeat commands to make HTML coding easier!
One way you can reduce the tedium of writing HTML is to make full use of your word processing program's copy and repeat functions. If you must enter several <LI> tags, for example, you can copy this tag to the Clipboard and insert it repeatedly. Microsoft Word users, note that you can use the Repeat command (Edit menu) to repeat the last editing action. Try typing <LI>, and then position the cursor where the next instance of <LI> should occur; choose Repeat, or use the Command-A keyboard shortcut.

Adding In-Line Images

Another appealing capability of the Web is that of embedding graphics and other multimedia objects in your document. The <IMG> tag makes it easy to include in-line images in your document.

Do you have a scanned photograph of yourself? If so, you can follow this tutorial. If not, use your browser to capture an in-line graphic from a Web page, just for purposes of experimentation. (To capture an in-line graphic with Netscape, point to the graphic and hold down the mouse key until the pop-up menu appears. Then choose Save This Image As from the pop-up menu and choose a name for the graphic. Be sure to store the graphic in the same folder as your test document.)

About In-Line Images

You'll learn more about in-line images in Chapter 14, but here's a quick overview. Most browsers can handle GIF images directly—and increasingly, they can also handle JPEG. JPEG graphics have many advantages; the JPEG compression format results in files that are considerably smaller than GIF graphics, by a factor of up to 4:1.

Whatever else you do with in-line graphics, keep them small. Millions of people are browsing the Web using slow, dial-up connections. It's very irritating to sit there while your browser downloads a huge graphic. Try to keep in-line images as small as possible, with a maximum of roughly 25 KB.

The <IMG> Tag

To add an in-line graphic to your document, you use the <IMG> tag. If your graphic is named "PORTRAIT.JPG," here's what the <IMG> tag looks like:

```
<IMG SRC="portrait.jpg">
```

In the above tag, SRC is an *attribute*, about which you'll learn more in the coming chapters. It identifies the location of the graphic. As this tag is written, the browser will assume that the graphic is located in the same directory as the document—and if it isn't, the browser will insert a placeholder instead of your graphic.

Please note the following:

- There's no stop tag.
- There's a space between "IMG" and "SRC".
- You must enclose the graphic's filename within quotes.
- Don't forget the equals sign!

Embedding the In-Line Graphic within the <H1> Tag

You've probably seen lots of Web pages that show an in-line image positioned flush left against the document's H1 heading, as in Figure 10.4. You can produce the same effect by positioning the <IMG> tag within the <H1> tag, as follows:

```
<H1><IMG SRC="portrait.jpg">Sue Thompson's Hot-
list</H1>
```

By default, the IMG tag aligns the text at the bottom of the graphic. You can change this by adding an ALIGN attribute within the IMG tag, as follows:

```
<H1><IMG ALIGN=MIDDLE SRC="portrait.jpg">Sue
Thompson's Hotlist</H1>
```

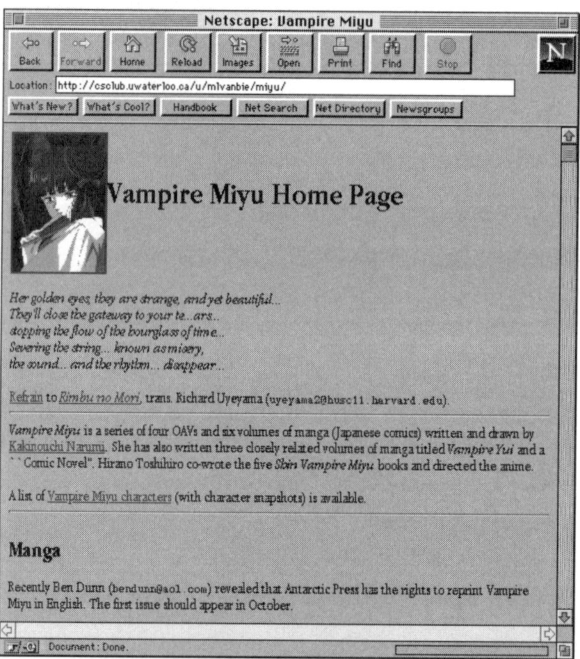

Figure 10.4 Web page with in-line graphic positioned flush left against Heading 1 (H1)

IMG

Purpose: Inserts an in-line image into the document.

Usage: <IMG SRC="*location of graphic file*">

Example: <IMG SRC="portrait.jpg">

Can Contain: None.

Can Be Contained By: <A>, <ADDRESS>, <B>, <CITE>, <CODE>, <DD>, <DT>, <EM>, <H1>, <H2>, <H3>, <H4>, <H5>, <H6>, <I>, <KBD>, <LI>, <P>, <SAMP>, <STRONG>, <TT>, <VAR>

Don't Forget: Unless you specify another location, the browser will assume that the graphic is located in the same directory as the HTML document containing this tag.

Hot Tip: Use the ALIGN attribute to control the position of the graphic when embedded within headings. For example, <IMG SRC ALIGN=MIDDLE SRC="portrait.jpg"> aligns the text at the middle of the graphic, which is positioned flush left. Use the WIDTH attribute to control the size of the graphic. WIDTH="3%" limits the width to 3% of the available window width.

This graphic's too big!
You can limit the size by using the WIDTH attribute, which specifies the percentage of the available window space that the graphic occupies. For example, the following <IMG> tag inserts a graphic but limits the size of the graphic to 1/3 the available window size: <IMG SRC="portrait.gif" WIDTH="33%">.

Adding Rules (Lines)

It's very easy to add horizontal rules (lines) to a hypertext document. Rules serve to divide a document into sections even more clearly than headings, so be sure to use rules to organize your information.

To create a rule, just insert the <HR> tag where you want it to appear.

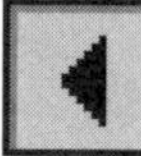

HR

Purpose: Inserts a rule that spans the active browser window.

Usage: <HR> (no stop tag)

Example: <HR>

Can Contain: None.

Can Be Contained By: <A>, <ADDRESS>, <B>, <CITE>, <CODE>, <DD>, <DT>, <EM>, <H1>, <H2>, <H3>, <H4>, <H5>, <H6>, <I>, <KBD>, <LI>, <P>, <PRE>, <SAMP>, <STRONG>, <TT>, <VAR>

Don't Forget: Use rules to demarcate the logical sections of your document.

Hot Tip: To make sure that the rule stands alone on a line, surround the rule with <P> tags, as in the following: <P>
</P>

Adding Your Address

On the Web, it's customary to add a note at the end of the document indicating who's responsible for it and when it was last updated. You can do this with the <ADDRESS> tag, which displays the information in a distinctive format.

To add an address tag at the bottom of your home page, type the following just before the </BODY> tag (but substitute your own name and e-mail address):

```
<ADDRESS>This document created by Sue Thompson
(suet@fictitious. com). Last modified 10/14/95.
</ADDRESS>
```

ADDRESS

Purpose: Shows the document's author and e-mail address in a distinctive format.

Usage: <ADDRESS> . . . </ADDRESS>

Example:	<ADDRESS>This document created by Sue Thompson (suet@fictitious.com). Last modified 10/14/95.</ADDRESS>
Can Contain:	<A>, <IMG>, , <EM>, <STRONG>, <CODE>, <SAMP>, <KBD>, <VAR>, <CITE>, <TT>, <B>, <I>, <P>
Can Be Contained By:	<BLOCKQUOTE>, <BODY>, <FORM>
Don't Forget:	Include your e-mail address and the date of last modification.
Hot Tip:	Enable e-mail replies using MAILTO.

Enabling E-mail Replies

Without any programming, you can enable a simple but very useful form of reader feedback: automatic e-mail replies. When the reader clicks your e-mail address, the browser—if it's capable of doing so—displays an e-mail reply box that is automatically addressed to you.

To enable e-mail replies, you use an <A> tag written as follows:

```
<A HREF = "mailto:e-mail address">e-mail
address</A>
```

Here's an example:

```
<A HREF="mailto:suet@fictitious.com">suet@ficti-
tious.com</A>
```

Note that the e-mail address is given twice. The first one doesn't appear; it's a hyperlink. The second instance appears in the document and is rendered with the usual hypertext formatting (with most browsers, blue color and underlining). You could just as well include the text, "Click here to send me e-mail," but some people would prefer to send you e-mail using their e-mail packages rather than the somewhat primitive e-mail capabilities of most browsers.

An Example

Here's a nice example of a personal home page, that of Kirsten E. Williams, a student at the University of Virginia. Kirsten's page includes information

about herself and her friends, her interests and concerns, and includes a resume as well. Kirsten makes use of all the HTML knowledge in this chapter. Take a look at the screen shot (Figure 10.5), and then have a look at the HTML code, which is reproduced here in its entirety

A few points to notice:

- Kirsten uses an <IMG> tag to insert a miniature version of a graphic in front of blocks of text (look for the <IMG SRC="ball.gif" WIDTH="3%"> tags).
- There's a good example of using nested character emphases ("*I'm not a scanning pro... **yet!***").
- Kirsten uses the <P ALIGN=CENTER> tag to center a graphic on the page.

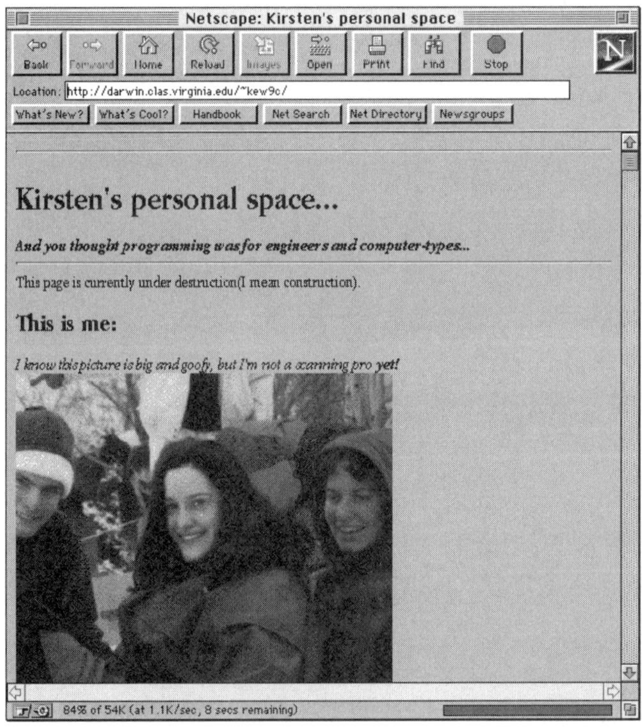

Figure 10.5 Kirsten Williams' home page

```
<HTML>
<HEAD>
<TITLE>Kirsten's personal space</TITLE>
</HEAD>

<BODY>
<HR>
<H1>Kirsten's personal space...</H1>

<I><B>And you thought programming was for engi-
neers and computer-types...</B></I>

<HR>

This page is currently under destruction(I mean
construction).

<H2>This is me:</H2>

<I>I know this picture is big and goofy, but I'm
not a scanning pro<B> yet!</B> </I>

<IMG SRC="kirsten.gif">

<P ALIGN=CENTER><IMG SRC="med.gif"></P>

<H2>General Kirsten info.:</H2>

<STRONG>

<IMG SRC="ball.gif" WIDTH="3%"><A HREF="http://
darwin.clas.virginia.edu/~kew9c/bio.html">Who is
she,</A> and why did they let her on the web?<BR>

<IMG SRC="ball.gif" WIDTH="3%"> And now the on-
line <A HREF="http://darwin.clas.virginia.edu/
~kew9c/resume.html">resume!</A><BR>

<IMG SRC="ball.gif" WIDTH="3%"> Meet my family
and friends. Check out my <A HREF="http://dar-
win.clas.virginia.edu/~kew9c/album.html">photo
album</A>!<BR>

</STRONG>

<H2>Fun stuff:</H2>

<STRONG>
```

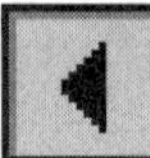

```
<BR> <IMG SRC="ball.gif" WIDTH="3%"> <B>Start
your day off right!</B>

<UL>

<LI>Check out <A HREF="http://www.butter-
fly.net:80/astro/">Real Astrology</A>for your
daily horoscope!</LI>

<LI>And while you're at it, get your <A
HREF="http://cad.ucla.edu/repository/useful/
tarot.html">tarot cards</A> read too.</LI>

</UL>

<IMG SRC="ball.gif" WIDTH="3%"> A haven for <A
HREF="http://darwin.clas.virginia.edu/~kew9c/
book.html">bookworms!</A><I> Featuring my own
"best seller list" updated weekly and links to
other sites for more good reads.</I><BR>

<IMG SRC-"ball.gif" WIDTH="3%"> <A HREF-"http://
darwin.clas.virginia.edu/~kew9c/quote2.html">
Quote of the week!</A> <I>People say the darndest
things!</I> (This list is updated weekly.)

<BR>

<IMG SRC="ball.gif" WIDTH="3%" alt"*"> <A
HREF="http://darwin.clas.virginia.edu/~kew9c/
music.html">Groovey music </A> you can tap your
toes to. <I>Featuring a list of songs currently
running through my head and links music-related
web pages. </I>(This list is updated weekly.)
<BR>

</STRONG>

<P ALIGN=CENTER><IMG SRC="med.gif"></P>

<ADDRESS> Please drop me a line at <A
HREF="mailto:kew9c@darwin.clas.vir-
ginia.edu">kew9c@virginia.edu</A></ADDRESS>

</BODY>
</HTML>
```

From Here

- Learn more about the HEAD of your document in Chapter 12.
- Learn all the BODY elements—plus all the cool attributes you can use—in Chapter 12.
- Delve into hyperlinks in Chapter 13.
- Learn more about graphics, and learn how to add movies, sounds, and animations to your documents, in Chapter 14.
- For advanced HTML, check out Chapter 15 on enabling user feedback with FORMS, Chapter 16 on clickable image maps, and Chapter 17 on tables.

Chapter 11

HTML Fundamentals

What's that you're saying? Enough already with this hands-on stuff? You want some theory and structure? Well, okay. You're like lots of Web publishers—willing to blindly follow recipes only so long. When it comes time to design your own Web publication, you want to understand the thinking behind the method. This chapter's for you.

Here, you'll learn the reasons why you did what you did in the last chapter, and prepare to learn more advanced HTML in Chapters 12–15. After reading this chapter, you'll understand the differences among the various versions of HTML, the ways you can use attributes to control how tags alter text, and the various tools you can use to generate HTML source code. You'll also be prepared to write HTML code that looks good on text-only Web browsers as well as graphical ones, and to use nested HTML tags to format text and graphics the way you want.

For the Time-Challenged

- HTML is a declarative markup language. It's based on defining the function or appearance of text with tags.
- HTML versions are really Document Type Definitions (DTDs) in Standard Generalized Markup Language (SGML). DTDs define the tags publishers can use to describe the text in their documents.
- Two major versions of HTML exist: version 2.0 and version 3.0. Almost all Web browsers support HTML 2.0, but HTML 2.0 doesn't support tables and other fancy formatting like HTML 3.0 does.
- On top of HTML 2.0 and HTML 3.0, there are the Netscape extensions to HTML 2.0. A set of tags that complement those included in HTML 2.0, only Netscape Navigator supports the Netscape extensions.
- Elements define the function of text and other media in HTML documents. Elements take the form of <ELEMENT> . . . </ELEMENT>.
- Attributes modify the function of elements. For example, the SRC attribute in <IMG SRC="boat.gif"> defines the graphic that an IMG element inserts in a document.
- You can nest many elements together to get special effects.
- HTML documents have a head section, which contains general information about the document and is of great interest to the spiders that feed search engines, and a body section, which contains the information you see displayed by a Web browser.
- There's a serious debate in the Web community about logical formatting as opposed to physical formatting. The <STRONG> tag is an example of logical formatting—it says "emphasize this text somehow." The <B> tag says "make this text bold."
- You can insert all the returns and spaces you want in your source code. This helps make your source code easy to read without altering your document's appearance to Web browser users.
- You can make HTML documents with an ASCII text editor or word processor. However, special HTML editors make coding HTML much easier. Converters exist for translating documents in various formats into HTML.

- Several types of Web browser exist. Graphical Web browsers are the most common, and allow visitors to view graphical images and fonts of different sizes. The latest graphical Web browsers support HTML 3.0, which allows tables, among other things. Some Web users have text-only browsers, though, so you have to keep them in mind when designing your site.
- Entry-level Web sites use the codes you learned in Chapter 10 (basic text and image formatting). More advanced sites use the material in Chapter 12 (more elaborate formatting). Really cool sites use the codes you'll learn about in Chapters 15–17, including clickable image maps, tables, and forms.

HTML: A Markup Language

You're probably used to thinking of computer programming languages as ways of encoding instructions for a computer to follow. Languages like C++, BASIC, FORTRAN, and Pascal are based on the model of a computer starting at the beginning of programs they create, and moving line by line through the program, doing whatever each line tells them to do. These languages, called *procedural languages,* rest on the idea of executing instructions in series over a span of time.

Other languages, including HTML, aren't based on the sequential execution of instructions. Instead, they rely on declared data and so are called *declarative languages*. COBOL is a good example of a declarative language, as is the database query language SQL. These languages require someone to define the state of certain things—the serial numbers of all the Bravo Units a company has sold or the way a Web browser should format a particular passage of text, for example. The programs then analyze this declared information and derive something useful from it. In the case of HTML, Web browsers process tagged text and yield attractively formatted Web documents.

An apt comparison may be made between PostScript and HTML. PostScript, a page-description language most frequently used to communicate page layouts to laser printers, is a procedural language. Though most PostScript code comes from programs (page layout and desktop publishing programs, typically), you can (if you're *really* hard up for something to do) sit

down with a PostScript compiler and write a program in PostScript. Your code would, in English translation, say things like "Place the text contained in variable BODY_TEXT in two columns, spaced one quarter of an inch apart and never approaching the page edges closer than an inch, and set the text in 12-point Regular Blathering Fool. Put a 10-percent gray screen over the entire page." In other words, you'd be laying out a procedure for the computer (or printer, which is really a specialized computer) to follow.

When coding in HTML, you're not telling the computer what to do, you're telling it how things *are*. HTML code says, "This passage is a Level 1 heading, this passage is a Level 2 heading, this passage is an Abstract, and this big passage is Body Text. A picture belongs over here." HTML code consists of a series of statements, not a series of commands—at least in the minds of purists. Lately, with the commercialization of the Web, HTML has become significantly more instructional. Is the <B> tag (which makes text bold, and which you learned about in the last chapter) a declaration—"This passage is bold"—or a command—"Format this passage in bold type"? You'll learn more about this debate later in this chapter and in Chapter 28.

HTML Versions

Like anything worth learning about, HTML is always changing. In the Web community, several factions argue about what they want HTML to do, and the various standard-making bodies have to make decisions about which new tags to include and which to leave out. As of this writing, HTML exists in at least three variations. Some sites embrace the older standards and guarantee themselves the largest possible audience, while other sites use the advanced features of the newer standard, but risk losing the patronage of those with browsers older than a few months.

This section discusses the differences among the various flavors of HTML and the advantages and disadvantages of using each of them. First, though, you'll learn the real significance of a "version" of HTML.

Document Type Definitions

This stuff falls into the category of that which you should know if you want to have a complete understanding of the topic, but which otherwise isn't much use. Read on in this subsection if you want to temporarily abandon practical applications of HTML and delve into the intricacies of the language's origins and defining characteristics.

Understand that HTML is a special kind of Standard Generalized Markup Language (SGML), a language used mainly in colleges and universities to facilitate the exchange of papers and other documents among researchers. SGML consists of a set of very broad protocols for marking up different types of documents with logical labels—things like "Here's my document's title" and "Here's a footnote." The rule sets that govern the marking up of each type of document are called Document Type Definitions (DTDs). HTML has several DTDs for hypertext documents, each of which represents a "version" of HTML. When someone "knows HTML," they really know one or two of the DTDs of SGML.

You can think of DTDs as lists of the tags with which you can mark up a particular kind of document. HTML DTDs tell what the <A> tag means, for instance, and explain what to do with the URL that follows the HREF attribute. But the <A> tag isn't a great example, because it's constant among all the various implementations of HTML. What are the differences among the versions? Read on and learn.

HTML Versions 2 and 3

The trouble with HTML versions is that there are at least two standard-setting bodies involved in hashing them out. Not only do the members of one organization have to reach a consensus about all the arcane issues that plague the development of SGML DTDs, they have to reconcile their organization's conclusions with those of the other standard-setting groups. For this reason, "standardization" of HTML versions lags far behind the state of the art in HTML—even further than standardization in other areas of personal computing, such as modem protocols.

HTML 2.0, for which a formal written standard will exist shortly, is old hat. Its main selling point is that nearly every Web browser supports it, and Web publishers can be sure that visitors to their documents will see a document formatted in some kind of coordinated fashion. The problem with HTML 2.0 is that its capabilities are so pedestrian. Serious HTML developers want to use slicker features supported only by various proposed HTML 3.0 standards and the Netscape extensions to HTML 2.0. You'll have to make a tradeoff between wide support (HTML 2.0) and cool formatting capabilities (HTML 3.0 and the Netscape extensions).

What's special about HTML 3.0, then? Lots of stuff that doesn't sound significant in print, but that makes the difference between a merely serviceable site and a really cool one (see "Levels of HTML Sophistication," later in this chapter). Some of the features supported by HTML include tables,

colored and patterned backgrounds, multicolored text, and a CENTER attribute for several text-formatting tags. Remember, experts are still haggling about the details of HTML 3.0, and by the time they decide those, HTML 4.0 will be the latest thing. Chapter 12 and Chapters 15–17 deal with many aspects of HTML 3.0 and how to use them in your documents.

Netscape Extensions

So what, then, are these Netscape extensions you're hearing so much about? They're one browser manufacturer's solution to the lack of features in HTML 2.0 and the plodding pace of the standards bodies. Netscape Communications, maker of the Netscape Navigator Web browser, decided that its browsers would support a special set of tags. Since Netscape Navigator is the most popular browser on the Web, the company's decision became a de facto standard immediately. Lots of HTML experts screamed when Netscape made this decision, since it opened the door for other Web browser manufacturers to do the same thing and create mutually incompatible versions of HTML. This hasn't happened yet, though, and it looks like most of the Netscape extensions will become part of the HTML 3.0 standard when it's finally adopted.

What happens when a browser sees a tag it doesn't support? In a nutshell, it ignores the tag. Here's some HTML code for creating a table—something that's supported by HTML 3.0-compliant browsers but not HTML 2.0-compliant browsers.

```
<TABLE COLSPEC="C20 C20 C20 C20" CELLPAD-
  DING=5>

<CAPTION ALIGN=top>An Example Table</CAP-
  TION>

<TR><TH></TH><TH>Cars

</TH><TH>Trucks</TH><TH>Buses</TH></TR>

<TR><TH>May</TH><TD>17</TD><TD>12</TD>
  <TD>12</TD></TR>

<TR><TH>June</TH><TD>15</TD><TD>14</TD>
  <TD>13</TD></TR>

</TABLE>
```

Take a look at Figure 11.1, which shows the table displayed by Netscape Navigator, which supports tables. A browser

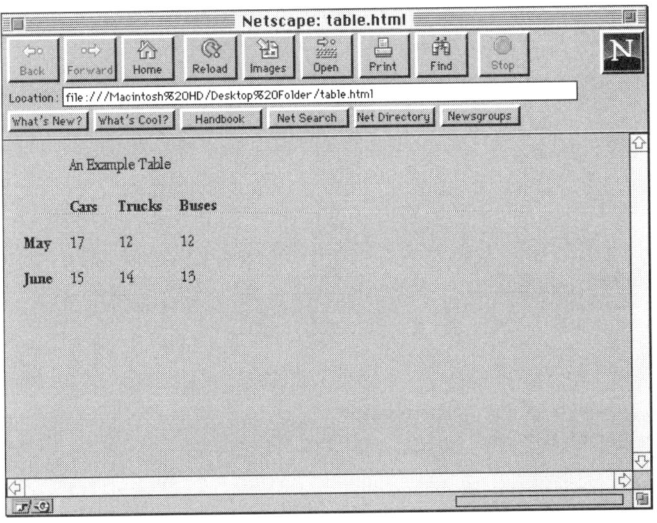

Figure 11.1 A table in Netscape Navigator

that doesn't support table tags would just show rows of numbers. That's why many people forego fancy formatting for the benefit of those with older browsers.

The Naming of Parts

The English poet Henry Reed, writing in 1945 about his army training, wrote "And today we will have the naming of parts." Reed's poem, part of *Lessons of the War,* depicts a training officer lecturing a group of recruits about the components of their rifles. This section doesn't purport to embody the irony or wit of Reed's poetry, but it's meant to do the same job as the officer Reed wrote about: to instruct the uninitiated about the tool of a trade.

Here, you'll learn the difference between an *element* and an *attribute,* learn what characters you can use in HTML source code and which characters you can't use, and learn how to combine elements to achieve special effects. You'll understand how logical formatting contrasts with physical formatting, and how you can use white space to make your code more readable.

As Reed wrote, today we have the naming of parts.

Elements (Tags)

In high school chemistry, you learned that elements comprise all matter. The same holds true, more or less, in HTML. Without elements, you'd have nothing but a disorganized collection of text, graphics, video, and sound files. Elements let you weave various hypermedia together into Web publications and link Web documents to one another.

In all cases, elements are the first set of characters to appear after the < character (later sets of characters may be attributes or values assigned to attributes. You'll learn about attributes later in this section). HEAD, U, BLOCKQUOTE, and CITE all are elements. They declare the nature or function of the text to which they're attached.

Usually, elements take this form:

```
<ELEMENT>...</ELEMENT>
```

In this arrangement, the <ELEMENT> tag defines the beginning of text defined by the element, and the </ELEMENT> tag defines the end. Here's an example:

```
<BLOCKQUOTE>A wide plain, where the widening Floss
hurries on between green banks to the sea, and the
loving tide, rushing to meet it, checks its pas-
sage with an impetuous embrace.</BLOCKQUOTE>
```

Note that BLOCKQUOTE elements surround the passage (the first sentence of George Eliot's *The Mill on the Floss*). When a Web browser looks at the code above, it will treat the text as defined by the BLOCKQUOTE element. Usually, that means it will indent the text from both margins and separate it from other text above and below.

Not all elements follow the <ELEMENT> . . . </ELEMENT> model, though. Many elements, particularly those found in document heads, are said to be *empty*; that is, they contain no text. The IMG element is an empty element. There is no </IMG> tag. The same holds true for the HR and META elements. These elements, along with several others, are inserted in text. They represent something that fits within the text (such as a graphic), but does not alter the text itself.

A few elements are not empty, but don't strictly require the </ELEMENT> portion of their syntax. For example, in a series of body-text paragraphs, you can get away with just putting <P> tags at the beginning of each paragraph, without worrying about putting </P> tags at the end of each paragraph. The <P> tag at the start of one paragraph implies the </P> tag at the end of the previous paragraph. Lists work the same way—you don't have to use the </LI> tag if you don't want to.

Element Nesting

You're not limited to tagging text with only one element. Often, you'll want to tag text with more than one element to achieve special effects. Taken literally, nearly all tags in HTML documents nest inside other tags, since the HTML, HEAD, and BODY elements surround large portions of documents and the tags those portions contain.

Here's an example of nested elements:

```
<ABSTRACT>In this article, the author explodes
the widely held conception that the character
Stella in Tennessee Williams' <CITE>A Streetcar
Named Desire</CITE> is a parallel to the declin-
ing culture of the Old South and instead argues
that she represents the results of a conflict
between post-World War II consumerism and Depres-
sion-era austerity.</ABSTRACT>
```

Figure 11.2 shows how a browser renders this code. Note that the entire passage is formatted as an abstract, but only "A Streetcar Named Desire" appears formatted as a citation. In this book, the boxes that summarize HTML elements show how various elements can and cannot nest.

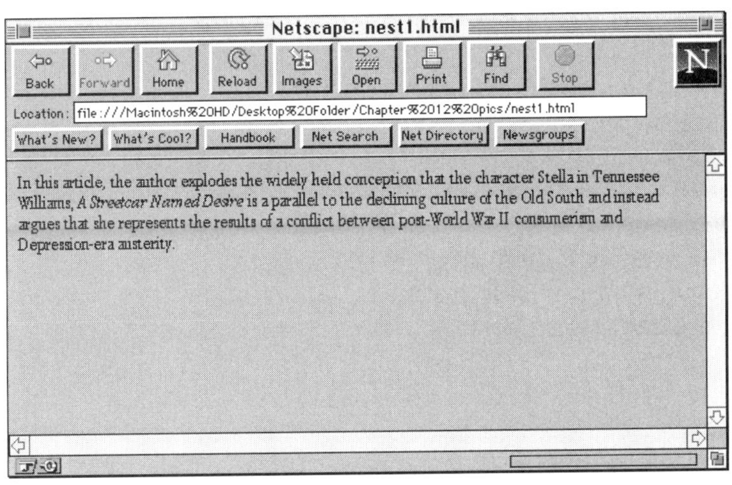

Figure 11.2 The results of nesting elements

Attributes

Elements aren't the whole story, though. You use *attributes* to modify the basic function of elements. Take the IMG element, for example. It inserts a graphic into an HTML document, but how does it insert that graphic? Is the top of the graphic flush with the top of the line of text, or is the bottom of the graphic level with the bottom of the text characters? Or should the center of the image align with the center of the line of text? You have to use attributes to specify how a Web browser should display the graphic. In the case of IMG and some other elements, you also have to specify the source of the graphic—a path to a graphics file.

In the IMG example, the ALIGN attribute is the attribute that determines the alignment of the graphic, and the SRC attribute specifies the source of the graphics file. The SRC attribute, in fact, is mandatory—you can't insert a graphic without telling the computer where to find the desired image file. The syntax looks like this:

```
<IMG SRC="glider.gif" ALIGN=MIDDLE>
```

In this example, the SRC attribute specifies that the in-line image comes from the image file called glider.gif and that the center of the image should align with the center of the text in the line. MIDDLE in this example is a value assigned to ALIGN—the other two options are TOP and BOTTOM. Many attributes take numerical values, such as the thickness of table grid elements in pixels or the amount of white space that should surround graphics.

Entities

In an HTML document, you can use any of the characters in the International Standards Organization (ISO) Latin-1 character set, which is also known as the ISO 8859/1 character set. Within this character set, you find the following:

- The first 128 characters of the 7-bit United States ASCII character set.
- An additional 128 characters that contain most of the accented and other characters needed to type words in European languages.

There's no problem with the first 128 characters, the ones included in the ASCII character set: You can type them on any computer keyboard, they'll appear on the screen, and they'll look fine when your HTML document is viewed by a Web browser. The problem lies with the next 128 characters.

These characters, commonly called *extended characters*, are coded differently by different computer manufacturers. If you use the Macintosh codes to insert an accented character in an HTML document, for instance, it won't be displayed correctly when your document is accessed by a program running on a Windows or UNIX system.

To deal with these discrepancies in extended character coding, you don't type the extended characters directly, the way you would if you were preparing a document with a word processing program. Instead, you use *entities* (also called *entity references*), which enable you to type the extended characters using a special code, which all HTML browsers recognize. For example, to include an "e" with an acute accent, you type the following code:

```
&eacute;
```

Note that you must begin the code with an ampersand (&) and end it with a semicolon. For a full list of the entity codes you can use, see Appendix B.

I typed an ampersand in my document but my browser ignores it!

HTML uses several ASCII characters for special purposes, such as the ampersand. If you use one of these characters in ordinary text, the browser will try to interpret the character as an expression (such as an entity code), and it may simply ignore the character if it can't make sense out of what follows.

To include a special character in ordinary text, type the following codes:

Character	Code
Ampersand (&)	&
Double quotation (")	"
Left angle bracket (<)	<
Right angle bracket (>)	&rt;

Overall Structure

In Chapter 10, you created a well-structured HTML document without really understanding what you were doing. Here, you'll learn what those <HTML>, <HEAD>, and <BODY> tags meant.

The HTML element is a holdover from the era of SGML, when it was important to specify which Document Type Definition a document

employed. In good HTML style, you put an <HTML> tag at the beginning, an </HTML> tag at the end, and nest all other elements inside the <HTML>. . .</HTML> pair. In practice, you don't have to include the HTML element—just like you don't *have* to wear pants and shirts that match. Using the tags is part of good style, though, so bracket your documents with <HTML>. . .</HTML> tags.

Aside from the overall <HTML>-tag bracketing, HTML documents have two distinct components: the document head, designated with the <HEAD>. . .</HEAD> tags, and the document body, defined by the <BODY>. . .</BODY> tags. The head contains information *about* the document, including the document's title and details about its creator. The body contains the stuff you see when you view the HTML code with a Web browser—the text and its attached formatting tags, and the images and rules that appear in the text.

Don't neglect your documents' heads just because visitors to your Web site can't see them. Web spiders—which feed data into search engines—pay special attention to the head section. With a carefully designed head, you can generate more search-engine hits on your site, and thereby draw more members of your target audience.

Logical Formatting vs. Physical Formatting

Debates about programming styles parallel debates about religion and politics—everyone has ideas, and it's nearly impossible to convince them that their ideas are wrong. In HTML, a debate rages about the extent to which tags should be logical (that is, the extent to which they should state the function of the text they define, and leave formatting to the browser) and the extent to which they should be physical (the extent to which they should say exactly how the browser should format text). Proponents of logical formatting say the true flexibility of markup languages lies in the ability of the Web browser—and the person who configures it—to make formatting decisions. Those who favor absolute formatting—and the ranks of this faction are swelling as the Web gets more commercial—say publishers should have control over the appearance of their publications.

Here's an example of logical and physical formatting tags that, in most browsers, yield the same results:

```
<P>The party was, like, a total
<STRONG>blast!</STRONG> There was this guy there
who ate, no joke, <B>fifteen</B> goldfish!</P>
```

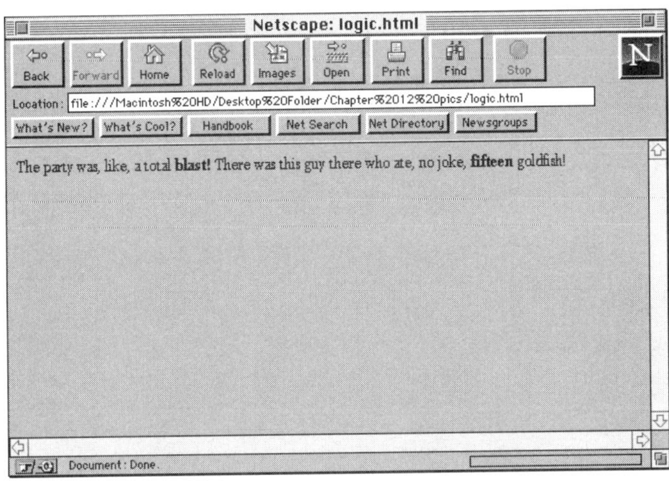

Figure 11.3 The identical results of logical and physical formatting tags

Figure 11.3 shows the code above as interpreted by a browser. Note that "blast!", tagged with the logical tag <STRONG>, is rendered the same as "fifteen," tagged with the physical tag <B>.

This book, lest it be featured at burnings sponsored by one faction or the other, doesn't endorse either position. Both sides' arguments make sense, and though it seems that the physical-formatting proponents have the upper hand now, something may change in a matter of months. Time will tell whether HTML remains a classic markup language, or a quasi-procedural language almost like PostScript.

Readability

As long as they're outside tags that protect preformatting (such as the <PRE> and <LIT> tags), you can insert all the spaces and returns you want into your HTML documents. Look at this example:

```
<P>Perhaps it was                    the middle of
January of the

present year that
I looked up and saw the mark on the wall.</P>
```

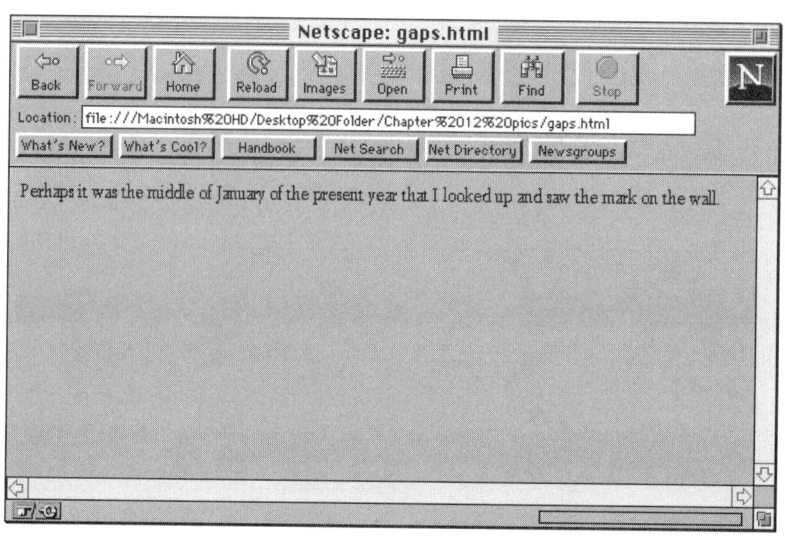

Figure 11.4 Space- and return-ridden code, interpreted by a browser

Now look at Figure 11.4. Virginia Woolf's prose appears as if the extra spaces and returns weren't there. Why is this an advantage? Because it enables you to make your source code easier to read. By inserting spaces and returns—white space—you can separate logical portions of your source code and thereby make it easier to understand. Don't hesitate to take advantage of this feature of HTML—you'll thank yourself later, when you have to modify old, complex HTML documents.

How to Create an HTML Document

Okay, all that's great, you say, but you want to know how to code HTML. What programs do you need—is there an HTML compiler or assembler? Should you look into buying HTML code libraries? No. There's no such thing as an HTML compiler, and HTML code libraries don't exist, though they probably soon will. All you really need to write HTML code on the cheap is a text editor. If you want, you can find a fancy HTML editor to absolve you of the need to type all those tedious tags. Or, if you already

have a document in one format and want to convert it to HTML, you can use a converter. This section explains the advantages and disadvantages of these programs for writing HTML code.

Word Processing Programs and Text Editors

You learned in Chapter 10 that HTML code is nothing more than ASCII text with some special character sequences thrown in among the normal text. Therefore, you can use an ASCII text editor to write and edit HTML source code. You probably have at least one text editor on your machine (if you don't, several good ones are available for free on the Web), so using a text editor is the most economical way to get into Web publishing. By using your word processing program (as long as it saves in ASCII format), you gain a few features on top of those offered by text editors—the ability to insert boilerplate text, for instance, and to use macros.

HTML Editors

If you're serious about HTML coding (you plan to do more than a couple of simple documents), get an HTML editor. These programs, most of which are freely distributed as shareware on the Web, are special-purpose word processing and page layout packages. Where a regular word processor would put a header in a large typeface, an HTML editor would surround the header text with the appropriate header tags. HTML editors also make it easy to enter values for attributes. When you tell it to insert a hyperlink, for example, editors may present you with a list of documents in the same directory and a list of targets (specified with the NAME attribute of the <A> tag) elsewhere in the same document. Editors ease the tedium of HTML.

Converters

Converters aren't as flexible as text editors, word processors, or HTML editors. Instead, they do only one utilitarian task: conversion of documents in a non-HTML format to HTML. Scores of shareware and freeware converters exist, and they translate everything from Microsoft Word documents to UNIX man pages (program documentation) into HTML.

To find a converter for the kind of document you want to convert to HTML, visit a search engine (such as InfoSeek or Lycos) and enter "HTML *whatever* converter," where *whatever* is the document flavor from which you want to convert, as the search criteria.

HTML Editor

HTML Editor, widely regarded as one of the best HTML authoring tools available for the Macintosh, appears on the CD-ROM that accompanies this book. A creation of Rick Giles, HTML Editor boasts a graphical toolbar and lots of intuitive dialog boxes that speed HTML coding.

The version of HTML Editor on the CD-ROM is shareware—you can evaluate it before you have to stop using it or pay the $25 registration fee. You'll learn how to use HTML Editor in Chapter 18.

HTML and Web Browsers

HTML code by itself isn't much fun—it's plain ASCII text, made less readable by the insertion of bracketed tags. For HTML to serve its purpose, a Web browser needs to look at the tagged ASCII text, evaluate the position and significance of the tags, and display an interpretation of the tagged text. Technically, a Web browser is called a *parser*, because it parses (sorts out) the tags from the text and uses the tags to decide how to display each passage of text.

The section earlier in this chapter that discussed the controversy about physical formatting versus logical formatting described an argument about the function of Web browsers. How much flexibility should browsers—and the people who configure them—have in deciding how to display text? HTML purists say they should have lots of flexibility, while many Web publishers say that the tags in HTML documents should leave little room for creative (and potentially ugly) interpretation.

This section describes some of the several kinds of browsers on the Web today, and tells you how to code for each of them.

Text-Only Web Browsers

They're in the minority, but they're still out there—people who use text-only browsers, that is. The introduction of the Web marked the establishment of a distinction among Internet users. Prior to the Web's advent, pretty much everyone with a modem and a computer that could emulate a VT-100 terminal had access to the same information. Now, if you don't have a computer that can handle the latest Web browsers and a fast modem or a network connection, you're at a serious disadvantage in terms of getting access to information. Lots of Web surfers in schools and libraries and in the Third World still use text-only (also called character-based) browsers.

As a Web publisher, you can make life easier for users of text-only browsers by attaching descriptive captions to your images, or by using the ALT attribute of the IMG element, which defines the text that appears in place of a graphic on a text-only browser. You may also want to have a text-only version of your document, both for users of character-based browsers and users of graphical browsers who don't want to wait for graphics to download.

Graphical Web Browsers

Most Web surfers use graphical browsers, such as Netscape Navigator or NCSA Mosaic. Graphical Web browsers have the ability to display different-sized typefaces and different fonts, as well as rules, icons, colored text, and graphics. Historians of the Internet likely will remember graphical Web browsers, along with the Web pages they traverse, as the Net's "killer app"—the application that brought the Internet out of academia and into the mainstream.

Most of this book deals with publishing for graphical Web browsers. Though you have to be mindful of those stuck using text-based Web browsers, assume that most of your audience will be able to look at fancy formatting and images. The extent to which a Web browser understands fancy formatting depends on which version of HTML it's designed for. Today, the most advanced Web browsers interpret HTML version 3.0.

HTML 3.0-Compliant Browsers

The latest Web browsers support HTML version 3.0—the version of HTML that allows tables and other fancy formatting tricks. If you want to code for the cutting-edge portion of the Web community, you'll want to use the semi-standard HTML 3.0 specification instead of the Netscape extensions (see the discussion of these HTML flavors earlier in this chapter). Netscape Navigator, the most popular Web browser, recognizes both the Netscape extensions and HTML 3.0 tags.

Levels of HTML Sophistication

In any area of expertise, someone with a little knowledge of the subject can differentiate those without a clue from those with average knowledge, and those with average knowledge from the experts. In personal computing generally, you know that people who have no interest in the Internet and have

little desire to squeeze every ounce of power from their computers aren't at the cutting edge of the field. Real computing experts want to publish on the Web, of course!

This section teaches you how to distinguish the amateur sites from the merely average sites and the fantastically cool sites. After reading this, you'll know what to look for before declaring a site the cat's pajamas.

Entry-Level HTML

This is what you learned in Chapter 10. Entry-level sites distinguish themselves from more advanced sites with their heavy reliance on single-column text layout and minimal use of graphics and other multimedia. Not only will you never see a table in beginners' sites; you'll never see text formatted with much other than the header tags and the body text tag. Clickable image maps and forms fall far outside the realm of comprehension of these sites' owners.

Pretty Cool HTML

Entry-level sites don't fool anyone using a graphical Web browser. They're minimalist, and they look the part. Once people have seen a lavishly illustrated site, with careful formatting and hierarchical organization, they'll turn up their noses at plain-vanilla text-oriented sites.

In Chapter 12, you'll learn to code enough HTML to impress most people, if for no other reason than that most Web users don't understand the HTML discussed in Chapters 15–17. This code will earn you entree into the Web-publishing mainstream. Your site will fall somewhere on the coolness continuum between functional and nifty, but it won't achieve the upper echelons of Web-surfer esteem.

Totally Boffo, Webmaster-Class HTML

This kind of HTML is what makes surfing fun. If you can achieve this level of coolness in your site, people who aren't even interested in your topic will check out your site just to see what you've done there. Some of the hallmarks of wondrous HTML:

- Forms (see Chapter 15)
- Clickable maps (see Chapter 16)
- Tables (see Chapter 17)

Even these things, with HTML editors easing their creation, have started to become vaguely déclassé, and by the time you read this you may have to stretch even further to achieve coolness. Java and HotJava likely will comprise a big part of the next wave of Web innovation, and VRML, though it's still in its larval stage, has great promise. Take a look at Chapter 20 for a discussion of these and other Web publishing horizons.

Don't forget, though, that just having "cool" features on your documents doesn't make them hot stuff. You can put tables together sloppily, or have slow, counterintuitive CGI scripts backing up your image maps. You have to have the content to back up the flash.

From Here

- Okay, class dismissed. Get back to the practical applications of HTML. In the next chapter, you'll learn HTML tricks slicker than those you saw in Chapter 10 and move into the Web-publishing mainstream. Chapter 12 also prepares you for the really cool stuff you'll learn in Chapters 15–17.

Chapter 12

Building Your Document

Now that you understand the fundamentals behind HTML, you're ready to move beyond the basic stuff you did in Chapter 10 and do some niftier stuff with HTML. Granted, the material here won't win you any raves—the tricks in Chapters 15–17 will do that—but this material will take you beyond the realm of the HTML novice. When you master these tags, you can say you've achieved HTML fluency for all practical purposes.

Making Your HTML Easier to Understand

You can get by with plain HTML code if your documents are simple, you are the only one who will modify them in the future, *and* you have a flawless memory. If, on the other hand, your documents employ complex tags and

features and other people will have to work with your code without your help, you should document the code in your HTML publications. This section is a guide to ways in which you can make your code easier to read, modify, and expand.

When typing HTML source code, do whatever you can to make it easier to read. You've already seen that Web browsers ignore extra spaces and line breaks in the source code—you have to use the <BR> tag to insert a line break in a line of text instead of just pressing Return, for example—but you can use this to your advantage. Insert lots of extra line breaks in your code to make it easier to read, breaking your code into logical units with white space.

You can also use the space key—which Web browsers ignore when it's outside text that appears in the document—to indent subsidiary document elements relative to higher-order ones. For example, you might indent all the items in a list three spaces, while leaving the <OL>, <UL>, or other list-definition tags on their own lines and flush with thc lcft margin. You can also use the Tab key for this purpose.

Using Comment Tags

On top of its ability to handle source code loaded with returns and spaces, HTML (like most advanced programming languages) has a procedure for encoding English-language comments in source code, and before you learn more advanced HTML tags and techniques, you should learn it. Web browsers ignore any text inside comment tags (which take the form <!-- ... ->), so you can surround helpful hints with comment tags to make the hints visible to human beings studying your HTML code but invisible to Web browsers. Remember that some browsers don't recognize comments that span more than one line, so surround each line of comments with its own set of comment tags.

Here's an example of HTML code with a comment buried inside it.

```
<P>Here's a list of the steps you need to follow
in order to play water polo. </P>
<!-- The following code creates an ordered list,
which the browser numbers automatically ->
<OL>
<LI> Find a ball.
<LI> Find a large body of water.
```

For the Time-Challenged

- Don't forget: you can insert returns and spaces in many places in your HTML source code without affecting the appearance of your document when a Web browser interprets it. Take advantage of this capability to make your documents easier to read.
- Use <!-- . . . -> tags to surround comments. Comments make it easier for others t-- understand your HTML code and modify it in your absence.
- Use the <BLOCKQUOTE> tag to distinguish a long text excerpt from the rest of the paper in which it appears.
- Use the <CITE> tag to highlight the title of a book or article.
- Use <DL>, <DT>, and <DD> tags to format text for use in a glossary or dictionary.
- Use the <OL> tag, in conjunction with the <LI> tag, to create a list of items that Web browsers number in sequence automatically.
- Use the <DIR> and <MENU> tags like <UL> tags. Many browsers format the three tags the same way.
- The <PRE> tag protects the spacing and returns in an imported passage of text. Use the <PRE> tag whenever you want to incorporate previously formatted text in your document.
- Use the <KBD> tag to distinguish text you want someone to type on a keyboard.
- Use the <STRIKE> tag in editorial and legal applications to show text that will be removed.
- The <ABSTRACT> tag distinguishes a document's abstract—its summary—from its body.
- The <BLINK> tag makes text flash on and off, but it can easily get annoying if overused.

```
<LI> Find a horse that can swim.
</OL>
```

Look at Figure 12.1 and note that the comment doesn't display when a Web browser interprets the code.

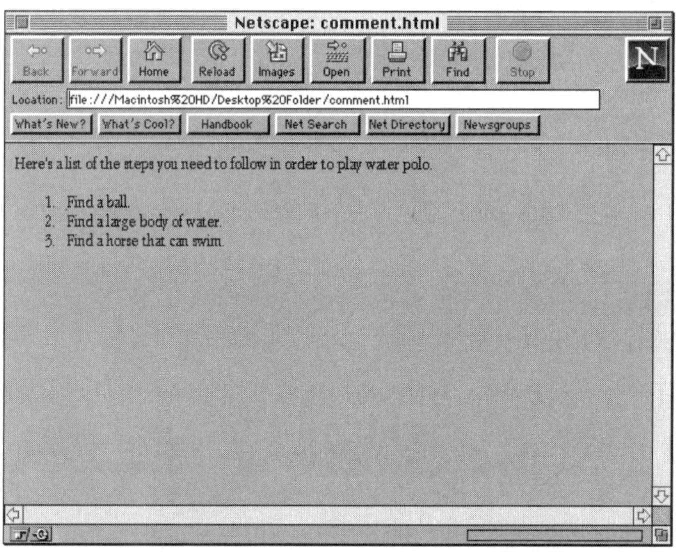

Figure 12.1 Comment hidden when document is displayed

<!--. . .->

Purpose: To allow HTML programmers to insert comments in their code, thereby making it easier for people to study and debug.

Usage: <!--. . .->

Example: <!--The tags in the next line create a form that prompts the user for a password.->

Can Contain: Text (the comment)

Can Be Contained By: None

Don't Forget: Not all Web browsers support multiple-line comments. Break your comments into chunks of less than line length, and enclose each chunk in <!--. . .-> characters.

Hot Tip: Use comments liberally, especially if other people will need to modify your code.

Referring to Other Works: The <BLOCKQUOTE> and <CITE> Tags

Since it's based on the academically oriented Standard Generalized Markup Language (SGML), HTML has lots of features that derive from the traditional organization of academic articles. Since one of the defining characteristics of academic writing is reference to past works, HTML has a couple of tags for distinguishing someone else's work from your own. The "Special Document Parts" section of this chapter covers some more of HTML's scholarly heritage.

Imagine you're writing a paper about Jonathan Swift for publication on the Web. You want to include an excerpt from his satirical classic, *A Modest Proposal*. If you were writing for publication on paper, you'd single space the excerpt and indent it from both margins, and underline the name of the essay or put it in italics. When coding in HTML, however, you'd write the following code:

```
<P>Swift's biting, irreverent wit is nowhere more
evident than in his <CITE>A Modest Proposal</CITE>,
in which he writes, </P><BLOCKQUOTE>I have been
assured by a very knowing American of my acquain-
tance in London, that a young healthy child well
nursed is at a year old, a most delicious, nourish-
ing, and wholesome food, whether stewed, roasted,
baked, or boiled; and I make no doubt that it will
equally serve in a fricasse or a ragout.</BLOCK-
QUOTE> <P>Swift's willingness to poke fun at "seri-
ous" topics also emerges in his <CITE>Gulliver's
Travels</CITE></P>...
```

The results of this code appear in Figure 12.2.

BLOCKQUOTE

Purpose: To set text off from other text as a quote excerpted from another source.

Usage: <BLOCKQUOTE>. . .</BLOCKQUOTE>

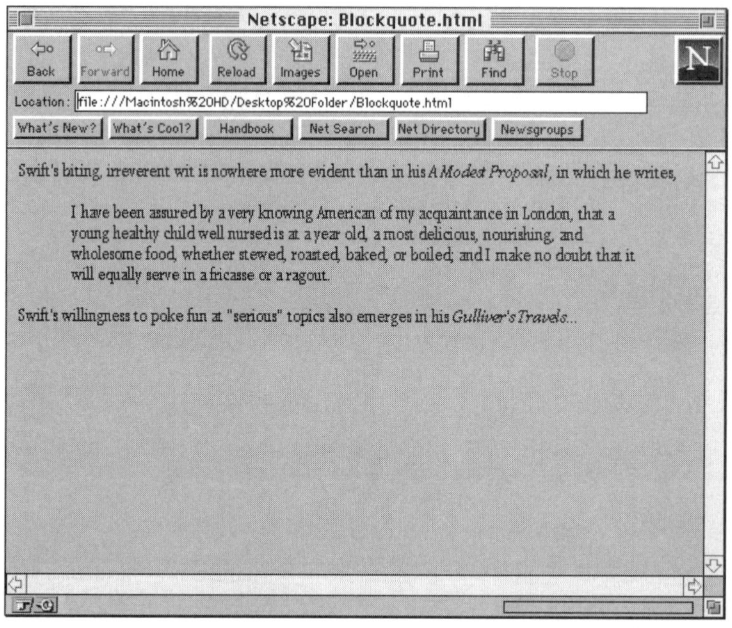

Figure 12.2 <BLOCKQUOTE>

Example: <BLOCKQUOTE> <P> When in the course of human events it becomes necessary to dissolve the political bands. . .</P> </BLOCKQUOTE>

Can Contain: <ADDRESS>, <BLOCKQUOTE>, <DIR>, <DL>, <FORM>, <H1>, <H2>, <H3>, <H4>, <H5>, <H6>, <HR>, <MENU>, <OL>, <P>, <PRE>, <UL>

Can Be Contained By: <BLOCKQUOTE>, <BODY>, <DD>, <FORM>, <LI>

Don't Forget: To add more white space around the quote, surround the text with <P>...</P> tags or other paragraph-separation tags, as in the example above.

Hot Tip: Always use <BLOCKQUOTE>, not other formatting tags, to distinguish excerpted material.

CITE

Purpose:	To define a short reference to another work, usually in a bibliography.
Usage:	<CITE>. . .</CITE>
Example:	<CITE>Terkel, Studs. <I>Working.</I> New York: Ballantine, 1972.</CITE>
Can Contain:	<A>, <B>, , <CITE>, <CODE>, <DFN>, <EM>, <I>, <IMG>, <KBD>, <SAMP>, <STRIKE>, <STRONG>, <TT>, <U>, <VAR>
Can Be Contained By:	<ADDRESS>, <B>, <CITE>, <CODE>, <DD>, <DT>, <DFN>, <EM>, <H1>, <H2>, <H3>, <H4>, <H5>, <H6>, <I>, <KBD>, <LI>, <P>, <PRE>, <SAMP>, <STRIKE>, <STRONG>, <TT>, <U>, <VAR>
Don't Forget:	Use the <CITE> tag for bibliographic references; use the <BLOCKQUOTE> tag for excerpted passages.

Creating a Dictionary or Glossary

You learned in Chapter 5 that one of the main Web publishing genres is documentation—text that explains a concept or a procedure. Often, documentation requires explanations of jargon or other specialized vocabulary, and that requires a dictionary or glossary. Use the three tags described below to organize a list of terms and their definitions.

To create a dictionary or glossary, you'll use three tags: the <DL> tag, the <DT> tag, and the <DD> tag. The <DL> tag identifies a dictionary-style list; the <DT> tag tells the Web browser to format the text it surrounds as a term in the dictionary; and the <DD> tag tells the browser to format the text it surrounds as a definition in the dictionary.

Here's an example of how to use the three dictionary tags:

```
<DL>
<DT>Onomatopoeia</DT>
```

```
<DD>Words that, when pronounced, sound like that
which they represent. Examples of onomatopoeia
include "splat," "bang," and "crackle."</DD>
<DT>Scansion</DT>
<DD>The arrangement of words in a poem on a
printed page. Loose scansion can give a poem an
airy feeling, while tight scansion can convey a
feeling of tension.</DD>
</DL>
```

Figure 12.3 shows how this code appears when interpreted by a Web browser.

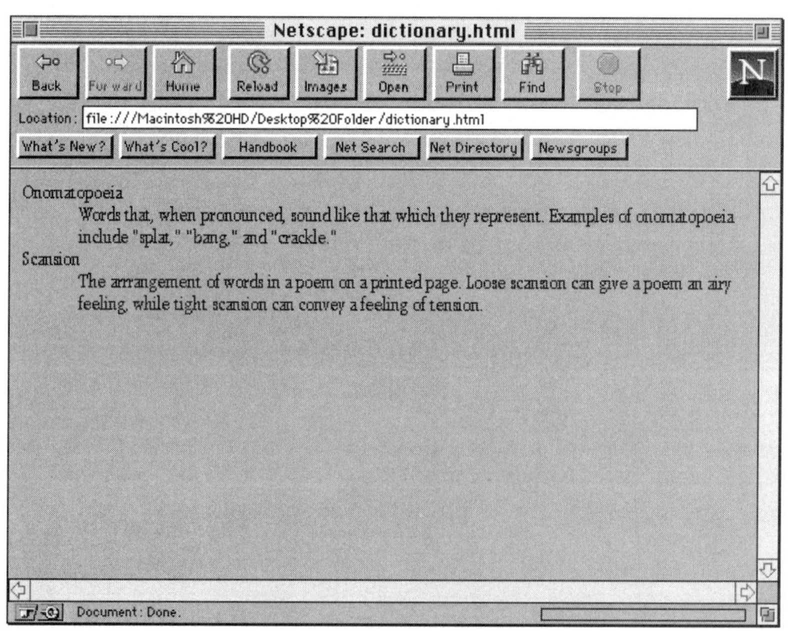

Figure 12.3 The dictionary tags in action

DL

Purpose: To identify a list of items as entries in a dictionary or glossary.

Usage: <DL>. . .</DL>

Example: <DL> <DT>Acoustic coupler</DT> <DD>An especially vocal lover.</DD> </DL>

Can Contain: <DL>, <DT>

Can Be Contained By: <BLOCKQUOTE>, <BODY>, <DD>, <FORM>, <LI>

Don't Forget: Organize the text inside <DL>...</DL> tags logically, with <DT>...</DT> and <DD>. . .</DD> tags, as in the example above.

Hot Tip: You can use the COMPACT attribute (written <DL COMPACT>...</DL>) to reduce the amount of space a dictionary list occupies.

DT

Purpose: To format text as a term in a dictionary or glossary.

Usage: <DT>. . .</DT>

Example: <DT>Acoustic coupler</DT>

Can Contain: <A>, <B>, <BR>, <CITE>, <CODE>, <DFN>, <EM>, <I>, <IMG>, <KBD>, <SAMP>, <STRIKE>, <STRONG>,<TT>, <U>, <VAR>

Can Be Contained By: <DL>

Don't Forget: Web browsers usually format <DT>-tagged text as flush left and bold or italic.

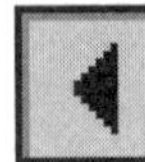

DD

Purpose:	To format text as a definition in a dictionary or glossary.
Usage:	<DD>. . .</DD>
Example:	<DD>An especially vocal lover.</DD>
Can Contain:	<A>, <B>, <BLOCKQUOTE>, , <CITE>, <CODE>, <DFN>, <DIR>, <DL>, <EM>, <FORM>, <I>, <IMG >, <KBD>, <MENU>, <OL>, <P>, <PRE>, <SAMP>, <STRIKE>, <STRONG>, <TT>,<U>, <UL>, <VAR>
Can Be Contained By:	<DL>

Other Lists

Not all the lists you'll want to include in your Web documents will take the form of dictionary entries and definitions. You may want to include a list of steps in a procedure, or a roster of people in an organization. You might also want to publish a list of the contents of a disk directory, or a price list. The tags in this section may come in handy for you.

Remember, you already learned about the unordered list (<UL>) tag in Chapter 10. It's similar to the <MENU> tag described in this section—try both (and view the results on various Web browsers) to see which better serves your needs.

Ordered Lists

Lots of good Web publications offer documentation for software and hardware products, and that means many Web publications have lists of procedural steps. How do Web publishers code ordered lists? With the <OL> tag, as in the following example:

```
<OL>
<LI>Open the drain valve.
<LI>Allow all the coolant to drain.
<LI>Loosen the fill cap slightly.
<LI>Allow pressure to fall.
</OL>
```

Figure 12.4 shows how a Web browser interprets this code.

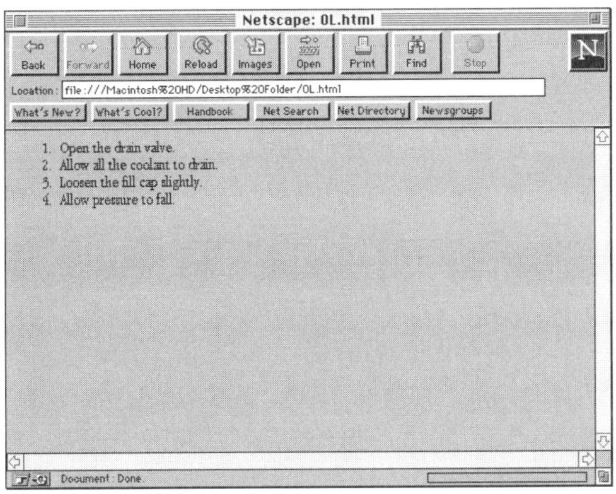

Figure 12.4 Ordered list

OL

Purpose: To identify an ordered list, in which the browser numbers list items sequentially.

Usage: <OL>. . .<OL>

Example: <OL><LI>Loosen wing nut. <LI>Clip red wire. </OL>

Can Contain: < LI>

Can Be Contained By: <BLOCKQUOTE>, <BODY>, <DD>, <FORM>, <LI>

Hot Tip: The COMPACT attribute reduces the space occupied by an ordered list.

Unordered Lists

Not happy with the way <UL> formats your data? Try the <DIR> or <MENU> tags. Some browsers try to arrange text tagged with <DIR> in columns, if space allows, with the first list item in the first column, the second item in the second column, and so on, wrapping around to a new row when space is exhausted.

Other browsers, including Netscape Navigator, treat <DIR> tags just like <UL> tags. <MENU> tags yield results very similar to <UL> tags, too. In Netscape Navigator, in fact, the two tags are treated the same.

Here's an example of <DIR> tags in action:

```
<DIR>
<LI>Apples
<LI>Bananas
<LI>Oranges
<LI>Kiwi
<LI>Mangoes
<LI>Strawberries
</DIR>
```

This code, interpreted by a Web browser, appears in Figure 12.5.

DIR

Purpose:	To identify a series of short lines of text (20 characters or fewer).
Usage:	<DIR>. . .</DIR>
Example:	<DIR> <LI>Hamburger: $0.89 <LI>Fries: $0.65 </DIR>
Can Contain:	<LI>
Can Be Contained By:	<BLOCKQUOTE>, <BODY>, <DD>, <FORM>, <LI>
Don't Forget:	If there's room, Web browsers will display items in a <DIR> list in columns across the screen. The first item in the list will appear in the first column, the second item in the second column, and so on, until the browser runs out of screen real estate and must start a second row.
Hot Tip:	To reduce the space occupied by a <DIR> list, use the COMPACT attribute (written <DIR COMPACT>. . .</DIR>).

If <DIR> tags don't do what you want, try <MENU> tags. Here's the same list formatted with <MENU> tags:

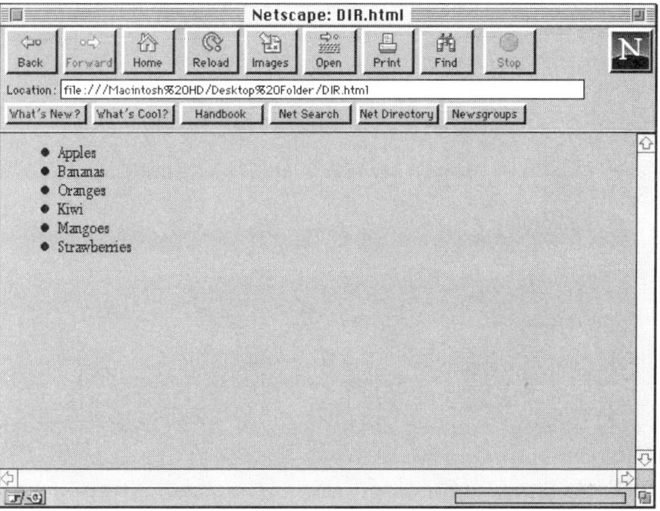

Figure 12.5 Unordered list (<DIR>) displayed by Netscape

```
<MENU>
<LI>Apples
<LI>Bananas
<LI>Oranges
<LI>Kiwi
<LI>Mangoes
<LI>Strawberries
</MENU>
```

This code, interpreted by a Web browser, appears in Figure 12.6. Note that in this browser, Netscape Navigator, <MENU> and <DIR> appear the same way. Other browsers try to display the list more compactly than a <UL> list.

If you'd like to specify how the bullet appears, try using the HTML 3.0 TYPE attribute (for example, <UL TYPE=square>). With HTML 3.0-compliant browsers, this produces a square bullet. You can also choose *disc* or *circle*.

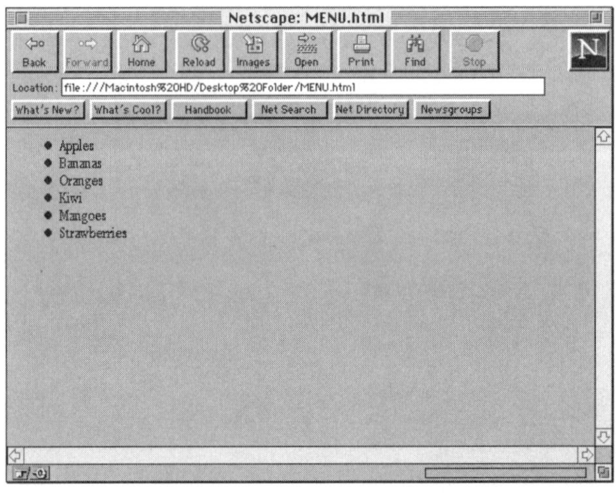

Figure 12.6 Menu list

MENU

Purpose: To define a list of short text items.

Usage: <MENU>. . .</MENU>

Example: <MENU> <LI> Music URLs <LI> Dance URLs </MENU>

Can Contain: <LI>

Can Be Contained By: <BLOCKQUOTE>, <BODY>, <DD>, <FORM>, <LI>

Don't Forget: <MENU> acts very much like <UL COMPACT>. Try both list syntaxes on your data to see which makes it look better in various browsers.

Hot Tip: Unless it helps you understand the logical function of a passage of text in a document, use less obscure tags, such as <UL>, for formatting lists.

Preformatted Text

Usually, surrounding excerpted text with <BLOCKQUOTE> tags solves the problem of formatting it as something taken from another work. Sometimes, however, the formatting of excerpted text is just as important as the words. In these cases—poetry, computer source code, and computer output, for example—use one of the preformatted text tags. You already learned about the <CODE> tag—used to identify computer source code—in Chapter 10.

If you want to encode text in which the placement of line breaks and spaces is important, and you don't want to insert a million <BR> tags or risk trusting the placement of those characters to Web browsers, use the <PRE> tag. Browsers usually render text surrounded by <PRE> tags in a monospace font, such as Courier, and they respect line breaks created with the Return key—there's no need for the <BR> tag within <PRE>-tagged text. Here's an example:

```
<P>Here's some text that the browser will format
in whatever way it wishes. Note that this line
wraps much further along than the lines below.
That's because I inserted line breaks—with the
Return key, not the BR tag—in the lines below.</P>

<PRE>Scientist fears worst;
predicts sky will fall soon

By George Arbogust
Baltimore Sun Staff Writer

According to University of Virginia
physicist Davis Bonner, Chicken
Little was right.
The world-renowned atmospheric dynamics
expert announced today that because of
a rare climatological phenomenon called
the "Spiral of Death," the altitude of
the uppermost reaches of the atmosphere
is decreasing. </PRE>
```

Figure 12.7 shows how a Web browser interprets this code.

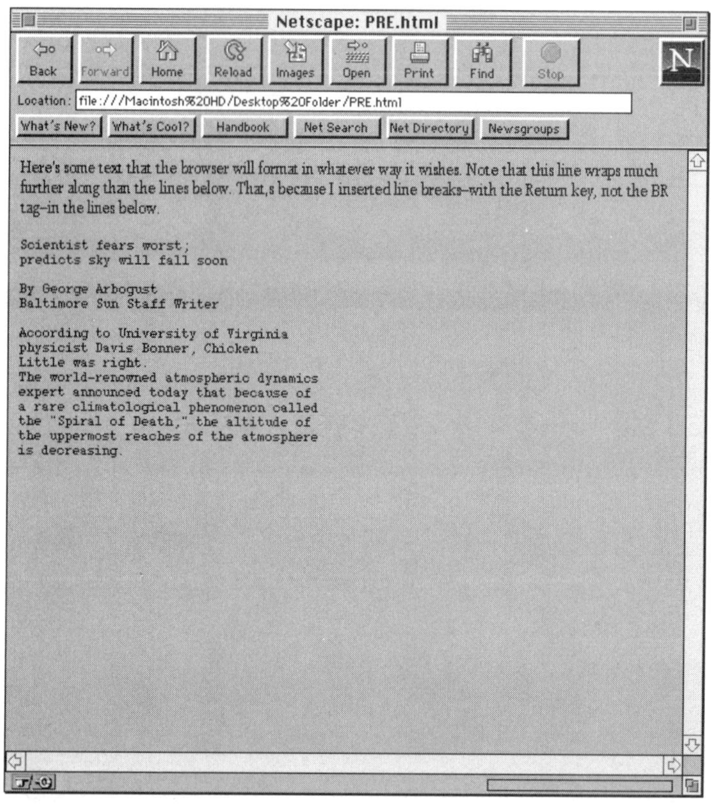

Figure 12.7 Preformatted text

PRE

Purpose: To preserve the line breaks and spaces in an excerpted passage of text.

Usage: <PRE>. . .</PRE>

Example: <PRE>By Jeffrey M. Leeds
Staff Reporter of the Los Angeles Times</PRE>

Can Contain: <A>, <B>, <CITE>, <CODE>, <DFN>, <EM>, <I>, <KBD>, <SAMP>, <STRIKE>, <STRONG>, <TT>, <U>, <VAR>

Can Be Contained By: <BLOCKQUOTE>, <BODY>, <DD>, <FORM>, <LI>

Don't Forget: Text formatted with the <PRE> tag usually appears in a monospace font like Courier. Also, <PRE> doesn't preserve spacing at the beginning of lines—to do that, consider using the little-supported <LIT> tag.

Hot Tip: <PRE> has an attribute—WIDTH, used <PRE WIDTH=X>. . .</PRE>—that lets you specify how many characters the Web browser should allow in each line (X, in the example above, represents the number of characters). Most browsers ignore this attribute, as it defeats the purpose of the <PRE> tag.

More Text-Formatting Tags

By now, you're familiar with several absolute text-formatting commands, including the <B> tag for boldface text and the <I> tag for italic text. Here are a few more absolute and logical formatting tags.

Representing Keyboard Input

Before long, you'll probably want to tell the reader of your Web publication to type something on a keyboard. How, in an HTML document, should you tag the text the reader is supposed to type? With the <KBD> tag, naturally. Here's how you use it.

```
<P>When you reach the BLORP! prompt, type:
<KBD>Self-destruct sequence one, one-a.</KBD> and
take off for the door.</P>
```

Figure 12.8 shows this code interpreted by a Web browser.

KBD

Purpose: To identify text as, in an example, text that would be entered into a computer via the keyboard.

Usage: <KBD>. . .</KBD>

Example: <P>Type <KBD>rlogin foo.foo.com</KBD> at the UNIX prompt.</P>

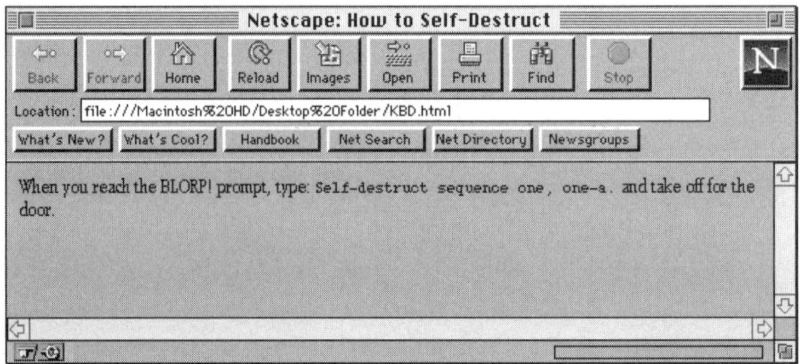

Figure 12.8 Keyboard input

Can Contain: <A>, <B>, <BR>, <CITE>, <CODE>, <DFN>, <EM>, <I>, <IMG>, <SAMP>, <STRIKE>, <STRONG>, <TT>, <U>, <VAR>

Can Be Contained By: <A>, <ADDRESS>, <B>, <CITE>, <CODE>, <DD>, <DT>, <DFN>, <EM>, <H1>, <H2>, <H3>, <H4>, <H5>, <H6>, <I>, <LI>, <P>, <PRE>, <SAMP>, <STRIKE>, <STRONG>, <TT>, <U>, <VAR>

Don't Forget: Web browsers usually render <KBD>-tagged text in monospace fonts, typically Courier.

Hot Tip: Try putting <KBD>-tagged text on its own line to further distinguish it from other text in your document.

Typing Variables

Reflecting HTML's origins in a scientific community, the <VAR> tag enables Web authors to represent math variables (generally, in italics).

VAR

Purpose: To indicate a variable.

Usage: <VAR>. . .</VAR>

Example: <VAR>x<\VAR>

Can Contain: <A>, <B>, <BR>, <CITE>, <CODE>, <EM>, <KBD>, <I>, <IMG>, <STRONG>, <SAMP>, <TT>, <VAR>

Can Be Contained By: <A>, <ADDRESS>, <B>, <CITE>, <CODE>, <DD>, <DT>, <EM>, <H1>, <H2>, <H3>, <H4>, <H5>, <H6>, <I>, <KBD>, <LI>, <P>, <PRE>, <SAMP>, <STRONG>, <TT>, <VAR>

Hot Tip: You can achieve the same results by using the <I> tag—and you'll know for sure that all browsers will display the variable in italics.

Representing Editorial Strikeouts

Sometimes, just deleting text isn't enough. When collaborating on a writing project or editing legal material, you'll want to cross words out, but keep them legible until all parties involved in the project can agree on what should be deleted permanently and what should not. In HTML, use the <STRIKE> tag to format text as stricken (usually with a horizontal line running through the center of the characters). Here's an example:

```
<P>It was a dark and stormy night. Suddenly, a
<STRIKE>bone-jarring series of revolver
shots</STRIKE>kiss rang out.</P>
<P>
<P>Author: I think the market's ready for a mushy
book. I altered your opening sentence accord-
ingly. THE EDITOR.(Apologies to Charles
Schulz.)</P>
```

Figure 12.9 shows this code rendered by a Web browser.

STRIKE

Purpose: To show characters as stricken, that is, deleted from a document but still visible for reference purposes.

Usage: <STRIKE>. . .</STRIKE>

Example: <P><STRIKE>We the men and women</STRIKE> We the People</P>

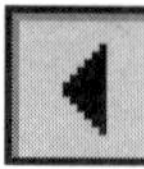

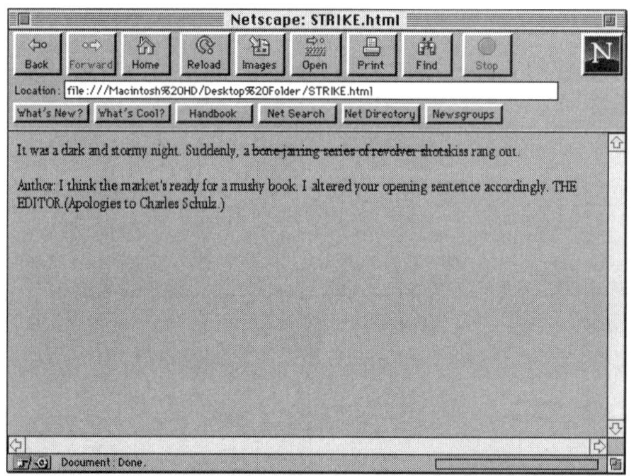

Figure 12.9 Editorial strikeout

Can Contain: <A>, <B>, <BR>, <CITE>, <CODE>, <DFN>, <EM>, <I>, <IMG>, <KBD>, <SAMP>, <STRONG>, <TT>, <U>, <VAR>

Can Be Contained By: <A>, <ADDRESS>, <B>, <CITE>, <CODE>, <DD>, <DT>, <DFN>, <EM>, <H1>, <H2>, <H3>, <H4>, <H5>, <H6>, <I>, <KBD>, <LI>, <P>, <PRE>, <SAMP>, <STRONG>, <TT>, <U>, <VAR>

Don't Forget: Don't use <STRIKE> unless someone else needs to approve deletions you've made. <STRIKE> tends to make your document look cluttered and muddy.

Hot Tip: Don't embed hyperlinks in <STRIKE>-tagged text. With the strikethrough line and the underscore most Web browsers attach to hyperlinks, the combination looks terrible and is logically confusing—does the link work, or not?

Identifying a Paper's Abstract

With its strong ties to academia, HTML has tags for identifying the parts of an academic paper. One of the tags that's useful in both academic and non-academic publishing is the <ABSTRACT> tag, which formats a summary of a document's contents differently from the body text itself, or at least separates the two. You can use the <ABSTRACT> tag to create an "executive summary" in nonacademic papers. Here's an example:

```
<ABSTRACT>In this paper, the author examines the
implications of multitasking operating systems on
the perceived stress levels of their users. Anec-
dotal evidence is presented that supports the
idea that human beings are capable of doing only
so much work each day, and that advances in tech-
nology can only boost that workload a little bit.
The author argues that further advances in com-
puting technology will only serve to annoy human
users and make them feel inadequate.</ABSTRACT>

<P>It's a well-known fact that the advent of per-
sonal computers hasn't brought the productivity
increases their marketers promised. Why is this?
The solution to the productivity enigma may lie
in the nature of human beings' relationship to
work, and about how much work is enough for one
workday.</P>
```

Figure 12.10 shows how a browser interprets this code.

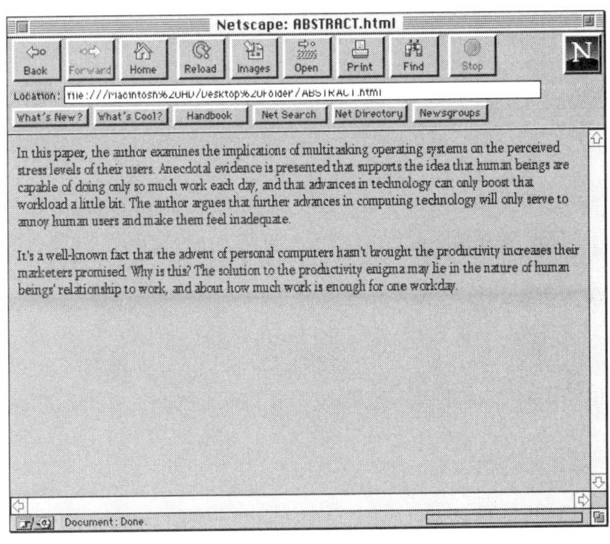

Figure 12.10 Abstract

Blinking Text!

Yes, you can make text in your documents flash on and off, too, thanks to one of the least-appreciated Netscape extensions. Some Web users find this effect pretty nifty, many others find it seriously annoying and consider it show-off-ish. Sometimes flashing text is nice for highlighting a link to something new or the most important aspect of your site. Evaluate the pros and cons on your own, and make your own decision. <BLINK> code looks like this:

```
<P>Check out the new <BLINK><A HREF="http://
foo.foo.com/~bill/html/gerbil.html>Gerbil
Page!</A></BLINK>
```

BLINK

Purpose:	To make text flash on and off.
Usage:	<BLINK>. . .</BLINK>
Example:	<P><BLINK>Today Only!</BLINK></P>
Can Contain:	<A>, <B>, , <CITE>, <CODE>, <DFN>, <EM>, <I>, <IMG>, <KBD>, <SAMP>, <STRONG>, <TT>, <U>, <VAR>
Can Be Contained By:	<A>, <ADDRESS>, <B>, <CITE>, <CODE>, <DD>, <DT>, <DFN>, <EM>, <I>, <H1>, <H2>, <H3>, <H4>, <H5>, <H6>, <KBD>, <LI>, <P>, <PRE>, <SAMP>, <STRONG>, <TT>, <U>, <VAR>
Don't Forget:	Lots of browsers—including nearly all text-only browsers—don't support the <BLINK> tag.
Hot Tip:	Use the <BLINK> tag sparingly. It's annoying after the initial "oh, cool!" effect wears off (about four seconds, on average) and HTML provides better ways of highlighting information.

Choosing Font Sizes

HTML is supposed to be a markup language—you identify the parts of the document, but the formatting choices are left up to the browser. As more people create Web pages for marketing and business purposes, however, there's been a push to increase Web authors' control over the document's appearance—and Netscape has been willing to oblige (all too willing, some say). Among the more controversial of the Netscape extensions is the <FONT> tag, which enables you to specify font size.

The <FONT> tag doesn't let you specify font sizes in points; instead, it uses SIZE attribute values ranging from 1 (the smallest) to 7 (the largest). Size 3 is the default font size for a document (if a document doesn't use a <FONT> tag, that's the size that Netscape uses to display the body text).

You can use the <FONT> tag in two ways:

- **By specifying the font size in absolute terms** (<FONT SIZE=5>. . . </FONT>). All the text within the tags is displayed in the size you've chosen.
- **By specifying the font size in relative terms** (<FONT SIZE=+2>. . . </FONT>. Within the tags, the font size is increased by two font sizes. To increase the font size, type a number from 1 to 7 with a plus sign; use a minus sign to decrease the font size.

I used the <FONT> tag to create headings, but they show up as ordinary text in Mosaic!
That's right. Not all broswers support the <FONT> tag. To create headings, use the headings tags (<H1>, <H2>, <H3>, etc.).

FONT

Purpose:	Specify the font size.
Usage:	<FONT>. . .</FONT>
Example:	<FONT SIZE=5>This will be shown in Font Size 5</FONT>
Can Contain:	<B>, <CODE>, <EM>, <I>, <STRONG>, <TT>
Can Be Contained By:	Most BODY tags.
Don't Forget:	You can specify the size in absolute terms (<FONT SIZE=3>) or in relative terms, increasing or decreasing the size from the base font size (default = 3): <FONT SIZE=+2>.
Hot Tip:	To change the base font setting from the default size 3, begin your document's body with the <BASEFONT> tag (for example, <BASEFONT SIZE=4>).

FROM HERE

- Between what you learned from this chapter and what you learned in Chapter 10, you know much more HTML than the average Web publisher. You can make cool-looking pages with graphics, fairly fancy formatting, and hyperlinks. But what if you want forms, or clickable image maps, or tables, or embedded multimedia? Read on.

Chapter 13

Adding Hyperlinks

The truly revolutionary capability of the Web is the ability to handle hyperlinks and thereby support the creation of hypertext documents. Hyperlinks give power back to the reader of a document, 600 years after it was taken away by the static printed word, and give them the ability to view the contents of one or several documents in whatever sequence they wish.

How can you incorporate hyperlinks in your document? It's really not hard: there's just one tag involved (you already learned a little about the <A> tag in Chapter 10) and a couple of important attributes. Before long, your Web publications will feature links within themselves and to other documents, both in your directory and elsewhere on the Web. You'll have links attached to in-line graphics, including small ones that look like icons, so you'll be able to simulate the appearance of a graphical user interface if you want.

For the Time-Challenged

- With the <A NAME="*keyword*"> . . . </A> tag and attribute combination, you can define a place in your document to which others can link instead of having to link to the top of your document.
- With the <A HREF="#*keyword*"> . . . </A> tag and attribute combination, you can jump to a defined location in the same document.
- You can follow the HREF attribute with the filename of the target document (if the target document is in the same directory as the document in which the hyperlink is embedded), a directory and filename of the target document (if the target document is on the same machine but in a different directory), or a complete URL.
- With the <A HREF="*URL#keyword*"> . . . </A> tag and attribute combination, you can establish a hyperlink to a location defined with the NAME attribute in another document.
- You can embed an <IMG> tag in an <A>. . .</A> tag to hyperlink an in-line image to another document.
- Be sure to describe, in text, what will happen if a user clicks a hyperlinked graphic. This is especially important for site viewers with character-based browsers, but it helps those with graphical browsers too.

Internal Hyperlinks

If you have a long Web document (one that takes up more than three screens when viewed on a Web browser), you'll want to use internal hyperlinks in it to help readers navigate. Often, section headings are copied to the top of a document, where they're hyperlinked to the start of the sections they describe. In this way, the copied, hyperlinked headings serve as a sort of table of contents. Often, when documents that were written for plain paper printing are converted to HTML, the person doing the conversion will insert some kind of internal navigation scheme to aid the reader and conceal the fact that the document was written before the author was Web-aware.

Internal hyperlinks also are useful for reference information. If the readers of your document will have to refer to an item of information, such as a mathematical equation or a passage of text, as they read a document, be sure to use internal hyperlinks to prevent the need for scrolling. Every paragraph or so, have a link that leads to the reference information, then have links near the reference passage that lead back to the various links in the text.

This section explains the technicalities of internal hyperlinks. Don't forget, you can combine the information here with the information in the section entitled "Attaching Graphics to Hyperlinks" if you want to create an icon-based internal navigation scheme.

Defining Targets to Which Hyperlinks Lead

In order to use internal hyperlinks, you must define the points (called *targets*) to which links will lead. You do this with the <A> tag—the same tag used to create a hyperlink—but with a special attribute, the "NAME" attribute. The NAME attribute allows you to assign a plain English (or French, or German) name, such as "Procedure" or "Conclusion" or "Shakespeare_Allusions," to a point in a document and make links lead to that particular point. If you want to name a point in a document, follow this example:

```
<A NAME="keyword">. . .</A>
```

"*Keyword*" is the word you want to use to represent that point in the document. Your keyword should be descriptive, since a word like "Third_Point" doesn't describe the function of the material around the named point very well. Something like "Reduced_Taxes" or "Health" is better.

The closing </A> tag isn't as important in this case as it is when you're defining a hyperlink with the HREF attribute. You should put the </A> tag immediately after the > character in the opening tag so you know precisely where the internal links will lead and you don't have bits of HTML code scattered around your document, making it hard to study and modify.

Linking to Other Points in the Same Document

Now that you've established targets to which hyperlinks can lead, you'll want to build hyperlinks that lead to them. Creating internal hyperlinks is just like building external ones, without the complete URL. You include only the # character and the keyword (which you learned how to define in the previous section) in an internal hyperlink. Internal hyperlinks should look like this:

```
<A HREF="#keyword">. . .</A>
```

When making a hyperlink to a point in the same document, as with all other hyperlinks, you need to be careful of where you place the </A> closing tag. Make sure you place the <A> tag before the text you want to link, and the </A> tag after it. Carefully placing your tags ensures that only words that accurately describe the linked material are treated as links.

The use of # and the keyword isn't limited to internal hyperlinks. If you want (and if your document is long enough to merit use of the NAME attribute, you probably should) you can include #*keyword* at the end of a complete URL. The next section discusses linking among different documents.

External Hyperlinks

One of the real beauties of the Web is the ability to link documents on widely separated servers. This section teaches you how to enable the people who visit your site to jump from one of your documents to another, or from one of your documents to a document maintained by someone else, who may be physically far away from you. This section also incorporates some of the lessons of the previous section, in that this section teaches you to link to points in a target document defined with the <A NAME="*keyword*">. . .</A> tag.

Linking to Documents on Another Server

You already learned how to do this in Chapter 10. To link a word or series of words to a document (usually, but not necessarily, on another server), use the following form:

```
<A HREF="http://www.donut.com/jones/
glazed.html">This text is linked to Marvin Jones'
Glazed Donut Page.</A>
```

That code will create a link in your document that leads to the URL http://www.donut.com/jones/glazed.html, the fictitious Glazed Donut Page, maintained by Marvin Jones. Since you already read about creating hyperlinks in Chapter 10, there's no need to elaborate on the basic concept here. You can learn about special applications of interdocument hyperlinks in the following sections.

Link to a Specific Point in Another Document

It won't do you much good to establish a hyperlink to a giant document if the information you want is buried deep in the document's text. For this reason, you can establish a link to a point established with the NAME attribute of the <A> tag in the other document.

The problem is, you can't insert named points in someone else's document. You have to count on them to organize their documents well by inserting named points to which you can link. If they didn't include such points when they created their document, you can ask them to insert the needed tags, but you can't do it for them (unless you can get permission to copy the document and reformat it properly as part of your site). If they don't put the tags in, all you can do is link to the top of their document and tell the reader of your document where he or she should look in the linked document for the needed information.

The HTML code for linking to a specific point in another document looks like this:

```
<A HREF="URL#keyword">. . .</A>
```

In the above example, "*URL*" is the URL of the document to which you're establishing a hyperlink, and "*keyword*" is the keyword established by a NAME attribute in an <A> tag in the target document.

If you need to do so, you can combine the NAME attribute with the HREF attribute to simultaneously establish a hyperlink and designate a point to which other hyperlinks can lead. A combination of the HREF attribute and the NAME attribute would look like this:

```
<A NAME="Kangaroo" HREF="http://www.koala.org/
documents/html/eucalyptus.html"> This point in
the document is both a point to which other
hypertext links can lead, and a hyperlink to a
document at koala.org.</A>
```

With the above code in your document, others would be able to refer to the #Kangaroo location in your document, and your site visitors could click the words "This point. . ." to jump to the document eucalyptus.html at koala.org.

Linking to Documents in the Same Directory (Relative URLs)

If you have a series of HTML documents in a single directory and you need to have many hyperlinks among them, it's cumbersome to type the complete

URL (machine name, domain name, directory, and filename) every time you want to make a hyperlink. Fortunately, you don't have to do that. HTML provides for *relative URLs*, which enable you to specify just part of the URL in order to save coding time. Relative URLs usually refer to documents in the same directory as the document in which the relative URL is embedded, as in the following example:

```
<A HREF="sting.html">This is a relative link to
sting.html.</A>
```

This relative URL would tell the browser to look in the current directory for a file called sting.html. There was no need to type the machine name, domain name, or directory path—they're all understood to be the same as the current document unless otherwise specified.

What if the document you want to link to is on the same machine, but in a different directory? No problem. To have the browser look in the directory www/music/spanish_language for sting.html, you'd use the following code:

```
<A HREF="/www/music/spanish_language/sting.html">
This is a relative link to sting.html, which is
in a different directory.</A>
```

Note that the forward slashes are UNIX symbols. That's what you use, even if you're going to put the document on a PC or Macintosh server. Remember that these lines "speak" to the browser, not directly to the operating system.

This relative link doesn't work!
Not surprising—they *are* pesky critters. Bear in mind that the frame of reference for writing relative URLs is the directory or folder in which the current document is stored. Suppose the current document is stored in

/htdocs/manual/chapters

A link to another document in the same directory need only include the filename:

"chapter1.html"

Suppose, though, that the /chapters folder contains the following folders: part1, part2, and part3. To link to a chapter in the part2 folder, you must include the folder name:

"part1/chapter2.html"

What if you want to link to a document that's *above* the current folder? You must use the UNIX parent directory symbol—two dots (..). To link to a document in the /htdocs/manual directory, which is one level up, you use this URL:

"../contents.html"

To link to a document *two* levels up, you use two parent directory symbols:

"../../intro.html"

To link to a document that's in an adjacent directory tree, you must use the parent directory symbols to go up—and then you can go over:

"../../moredocs/newstuff/hot.html"

Fun, huh? It's much easier to link to documents *below* the current document, but sometimes this isn't possible.

ATTACHING HYPERLINKS TO GRAPHICS

You can combine two of the Web's coolest features by nesting an in-line graphic in a hyperlink tag. By doing this, you can create a graphical user interface that approximates that of the Macintosh or Microsoft Windows 95. You can also, if your site is some kind of image archive, provide a small rendition of each image in your collection to help people decide if they want to commit to downloading the large version or not.

Coding Hyperlinked Graphics

To treat an image as a hyperlink to another document, put an <IMG> tag inside an <A> tag with an HREF attribute. In the following example, the picture called sting.jpg is linked (via a relative URL—see the previous section) to a document called sting.html:

```
<A HREF="/www/music/spanish_language/sting.html">
<IMG SRC="sting.jpg"></A>
```

When a browser interprets this code, the browser will display sting.jpg (usually surrounded by a colored border) and will retrieve sting.html when the viewer of your document clicks the image. Don't assume that images are

self-explanatory, though—include some text to explain where the graphics' links lead.

You'll learn about creating image maps—fancy graphics that have different hyperlinks in different portions of themselves—in Chapter 16.

Being Considerate of Those with Text-Only Browsers

Though their ranks are thinning, there is still a significant number of Web surfers whose browsers can't display graphics. Graphical browsers require computers of significant power—computers that are beyond the means of lots of people. Browsers like Lynx show a characters-only rendition of Web pages, which is fine, except when a graphic represents a hyperlink. Then, character-based browsers display "[image]" or something equally cryptic, and users are left to guess what happens if they follow hyperlinks attached to in-line graphics.

HTML, fortunately, offers a solution to this problem: the ALT attribute. Use the ALT attribute inside the <IMG> tag to explain what a graphic depicts. In the following example, the ALT tag is used to explain sting.jpg:

```
<A HREF="/www/music/spanish_language/sting.html">
<IMG SRC="sting.jpg" ALT="A picture of Sting per-
forming at a concert."></A>
```

The ALT attribute, as used above, explains what the picture shows—but doesn't say what the hyperlink does. Users of both graphical and text-based browsers will need explanatory text before they can decide whether to follow a link.

From Here

- Hyperlinks are probably the biggest single appeal of publishing on the Web, but the ability to include multimedia in presentations is a big draw, too. In the next chapter, you'll learn how to incorporate still graphics, sounds, and video into your Web publication.

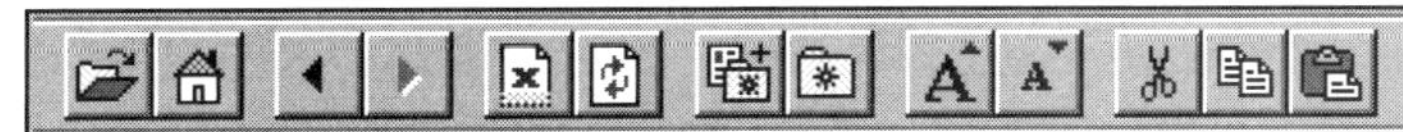

Chapter 14

Adding Multimedia

Like the days of black-and-white television, the era of text-only Web pages is past. Though a small minority of people still browse the Web with character-based browsers such as Lynx (just as some people still watch black-and-white television), most of your audience will have a multimedia-capable browser. To keep the attention of your audience, you'll have to take advantage of multimedia and engage as many of your viewers' senses as possible.

It may be true that the only reason text predominates on the Web is its past dominance of communication. People have been communicating at a distance with written words for thousands of years; long-distance audio and video communications are a phenomenon unique to this century. Lots of tools exist for writing text, while relatively few exist that a lay person can use to generate sound and video communications. Perhaps someday audio or video will rule the Web, and text will be an anomaly.

This chapter doesn't address producing multimedia files—that's dealt with in Chapters 21 through 25. This chapter discusses the advisability of including multimedia features in your Web site, and explains the HTML required to embed multimedia in your documents. This chapter shows how you can use small in-line graphics as icons to keep links to your multimedia files visible, yet unobtrusive. Consider using some of the icons on the CD-ROM included with this book.

Though most browsers have built-in support for GIF and JPEG still graphics, few browsers have native sound and video support. Helper applications are needed in order for these programs to run. Do your site's visitors a favor and provide the viewers needed to take full advantage of the multimedia at your site. This reduces the risk of viewers taking off to find helper applications, then getting sidetracked and never returning to your publication.

For the Time-Challenged

- Embedded multimedia, when used correctly, can communicate your message faster than text. Though it's kind of special now, sound, video, and graphics may comprise the bulk of the information on the Web someday.
- Embed still graphics with HTML code such as the following: <IMG SRC="smiley.gif" ALIGN=middle ALT="Smiley face">.
- Embedding sound, video, and animation files is just like creating hyperlinks to other HTML documents.
- The HTML code for embedding a sound looks like this: <A HREF="toodle.wav"> <IMG SRC="wavicon.gif" ALIGN=middle ALT=".wav sound file"></A>Click here to hear my kazoo skills (a 150K .wav file).
- The HTML code for embedding a video or animation clip looks like this: <A HREF="Patti_on_bike.mpg"> <IMG SRC= "mpegicon.gif" ALIGN=middle ALT=".mpeg video file"></A>Click here to see my kid ride her bike (a 500K .mpeg file).
- You should always attach an icon to linked multimedia files and indicate how large a file is before your reader commits to downloading it.

Adding Still Graphics

Still graphics, large and small, are everywhere on the Web. This section explains how to embed still graphics (as opposed to moving graphics, which are covered in the "Adding Video and Animation" section) in your Web page.

Generally, when planning which graphics to include, think small. Smaller is better, since viewers don't have to wait a long time for small, icon-sized graphics to download but still benefit from the visual cues they provide. Also, try to repeat small graphics, since that way Web browsers need only download a graphics file once, then pull it out of their cache for subsequent uses.

If you're interested in producing graphics to include in your Web site, take a look at Chapter 22.

Why Add Still Graphics?

It's a cliché, but it's generally true: A picture is worth a thousand words. On the Web, where communicating your message to a site visitor before he or she clicks away is key, graphics can send a signal that either satiates your visitors' needs right away or invites them to hang around. Graphics can also enhance the appeal of the other media on your pages. A good icon can induce visitors to play a sound or video file they otherwise might not play, or add a dimension of interpretation that text alone could not provide.

Also, graphics appeal to the members of an increasingly nonverbal society. Not only is a large portion of the population of Web users young, and therefore used to absorbing visual information from television and heavily illustrated magazines, but also many Web users don't speak the same language you speak. Simple icons that illustrate what a link does help those non-English speakers trying to navigate the Web. Additionally, a small but growing portion of the Web population is *very* young—children. If you have any interest in having early elementary-school-age children visit your site, make sure your graphics help compensate for their limited reading ability.

HTML for Still Graphics

Coding HTML to embed still graphics differs from coding to embed other kinds of graphics in that browsers display still graphics automatically (unless you tell them not to), while there's not yet a way to play sound or video files without special instructions from the Web browser's user. Embedded still

graphics have their own tag—the <IMG> tag—and don't rely on hyperlinks to files that must be clicked. If you want, however, you can treat JPEG or GIF files like sound and video files by having visitors access them by following a hyperlink. This technique works best for large images that site visitors most likely will want to download.

The <IMG> tag is open—there's no </IMG> tag—and can take up to three attributes. The attributes are:

SRC="..."	Defines the location of the graphic to be embedded in the document. A URL or a relative URL can replace the ellipsis.
ALT="..."	Provides the text that is displayed in place of the graphic if a browser displays text only or has its image-interpretation feature turned off.
ALIGN="..."	Defines the vertical position of the graphic relative to the line of text in which it appears. TOP, MIDDLE, or BOTTOM can replace the ellipsis. TOP aligns the uppermost portion of the graphic with the top of the characters in the line; MIDDLE aligns the center of the graphic with the center of the characters; and BOTTOM aligns the bottom of the graphic with the bottom of the characters in the line.

A typical use of the <IMG> tag follows.

```
<IMG SRC="smiley.gif" ALIGN=middle ALT="Smiley
face">
```

Another example of how you can use the <IMG> tag appears in Figure 14.1, with the results pictured in Figure 14.2.

Adding Sound

This section teaches how to attach sounds to your Web document. The process isn't complex—it's the same as establishing a hyperlink to another Web page—but when it's done correctly, sound adds a lot to a site's overall appeal. Don't forget to add icons to your links to embedded sounds, since

Figure 14.1 HTML code for an in-line graphic

icons will tip off visitors to your site about what's at the other end of a link. Several sound icons appear on the CD-ROM enclosed with this book.

If you're interested in producing sounds to include in your Web site, take a look at Chapter 23.

Why Add Sound?

Viewers' eyes get a workout when browsing the Web. Viewers read text, look at icons, and absorb large graphics. Video, however cool it is, still engages the viewer's vision. Adding sound files to your site engages another of your visitors' five senses, and thereby draws them further into the total multimedia experience your site represents. Current technology limits Web publishers to engaging two of the five senses (maybe later editions of this

Figure 14.2 The resulting in-line graphic viewed in Netscape Navigator

book will have sections on "Adding Smells," "Adding Tastes," and "Adding Tactile Feedback"), so it's critical that you pay attention to them both.

Certain kinds of information can only be communicated fully in sound format. Though you can display music graphically (through musical notation), reading music isn't the same as hearing it performed. A large portion of the Web population can't read music, so displaying music solely in written form cuts them out from experiencing it. You'll need to learn how to embed sound files in your pages if communicating naturally audible information is a goal of your site.

HTML for Sound

If you understand hyperlinks, you understand how to embed sounds in a document. As of this writing, there's no popular way to play a sound automatically when a Web browser loads a page, though Java and HotJava (discussed in Chapter 20) are promising. For now, you have to rely on your reader clicking a hyperlink connected to a sound file, which then downloads to his or her machine for handling by a helper application.

Construction of a hyperlink to a sound file mimics construction of a hyperlink to a video file or another HTML document. The code looks like this:

```
<A HREF="toodle.wav">Click here to hear my kazoo
skills.</A>
```

This code, when viewed in a browser, will yield the words "Click here to hear my kazoo skills." The words will be hyperlinked to the file "toodle.wav," which will download and be played by the application that the browser associates with the .WAV extension.

Good Web page design, however, dictates that you provide a visual clue as to what's at the other end of a link—an icon that shows that a link connects to a sound file. You should also give information about the size of the file, so viewers of your site can anticipate how long they will have to wait for the file to download. With RealAudio, a visitor to your site doesn't have to download the whole file before it starts to play, but it's still a good idea to say how big a file is. The following is a more proper way of embedding a sound file:

```
<A HREF="toodle.wav"> <IMG SRC= "wavicon.gif"
ALIGN=middle ALT=".wav sound file"></A>Click here
to hear my kazoo skills (a 150K .wav file).
```

This code yields an active icon—an icon you can click to follow a hyperlink—and a detailed explanation of the linked file and its size. There's no ambiguity about what the link does.

Another example of embedded sound code appears in Figure 14.3, with the results pictured in Figure 14.4.

Adding Video and Animation

Adding video and animation to your site adds a lot to its appeal, mainly since so few sites feature moving graphics. This section teaches how to embed video and animation files in your HTML documents—a process that's identical to embedding sounds. It's important with video, as with

Figure 14.3 HTML code for linking a sound file to an in-line graphic (an icon).

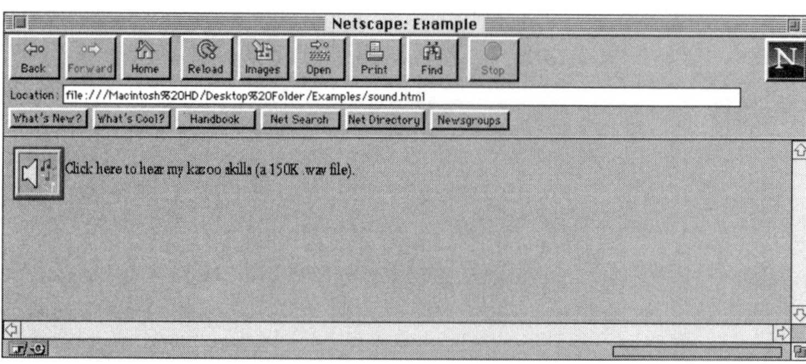

Figure 14.4 The resulting icon (linked to a sound file) in Netscape Navigator.

sounds, to label links with icons and to give some indication of how long a file will take to download.

If you're interested in producing videos and animations to include in your Web site, take a look at Chapter 24.

Why Add Video and Animation?

Video and animation are the fine wine grapes of Web publishing: they're rare, and when you can pull them off successfully, they're delicious. It's unusual to find video on the Web that simultaneously entertains, communicates a message, and doesn't clog communications channels. When a video or animation clip succeeds in all three criteria, it dramatically improves the quality of the site on which it appears.

Also, video and animation approximate television, a medium from which many Web users are used to absorbing information. For this reason, messages you communicate in the form of video files may be better absorbed. Visitors to your site may pay extra attention to video and animation clips, both because they're novelties and because the visitors had to wait a while for the clips to download and don't want their time investment to go to waste.

HTML for Video and Animation

The HTML for embedding video is identical to the process for embedding sound, which is to say it's just like building a hyperlink to another Web document. As with sound, there's no popular way to play a video automatically when a Web browser loads a page, though Java and HotJava (discussed in Chapter 20) are promising. For now, you have to rely on your reader clicking a hyperlink connected to a video or animation file, which then downloads to his or her machine for handling by a helper application.

The basic code for embedding a video clip looks like this:

```
<A HREF="Patti_on_bike.mpg">Click here to see my
kid ride her bicycle.</A>
```

This code, when viewed in a browser, will yield the words "Click here to see my kid ride her bicycle." The words will be hyperlinked to the file "Patti_on_bike.mpg," which will download and be played by the application the browser associates with the .WAV extension.

Good Web page design, however, dictates that you provide a visual clue as to what's at the other end of a link—an icon that shows that a link connects to a video file. You should also give information about the size of the

file, so viewers of your site can anticipate how long they will have to wait for the file to download. The following is a more proper way of embedding a sound file:

```
<A HREF="Patti_on_bike.mpg"> <IMG SRC="mpeg-
icon.gif" ALIGN=middle ALT=".mpeg video file">
</A>Click here to see my kid ride her bike (a 500K
.mpeg file).
```

This code yields an active icon—an icon you can click to follow a hyperlink—and a detailed explanation of the linked file and its size. There's no ambiguity about what the link does.

Another example of embedded video code appears in Figure 14.5, with the results pictured in Figure 14.6.

Figure 14.5 HTML code for linking a video file to an in-line graphic (an icon)

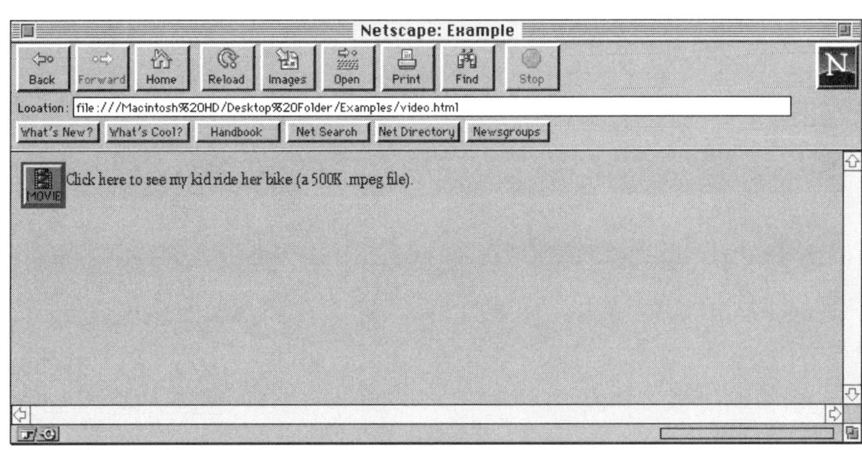

Figure 14.6 The resulting icon (linked to a video file) viewed in Netscape Navigator

From Here

- Multimedia gets raves, but it's the status quo on the Web. To make your site stand out, you need forms, image maps, and tables—HTML programming tricks discussed in the next three chapters.

Chapter 15

Enabling User Feedback

To create a top-flight Web site, you need to provide ways for your readers to interact with your site—and with you. In this chapter, you'll learn how to use HTML tags that enable user feedback. Although most of them require server-side scripts to process the data originated by users, you'll be happy to learn that one of them—the MAILTO URL—can be implemented without any scripts or programming.

Please bear in mind that not all browsers are capable of dealing with forms. However, most are—and the trend is in the direction of forms capabilities for all browsers. The other thing you'll need to consider is that the FORM tags discussed in this chapter can produce HTML documents with interactive features such as list boxes and radio buttons, but these features won't do anything unless there's a script to handle them. And with most servers, you'll be in for a bout of programming—or a

time-clocked session with a CGI programmer. If you're using MacHTTP or WebSTAR, you're in luck—you can take advantage of user-friendly utilities that enable you to process forms without doing any programming whatsoever.

This chapter fully introduces all the tags you'll need to understand in order to create an interactive Web document. You'll also find an introduction to the forms-processing utilities included with this book: NetForms and TR-WWW.

For the Time-Challenged

- You can use several HTML tags to create interactive elements in your Web presentations, but most of them won't do anything unless you can provide a server-side script.
- The exception to this rule is the MAILTO URL, which enables your readers to send you e-mail.
- Within the environment set up by a <FORM> tag, the user makes choices and enters text. When the user clicks the Submit button, the browser sends this information to a script in the form of name + value pairs. The script then decodes the incoming information and does something—at the minimum, writing the incoming information to a document and sending a confirmation. Some scripts do much fancier things, but they require equally fancy programming.
- Use the <INPUT> tag within the <FORM> container to create single-line text boxes, check boxes, radio buttons, and the Submit and Reset buttons.
- Use the <SELECT> and <OPTION> tags to create drop-down list boxes.
- Use the <TEXTAREA> tag to create a scrollable text box for lengthy user feedback.
- If you're using MacHTTP or WebSTAR, you can take advantage of several easy-to-use utilities that process forms without requiring any programming. These include NetForms and TR-WWW, both of which are included on this book's CD-ROM disc.

HTML Attributes and Tags for Enabling User Feedback

This chapter discusses the following HTML attributes and tags. Here's a quick overview:

- **The MAILTO URL** When used with the <A> tag, this attribute opens an e-mail dialog box enabling the user to send e-mail to you. The MAILTO URL does not require a script, but not all browsers are equipped to display an e-mail dialog box when this URL is clicked.
- **<ISINDEX>** The <ISINDEX> tag opens a simple text search box, which enables the user to type keywords for searches. This tag won't do anything unless there's a script to process the search box's output.
- **<FORM>** The FORM tag creates an environment within which you can use the <INPUT>, <SELECT>, and <TEXTAREA> tags to create user-friendly input fields.
- **<INPUT>** With its various attributes, the <INPUT> tag provides many of the tools you need to create highly interactive Web documents, replete with check boxes, radio buttons, fill-in text boxes, and more. Included are two essential buttons, Submit and Reset. Submit sends the filled-out form data to a script, while Reset clears all the user's choices.
- **<SELECT>** This tag enables you to create drop-down list boxes with as many predetermined options as you wish.
- **<TEXTAREA>** This tag creates a large, scrollable text box, within which your readers can wax prolific in providing feedback to you.

The following sections discuss these attributes and tags in more detail.

I created these tags, and the check boxes and stuff appear in my document, but they don't *do* anything!
That's right. The <FORM> tag creates an environment in which you can add interactive features to your documents. When you click the Submit button, the browser originates a message—but it must be pointed to a specific script, which in turn must be designed to handle the information it's getting. If there's no script, your form won't do anything.

Enabling User Feedback the Easy Way: Using the MAILTO URL

By far the easiest way to enable user feedback is to use the MAILTO URL, which looks like an ordinary hyperlink on-screen but performs a very different function. When you click a MAILTO URL, your browser opens an e-mail dialog box, which is (usually) preconfigured with the appropriate e-mail address. The user can then type a message and click the OK or Send buttons to send feedback.

Please note that not all browsers support the MAILTO URL. If somebody accessing your site is using a browser that doesn't support MAILTO, an error message will appear when the MAILTO URL is accessed. Happily, almost all of today's popular browsers (including Mosaic 2.0 and Netscape) support MAILTO. Still, it's considered good Web manners to include a note such as this one: "If your browser doesn't support e-mail, use your e-mail program to send a message to [your e-mail address]."

To create a MAILTO URL for the e-mail address "webmaster@homely_house.rivendell.edu," you type the following:

```
<A HREF="mailto: webmaster@homely_house.riven-
dell.edu"></A>
```

Any text enclosed within the beginning and closing <A> tags is rendered as a hyperlink.

How Forms and Scripts Work

Apart from the MAILTO URL, there's no convenient way to enable user feedback without employing scripts. A script is a brief program that provides a Web server with the ability to deal with user feedback.

In very general terms, here's how a script works:

1. **A Web user accesses a Web document that contains a <FORM> tag.** Within the <FORM> tag are one or more <INPUT> tags, which create input areas on the screen. Each of these input areas has a unique, identifying name.

Solutions

Signing Your Page

You can use the MAILTO URL with the <ADDRESS> tag to create a nice-looking signature to your Web pages. For a reply to "webmaster@homely_house.rivendell.com," you'd code the tag as follows:

```
<ADDRESS> Please send comments or suggestions to
<<A HREF="mailto: webmaster@homely_house.riven-
dell.edu"> webmaster@homely_house.rivendell.
edu </A> </ADDRESS>
```

Note that the e-mail address appears twice in the code; that's intentional. One of them is the MAILTO URL; the other appears as the text of the hyperlink, so that someone who prefers to use an e-mail program (rather than a browser's built-in e-mail capabilities) can do so by copying the e-mail address to the Clipboard and pasting it in the To: field of the e-mail program. On-screen, this code looks like this:

Please send comments or suggestions to webmaster@homely house.rivendell.edu

2. **The user fills out information on the screen and clicks the Submit button.** If a mistake is made, the user can correct the mistake before clicking Submit. To clear all the input, the user can click Reset.
3. **The browser originates a message and sends it to the server.** For each input field, the browser sends the name of the input field plus the value chosen by the user (such as the text that was entered in a text box).
4. **The server passes the message to the script.** The script is designed to *parse*, or make sense out of, the name + value pairs submitted by the browser.
5. **The script interprets the message and performs the requested action.** This may involve performing a search, recording the user's input, or generating a list. Lots of scripts don't do much

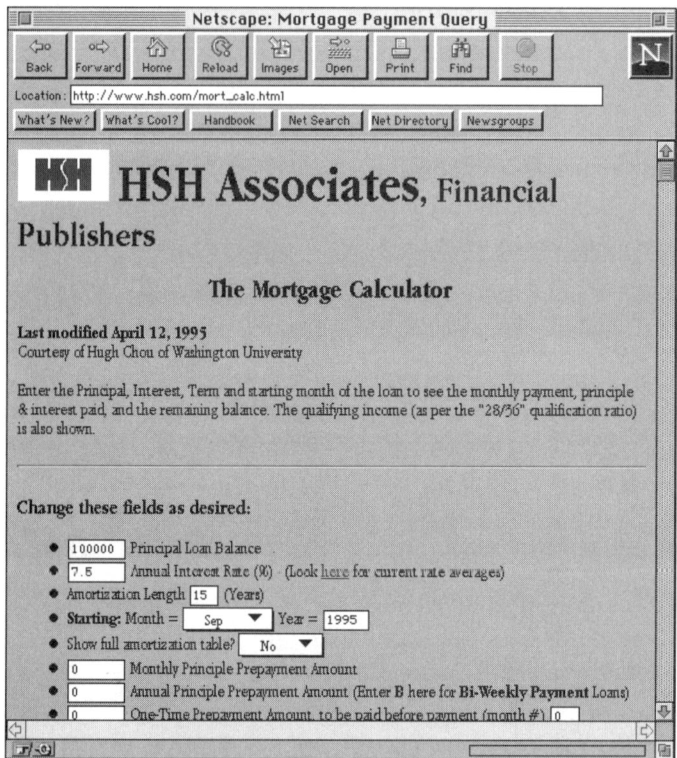

Figure 15.1 Mortgage interest calculator created with FORM tags

more than parse (decode) the incoming name + value pairs, write them to a file in a nice, bulleted list, and send the user a confirmation message stating that the data has been received. Some scripts do much fancier stuff.

6. **Optionally, the script prepares an HTML page reporting on the results of its action.** For example, the page may show the results of a search.

7. **The server sends the new page, or at least a confirmation message, to the browser.**

Here's an example of how FORM tags and scripts work in tandem. Figure 15.1 shows a very nice mortgage calculator, offered by HSH Associates

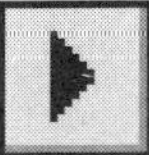

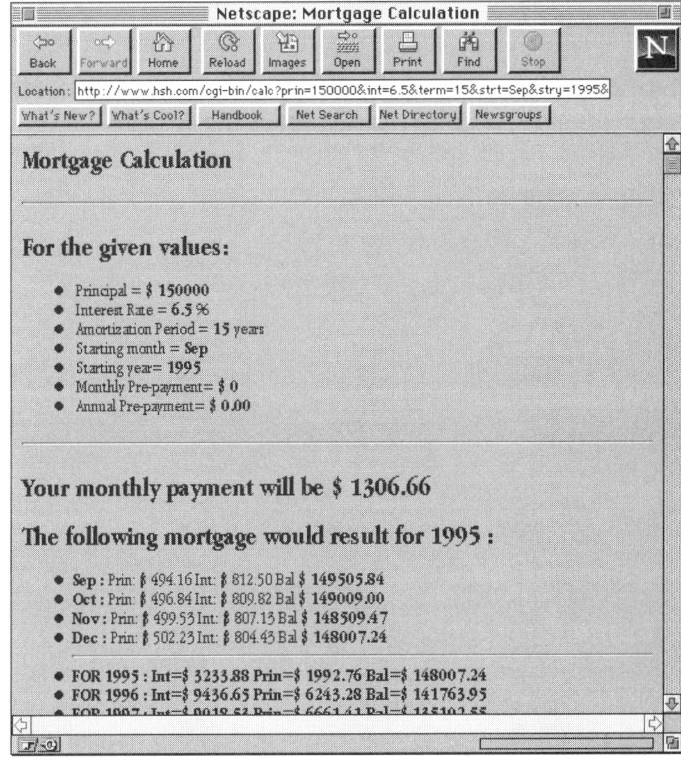

Figure 15.2 Page generated by script

(http://www.hsh.com/mort_calc.html). When you fill in the various boxes and options and click Calculate Mortgage, your browser sends a message to the script that's identified in the <FORM> tag (www.hsh.com/cgi-bin/calc). This script parses and processes the data, and generates a new HTML page (Figure 15.2) on the fly.

Enabling Searches with <ISINDEX>

The <ISINDEX> tag requires a server-side script, as do all the rest of the tags discussed in this chapter. Please note, though, that this tag is infre-

quently used these days, since it's much easier to create a useful search entry form with the <FORM> tag.

<ISINDEX> tells the browser to display a search text box such as the one shown in Figure 15.3. The user can then type in one or more search words and press Enter to initiate the search—but please remember, this tag doesn't do anything unless there's a script to field the output of this tag.

<ISINDEX> isn't very difficult to code; you just place the <ISINDEX> tag within the <HEAD> element, as follows:

```
<HEAD>
<TITLE>A Searchable Document</TITLE>
<ISINDEX>
<P>Please type your search terms.</P>
</HEAD>
```

After the user presses Enter, the browser creates a new URL, which it sends to the server for processing. For example, suppose the user types "California," "Chardonnay," and "Reviews" in the text box. The browser adds the following to the current document's URL:

```
California+Chardonnay+Review
```

When this URL is sent to the server, the server looks for the appropriate script, which must be prepared in advance and in anticipation of the types of searches users want to make. The server then prepares a list of items or documents that correspond to the search words, if any, and

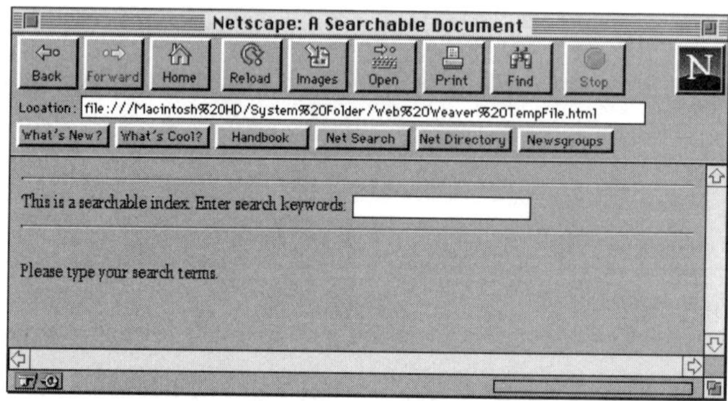

Figure 15.3 How Netscape displays the <ISINDEX> tag in a document

sends this list back to the browser in the form of a new HTML document.

Using the <FORM> Tag

To create a Web document with interactive capabilities, you begin by adding the <FORM> tag to your document. The beginning and end <FORM> tags (<FORM>. . .</FORM>) enclose all the HTML that displays elements such as radio buttons, check boxes, and text entry areas.

The <FORM> tag has two required attributes:

- **METHOD** This attribute has two possible settings, METHOD=GET and METHOD=POST. The POST method is the best one for most servers, but check your server's documentation. In the POST message, the form's output is sent as a separate message. The GET option appends the form's output to a URL, very much like the <ISINDEX> output does.
- **ACTION** Here, you name the script that is designed to receive the form data.

A completed <FORM> tag looks like this:

```
<FORM METHOD="post" ACTION="cgi-win/poly-
form.exe"></FORM>
```

FORM

Purpose:	Creates the environment within which <INPUT> tags can be used to add interactive features to your Web documents.
Usage:	<FORM>...</FORM>
Example:	<FORM METHOD="post" ACTION="cgi-win/polyform.exe"> <P>Please type your name:<INPUT TYPE=text NAME="username"> </FORM>
Can Contain:	<INPUT>, <SELECT>, and most BODY tags

Can Be Contained By:	<BODY>
Don't Forget:	The METHOD attribute specifies how the data is sent to the server. With the GET option, the data is appended to the URL. With the POST option, the data is sent as a separate message. Most servers are designed to work with the POST option. The ACTION attribute is required. It names the script that handles the form's output.
Hot Tip:	Although it's possible to create more than one form in a single Web document, it doesn't make sense to do so—when the user clicks the Submit button for the first button, the browser displays the response page, so the user would have to use the Back button to redisplay the second form. One page, one form.

USING THE <INPUT> TAG

By itself, the <FORM> tag doesn't do anything. To make interactive input areas appear on-screen, you must use the <INPUT> tag. Here are some important facts about the <INPUT> tag:

- You can add two or more <INPUT> tags to your document, but you must place them all within the <FORM> tag.
- The most important <INPUT> attribute is NAME. This attribute assigns a name to the values the user chooses. For example, suppose you name a text box "username," and the user types "bp." When the user clicks the Submit button, the browser sends the name + value pair "username = bp" to the script. Use quotes around the name that you choose (as in <INPUT NAME="username">
- Another important <INPUT> attribute is TYPE. This attribute enables you to select the type of input area you want (such as text area, check box, radio button, and more).

Here's a quick overview of the TYPE options currently available (later sections of this chapter go into most of these in greater detail):

Text	This option creates a text box in which the user can type information.
Password	Like the text option, this one creates a text box, but the text the user types is obscured by asterisks.
Checkbox	This option creates a check box; each check box has a unique name, and it can have only two values: checked and unchecked.
Radio	In a group of radio buttons that all have the same name, only one can be chosen. You can have more than one group of buttons in a form.
Image	This option displays a graphic, the location of which must be identified in the same way you do using the IMG SRC attribute. Clicking the image submits the form, and what's more, the coordinates of the mouse click. A really clever script programmer could use this capability to advantage, but some fancy programming would be required.
Hidden	This option is used in advanced scriptwriting. It enables programmers to write a script that constructs a new document on the fly, drawing on portions of two other ones.
Submit	This option creates a Submit button that, when clicked, submits the form data to the server.
Reset	This option creates a Reset button that, when clicked, clears all the user's data and restores the default settings in the form.

The TYPE options don't include all the possible input areas you can define, as you'll see in the next two sections.

INPUT

Purpose: Creates a text box, radio button, check box, clickable image, hidden message, Submit button, or Reset button.

Usage: <INPUT> (no end tag needed)

Example: <INPUT NAME="Your_Name" TYPE="text" VALUE="Type your name here" SIZE="40" ALIGN=left>

Can Contain: None (not a container tag)

Can Be Contained By: <FORM>

Don't Forget: To determine the input field type, you use the TYPE attribute. The NAME attribute is required. The <INPUT> tag must be enclosed within beginning and ending <FORM> tags.

Hot Tip: Use the VALUE attribute (for example, VALUE="Type your name here") to define a default entry, which the user can change. In a radio button or check box, use VALUE="Checked" to show a dot or check mark.

Adding a Text Box

To add a single-line text box to your document, you can use the <INPUT> tag with the TYPE="text" attribute, as in the following example. Note the explanatory text that's added to the <INPUT> tag. And remember, this tag must be positioned within <FORM>...</FORM> tags, or it won't show up in your browser.

```
<P>Please type your name here: <INPUT TYPE="text"
NAME="User_Name" SIZE="50" MAXLENGTH="100"></P>
```

Figure 15.4 shows what this code looks like on-screen.

I just tried this but I can't get the text box to display!
Did you enclose the <INPUT> tags within the <FORM> tags (<FORM>. . .</FORM>)? Also, check for mistakes—did you leave off the trailing angle bracket? If there are any errors, your browser will ignore the tag.

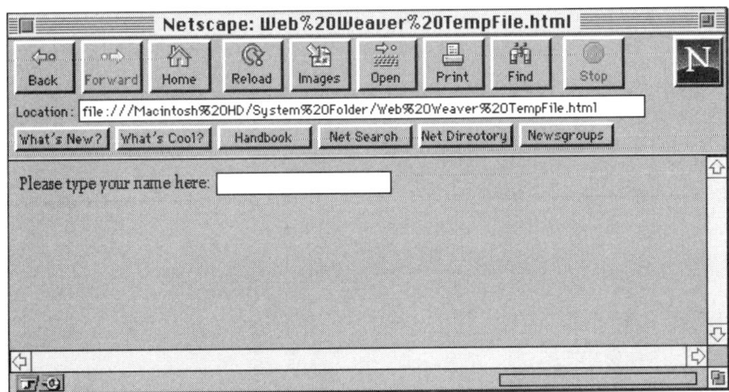

Figure 15.4 Text box created with <INPUT TYPE="text"> tag

If you create an <INPUT TYPE="text"> tag, you can use the following atttributes:

- NAME (required) Here, you give a name to the data the user will type. For example, suppose you are creating a form that asks people to type their favorite color. You could name this text box "color" (NAME="color").
- ALIGN (optional) By default, text is aligned flush left. You can change the alignment to centered or flush right, if you wish.
- VALUE (optional) If you would like the text box to contain some default text, which the user can leave or change as desired, you can use this attribute. For example, you could show a default value of "blue" in the Color box (VALUE="Blue").
- SIZE (optional) Specifies the visible length of the text box, in characters. The attribute SIZE=50 specifies a text box 50 characters in length. *Note:* The user can enter a longer entry, up to the maximum permitted by the MAXLENGTH attribute.
- MAXLENGTH (optional) Specifies the maximum number of characters the user can type in a text box. The attribute MAXLENGTH=120 limits total text input to 120 characters.

Adding Radio Buttons

When you add two or more radio buttons in a group, the user expects to be able to click just one of them (and have the other ones blanked automatically)—and that's just what the TYPE="radio" attribute does. To create a bank of radio buttons, you assign all the buttons to the same name, using the NAME attribute, and give each button a distinctive value using the VALUE attribute. The following illustrates the HTML needed to set up a bank of radio buttons:

```
<P>Indicate your level of experience with wine:</P>
<INPUT NAME="Experience" TYPE="radio" VALUE="Begin-
ner"> Beginner <BR>
<INPUT NAME="Experience" TYPE="radio" VALUE="Nov-
ice"> Novice <BR>
<INPUT NAME="Experience" TYPE="radio" VALUE="Expe-
rienced"> Experienced <BR>
<INPUT NAME="Experience" TYPE="radio" VALUE="Con-
noisseur"> Connoisseur <BR>
```

Figure 15.5 shows how these radio buttons appear in Netscape.

The following attributes are used with radio buttons:

- **NAME** (required) To create a bank of radio buttons, in which the user can only choose one of them, you use the same NAME for all (for example, NAME="Experience")
- **VALUE** (required) In radio buttons, the VALUE attribute is required because it identifies the value that will be sent by the browser in the name + value pair. In a bank of radio buttons that share the same NAME, each button should have a unique VALUE (for example, VALUE="Novice").
- **CHECKED** (optional) If you add this attribute to one of the radio buttons in a bank of buttons, the option will appear with a dot within the circle. The user can change this, but the setting reverts to this option if the user clicks the Reset button.

To mark one of the radio buttons in a bank of buttons as the default (marked) value, use the CHECKED attribute, as in this example:

```
<INPUT NAME="Experience" CHECKED
TYPE="radio" VALUE="Novice" > Novice <BR>
```

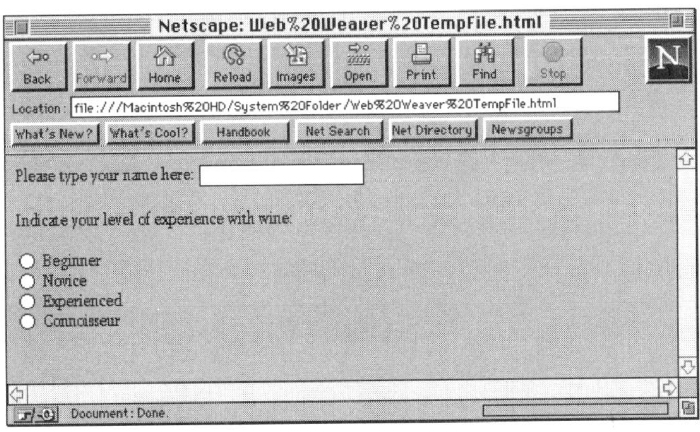

Figure 15.5 Radio buttons

Adding a Check Box

Check boxes are like radio buttons in that the user can choose an option by clicking the option on or off. However, the user can choose more than one check box. Each check box has its own name (such as NAME="Sweet"). By default, the VALUE of each check box is "off," so an unchecked box isn't included when the browser sends the name + value pairs. If the check box is checked, then the VALUE changes to "checked," and the name + value is included in the messsage. Here's an example of a bank of check boxes:

```
<P> Take a sip of Pinot Noir.<BR>
How would you best describe the tastes you just
experienced?<BR>
(Click more than one taste, if you wish)<P>
<INPUT NAME="Strawberry" TYPE="checkbox"> Straw-
berry<BR>
<INPUT NAME="Cedar" TYPE=CHECKBOX > Cedar <BR>
<INPUT NAME="Blackberry" TYPE="checkbox" >Black-
berry<BR>
<INPUT NAME="Raspberry" TYPE="checkbox" > Rasp-
berry<BR>
<INPUT NAME="Tobacco" TYPE="checkbox" > Tobacco
<BR>
```

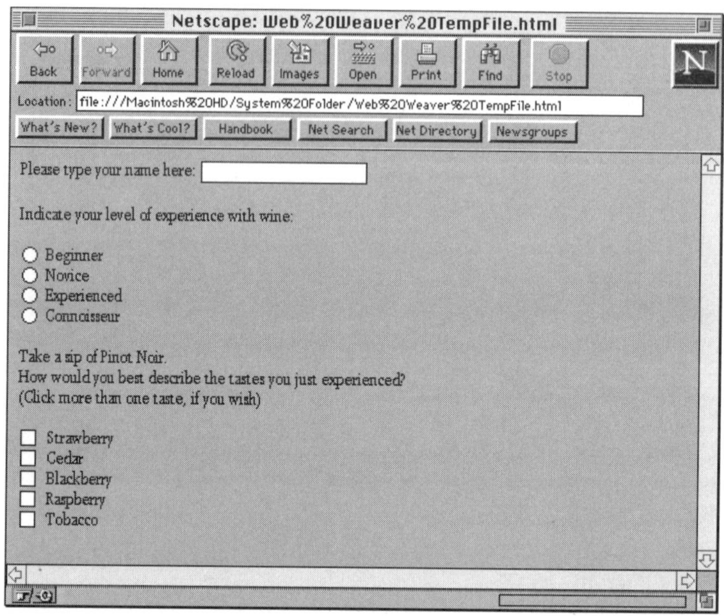

Figure 15.6 Check boxes

Figure 15.6 shows how these check boxes appear in Netscape.

The following attributes are used with check boxes:

- **NAME** (required) In a group of check boxes, each check box should have its own NAME (as in NAME="Strawberry").
- **CHECKED** (optional) If you add this attribute to a check box, the box will appear with an "X" within the circle. The user can change this, but the setting reverts to this option if the user clicks the Reset button.

To turn on check boxes by default, use the CHECKED attribute, as in this example:

```
<INPUT NAME="Blackberry" TYPE="checkbox"
CHECKED>
```

Adding the Submit and Reset Buttons

These buttons are very easy to add. Here's the HTML:

```
<INPUT TYPE="Submit"><BR>
<INPUT TYPE="Reset">
```

Figure 15.7 shows Submit and Reset buttons, as displayed by Netscape.

By default, the Submit button displays the text "Submit" on the button, while the Reset button displays—you guessed it—"Reset". You can change these defaults by using the VALUE attribute, as in the following examples:

```
<INPUT TYPE="Submit" VALUE="Submit
Comments"> <INPUT TYPE="Reset"
VALUE="Clear Form">
```

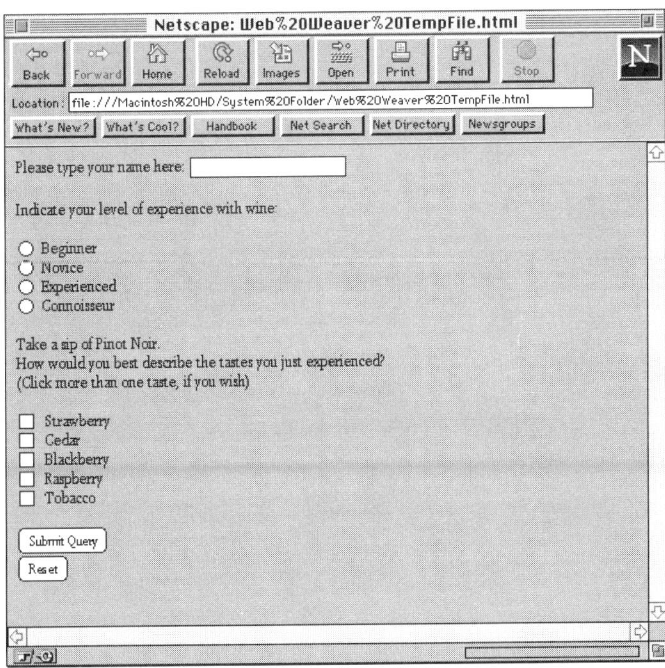

Figure 15.7 Submit and Reset buttons

Adding a Drop-Down List Box

In a drop-down list box, the user can select from a list of predefined options. In many cases, list boxes are a better choice than text fields in that a list box enables you to group responses together because they are all spelled in exactly the same way. Suppose, for example, you ask your readers to identify the wine they're tasting; in a text box, some might type "Chardonnay," while others type "Chard," "Chartoney," or maybe just "White wine."

To create a drop-down list box, you use the <SELECT> and <OPTION> tags:

```
<P>What is the red wine varietal you are tast-
ing?</P>
<SELECT NAME="Varietal">
<OPTION>Cabernet Sauvignon
<OPTION SELECTED>Pinot Noir
<OPTION>Merlot
<OPTION>Zinfandel
<OPTION>Cabernet Franc
<OPTION>Syrah
<OPTION>Blend or not sure
</SELECT></P>
```

Figure 15.8 shows the list box before it's clicked, while Figure 15.9 shows the entire list.

To define one of the options in the list as the default value, so that it appears in the text box, use the SELECTED attribute (<OPTION SELECTED>).

SELECT

Purpose: Creates an environment for the <OPTION> tag, which you can use to create a drop-down list box within a <FORM> environment.

Usage: <SELECT>. . .</SELECT>

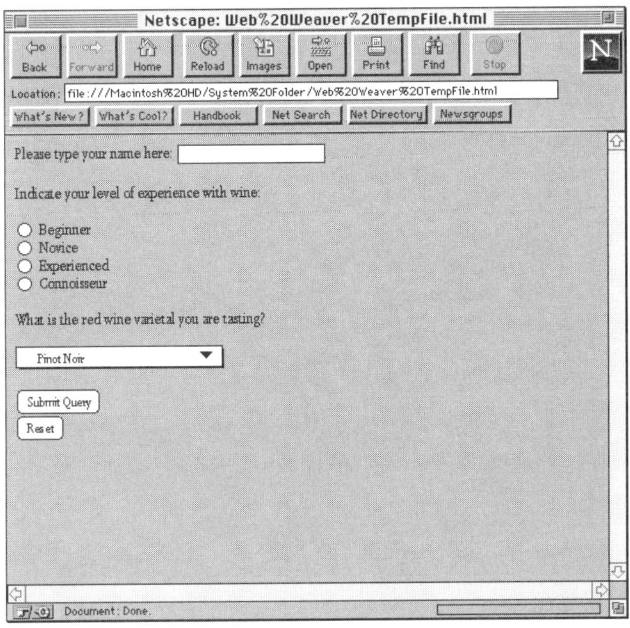

Figure 15.8 Drop-down list box (before clicking the down arrow)

Example:

```
<SELECT>
    <OPTION>Red
    <OPTION>White
    <OPTION>Rose
</SELECT>
```

Can Contain: <OPTION>

Can Be Contained By: <FORM>

Don't Forget: By itself, the <SELECT> tag doesn't create a list; you must use the <OPTION> tag to define the items that appear in the drop-down list.

Hot Tip: You can use the SIZE attribute to determine the number of choices that appear on-screen, within the text box. The default is one. If you use the attribute <SELECT SIZE=5>, five of the options appear within an enlarged text box.

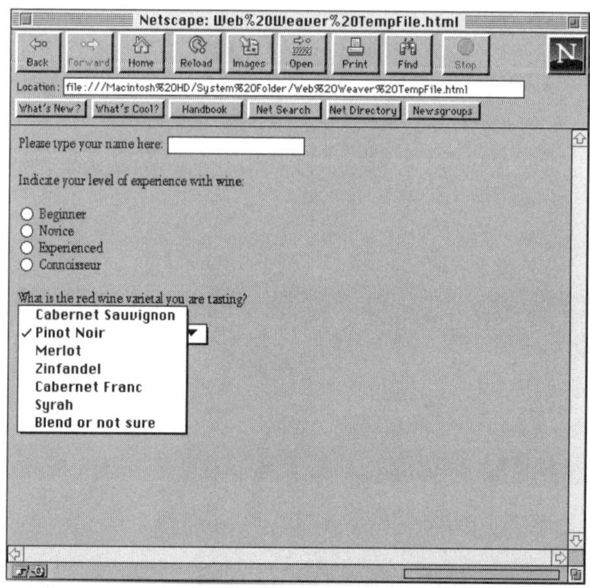

Figure 15.9 Drop-down list (the whole list displayed)

OPTION

Purpose:	Creates an item in a drop-down list box.
Usage:	<OPTION> (no end tag)
Example:	<OPTION>Rhode Island
Can Contain:	Text emphasis tags
Can Be Contained By:	<SELECT>
Don't Forget:	To create the drop-down list, you must surround the <OPTION> tags with <SELECT> tags.
Hot Tip:	To mark one of the options as the one that appears by default in the list box, use the SELECTED attribute (<OPTION SELECTED>).

Adding a Text Entry Area

If you would like to provide your readers with the ability to enter more than a single line of text, the <TEXTAREA> tag is just the ticket. Here's the HTML that creates a scrollable text box:

```
<P>Pleasc type any additional comments you might
have:</P>
<TEXTAREA NAME="Verbiage" ROWS="10" COLS="50">
</TEXTAREA>
```

Note that an end tag is required (</TEXTAREA>). Figure 15.10 shows the results of this tag.

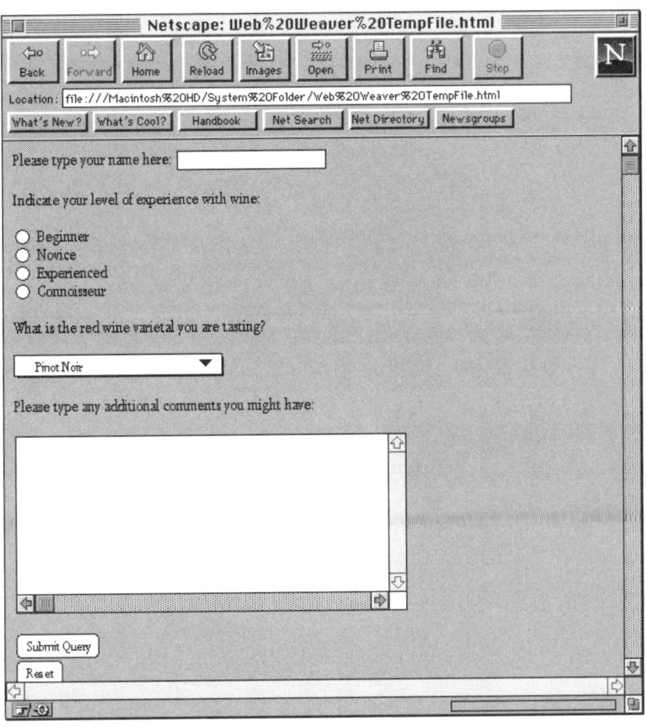

Figure 15.10 <TEXTAREA> for unlimited text entry

You must use the following attributes with the <TEXTAREA> tag:

- **NAME** This attribute specifies the variable name so that the text will be associated with a name + value pair.
- **ROWS** This attribute specifies the default number of rows (in lines) that are visible on-screen.
- **COLS** This attribute specifies the width of the text entry window, in characters.

TEXTAREA

Purpose:	Creates a text box for text entries of more than one line.
Usage:	<TEXTAREA></TEXTAREA>
Example:	<TEXTAREA NAME="Verbiage" ROWS="10" COLS="50"></TEXTAREA>
Can Contain:	No HTML tags are permitted within the <TEXTAREA> container—just text (see the Hot Tip).
Can Be Contained By:	<FORM>
Don't Forget:	To create a single-line text entry area, use the <INPUT TYPE=text> tag.
Hot Tip:	If you include any text within the beginning <TEXTAREA> and ending </TEXTAREA> tags, this text is displayed as the default text, which the user can modify or erase. Don't use any HTML tags in this text.

Adding Scripts Using NetForms and TR-WWW

The two leading Web servers for Macintoshes, MacHTTP (shareware) and WebSTAR (commercial), follow the guidelines of the Common Gateway Interface (CGI) standard. On Macintoshes, the scripting language that is most widely used is AppleScript, which is packaged with every copy of Mac OS (System 7.5 and later). AppleScript isn't difficult to learn and many Web authors have been able to obtain and modify scripts that are designed to work with these servers.

If you don't have time to learn AppleScript, you'll be glad to know that script utilities exist that enable you to create highly interactive documents without any programming. And two of the best of them are included on this book's CD-ROM disc:

- **NetForms** This amazing utility adds a level of interactivity to your documents that goes far beyond what this chapter has discussed. With NetForms, you can set up forms that visitors to your site fill out. When these forms are submitted, NetForms processes them and then—here's the good part—creates new, publicly accessible HTML documents that contain your visitor's contributions. This is great for conferencing; in fact, NetForms includes a ready-to-use sample application that enables you to set up a conferencing system at your site. Visitors can contribute their feedback, see their comments added to a list of contributions, view other peoples' contributions, and even comment on other peoples' contributions. Talk about interactivity! Other sample applications include forms for uploading recipes and creating a mailing list. To expand these examples, you'd need to learn how to use some of the special tags that NetForms adds to HTML, but it's easy to modify the existing applications without learning anything new.
- **TR-WWW** This program enables the people visiting your site to search all the text or HTML documents that you've placed in a special Docs folder. It's fast and incredibly easy to set up. Best of all, it doesn't require any pre-indexing, so you don't have to go through a lengthy process of re-indexing the documents after you add new documents to the folder.

Using NetForms

NetForms, an extremely cool product of Maxum Development, provides a very high degree of interactivity for Web documents, but doesn't require you to learn a programming language. The secret lies in the Forms Definition Markup Language (FDML). You can think of FDML as an extension to HTML; it consists of tags that you can add to Web documents. These tags tell NetForms how to process the form you're submitting, freeing you from the need to write a server-side script.

What's so cool about NetForms is that it goes beyond merely processing forms. It also provides a means for people visiting your site to contribute their own material. The best way to understand this is to see it in action, so Maxum provides three sample applications with NetForms:

Recipes	Users contribute recipes; after they do, their recipes are added to the recipe book, and they can browse the recipes they have contributed.
Feedback	Users can contribute feedback to a conference of their choice (Figure 15.11) Subsequently, they can see the messages they have contributed (Figure 15.12), and they can even write

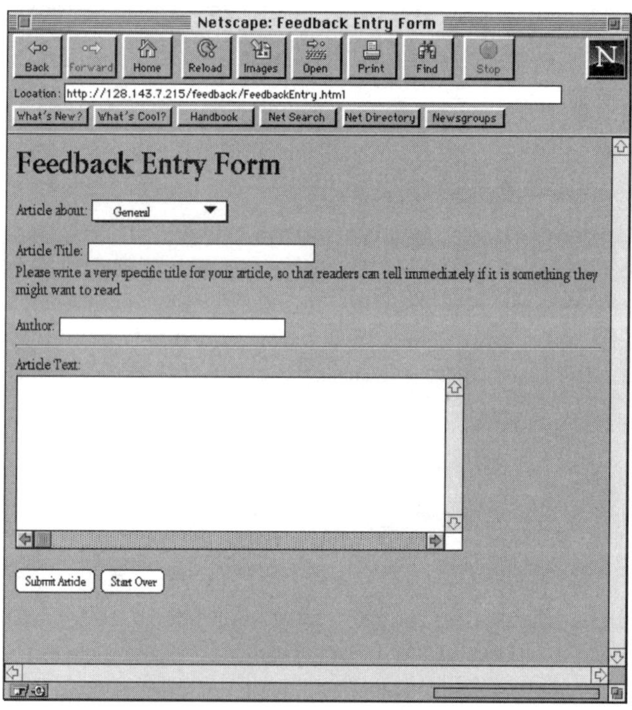

Figure 15.11 Feedback with NetForms

	additional comments on comments that have been previously contributed.
Mailing List	Users fill out a mailing list form, which is added to a text file that is formatted for exporting to database programs.

Just by modifying these programs, you can add a lot of interactivity to your site.

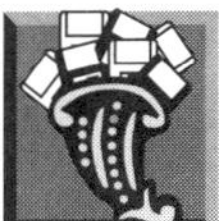

For more information on NetForms, check out Maxum Development's home page at http://www.maxum.com/maxum/. Be sure to check out the following document, which shows you how to modify the Forum example to suit your site's particular needs:

http://maxum.catalogue.com/maxum/nffaq/feedbackchanges.html

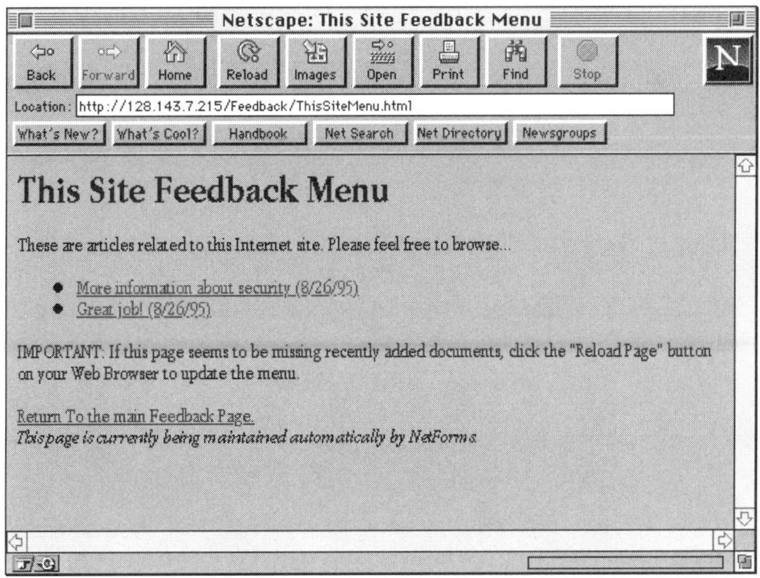

Figure 15.12 Reading contributions

Searching Document Databases with TR-WWW

If you would like to allow visitors to your site to search large databases of text or HTML documents, TR-WWW enables you to do so without any programming. You'll find a copy of TR-WWW on the CD-ROM disc enclosed with this book, and you'll also find complete installation instructions.

TR stands for Total Research, a complete research system for dealing with unstructured textual information. TR was developed by Chris Priestley, and it is a commercial, fully supported product with a large user base. TR-WWW is a modified version of TR designed to work with MacHTTP. The program is by Adrian Vanzyl at Monash Medical Informatics, in Monash, Australia. Please note that TR-WWW is shareware and requires a payment of $50 for educational or nonprofit organizations, and $300 for commercial endeavors.

After installing TR-WWW, you initiate a search by accessing the tr-www.cgi file with your Web browser, or by creating a form (see Figure 15.13) in which the ACTION attribute in the <FORM> tag points to tr-

Netscape: Search the Undergraduate Thesis Manual

Back Forward Home Reload Images Open Print Find Stop

Location: file:///Macintosh%20HD/MacHTTP%202.2/MacHTTP%20Software%20&%20Docs/Docs/Th

What's New? What's Cool? Handbook Net Search Net Directory Newsgroups

Search the Undergraduate Thesis Manual

Please type in a search term, select the appropriate options, and then click on Search to run the search

Enter search word [ ] Search

Choose type of search to perform:
Context Find ◉ Relevance Find ○

For Context finds, choose the number of hits to return [40] (range 10 to 200).

Select the variant Boolean relationship between the first and remaining words:
[OR ▼]

For NEAR and NOTNEAR type searches, set the nearness [40] (suggested range 10 to 200).

Please choose a document set from the list to search: [Thesis ▼]

Figure 15.13 TR-WWW search form

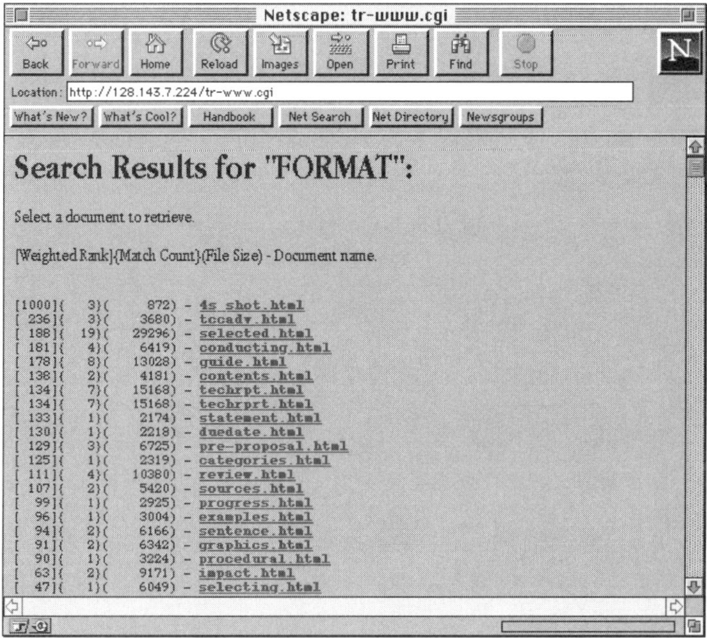

Figure 15.14 Search results ranked by relevance

www.cgi. The search form includes a variety of sophisticated search options, including Boolean searching using the AND, OR, and PHRASE options.

The results of a TR-WWW search can be displayed as a keyword in context (KWIC) list (the default option), which is hard to read and understand, or (better) a list of document hits ranked by relevance (Figure 15.14).

From Here

- In this chapter, you've mastered one of the two key elements of user interactivity—forms. The next chapter tackles clickable maps, which enable users to choose items from a graphic.

Chapter 16

Creating Image Maps

An image map (also called a clickable map) is a graphic that contains two or more hyperlinks, each tied to a particular region of the image. The linkage of graphic region and URLs is accomplished by means of a map file, a text file that contains the definitions of the various clickable areas on the graphic, along with their associated URLs. The definitions consist of specific areas that are delineated in terms of the mouse's position within the graphic. When someone accessing your site displays a clickable graphic and clicks part of it, the browser detects the mouse's position and sends this information to the image map script. Using the map file as a reference, the script determines which URL to send back to the browser.

Unlike in-line images, which can be linked to a URL by using the <A> tag, image maps require preparation and scripts in order to function—and it used to be a very arduous process. You had to calculate. The good news is

that, thanks to a spate of user-friendly utilities, it's now possible to create image maps with "what-you-see-is-what-you-get" (WYSIWYG) graphics editors, and you can install them on Macintosh servers without doing any programming.

Image maps solve one of the most persistent problems of Web document design: The need to gain control over your presentation's graphical appearance without sacrificing the interactivity of HTML. Most of today's hottest new sites present a welcome page that includes an image map marquee, like the one shown in Figure 16.1. The use of image maps in this way permits Web designers to kill two birds with one stone: You can establish a consistent look for your pages at the same time that you provide navigation buttons.

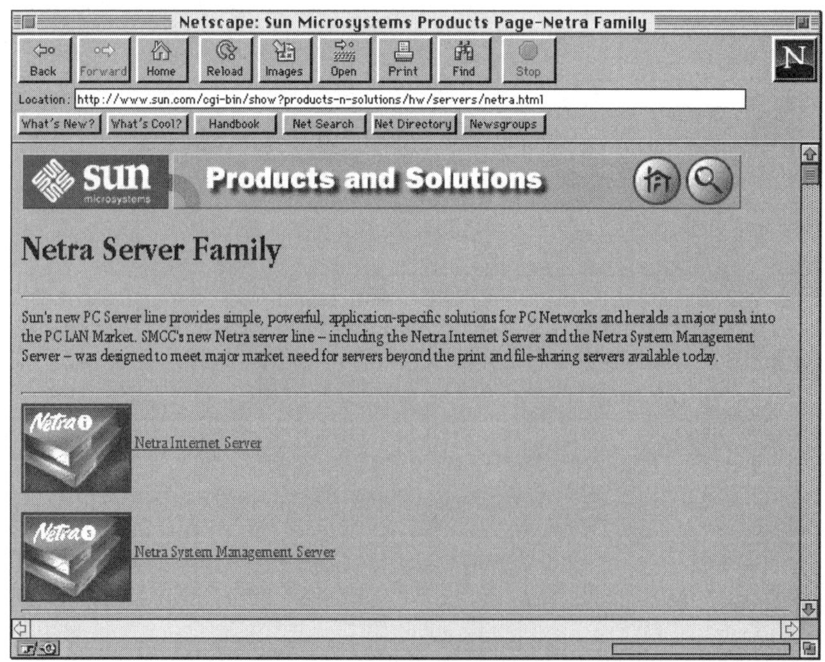

Figure 16.1 Image map as marquee

For the Time-Challenged

- Not all graphics are suitable as clickable maps. You must be able to mark squares, rectangles, circles, ellipses, or polygons within the graphic, and assign these shapes to URLs.
- Image map editors enable you to define these shapes on-screen with a mouse, and also enable you to link each shape with a URL. Finally, the image map editor creates the .MAP file, which the image map script uses to link mouse coordinates with specific Web documents.
- If you're using Mac-ImageMap, the CGI image map script that comes on this book's CD-ROM disc, you should install the software to a folder called imagemap and place this folder within MacHTTP's or WebSTAR's folder.
- When you create an HTML document that contains a link to the clickable map, you use the ISMAP attribute. To hide the border that browsers place around URL-linked graphics, add the BORDER=0 attribute to the <IMG> tag.
- To get your image map to work, you'll need to modify Mac-ImageMap's imagemap.config file so that the program knows how to link the image map (.MAP) file and the file containing the graphic.

Creating the Graphic

Not every graphic is suitable for use as an image map. To use map editors such as WebMap, you need to be able to identify clickable regions that have the following geometric shapes:

- Squares
- Rectangles
- Circles
- Ellipses (Ovals)
- Polygons

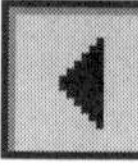

Figure 16.2 displays an example of the shapes that a popular Macintosh map editor, WebMap, can assign to shapes within a graphic.

Remember that your primary purpose in creating an image map is to link the graphic in some visual way with the contents of your site. In Figure 16.3, you see a Gantt chart that's doing double duty: At the same time that it provides a visual map to a complex, year-long project (a senior thesis project), it also provides access to documents that explain each assignment. If you click on the bar next to Doing the Research, for instance, you see a document explaining how to conduct the research project. This graphic provides an excellent example of a good candidate for image map-making for another reason: The rectangular areas are exceptionally easy to identify and link with specific URLs.

Introducing Image Map Editors

An indispensable tool for making image maps is an image map editor. Image map editors enable you to define these shapes on-screen with a mouse, and

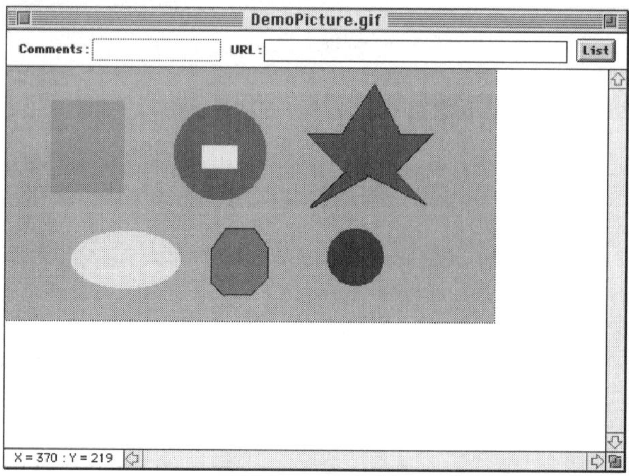

Figure 16.2 Shapes in WebMap

also enable you to link each shape with a URL. Finally, the image map editor creates the .MAP file, which the image map script uses to link mouse coordinates with specific Web documents.

In the Macintosh world, the image map editor of choice is WebMap 1.0.1, a shareware program that's included on this book's CD-ROM disc.

If you like WebMap, you'll surely want to upgrade to the commercial version ($25). For more information on this version, WebMap 2.0, check out the WebMap home page at http://www.city.net/cnx/software/webmap.html. You can download the software from this site (it's set to expire at a certain date). Send your $25 (payable to City Net Express)

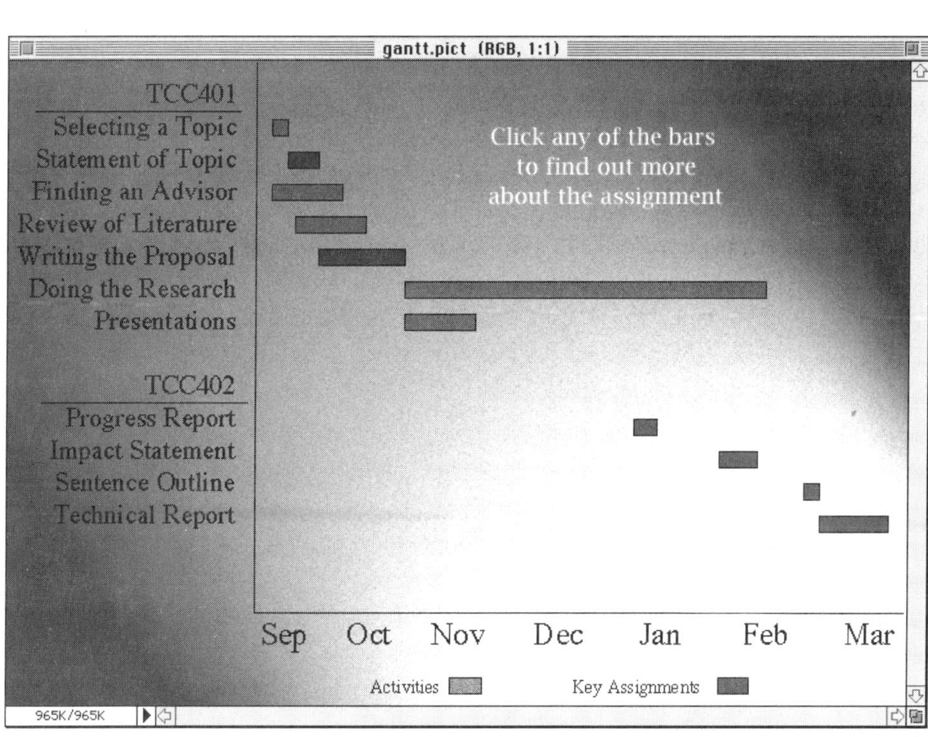

Figure 16.3 Gantt chart with clickable bars

to the following address, and you'll receive a numerical key that unlocks the software for your use:

City Net Express
3531 SE 11th Ave.
Portland, OR 97202
USA

Linking Shapes and URLs with WebMap

WebMap is easy to use. The program enables you to open a GIF graphic on which you can draw rectangles, circles, ovals, polygons, and points. You can then individually or collectively select these shapes, move them, resize them, or delete them, if you wish. Each shape can be linked to a specific URL. This section doesn't go into all the details of working with WebMap, but it's plenty to help you get started. The program comes with a good Help file (accessible through the Apple menu) that contains additional information about WebMap features.

Enclosing the Shape

After you display a document with WebMap (see Figure 16.4), you'll see a toolbar with the drawing tools available in this version: rectangles, circles/ovals, and polygons. To draw with one of these tools, just click it and click the mouse where you want the shape to be positioned. Then move the mouse until you've enclosed the shape that you want to link with a URL.

Linking a Shape to a URL

After you draw the shape, you'll see an entry in the list box to the right of the graphic window. If you double-click this entry, you'll see a dialog box that enables you to link the shape to a URL. You can type absolute or relative URLs. If you use relative URLs, bear in mind that the document's position is relative to the folder in which MacHTTP or WebSTAR is stored. Since other utilities require Web documents to be stored in folders within the server's directory, you'll probably have a Docs folder in which the documents are stored. Begin the relative URL with a slash mark, as in the following example:

/Docs/Thesis/overview.html

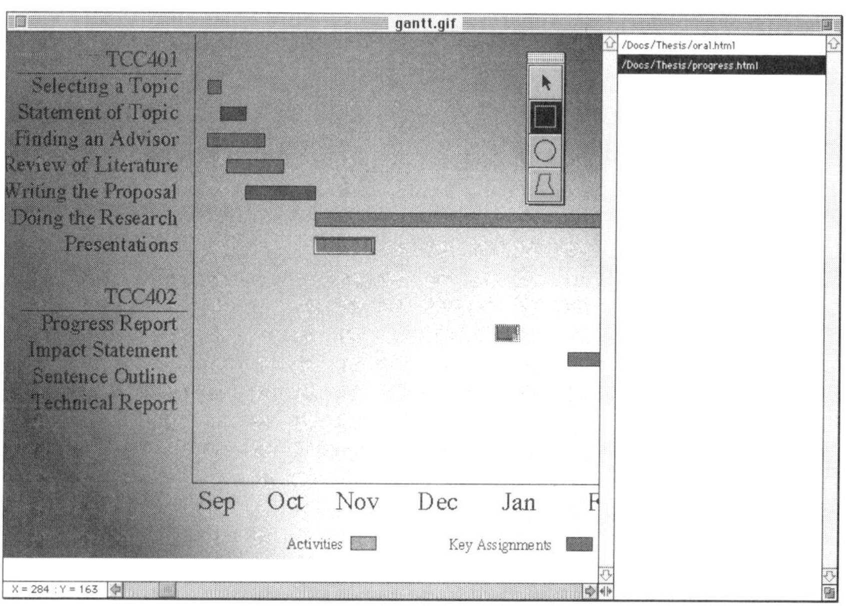

Figure 16.4 Gantt chart with clickable bars

This is necessary because the image map CGI, as explained below, appends the relative URL to the site's domain name; without the beginning backslash, the URL won't work.

When you're finished linking shapes to URLs, choose Save from the File menu—but don't quit WebMap just yet. You still need to write the image map file, as explained in the following section.

You can link undefined regions of the graphic with a default URL, so that a document appears if the user clicks the graphic's background. To define the default URL, choose Set Default URL from the Edit menu.

Writing the Image Map File

When you're done linking shapes with URLs, you need to write the image map file. To do so, choose Export as Text from the File menu. Important: click the

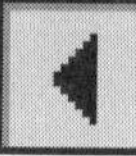

NCSA option button. Be sure to name the file with the three-letter extension .MAP. Place the image map within a folder called imagemap, and make sure this folder is placed within MacHTTP's or WebSTAR's folder.

Installing the Image Map Script

Like most of the interactive features discussed in the previous chapter, image maps require a server-side script in order to function. The good news is that you can obtain scripts that require no programming on your part. One of them, Mac-ImageMap, is included on the CD-ROM disc packaged with this book.

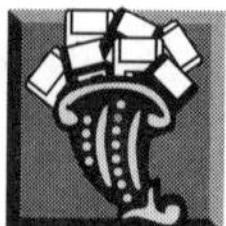

For more information on Mac-ImageMap, check out the Mac-ImageMap home page at

http://weyl.zib-berlin.de/imagemap/Mac-ImageMap.html

To install Mac-ImageMap, place the program's folder within the MacHTTP or WebSTAR folder. (This is important—the folder *must* be within the server's folder.)

Creating the HTML Document

The next-to-last step that you need to take to set up your image map involves creating the HTML document containing the link to the graphic. To write the hyperlink that references Mac-ImageMap and the graphic, you write a tag such as the following:

```
<A HREF="http://your.host/imagemap/
imagemap.cgi$mapname"><IMG SRC="http://your.host/
imagemap/your_example/map_picture.gif" ISMAP></A>
```

Note that this example assumes that Mac-ImageMap is stored in a folder called imagemap, and that this folder is placed within the MacHTTP or WebSTAR folder.

When you include an <IMG> tag within the <A> container, the map functions as a hyperlink—and your browser puts a big, ugly blue border around it. To avoid this, you can use the BORDER=0 attribute (zero, not the letter O) of the <IMG> tag, as in the following example:

```
<A HREF="http://gatchaman.tcc.vir-
ginia.edu/imagemap/
imagemap.cgi$gantt.map<IMG SRC="http://
gatchaman.tcc.virginia.edu/imagemap/
gantt.gif" ISMAP BORDER=0></A>
```

This tag is one of the Netscape extensions and might not be supported by all browsers.

Adding Your Map to the Image Map Configuration File

With Mac-ImageMap, there's one more task you need to perform before you can test your image map: telling the program that there's a connection between a given image map file (*.MAP) and the corresponding GIF. (The program wouldn't know unless you provided this information.) To do this, open the file imagemap.config, which you'll find in Mac-ImageMap's imagemap folder. Add a line to the file that links the map file name and graphics file name as follows:

```
name of the map file : name and location of the
graphics file
```

Let's say you created a map file named gantt.map and a graphics file called gantt.gif. If you've stored the graphics file in the same folder (imagemap) as the map file (a very good idea, incidentally), you can type this line like this:

```
gantt.map : gantt.gif
```

Note the colon—and also note the space before and after the colon. These spaces are required.

Save the file and exit.

Testing the Image Map

To test your image map, you must have started your server and accessed the document containing the image map from the network. (The test won't

work if you open the file as a local file.) After loading the document, try clicking all the shapes you defined. If something goes wrong, the likely culprits are as follows:

- In WebMap, did you type the URLs correctly? If you're using relative references, did you remember to place a slash mark (/) at the beginning of the URL?
- Did you click the NCSA option when you used WebMap to save the image map file? Mac-ImageMap won't work with the CERN image map format.
- Did you install the Mac-ImageMap software within the MacHTTP or WebSTAR folders?
- Did you link the image map file and graphics file by adding a line to the imagemap.config file? Did you remember to put spaces before and after the colon?

From Here

- Moving right along in this book's survey of advanced HTML, the next chapter tackles one of the most exciting additions: tables.
- If you get tired of doing all that HTML coding by hand (and who doesn't?), check out an HTML editor. You'll find an introduction to HTML Editor, an editor included on this book's CD-ROM disc, in Chapter 18.

Chapter 17

Creating Tables

One of the newest and most useful features of HTML 3.0 is the <TABLE> tag, which enables you to create nicely formatted tables (see Figure 17.1). HTML 3.0's table capabilities can be used for multiple column layouts, too, such as the *Wall Street Journal* daily investment newsletter shown in Figure 17.2. That's the good news. The bad news is that many browsers don't yet support tables. Happily, the two that do—Mosaic and Netscape—are the two most frequently used browsers on the Web.

Before adding tables to the documents in your Web site, consider that someone accessing your site with a browser that isn't capable of formatting tables is going to see a jumble of unformatted text. Do you want a site with pages that look extra nice—or would you rather make sure that everyone can read the content you have to offer? It's your call.

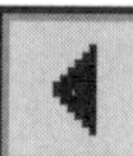

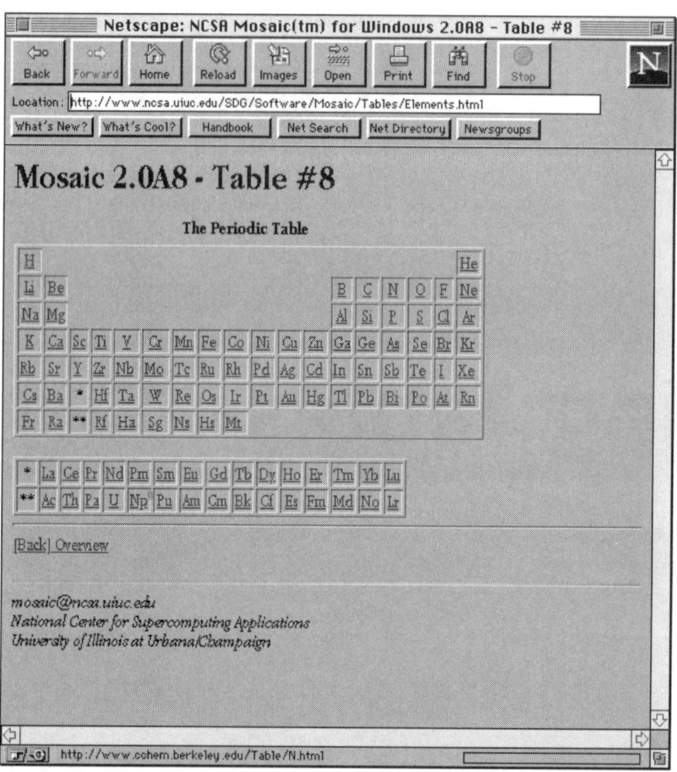

Figure 17.1 Table (displayed with Netscape Navigator)

As you work through this chapter, you will surely agree that the HTML 3.0 <TABLE> tag and related tags are difficult to work with. But there's a reason—they weren't *meant* to be worked with. The design of these tags is optimized so that editor programs can automate the table-creation process. Although this chapter discusses manual table formatting, you would be well advised to forget the manual formatting and create tables with a WYSIWYG editor. Perhaps by the time you read this, you'll find an HTML editor that can handle tables using WYSIWYG capabilities (such editors already exist for Microsoft Windows systems, so they'll be along shortly for the Mac).

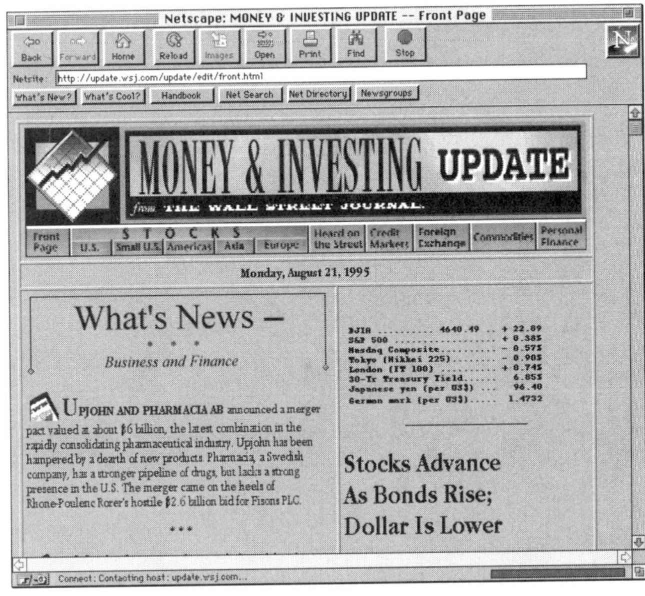

Figure 17.2 *Wall Street Journal* investment newsletter (formatted with <TABLE> tags)

Before trying to code your table, make a pencil sketch of what your table is supposed to look like. How many columns of data does it require? Do you have headings that span two or more columns? How would you like the data aligned? It's easier to code the table once you've made basic decisions such as these.

The Basics: The <TABLE> Tag

To create a table in your HTML document, you use the <TABLE> tag. Here's the basic point about this tag: You create your table row by row,

showing the logical relationships among the parts of the table. The exact details of the physical layout are handled by the browser. These details include the width of individual cells. The width is adjusted depending on the size of the current display font and the width of the current window.

When you create a table, you also use the following tags:

<TR>...</TR>	This tag defines a row of data in the table.
<TH>...</TH>	This tag defines a table heading, which is normally displayed with emphasis (bold).
<TD>...</TD>	This tag defines a table data item.

The following HTML code illustrates the fundamentals of creating a table with the <TABLE>, <TH>, and <TR> tags. Note that, within the <TABLE> environment, the <TR> tags are used to define individual rows of the table. Figure 17.3 shows what this table looks like.

For the Time-Challenged

- In HTML 3.0, a table begins with the <TABLE> tag, and ends with </TABLE>.
- A table consists of rows and columns, which together form table cells.
- You define the table row by row, using the <TR> tag.
- To create headings within cells, you use the <TH> tag. The heading will be shown in emphasized type (bold). By default, headings are centered.
- To create a data cell, you use the <TD> tag. By default, data is aligned flush left.
- You can control the horizontal and vertical alignment of table data using the ALIGN and VALIGN attributes of the <TH> and <TD> tags.
- The Netscape extensions give you ways to increase your table's visual appeal, but the effects may not be seen by people using browsers other than Netscape.

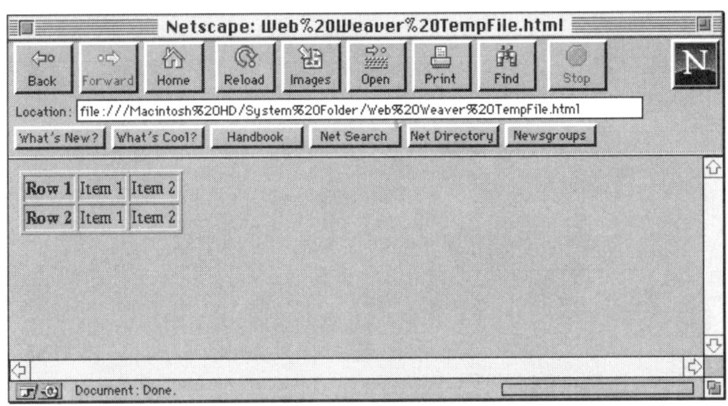

Figure 17.3 A simple table

```
<TABLE BORDER>
  <TR>
      <TH>Row 1
      <TD>Item 1</TD>
      <TD>Item 2</TD>
  </TR>
  <TR>
      <TH>Row 2
      <TD>Item 1</TD>
      <TD>Item 2</TD>
  </TR>
</TABLE>
```

The <TABLE> tag's BORDER attribute (<TABLE BORDER>) automatically creates a border around the table and each cell. Just how the border appears depends on the browser you're using.

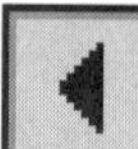

TABLE

Purpose: Creates a table.

Usage: <TABLE>. . .</TABLE>

Example:

```
<TABLE>
  <TR>
    <TH>Row 1</TH>
    <TD>Item 1</TD>
    <TD>Item 2</TD>
  </TR>
  <TR>
    <TH>Row 2</TH>
    <TD>Item 1</TD>
    <TD>Item 2</TD>
  </TR>
</TABLE>
```

Can Contain: <TR>, <TH>, and <TD> are used to define table rows;
 is useful to break a lengthy line within a table cell; you can also use any of the other tags normally used within the <BODY> environment.

Can Be Contained By: <BODY>. . .</BODY>

Don't Forget: You set up your table by defining the table rows with <TR>.

Hot Tip: The BORDER attribute (<TABLE BORDER>) adds a border around the cells in your table.

TR

Purpose: Within a <TABLE> environment, creates a row of data cells.

Usage: <TR>. . .</TR>

Example:

```
<TABLE>
  <TR>
    <TH>Row 1</TH>
    <TD>Item 1</TD>
    <TD>Item 2</TD>
  </TR>
</TABLE>
```

Can Contain: <TD> and <TH> are used to create table data cell items and table headers.
 is useful to break a lengthy line within a table cell; you can also use any of the other tags normally used within the <BODY> environment.

Can Be Contained By: <TABLE>. . .</TABLE>

Don't Forget: Within a <TR> environment, you can use the <TH> tag to create a header item, which is normally displayed in bold.

Hot Tip: By default, heading cells are centered horizontally and vertically within the cell space. When used with the <TR> tag, the ALIGN and VALIGN attributes allow you to define the default horizontal and vertical alignments for the entire row (<TR ALIGN=LEFT>, <TR ALIGN=CENTER>, <TR ALIGN=RIGHT>, <TR VALIGN=TOP>, <TR VALIGN=CENTER>, <TR VALIGN=BOTTOM>)

TH

Purpose: Within a <TR> environment, creates a table heading (displayed in bold by most browsers). The heading is displayed in a cell like those created by <TD>.

Usage: <TH>. . .</TH>

Example:

```
<TR>
  <TH>Row 1</TH>
  <TD>Item 1</TD>
  <TD>Item 2</TD>
</TR>
```

Can Contain: Any of the other tags normally used within the <BODY> environment.

Can Be Contained By: <TR>. . .</TR>

Don't Forget: By default, the table header is aligned at the center of the cell, both horizontally and vertically.

Hot Tip: The ALIGN and VALIGN attributes allow you to define the horizontal and vertical alignments (<TH ALIGN=LEFT>, <TH ALIGN=CENTER>, <TH ALIGN=RIGHT>, <TH VALIGN=TOP>, <TH VALIGN=CENTER>, <TH VALIGN=BOTTOM>). To span columns, use the COLSPAN=number attribute; to span rows, use the ROWSPAN=number attribute (for example, <TH COLSPAN=2> spans two rows).

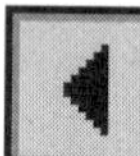

TD

Purpose: Adds a data cell to a table defined by the <TABLE> tag.

Usage: <TD>. . .</TD>

Example:

```
<TR>
  <TH>Row 1</TH>
  <TD>Item 1</TD>
  <TD>Item 2</TD>
</TR>
```

Can Contain: Within the cell, you can use emphases and any other tag that's normally used within <BODY>.

Can Be Contained By: <TR>. . .</TR>

Don't Forget: By default, the table data item is aligned at the center of the cell, both horizontally and vertically

Hot Tip: The ALIGN and VALIGN attributes allow you to define the horizontal and vertical alignments (<TH ALIGN=LEFT>, <TH ALIGN=CENTER>, <TH ALIGN=RIGHT>, <TH VALIGN=TOP>, <TH VALIGN=CENTER>, <TH VALIGN=BOTTOM>). To span columns, use the COLSPAN=*number* attribute; to span rows, use the ROWSPAN=*number* attribute (for example, <TD COLSPAN=2> spans two rows).

Creating a Horizontal Header

You've already learned how to create row headings using the <TH> tag. But how do you create a row of headings across the top of the table, as shown in Figure 17.4? There are a couple of tricks that you can use.

First, create the first row of your table using nothing but <TH> tags—don't use <TD>—as in the following example:

```
<TR>
  <TH></TH>
  <TH>Chardonnay</TH>
  <TH>Sauvignon Blanc</TH>
```

```
    <TH>Cabernet Sauvignon</TH>
    <TH>Merlot</TH>
    <TH>Pinot Noir</TH>
</TR>
```

In Figure 17.4, note that there's an empty cell. The first column doesn't require a heading, so this empty cell is needed to make the table look right. To create the empty cell, you can use <TH></TH> or <TD></TD>. Note that there's nothing between these tags, and the result is a blank space in the table.

Second, add rows with the same number of items, as in the following:

```
<TR>
  <TH></TH>
  <TH>Chardonnay</TH>
  <TH>Sauvignon Blanc</TH>
  <TH>Cabernet Sauvignon</TH>
  <TH>Merlot</TH>
  <TH>Pinot Noir</TH>
</TR>
<TR>
  <TH>Best with:</TH>
  <TD>Appetizers, cheese</TD>
```

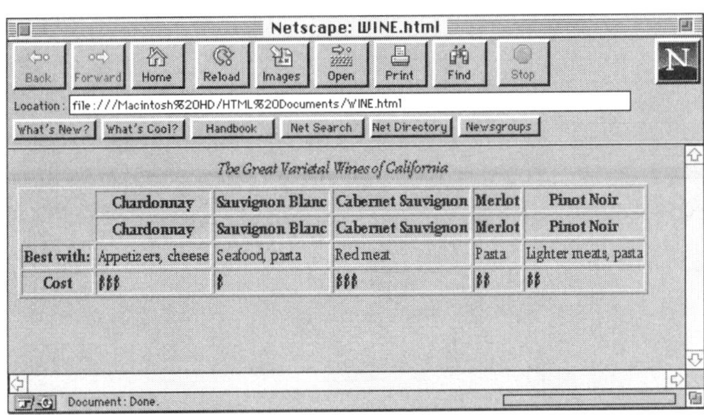

	Chardonnay	Sauvignon Blanc	Cabernet Sauvignon	Merlot	Pinot Noir
	Chardonnay	Sauvignon Blanc	Cabernet Sauvignon	Merlot	Pinot Noir
Best with:	Appetizers, cheese	Seafood, pasta	Red meat	Pasta	Lighter meats, pasta
Cost	$$$	$	$$$	$$	$$

Figure 17.4 Table with horizontal row of headings

```
    <TD>Seafood, pasta</TD>
    <TD>Red meat
    <TD>Pasta</TD>
    <TD>Lighter meats, pasta</TD>
  </TR>
  <TR>
    <TH>Cost</TH>
    <TD>$$$</TD>
    <TD>$</TD>
    <TD>$$$</TD>
    <TD>$$</TD>
    <TD>$$</TD>
  </TR>
```

Adding a Caption

Tables don't have to have captions—they're optional. If you wish to add a caption, you can do so using an ordinary text paragraph (<P>. . .</P>), or you can use the <CAPTION> tag. The caption tag goes just after the <TABLE> tag. By default (with most browers), the caption is centered at the top of the table, as shown in Figure 17.4.

Here's the HTML that adds the caption shown in Figure 17.4:

```
<TABLE BORDER>
  <CAPTION><EM>The Great Varietal Wines of
    California</EM>
  <TR>
  [...]
</TABLE>
```

CAPTION

Purpose: Adds a caption to a table or figure.

Usage: <CAPTION>. . .</CAPTION>

Example:

```
<TABLE>
<CAPTION>Caption Text</CAPTION>
</TABLE>
```

Can Contain: You may wish to add emphasis to the caption text, such as <EM> or <B>.

Can Be Contained By: <FIG>, <TABLE>

Don't Forget: The <CAPTION> tag must be placed within the <FIG> or <TABLE> tags.

Hot Tip: To place the caption at the bottom of the table or figure, use the ALIGN=BOTTOM attribute (<CAPTION ALIGN=BOTTOM>).

Aligning Text within Table Cells

By default, heading cells are centered horizontally and vertically within the cell, while data cells are centered only vertically; horizontally, they're aligned flush left. Take a look at Figure 17.5, and you'll see what I mean.

To modify the default alignments, you can use the following attributes of the <TH> and <TD> tags:

- **VALIGN (VALIGN=TOP, VALIGN=MIDDLE, VALIGN=BOTTOM)** Use these attributes to control the vertical alignment of the text within the data cell (for example, <TD VALIGN=TOP> positions the text at the top of the data cell).

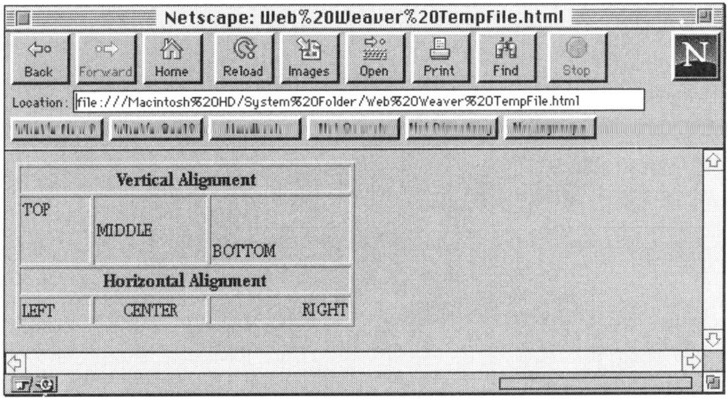

Figure 17.5 Horizontal and vertical alignments within data cells

- **ALIGN (ALIGN=LEFT, ALIGN=CENTER, ALIGN=RIGHT)** Use these attributes to control the horizontal alignment of the text within the data cell (for example, <TD ALIGN=RIGHT> positions the text flush right within the data cell).

Spanning Rows and Columns

Sometimes you may wish to create a header cell that spans two or more columns, like the headers shown in Figure 17.6. In that figure, note the following:

- There is a large, blank area in the upper left of the table; this is a blank cell that spans two columns and two rows.
- The "Microprocessor" heading spans two columns.
- The "Amount of Installed RAM" heading spans two rows.

To span columns and rows, you use the COLSPAN and ROWSPAN attributes, which work with the <TH> and <TD> tags. For example, the tag

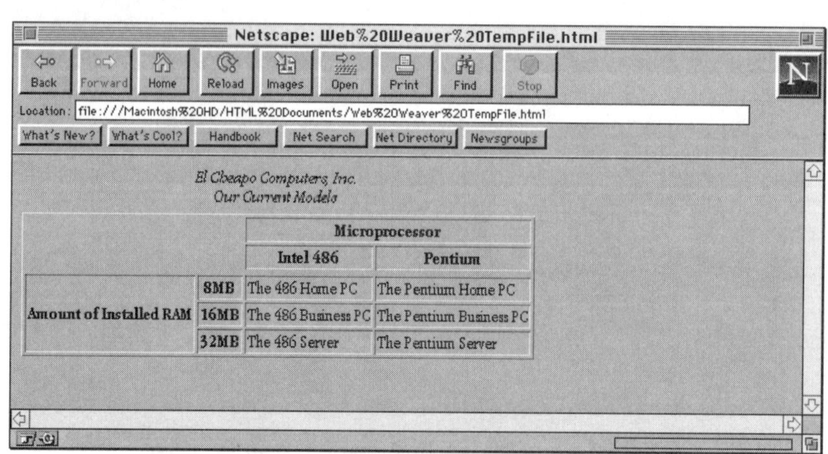

Figure 17.6 Spanning columns and rows

<TH COLSPAN=3> spans three columns, while the tag <TH ROWSPAN=3> spans three rows.

Here's the HTML that produced the table shown in Figure 17.6:

```
<TABLE BORDER>
  <CAPTION>
    <EM>El Cheapo Computers, Inc.<BR>
    Our Current Models</EM>
  </CAPTION>
  <TR>
    <TH COLSPAN=2></TH>
    <TH COLSPAN=2>Microprocessor</TH>
  </TR>
  <TR>
    <TH COLSPAN=2></TH>
    <TH>Intel 486</TH>
    <TH>Pentium</TH>
  <TR>
  <TR>
    <TH ROWSPAN=3>Amount of Installed RAM</TH>
    <TH>8MB</TH>
    <TD>The 486 Home PC</TD>
    <TD>The Pentium Home PC</TD>
  </TR>
  <TR>
    <TH>16MB</TH>
    <TD>The 486 Business PC</TD>
    <TD>The Pentium Business PC</TD>
  </TR>
  <TR>
    <TH>32MB</TH>
    <TD>The 486 Server</TD>
    <TD>The Pentium Server</TD>
</TABLE>
```

The Netscape Extensions to the <TABLE> Tag

If you're willing to risk adding some features that non-Netscape browsers won't be able to format, you can add some visual spice to your tables by

using the Netscape table extensions. Here's a quick overview of what you can do:

- **<TABLE WIDTH =** ***percent*****>** When used with the <TABLE> tag, the WIDTH attribute specifies how much horizontal space the whole table should occupy on the current display window. To make sure the table spans the whole display window, use <TABLE WIDTH=100%> (see Figure 17.7). If you prefer, you can type an exact pixel width.
- **<TH WIDTH=*percent*>, <TD WIDTH=*percent*>** Here, the WIDTH attribute specifies how wide a particular column should be. To specify that a particular column should occupy 25% of the current window, use <TH WIDTH=*percent*>. See Figure 17.8 for an example of reducing a column's width with the WIDTH attribute. You can also type an exact pixel width, if you prefer.
- **<TABLE CELLSPACING=*number*>** The CELLSPACING attribute controls the width of the borders separating cells. By default, the cells are separated by a border 2 pixels wide. See Figure 17.9 for an example of increasing the CELLSPACING attribute to 10.
- **<TABLE CELLPADDING=*number*>** The CELLPADDING attribute controls the amount of blank space *within* the cell (the default is 1 pixel). Figure 17.10 shows the effect of changing the CELLPADDING to 10.

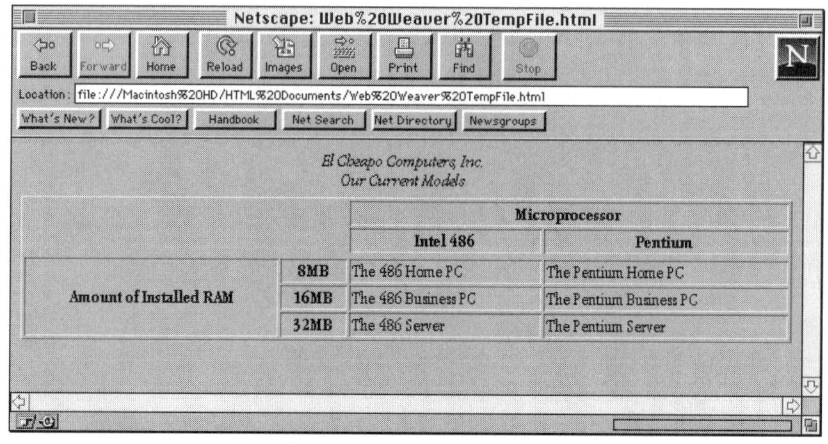

Figure 17.7 Table width set to 100% with WIDTH attribute

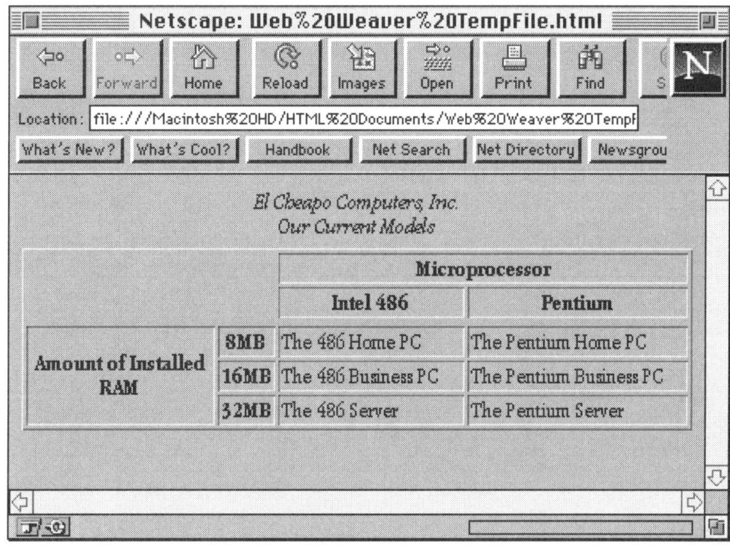

Figure 17.8 First column width set to 15% with WIDTH attribute

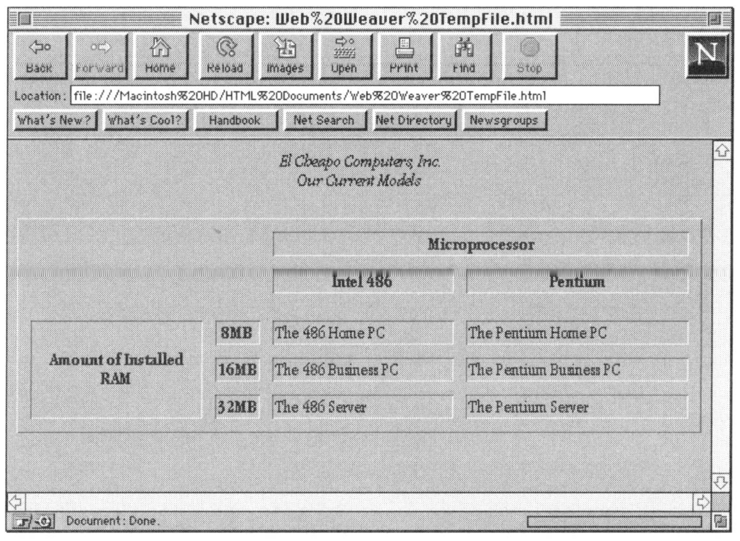

Figure 17.9 CELLSPACING attribute set to 10

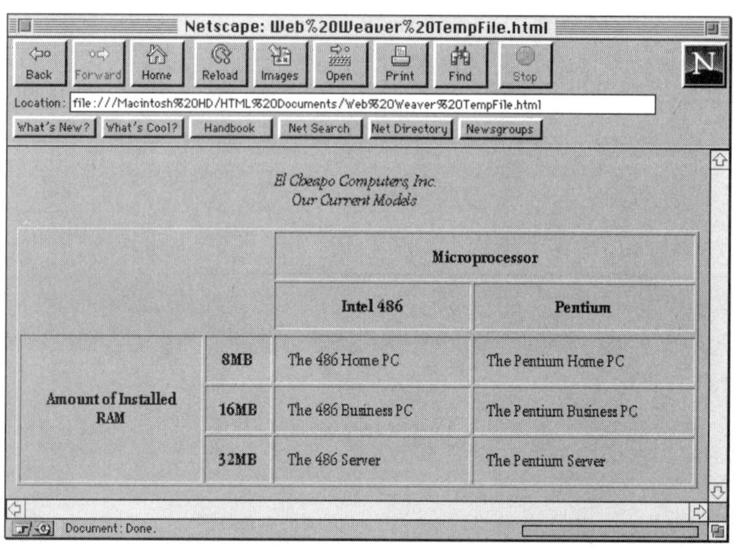

Figure 17.10 CELLPADDING attribute set to 10

Chapter 18

Using HTML Editor

The CD-ROM disc included with this book contains several valuable treasures, but one of the coolest is HTML Editor. Created by Dr. Rick Giles, a professor at Acadia University in Nova Scotia who enjoys canoeing and blues harmonica, HTML Editor frees you of the need to type long, elaborate HTML tags. It helps you organize your HTML documents logically, and enables you to concentrate on the content of your site rather than on the technical aspects of HTML.

In this chapter, you'll learn how to move HTML Editor from the CD-ROM disc to your Macintosh's hard drive and set it up for use. You'll learn the significance of the different parts of HTML Editor's screen display and how to use them to speed insertion of hyperlinks and other elements into your documents. Finally, you'll learn how to test the documents you create in HTML Editor; then you'll be ready to move on to the next chapter, which teaches you how to publicize the site you've created.

Rick Giles has a great set of documentation for HTML Editor on the Web. His manual is a well-organized collection of hyperlinks with which you should be able to find the answer to just about any question—or send electronic mail to Rick if you can't! You'll find the on-line manual and reference guide at

http://dragon.acadiau.ca/~giles/HTML_Editor/Documentation.html

You can download the latest version of HTML Editor from that site, too, if the version on the CD-ROM disc goes out of date.

For the Time-Challenged

- An HTML editor called, appropriately, HTML Editor appears on the CD-ROM disc that accompanies this book.
- You can install the uncompressed files on your hard disk by copying them directly from the CD-ROM disc to a special folder.
- HTML Editor's strength is in its ability to format body text elements. Usually, you just highlight the text you want to tag and click the appropriate button.
- Using the User Tags palette, you can speed the insertion of tags that HTML Editor doesn't support natively.
- Compensate for HTML Editor's poor basic-structure formatting ability by making a template—a file that you open each time you start HTML Editor, then save under a new name. The file can contain all the structural elements and any other features that you want in all your documents.
- Insert images and hyperlinks in your documents by positioning the cursor, clicking the Anchor or Image button, respectively, and entering a URL in the dialog box that appears.

Getting Started with HTML Editor

This section teaches you how to set up HTML Editor on your Macintosh's hard disk. If you want (to save disk space, perhaps), you can run HTML Editor directly from the CD-ROM disc—it's not compressed. Most likely, though, you'll want to copy the files from the CD-ROM disc to your hard disk so you can run the program with another disc in the CD-ROM drive. That way, you'll be able to listen to your favorite tunes while you weave your web.

This section also teaches you the significance of the various screen elements you'll see when you start HTML Editor. Once you learn what each screen element does, you'll be ready to move on to the next section, which teaches you how to write HTML with HTML Editor's aid.

Installing HTML Editor

In order to copy the HTML Editor files to your hard disk, you must first create a place to keep them. From the desktop, double-click your hard disk icon. You'll see all the files and folders in the main disk directory. Choose File, New Folder, and a new folder will pop up. Name the folder HTML Editor and open it.

Next, take the CD-ROM disc from the pouch inside the back cover of this book and put it in your Macintosh's CD-ROM drive. Double-click the CD-ROM icon, and open the HTML Editor folder. You'll see several files; select them all. Drag the selected files to the HTML Editor folder (the one you created on your hard disk) and let your Mac chug for a while while it copies the files.

When the CD-ROM drive stops spinning, close the CD-ROM folders. Double-click the HTML Editor icon that represents the copy of the program on your hard disk (The HTML Editor icon consists of a hand holding a pen and writing on a sheet of paper, superimposed in a big orange "W3"), and the program will start—your Mac's screen will look like Figure 18.1. Whoa! What's all that stuff? Keep reading.

Understanding HTML Editor's Display

Take a look at the button bar that tops the HTML Editor window. It features four drop-down lists, 11 pushbuttons labeled with icons, and a button bearing the words "Hide Tags." Here's a brief rundown of what those on-screen

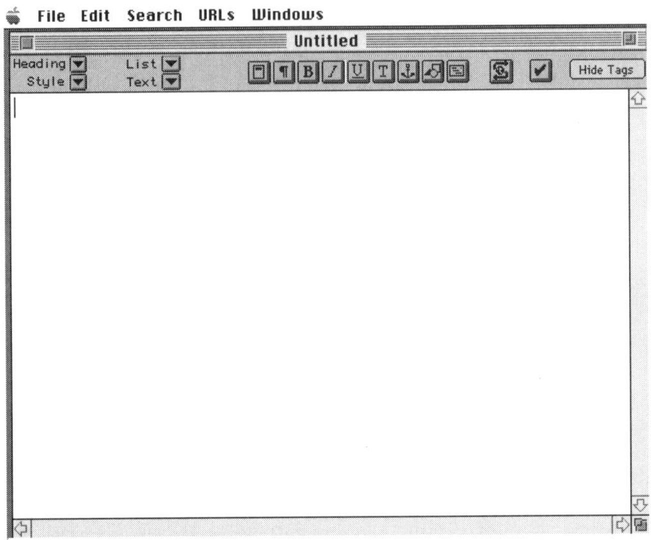

Figure 18.1 The HTML Editor display at startup

tools are called and what they do. This list correspond to the order in which the buttons appear, left to right.

Heading menu	Used to designate text with <H1>, <H2>, <H3>, <H4>, <H5>, or <H6> tags.
Style menu	Used to designate text with <EM>, <STRONG>, <CODE>, <SAMP>, <KBD>, <DFN> and <CITE> tags.
List menu	Used to tag text with <DL>, <DIR>, <MENU>, <OL>, or <UL> tags.
Text menu	Used to tag text with <LISTING>, <PRE>, <BLOCKQUOTE>, or comment tags.
Title button	Attaches the <TITLE> tag.
Paragraph button	Inserts the <P> tag.
Bold button	Inserts the <B> tag.
Italic button	Inserts the <I> tag.

Underline button	Inserts the little-supported <U> tag.
Typewriter button	Inserts the <TT> tag.
Anchor button	Inserts the <A> tag.
Image button	Inserts the <IMG> tag.
Address button	Inserts the <ADDRESS> tag.
Browser button	Starts your Web browser and tells it to display your document. The button keeps the Mosaic icon even when you configure HTML Editor to start another browser.
Restyle button	Renders any hand-typed tags in gray, and formats the hand-tagged text if HTML Editor knows how to do so.
Hide Tags button	Hides the tags to provide a crude WYSIWYG rendition of your document. When the tags are hidden, this button says Show Tags.

HTML Editor's menus generally follow Macintosh conventions, but they contain one neat but sort of arcane feature you'll need to learn to use. First, choose Windows, User Tags from the menu bar to see why HTML Editor is so flexible. The User Tags palette (Figure 18.2) lets you keep up with the latest HTML tags by adding them to a list. Add tags to the palette by clicking the Add button and typing the new tags into the dialog box. To insert the tags into your documents, double-click them.

Figure 18.2 User Tags palcttc

Writing HTML with HTML Editor

Now that you're oriented to HTML Editor's layout, it's time to do something with it. This section covers the routines you'll follow in coding HTML documents with HTML Editor. Remember, this section covers only the program's built-in functions—you can always add to them by adding new tags to the User Tags palette.

The Initial Codes

Here's a real shortcoming of HTML Editor: it provides no facility for automatically entering <HTML>, <HEAD>, <BODY>, or other tags that define the overall structure of HTML documents. You have to type these in by hand, or enter them in the User Tags palette and double-click them each time you want to insert them. If this annoys you (and if it doesn't, go into the bathroom and see if your pupils are the same size), set up a template. A template in HTML Editor is nothing more than a file containing basic elements that you open and then promptly save under a new name. This way, you can alter your basic template to fit your needs (by adding a company logo at the top, for example) whenever you want.

Creating the Body

Fortunately, HTML Editor makes up for its poor head-formatting capabilities with a lot of versatility in the body-formatting department. Most of the buttons and menus mentioned in the last section have to do with attaching formatting tags to body text. The User Tags palette still applies here, though it's not the only tool available, so you can teach HTML Editor to insert newly supported tags as they appear on the Web scene.

To designate text as body text (tagged with <P>), highlight the text and click the Paragraph button. You'll see small gray <P>. . .</P> tags appear at either end of the selection, and HTML Editor will format the text according to its definition of how the <P> tag should be interpreted.

HTML Editor handles headings the same way, except you have to click the Heading menu and pick the proper heading type from the list that pops up.

The way HTML Editor handles lists is pretty nifty, too—you highlight the text you want to include in your list, then choose the type of list you want from the List menu. HTML Editor automatically surrounds the list with the proper list tags (<UL>, <DL>, <OL>, or whatever) and puts <LI> tags in front of each list item. Look at Figure 18.3 to see how HTML Editor handles tag and text formatting.

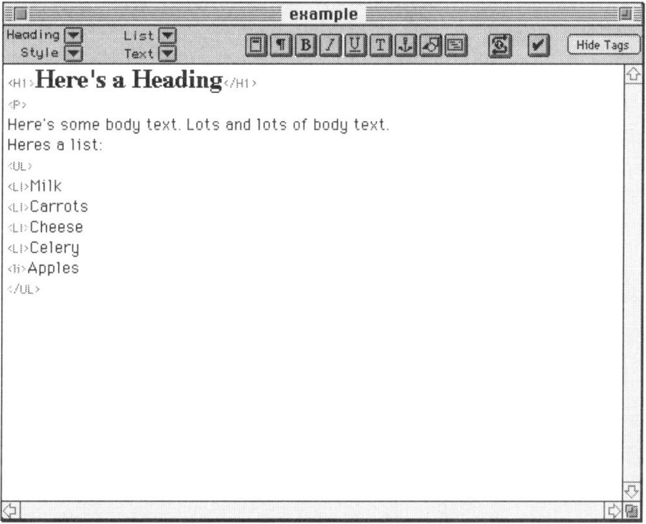

Figure 18.3 Text formatted in HTML Editor

Adding Hyperlinks

To insert a hyperlink into your document, highlight the text to which you want to attach the hyperlink and click the Anchor button. You'll see the Anchor dialog box (Figure 18.4). Type the URL—relative or absolute—to which the link should lead in the Name or Reference box (if you've referred to URLs before, they're listed in the box and you can choose from among them). If you're making a hyperlink to a remote Web resource, you can click the Construct button in the Anchor dialog box, which will call up the Reference dialog box. With the Reference dialog box, you can build URLs with some help from the program, but you'll still have to type the machine and directory names yourself.

Adding Images

The procedure for adding images mirrors the procedure for adding hyperlinks. Position the cursor where you want the image to go, and click the Image button. You'll see the Image dialog box (Figure 18.5), in which you can either enter the image file's URL yourself or click the Relative or Complete buttons, both of which let you choose an image from a folder window.

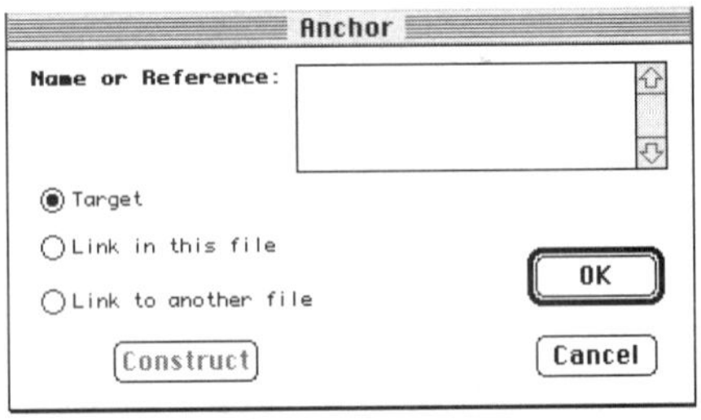

Figure 18.4 The Anchor dialog box

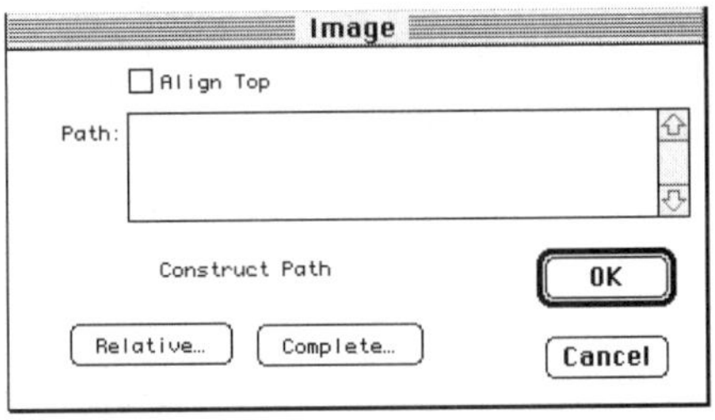

Figure 18.5 The Image dialog box

The difference between the two is that Complete inserts the whole URL of the image file, while Relative inserts only part of it. Note that HTML Editor only lets you attach the TOP value to the ALIGN attribute—you have to type other attributes by hand.

Testing Your Document

HTML Editor boasts a "semi-WYSIWYG" display. It can't be true what-you-see-is-what-you-get because, as you learned in Chapter 11, you never

know how—or even if—a browser will interpret a particular HTML element. To test your page, you'll want to load it into your Web browser.

HTML Editor makes it easy to do this, but its interface clues are somewhat arcane. To summon your Web browser and load your document into it, you click the Browser button—the one labeled with the Mosaic swash-and-globe icon. Even when you configure HTML Editor to start a different browser, as you'll learn to do in the next paragraph, the Mosaic icon remains on the button. This is an annoying but not crippling bug in the program.

To configure HTML Editor to start your browser, choose Edit, Preferences and click the lower Select button. Find your browser in the dialog box and click OK. Click OK in the Preferences dialog box, too, and the Browser button, when clicked, will start the browser you designated.

From Here

- Okay, you're up and running with a good HTML authoring tool. Now you're ready to learn how to publicize the sites you create with it.

Chapter 19

Publicizing Your Site

Once you've created your Web site, think back to the people you had in mind when you first planned your pages. Now is the time to let them know that a resource they will find useful has been posted to the Web. This chapter covers the various means by which you can let potential visitors to your site know it's available to them.

Direct Publicity

The marketers who send unsolicited snail mail know that people like to get mail—it makes them feel loved. Knowing this, they flood mailboxes with

flyers and brochures, hoping that some of the people they spam with junk mail will be persuaded to buy a product or service from them. Direct marketers have found that direct mailings have a much higher response rate than less targeted advertising, such as radio and television commercials.

You don't need to approach the advertising of your newly created site quite so cynically, but you can take a hint from junk mailers and know that by sending information about your product (your site) to the people it's designed for, you stand a better chance of winning attention for it than if you rely entirely on broadcast advertising. Your site will certainly gain more attention if you advertise it carefully than if you don't advertise at all and count on word-of-mouth and happenstance to garner attention for your site.

You should have identified your audience by now—so you should know how to reach its members, too. Take advantage of this fact and bring the news of your site directly to the people it's designed to interest. Write to them directly, if you can, or do the next best thing and post to a mailing list or Usenet newsgroup. This section deals with some of the ways in which you might be able to gain access to the electronic mailboxes of the people you want to use your Web resource.

For the Time-Challenged

- In order for your site to serve its purpose, you have to advertise.
- If you can, send e-mail directly to people you know will be interested in your site. Direct electronic mail gets a great response rate.
- Post announcements where you know people interested in your site's topic will see them. Mailing lists are best; Usenet newsgroups are good, too.
- Make sure you fill out the URL-addition forms at any search engines, including Lycos, that accept site submissions.
- Submit your site's information to the maintainers of the various What's New sites on the Web, including those run by Netscape and NCSA Mosaic.
- Post a notice to comp.infosystems.www.announce.

Tell Your Friends

It sounds simplistic and decidedly low-tech, but an old-fashioned invitation to friends to visit your site can improve traffic there tremendously. Your friends are also likely to include links to your site on their pages, making it more likely that casual Web surfers will happen across your resource. This is one way webs grow—with one friend linking to another's site, and so on.

It's also likely that at least some of your friends have interests similar to yours, so the links from their site can help draw more people from your target group to your resource.

Post to Mailing Lists

Though they're harder to find than Usenet newsgroups, mailing lists are second only to direct personal mail as an advertising medium. They get your message into the electronic mailboxes of the people you want to know about your site, forcing them to pay attention to your message for at least long enough to read your name and the subject header.

Since members of your target audience may *only* read your name and subject header before deleting your announcement, make sure you're descriptive in your choice of words. Something like "NEW RESEARCH AID" probably won't get much attention, but something like "BOTANISTS: Web Guide to Orchid Species Available" will at least merit a read from those interested in orchid taxonomy. Remember, the Web and Internet are different from television, radio, and other broadcast media because few people use the Web and Net just for fun—they're usually doing something related to their work. Assume that the people who read your mailing-list posting are in a hurry: explain the resource, give the URL (on a separate line so it's easy to copy and paste), and let the site speak for itself to whomever decided to give it a visit.

To locate lists of people interested in the subject of your site, visit the various search facilities on the Web (InfoSeek, Lycos, Webcrawler—a whole list appears in Chapter 7) and hunt for words related to your site's topic. Very often, mailing list moderators will include a mention of their lists on their home pages, so a full-text searching engine like Webcrawler may be your best bet, in case the moderator mentions the list near the bottom of his or her home page.

It's possible that the mailing lists you most want to advertise on are closed lists—you must be invited to join, or there's some sort of screening process. Often, the screening process is perfunctory, and consists entirely of

a check to see if you're on a list of people who disrupted the list in the past. If the screening process is more severe, as in the case of lists that require members to be college professors or other recognized experts in a field, send a message to the moderator or another individual on the list. Explain how you think members of the list will benefit by knowing about your resource, and ask the person to forward your material to the list.

Post to Usenet Newsgroups

Usenet newsgroups are not as good a place to advertise your new site as mailing lists and direct electronic mail for two reasons:

1. Usenet postings do not directly enter people's electronic mailboxes. It's easy for potential users of your site to miss your information because they chose not to read Usenet postings during the time your advertisement was posted.
2. Many fewer people use Usenet than use electronic mail. Those newsreaders that are easy to install (tin and trn, especially) are hard to understand, and those that are easy to understand (such as Free Agent and WinVN) are difficult to install. For these reasons, many people shun Usenet and stick with relatively easy-to-understand electronic mail.

To circumvent these potential problems, don't rely on Usenet totally. Instead, post notices to mailing lists and try some of the advertising methods suggested in the "Indirect Publicity" section of this chapter. The more places you make your site known, the more attention it will get.

When you do post to Usenet, follow general Usenet etiquette and frame your post carefully to ensure maximum impact:

- Keep your header brief and descriptive. Make sure that it says your post is about a new Web resource, and what that resource is for.
- Post your message several times—once a week for three weeks, say. This helps ensure that people hear about your site even if they missed your first posting because they were away or for some other reason were not using Usenet. Don't post too much to one group, though. Your site is only new for so long, and if you post the same message repeatedly, you'll annoy more people than you inform.

- Don't spam—post your announcement to two or three relevant newsgroups only. Resist the urge to post a copy of your message to every newsgroup with a topic tangentially related to that of your site. It's really bad netiquette to stray from the topic of a discussion group, especially when you're not a regular participant in that group.

Indirect Publicity

The whole point of carefully identifying your audience before getting into the specifics of planning and building your site was to decide who you wanted to make your site appeal to. Still, you should spread the word of your site to the general Web community, if for no other reason than to showcase cool HTML techniques in your site and give others ideas for how they might incorporate your organizational techniques into a site specializing in another topic.

Most of the people who peruse the resources described in this chapter have an interest in the Web for the Web's sake. They want to see neat HTML tricks and clever organizational techniques. Using the techniques described in this section probably won't bring in many more members of your target audience, but it will bring in some Webmasters, who may choose to tell friends interested in your subject about your site.

Search Facilities

Some search facilities, including the very popular Lycos search engine, have forms that allow you to add the URL of your site to the search engine's database. Adding your site to the database ensures that anyone who searches for the subject of your site—at least in the way you describe it on the submission form—will see the URL for your site.

What's New Pages

There are several What's New pages on the Web. These pages are supposed to showcase the latest additions to the Web and enable Web surfers to find new and potentially useful or interesting sites quickly. These What's New sites usually are based on a submission process: You send in the information

about your site, and the maintainers of the What's New pages decide if it's worth advertising.

The most frequently visited What's New sites are those affiliated with Web browser manufacturers. Typically, Web browsers call up their manufacturers' home pages when they first connect to the Web, and the What's New pages can be reached from there. The two biggest What's New pages (maintained by the two biggest Web browser developers) are:

- **The Netscape What's New Page** (http://home.netscape.com/home/whats-new.html) Submit your site's information to the Netscape editors by filling out the form at http://home.netscape.com/escapes/submit_new.html.
- **The NCSA Mosaic What's New Archive** (http://www.ncsa.uiuc.edu/SDG/Software/Mosaic/Docs/archive-whats-new.html) To have your site considered for inclusion in the archive, send electronic mail to whats-new@ncsa.uiuc.edu. Unlike the Netscape What's New Page, the Mosaic archive is exactly that—you can find the "new" sites posted anytime in the past two years.

Usenet Newsgroup comp.infosystems.www.announce

There's a Usenet newsgroup specifically for announcing new Web resources. It's called comp.infosystems.www.announce, and it's carried on all Usenet servers that handle the standard hierarchies. Post a brief description of your site to the newsgroup as a courtesy, but don't expect a lot of traffic to result from your posting. Comp.infosystems.www.announce is read mainly by Webmasters and other computer types, so unless your target audience includes these people, you won't draw much more of your market by posting there.

From Here

- By now, you've built a Web page and have made it known to the Web community. Now it's time to jazz up your page with multimedia—the graphics, sounds, and video clips that make the Web stand out from the rest of the Internet. Chapter 21 deals with collecting multimedia with scanners, microphones, and camcorders.

Chapter 20

Web Publishing Horizons

The Web is not a static medium. Television and radio haven't changed much in the past twenty years, but the entire development of the Web has happened in the past five years. Things are changing fast on the Web, and as a Web publisher, you need to be up on the latest innovations in order to keep the attention of your audience and to avoid becoming the equivalent of the only television station in town that broadcasts in black and white.

Late innovations on the Web—things that haven't yet been widely implemented, but probably will be before long—include Sun Microsystems' Java and HotJava, which will enable you to embed entire programs in your HTML documents, and Virtual Reality Modeling Language (VRML), which allows you to create three-dimensional Web documents.

This chapter doesn't aim to explain Java, HotJava, or VRML in depth—each section in this chapter merits its own book, and the technology is so new as to be very fluid anyway. Instead, this chapter serves as a heads-up notice to you as a Web publisher. You should keep the issues discussed here in mind as your site, and the rest of the Web, develops so that you can keep on top of the wave of technology that is part of the Web as a publishing medium.

For the Time-Challenged

- Virtual Reality Modeling Language (VRML, pronounced "vermal") is a set of markup codes that can be used to simulate three-dimensional spaces on the Web. The idea behind VRML is the elimination of "interfaces" by making computer applications interact naturally with human beings.
- VRML is still deep in the development stages. It will be a while before mainstream Web browsers support its tag definitions, though browsers like WorldView, VRweb, and WebFX already do.
- VRML 2.0 (the current standard is 1.0) will support such things as real-time interaction with others on the Web and the use of video as a texture for virtual surfaces. It will also probably support a virtual implementation of the laws of physics: virtual objects, when dropped, will fall.
- Go to http://vrml.wired.com/ for the latest information on VRML and its development.
- Java is a developmental programming language, designed by Sun Microsystems, that is loosely based on C++. It will work with the HotJava browser to enable HTML developers to embed applets in their Web pages. Sun claims Java is notable for its portability (it runs on any platform for which there is a HotJava browser).
- HotJava is a developmental Web browser. It differs from NCSA Mosaic and Netscape Navigator in that it recognizes the <APP> tag—the HTML tag with which you embed Java programs in HTML documents.
- You may want to investigate including VRML and Java technology into your site, if for no other reason than that sites with snazzy new features tend to get more attention than sites with yesterday's technology.

Virtual Reality Modeling Language (VRML)

Since the invention of electronic computers, there have been interfaces—the means (button bars, command lines, voice recognition systems, whatever) by which human beings communicate with machines. We've grown used to having to remember arcane commands, but some people realize that the goal of technology should be integration with the way human beings think. There shouldn't be a distinction between commands we issue to other people and commands we issue to machines. Mark D. Pesce and Tony Parisi realized that the Web needs an interface that approximates the real world. Their area of expertise is virtual reality "interfaces" for the Web.

Though the point-and-click concept behind modern Web navigation is intuitive, it's not life-like (you wouldn't point-and-click to get a cup of coffee in the morning). VRML (rhymes with "thermal") opens the door to virtual reality navigation of the Web. Though it's still very much in its infancy, VRML or a VRML-like Web navigation tool may enable you to "walk" from one piece of data to another, or fold a message into a "paper" airplane and fly it to its intended recipient. It's a new field (the first VRML helper application, Labyrinth, came out in mid-1994) and it's hard to say where it will lead.

How Does VRML Work?

VRML is a set of tags—as yet not standard and still being debated by a small group of experts—that allows Web browsers to display virtual environments defined in a VRML document created by a VRML programmer. In theory, VRML environments can take infinite forms. They can be just like the existing graphical Web interfaces supported by Netscape Navigator and NCSA Mosaic, or they can be much more elaborate three-dimensional worlds that you navigate with a special glove or some sort of whole-body interface. Popular browsers don't support VRML yet—you need a VRML-capable browser such as WorldView, VRweb, or WebFX.

As it stands, only VRML 1.0 is complete. Work continues on VRML 1.1 and 2.0. By version 2.0, VRML should support the following:

- Sound
- Animation

- Video files as textures (i.e., for use on a virtual television screen)
- Multiple participants (interaction with others in a single VRML environment)

How Can You Find Out More about VRML?

The state of the art in VRML changes almost daily. If you're interested in keeping up with developments in this new technology, you have to follow it on the Web. Your first stop should be the VRML Frequently Asked Questions document at http://www.oki.com/vrml/VRML_FAQ.html. Also look at the VRML Forum (http://vrml.wired.com/), where the latest information about VRML and the debate surrounding it appear.

Having looked at those sites and experimented with VRML a little yourself, you may want to join the WWW-VRML mailing list. This list, run by Mark Pesce, is the governing body for VRML—if you contribute meaningfully to this list, you stand a good chance of influencing the next VRML specification. Don't join if you're not familiar with VRML, since it's not a teaching list, and don't join if you shy away from technical discussions about programming languages. If you think you can contribute, though, send mail to majordomo@wired.com, leave the subject line blank, and put "subscribe www-vrml <your electronic mail address>" (without the quotes or brackets) in the message body.

Java and HotJava

In Chapter 14, you saw that it's easy to have graphics display as soon as someone calls up the Web page in which they're embedded, but before sounds, videos, or animations can play, users must click a special hyperlink. That detracts from your site. Wouldn't it be tremendously cool if, when someone loaded one of your pages, they heard a piece of music that played continuously while they viewed your page? Or if you could create a border for your page made up of animated guppies that swam in a rectangular path around their screen?

You've also probably encountered sites at which you fill out a form, send the data back to a server that performs a calculation, and then you receive some kind of report back from the server. Wouldn't it be much nicer to have the program loaded on your computer, and not have to send data to a distant computer, wait for free processor time there, and wait for the calculated results to return to you?

With Java and HotJava, to be released in 1996, Sun Microsystems may have made those things possible.

What's Java?

Java is a programming language loosely modeled after C++. It's used to write applications that you can embed in Web documents and run with the HotJava browser.

One of the cool things about Java is its distributed design. A traditional program on your computer, originally written in C++ or Visual Basic, say, might draw on routines stored in libraries in various directories. Java programs do the same thing, except they can draw on library routines stored anywhere on the Web. If Sun decides to upgrade one of its important library files, you wouldn't have to find it, download it, and replace the version on your computer. Instead, a Java program would know where to look for the routine and automatically get the latest version.

Java can run on virtually any platform. Whether you have a Macintosh or Windows 95-based computer, a UNIX or LINUX workstation, or a NeXT workstation running NeXTStep, Java programs will run. Java programs are device-independent, meaning they aren't compiled for particular computers. Instead, programmers tailor, or "port," the HotJava browser to particular machines, and then the browsers interpret the generic Java code to run on those machines.

For more information, read the Java White Paper at http://java.sun.com/1.0alpha3/doc/overview/java/index.html.

I want to attach a Java applet to a page of mine. How do I do that?

You embed Java applets with the <APP> tag. The <APP> tag is an open tag with one important attribute: CLASS. A typical use of the <APP> tag looks like this:

```
<APP CLASS="DonutCounter">
```

This code makes the browser look in the CLASSES directory—all Java programs should be kept in the CLASSES directory, which branches from the directory that holds your HTML documents—for a program called DonutCounter.class. The program will then run.

If a browser that does not understand the meaning of the <APP> tag encounters one, the browser will ignore the tag.

What's HotJava?

HotJava is a Web browser like Netscape Navigator or NCSA Mosaic except for its ability to handle the <APP> tag and the Java programming language. At this writing, HotJava is in alpha testing (early testing, generally within Sun) and should be out sometime in 1996.

The HotJava White Paper (http://java.sun.com/1.0alpha3/doc/overview/hotjava/index.html) calls HotJava "the coordinator of a federation of pieces." It draws on resources all over the Web and makes them appear in a logical order on your computer. The implications of this capability may prove tremendous. It means, for example, that you won't need helper applications installed on your computer—HotJava will know where on the Web to find the Java code to handle all media. It also means you'll always have up-to-date versions of all your software programs, since HotJava will be able to hunt for new program components and download them without special attention from you (unless, of course, you have to pay for the upgrades—and HotJava can handle secure transactions, so it can probably handle that, too).

What Do Java and HotJava Mean to You?

Right now, not much. Test versions of HotJava and Java for personal computers don't exist yet: It will be months before they make it out of testing, and another couple of months to see if they catch on. A potential flaw in HotJava is in bandwidth conservation—having to scurry all over the Web downloading bits of code might take a long time, especially on a slow dial-in connection, so Java and HotJava may not be the utopian browsing solutions Sun's literature makes them out to be. On the other hand, Sun may have figured out a way to compress the needed information and transmit it very quickly, and Java and HotJava may be the Perl and Netscape Navigator of late 1996 and beyond.

The technology is exciting, and if your site uses Java technology when HotJava first comes out, it will get a lot of traffic. The issue to consider is whether HotJava will be a fad or a long-term Web staple, and whether it is worth your time to learn Java and develop a page that incorporates it. Keep an eye on the Java site (http://java.sun.com/) for the latest news.

FROM HERE

- Read on to learn how you can produce multimedia for your Web site.

Part IV

Producing Multimedia

Chapter 21

Capturing Multimedia Material

Scanners, Microphones, and Camcorders

This chapter deals with the mechanics of acquiring multimedia information for inclusion in your Web publication. Discussions of scanners, sound hardware, and video hardware, as well as supporting software, are included in the following sections.

This chapter does not purport to be an exhaustive authority on capturing still images, sound, and video. Entire books—indeed, entire college-level courses of study—are devoted to these topics. This chapter is intended to give you a general overview of what is involved in collecting nontextual information. The ability to handle multimedia information is one of the Web's strong points; you'd be foolish not to take advantage of it.

Chapters 22, 23, and 24 deal with what to do with multimedia material once you've acquired it, since raw images, sounds, and video "footage" (the word, which stems from linear feet of film, is now technically obsolete)

require editing before they can be used with full effect. Chapter 22 deals with still graphics production, Chapter 23 with sound production, and Chapter 24 with video production. Chapter 25 explains how to use Adobe Acrobat software to incorporate documents with formatting beyond the capabilities of HTML into your Web site.

For the Time-Challenged

- Scanners are used to translate printed images into digital information in the form of graphics files.
- Scanners are operated with a special scanning program or a special routine in a large image-editing program like Adobe Photoshop.
- Before selecting an image, sound, or video clip for inclusion in your Web site, you should make sure the image or clip isn't copyrighted. You can get into serious legal trouble if you use copyrighted information, especially for profit-making purposes.
- Any multimedia item that you include in your site should be small, both dimensionally and in terms of storage required. Big multimedia files render your site unusable because they vastly increase the time required for downloading.
- To record sounds, you need a microphone and a sound card with a jack to accept the microphone. You'll also need a recording program such as Alchemy, Deck II, Session Software, or DigiTrax.
- If you need to record sounds in the field, away from your computer, you can record them on a cassette deck, then later feed the output of the cassette deck into the Line In jack of your sound card.
- To capture video images for inclusion in Web publications, you need a camcorder and a video capture card, as well as video capture software. You can use any camcorder, but a professional model with interchangeable lenses and advanced editing features will give better results.

SCANNERS

You've probably seen a scanner—the big flat thing on the desk of the desktop publishing guru at the office, or in the little computer room at Kinko's Copies. It's likely, though, that you've never used one. You know scanners are used to translate printed graphics into a form the computer can use, but you don't know the specifics. Now you want to include graphics in your Web publication and it seems you need to use a scanner in order to do that. This section explains the rudiments of translating printed images into machine-readable graphics files.

What's a Scanner?

A scanner is any device that interprets visual information in a way that makes it useful to computers. Under this definition, the bar-code readers and automatic door sensors at the supermarket are scanners, just like the flatbed scanners that translate printed information into digitized data. The scanners used to encode graphical data for the Web are flatbed scanners—those with glass panels like copier machines—or hand-held scanners, which you drag manually across material to be scanned.

Scanners are also distinguished by their ability to handle color information. Though grayscale scanners exist and are somewhat less expensive than color-capable scanners, the price difference isn't significant and color graphics are de rigueur on the Web. Color scanners are distinguished primarily by the color depths they handle. The best scanners have 24-bit color depth—they record each pixel of an image with 24 bits of data. Other scanners, which are entirely adequate for most Web work, have color depths of 8 bits. They assign 8 bits of data to record the color information for each pixel.

Resolution is a measure of the sharpness of images generated by a scanner. There are two kinds of resolution: hardware and interpolated. Hardware resolution is a real measure of a scanner's quality, since it is determined by the number of charge-coupled devices (the electronic devices that sense light reflected from the image to be scanned) in the scan head and the speed of the stepper motor that moves the scan head across the image. 300 dot by 600 line hardware resolution is good; 600 by 600 resolution is great; 600 by 1200 is excellent. Interpolated resolution, which uses a software algorithm to fill in extra pixels between those actually scanned, should be 600 by 1200 or better.

How much can you expect to pay for a scanner? As with a lot of things, you generally get what you pay for. A low-end hand-held scanner with 8-bit color depth and 300 by 300 resolution can be had for $250 or so, but you can expect to pay between $600 and $1000 for much nicer—and much more versatile—flatbed scanners.

Scanning Software

A scanner isn't much good without software to support it by handling file management tasks and basic image cropping and editing duties. Though your scanner may come bundled with a rudimentary scanning software package, a better program is almost certainly worth the extra investment. Good scanning software makes scanning images and preparing them for publication much easier.

What should you look for in scanning software? There's only so much to be done by software in the scanning process itself, and many programs handle the necessary tasks well. Make sure the program you choose allows you to adjust the color depth and resolution of the graphics file output and allows you to save the files in a variety of different formats. Also—this sounds silly, but it's vital—make sure your scanning software works with your scanner. Sometimes special libraries of code are needed to make programs work with certain hardware.

Scanning, in fact, is often an ancillary function of image-editing software. Programs like Adobe Photoshop, which are designed mainly to modify graphics files, can support scanning. Photoshop or a similar graphics-editing package is probably your best bet for scanner software.

Selecting Graphics for Scanning

The biggest concern when selecting graphics for scanning and subsequent inclusion in your Web publication is not the range of colors included in a graphic or the difference between its darkest colors and its lightest ones, though those criteria are important. The overriding concern in picking images to be scanned is copyright: whether the image you want to scan is in the public domain, or if someone owns the rights to it and can prohibit you from reproducing it.

All corporate logos fall into the protected category—if your name is Alice Teresa Thompson you can't legally put an AT&T logo on your site just to be cute. Most photographs in newspapers and magazines are copyrighted either by the publisher or the photographer, so you can't legally scan and

republish them. A good rule of thumb is to assume that an image is copyrighted unless an authoritative source—such as a note on the case for a CD-ROM disc full of images—says otherwise.

My site is already loaded with images that are probably copyrighted! How much trouble am I in?
You're in violation of the law, to be sure, but don't expect FBI agents to knock on your door any time soon. If you're using the images in a way that neither earns money for you nor detracts from the income of someone else, the worst you can expect is a letter from a lawyer warning you of possible legal action and telling you to take the images off the Web.

Corporations actually face something of a dilemma concerning use of copyrighted information on the Web: If somebody uses a copyrighted image to promote a product or company, are they harming the company or doing it a favor? Time will show the ways in which copyright law will change in the age of the Web. Chapter 27 offers a more in-depth discussion of Web copyright issues.

Once you've established that an image is not copyrighted and may be used in your Web publication, evaluate it for its technical suitability. Make sure the graphic is small, since giant pictures make sites take forever to download. Also, make sure the image has a good range of colors and a strong contrast between its dark portions and its light portions. You're ready to move on to actually scanning the image for modification in a graphics-editing program.

Scanning and Cropping

Place the image to be scanned on the glass deck of a flatbed scanner (or lay it on a flat surface for scanning with a hand-held scanner) and start your scanning software. The program you use probably gives you the option to set the scan resolution and adjust the color depth. Remember, scanners are designed to digitize images for printing on laser printers, which are capable of much higher resolutions and color depths than any monitor on which your Web publication will be viewed. Avoid setting the scanner for its greatest resolution and color depth, since those settings will result in a giant graphics file that will effectively go to waste on the Web, where its fineness cannot be seen.

Make sure to use the preview feature of your scanning program. Most scanning programs allow you to make a preliminary scan of an image, designate the part of it you want to include in the output file, and scan only that portion of the document in detail. Use the preview feature to save yourself trouble later—by using it, you'll save the hassle of having to trim unwanted parts of the image during the editing process (described in Chapter 22).

Graphics Libraries

The best way to get graphics for use on the Web is from a graphics library. Graphics libraries are CD-ROM discs packed with images of all sorts: photographs, line art, and graphical elements such as rules and boxes. There are several advantages to using graphics libraries such as the one encoded on the CD-ROM included with this book:

- There's no need to buy a scanner or elaborate, expensive editing software. All the scanning and editing is done for you.
- You can rest assured (if the library comes from a reputable manufacturer) that there are no legal strings attached to the artwork. You won't have to worry about getting a call from an angry photographer's lawyer demanding that you pay royalties.
- You're absolved of the need to develop artistic talent. Usually, professional graphic artists create the images included in graphics libraries and their work is of high quality (though there's a large variation in quality among collections of artwork).

What Do I Do Now?

Now that you've acquired, by whatever means, a graphic image in computer-readable format, what do you do with it? Chances are, the image could use some tweaking before you're happy with releasing it to the Web. Chapter 22 is for you. In that chapter, you'll learn how to use image-editing software such as Adobe Photoshop to modify graphics to your (and your audience's) liking.

Microphones

Your Web presentation won't be complete without sound, although sound is, compared to text and graphics, new to the stable of options Web authors

have for communicating their messages. In fact, many people don't think of a presentation as employing "multimedia" if it uses only text and still graphics. You need sound (and video) if you really want to get the attention of Web surfers raised on radio and television.

Many books have been written on communicating messages with sound (radio is a field of study in itself), and this section does not aim to compete with them. Here, you'll learn the basics of collecting sounds for use on the Web, as well as some essential information about sound-recording software and sound file formats.

Audio Hardware

Macintosh computers come with built-in sound support. Many late-model Macs have jacks for speakers and a microphone, but older and low-end Macs require a sound card—a special piece of hardware that fits into a NuBus slot. You can get a good-quality sound card for less than $200.

The actual conversion of sound waves into electrical impulses is handled by a microphone. You can plug a $10 microphone from the local electronics or stereo store into your Mac, or use the gray disk-shaped microphone that came with the system, but you'll get better sound quality if you use a better microphone that costs $30 to $50. You can drop several thousand dollars on a studio-quality microphone, but it's unlikely (unless your site is targeted at recording professionals) that visitors to your site will have the playback equipment to appreciate the improved quality.

Audio Software

You'll need software that enables you to control your sound hardware. The Mac System comes with Sound, which you access via the Apple menu, but the capabilities of Sound are very limited. If you're interested in producing sounds for the Web, invest in a program like Alchemy, Deck II, Session Software, or DigiTrax.

Recording in the Field

It's hard to record digitized sounds directly if they exist away from your computer. Bird calls, for example, or the sound of warning bells at a railroad grade crossing are hard to capture, as they require you to travel to a location remote from your computer and work in an area in which there is no electricity. Unless you have access to a high-end PowerBook, you're stuck with having to dub sounds taped on a traditional cassette.

To digitize a taped sound, connect the Line Out jack of your tape deck with the Line In jack of your computer. Play the cassette and record the signals coming into the Line In jack as if it were connected to a microphone. Though sound will be fine if you work with good-quality analog cassettes, you'll have better luck with digital audio tapes (DATs), which record with near-CD quality.

Prerecorded Sound Clips

As with graphics, your safest bet in terms of copyright law, technical quality and artistic merit is a collection of prerecorded sound files. Collections are available from several manufacturers, and there's a library of sounds on the CD-ROM included with this book. You can modify the sounds, which are licensed to be used by anyone who pays for them, as much as you wish, and chances are good you'll find a high-quality sound that matches your needs. Though the hardware and software required for sound collecting and editing is not as elaborate as that needed for still graphics or videos, recording sounds that cannot be heard within a few feet of your desktop is a chore, and it's probably worth it to invest in a library of prerecorded sounds.

What Do I Do Now?

After acquiring sounds, you need to modify and combine them before publishing them on your Web site. Chapter 23 teaches the technical and artistic aspects of sound editing.

CAMCORDERS

Video adds a lot to a Web publication. It draws viewers' attention because it is a moving picture in an environment that otherwise consists of static pictures. The production costs of video, both in terms of time and money, are greater than those of other media, and the cost prohibits many Web publishers from using video. If you can afford the cost, though, video will virtually guarantee that your site gets visited more often than sites without motion pictures.

This section deals with capturing live-action video, as opposed to animation, which can be done entirely with a standard high-end Macintosh system. Here, you'll learn how to capture video in the real world and transfer it to your computer.

Selecting a Camcorder and Tape

A camcorder senses light reflected from a subject and converts that sensed light into an electrical signal that it records on a magnetic tape. All camcorders serve that purpose, but there is considerable variation among camcorders in the quality and versatility with which they perform that task.

What kind of camcorder do you need to capture video images for Web publishing? Again, it depends on your needs. If you're just shooting one clip of the company president promoting the company's stock, you can probably get by with the VHS camcorder you bought to tape your kid's birthday party. If you have a more elaborate project in mind, you'll want a fancier camcorder. The Canon L2 offers interchangeable lenses, autofocus capability, and a variety of other attractive features that make it the camera of choice among videographers who don't want to invest in studio-quality equipment. Even the L2 will probably cost more than the rest of your computer system, so it's not an investment to be made unless you plan to do a lot of videotaping, for the Web or for traditional tape publication.

Buy top-quality tapes for your camcorder. Standard 8-millimeter tape will work, but Hi-8 tapes are better because there is very little degradation in image quality from one generation to the next and the tape maintains high resolution even after extensive editing. High-quality tapes also promise not to break or jam—which cheap tapes often seem to do at critical times in a taping session.

Other Video Hardware

In addition to the camcorder, you'll need a video capture card to convert analog video signals (either from the camera or from a recorded tape) into digital files that can be read by the computer. Video capture cards, such as the VideoVision Studio or Targa 2000, plug into NuBus slots and have ports that accommodate input from a VCR or camcorder. Video capture cards aren't cheap: the VideoVision Studio lists for $4,499 and the Targa 2000 lists for $5,495.

You'll also need a strong video adapter (the card that connects to your monitor). Make sure the card you choose has a 64- or 128-bit data bus and at least 2 MB of VRAM. Motion video puts gigantic demands on graphics hardware, so make sure your monitor is of high quality too. Experts say 40 MB of RAM is the minimum for video-capturing systems, and many desktop video producers use large arrays of hard disks (such as FWB's SledgeHammer*FT array or one of MicroNet Technologies' Raven arrays) for nonvolatile storage.

Video-Editing Software

You'll need a program to control your video hardware. The Avid Media Suite Pro offers support for high-resolution images, as well as support for Adobe Photoshop plug-in programs. Media Suite Pro is a start-to-finish video-capture solution, since it can handle the mechanics of capturing a video signal as well as editing frames of video. Adobe Premiere, another video-editing software package, doesn't handle physical capturing of video, but is very good at editing the contents of video files. Again, desktop video production isn't cheap. Expect to pay $1000 or more for the various software components of your editing system.

You can learn how to use video-editing software in Chapter 24.

Camera, Lighting, and Sound Technique

You can spend years in school learning about how to record moving subjects on videotape, and even then you need to spend years accumulating experience before you're considered any sort of an expert. This book can't begin to cover the details of good videotaping technique, but there are a few things you should keep in mind:

- Don't overuse your camera's zoom feature. It's best to cut directly from a wide-angle shot to a close-up, without the bore of watching the camera zoom in. Worst of all is zooming in and out on a static subject in a futile attempt to make it appear more exciting.
- Use some kind of stabilizer. Put your camcorder on a tripod or monopod, or just brace it against something stable while shooting. This will prevent "the wobblies"—an annoying characteristic of amateur video.
- Light your subject carefully. Bright sunlight isn't the best lighting for video, since it creates harsh shadows. Learn to use filler lights to soften shadows and bring out detail.
- Don't rely on the little microphone that's built into your camcorder. Instead, get a microphone that can be placed close to the sound source or clipped to the speaker's clothing.
- Shoot efficiently to minimize the need for editing later. If you can avoid shooting useless material, you won't have to waste time cutting it out.

Prerecorded Video Clips

As with still graphics and sounds, libraries of video clips are available. It is less likely these clips will be useful to you, though, since you probably want a video of a specific thing, such as your company president speaking or a salesman pitching your company's product. A generic video of a bear cub running around or a sailboat racing across a harbor probably won't solve all your video needs, but such clips might be useful as parts of a larger video presentation. And remember, clips on video libraries published by reputable manufacturers are royalty-free.

What Do I Do Now?

Capturing motion pictures for use in a presentation is just the beginning. You'll want to edit the files you've created, add titles, and include special effects. You might want to add voice-over narration or integrate animation with your live-action video. Chapter 24 covers all these topics in some depth.

From Here

- The next three chapters teach you what to do with the material you learned how to capture in this chapter. You'll learn how to prepare still images for the Web by cutting out the extraneous parts and giving them, where appropriate, a transparent background. You'll learn how to alter sound files by adding special effects. And you'll learn how to edit videos and add titles to them.

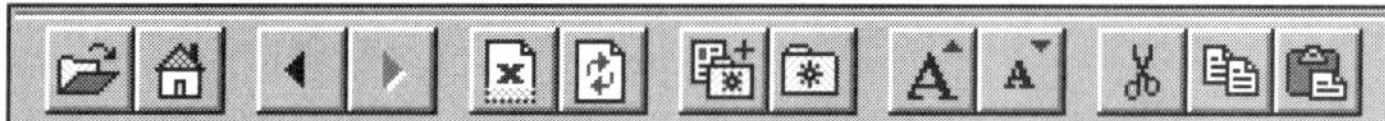

Chapter 22

Producing Still Graphics

The age of text-based interfaces for personal computers ended in 1988 with the wide adoption of Microsoft Windows 3.0, DesqView, and other graphical user interfaces (long after the Mac adopted them). Text-based interfaces survived on the Internet, however, until the Web made them obsolete in 1992 or so. The ability to embed graphics in text is one of the main reasons the Web caught on initially, and one of the reasons it remains the fastest-growing portion of the Internet today. Though it's neat to embed sound, video, and other special files in Web publications, no media but text and still graphics display automatically, without a helper application. You can't beat still graphics in terms of impressiveness per unit of time invested.

This chapter teaches you how to prepare graphics for publication on the Web. In Chapter 21, you learned how to capture printed images with a

scanner. This chapter shows you how to alter those images so they suit your site visitors'—and your own—needs. Among other things, this chapter shows you how to make GIF image files with transparent backgrounds, which can make your site look very clean and professional. Remember, though, that graphics is a giant field—lots of people make a living in it—and this section is merely an introduction to basic Web graphics skills.

For the Time-Challenged

- You can characterize Web graphics by their resolution (sharpness), color depth (the number of colors they contain), and the amount of memory they occupy.
- GIF images have poor compression (they usually take up a lot of storage space), but they can have transparent backgrounds (at least, images in GIF version 89a can). They're well suited to making icons, rules, and other small elements.
- JPEG images have good compression, but lower image quality and no transparency capability. JPEG images are good for large graphics, such as photographs.
- Adobe Photoshop is a very powerful image-editing program that allows you to create and edit images in innumerable ways. It's very expensive, though, and its elaborate features take some time to learn.
- Use Transparency to create GIF images with transparent backgrounds. To do so, open a GIF graphic in Transparency, click the region you want to make transparent, and hold the mouse button down. A palette of all the colors that appear in the graphic will fly out from the point you clicked, with the one you clicked shown as an "X." Release the mouse button if Transparency picked the right color, or select another color from the palette (you can choose the "None" box, above the palette, if you want no transparent colors). Choose File, Save as GIF89, and you've created a transparent GIF.
- Try to keep your Web images simple, small, and repetitive. By doing so, you'll save visitors to your site from having to wait while big images download. You'll also allow them to learn what certain icons and buttons mean—something they could not do if you didn't use the same images repeatedly throughout your site.

A Brief Introduction to Image File Formats

Image file formats are the ways in which your computer encodes the information that defines an image in a machine-readable format. Image file formats take the color, brightness, and contrast values that make images appear as they do and convert them into bits of data. Several image file formats exist, and each has strong points and shortcomings.

Before learning about the various file formats, though, you need to understand some basic facts about computer graphics. Some important terms:

- **Resolution** The sharpness of a graphic. Usually, you describe resolution in terms of pixels and lines, as in, "This is a 640-pixel by 480-line image." That means the image is 640 pixels wide and 480 scan lines tall—standard VGA size. Unless you're planning for visitors to your site to print your graphics out, you can get away with lower resolutions than in paper publications, as monitor resolutions fall far short of laser printer resolutions.
- **Color depth** The number of colors in a graphic. You describe color depth in terms of the number of bits used to encode each pixel, as in "24-bit graphics" or "4-bit GIF." A 4-bit image, though it can cost much more than 50 cents, contains only 16 colors and fits into a small file. A 24-bit image, in contrast, features more than 16.7 million colors—more than the human eye can distinguish—and requires a lot of storage space. Generally, keep your color depths low to avoid overloading your server with requests for giant files.
- **Compression** The ability of an image file format to fit a lot of graphics data into a small file. Compression varies from one file format to another, and often there's some kind of trade-off for high compression, such as a slight loss of color depth.

Although there are lots of image file formats, only two matter to those using a Macintosh to publish on the Web. Read about GIF graphics and the JPEG format in the sections that follow.

GIF Images

The Graphics Interchange Format (GIF) has been on the Web since its earliest days. Every major graphical Web browser displays GIF images without a helper application, and lots of shareware GIF editors exist to make creating

and modifying images easy. GIF images are known for their accurate reproduction of color, but also have a reputation for being big—JPEG images, described in the next section, employ a much better compression scheme.

Of most interest to Web publishers is GIF version 89a, which allows the use of a transparent "color"—a code, treated just like codes for red and blue, that makes pixels tagged with it assume the color of the background behind the image. You'll learn how to make GIF images with transparent backgrounds later in this chapter.

Do I have to pay a royalty for using a GIF image?
Although GIF images use a patented compression technique, you don't need to worry about getting a call from an attorney if you use a GIF image. A royalty must be paid, though, by companies that make software capable of creating and storing images in the GIF format.

JPEG Images

Developed by the Joint Photographic Experts Group (JPEG) of the International Standards Organization, the JPEG image file format employs an ingenious compression scheme with which it can pack huge images into fairly small files. The compression scheme relies upon tricking the brain by taking advantage of the fact that it can perceive differences in color less readily than differences in brightness. The JPEG format throws out some color information in order to conserve storage space—that's why it's said to use *lossy compression*—and keeps brightness information, which it uses to distinguish among different areas that once were of slightly different colors.

Most graphical Web browsers support JPEG images without a helper application now, so it's safe to include them in your Web publication. The JPEG format doesn't support transparent backgrounds (as GIF images do), so they're not useful as icons or other small elements, but because of its superior compression, it's preferred for large images. JPEG images download much faster than GIF images that take up the same screen space.

Using Adobe Photoshop

Experts regard Adobe Photoshop as the best image editor on the market. It's hugely powerful (it can handle everything from controlling a scanner to drawing an image freehand) and it's expandable (plug-in modules, sold by a

number of publishers, add specialized capabilities to Photoshop's impressive array of standard features). Photoshop provides you with the tools to create professional-caliber artwork on your computer.

On the other hand, Photoshop isn't cheap. It sells for about $500, and specialized plug-in modules can run $100 apiece. Scanners and other hardware you may want to use in conjunction with Photoshop will increase your total bill significantly. You'll want to stick with shareware image editors and prepackaged collections of artwork (such as the one on the CD-ROM included with this book) if you're not ready to sink a lot of money into Photoshop and the hardware to support it.

Creating New Images

Photoshop excels in editing imported images, such as scans or CD-ROM clip art, but it's also more than adequate for creating new artwork from scratch. Before you start creating new graphics with Photoshop, though, you'll need to understand the function of some of the tools available to you. Some of the most important ones include:

- **The Pencil Tool** Used to draw freehand lines. You can adjust the thickness and color of the line the Pencil tool draws by choosing options from the Brushes and Colors dialog boxes.
- **The Type Tool** Prints letters and numerals on your graphic. The Type tool is useful for creating buttons and descriptive icons.
- **The Paint Bucket Tool** Fills any selected area with a color.
- **The Dodge Tool** (the tool that looks like a circle on a stick) Simulates the photographic technique of "dodging," that is, hiding a small portion of an image from light so that it's lighter than the rest of the image.

You can use these tools and the others (Figure 22.1) with great flexibility, but remember that Photoshop can't handle GIF images without a special plug-in addition. You'll have to use another program to convert Photoshop images (in TIFF format or another non-Web format) into GIFs, to which you can add transparent backgrounds.

Altering Images

On the rare occasion that image-editing software makes it into the news, it's because someone used it to alter a photograph and then represented the photograph as an accurate representation of something. *National Geographic*

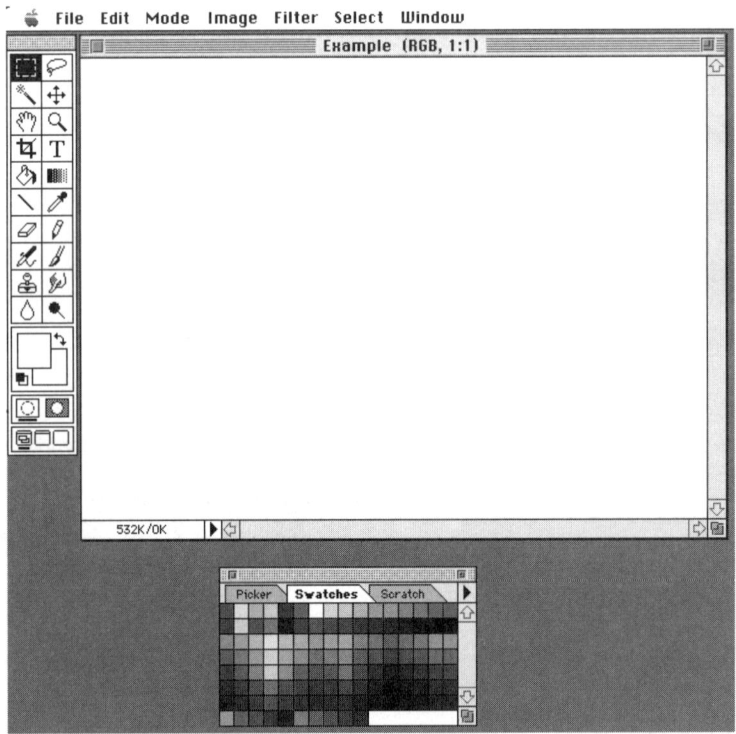

Figure 22.1 A new Photoshop document, with various Photoshop tool and color windows open

magazine's editors got into trouble once for moving one of the pyramids at Giza, Egypt, in a photograph to better fit on the magazine's cover. Photoshop will allow you to do tricks like that, and leaves the ethics of such editing up to you.

The Magic Wand tool identifies object edges automatically and therefore makes it easy for you to cut objects, such as pyramids, out of one portion of the image and either delete them entirely or paste them somewhere else. The Magic Wand tool works best in images with clearly defined elements—if different portions of the image are hard to distinguish, the Magic Wand's magic gets befuddled and you may have to help it identify the portion of the image you want to select. You can also select circular or angular regions of the image—see Figure 22.2.

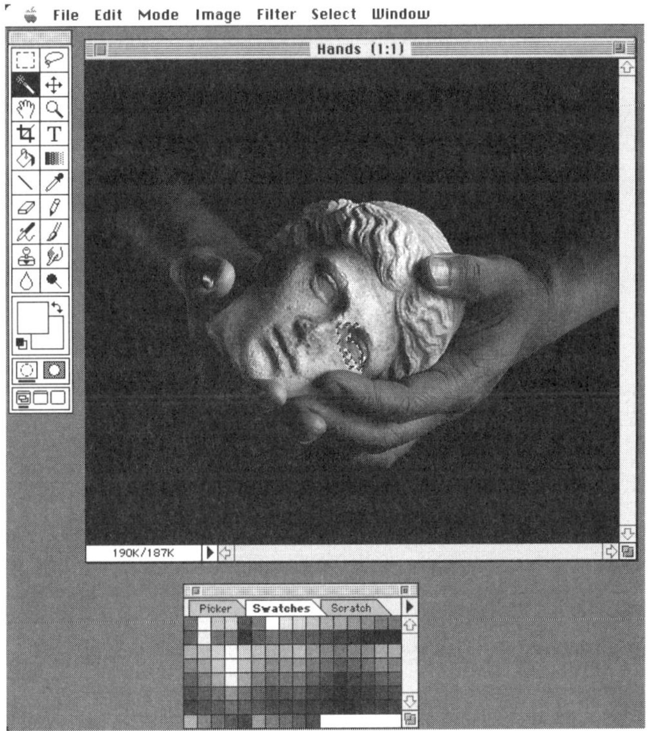

Figure 22.2 A scanned document in Photoshop, with a region selected for editing with the Magic Wand tool

The Rubber Stamp tool lets you blot out a portion of your image easily. Imagine you have a picture of yourself and your once-significant other at the beach, and, in a fit of anger, you decide to remove your ex from the picture. With the Rubber Stamp tool, you can carry out your petty revenge quickly and easily: just select the Rubber Stamp tool and hold down the Option key while you click on some nondescript sandy portion of the beach scene. This "loads" the Rubber Stamp tool. Then, perhaps giggling happily, you can release the Option key and click with the Rubber Stamp tool all over your one-time love. This covers the image of him or her with the image of the sand, effectively removing him or her from the scene.

Using Transparency

Written by Aaron Giles, Transparency defines the phrase "quick-and-dirty." It does one job—making transparent GIF images on the Mac—does it well, and does absolutely nothing else. The documentation that comes with Transparency is less than two pages long, and it includes more than a page about the GIF format in general, WWW browser support for transparent GIF images, and the revision history of the program. There's not a lot involved in understanding Transparency. In this section, you'll learn how to acquire Transparency on the Web and how to use it to make slick-looking buttons, icons, rules, and other images with transparent backgrounds.

Acquiring Transparency

You should check the Cornell University ftp archive (ftp://ftp.med.cornell.edu/pub/aarong/transparency) for the latest version of Transparency. When you download the stuffed file, you'll get the Transparency executable file, as well as a set of release notes and the Transparency documentation.

Making Transparent GIF Backgrounds

The process by which you give images transparent backgrounds with Transparency is fairly easy, once you understand the steps, but it's far from intuitive. You have to follow these steps carefully in order to create a transparent background—the process isn't one you'd soon figure out on your own.

1. Identify an image suitable for a transparent background. You want an image in which the foreground image is distinct from the background image. The picture of the tree shown in Figure 22.3 is a good example. The tree is clearly separated from the white background. If the tree had been in a jungle or something, this would not be a good picture to use.
2. To make the white background transparent, click the background and hold the mouse button down. You'll see a palette of all the colors that appear in the graphic fly out from the point you clicked, with white shown as an "X" (Figure 22.4). Release the mouse button if Transparency picked the right color (in this case, it did), or select another color from the palette (you can choose the "None" box, above the palette, if you want no transparent colors).

Figure 22.3 An image that needs a transparent background

Figure 22.4 A palette of colors in Transparency, with the color to be made transparent crossed out

Figure 22.5 Transparency's File menu

3. Choose Save as GIF89 from the File menu (Figure 22.5), and you've created a transparent GIF. Try opening your trial image in your Web browser as a test. You'll see that the background hides equally well in dark backgrounds (Figure 22.6) and in light ones (Figure 22.7).

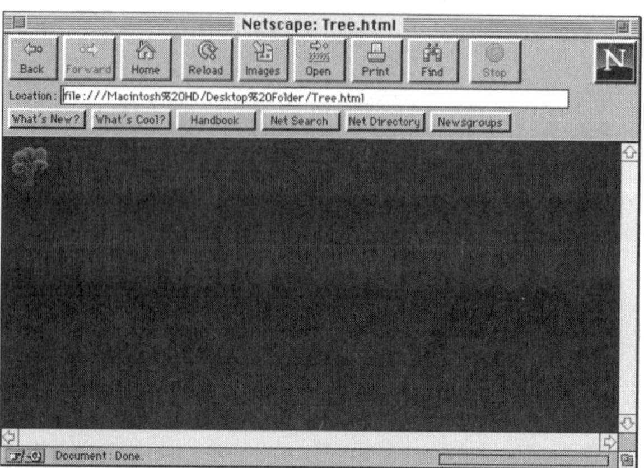

Figure 22.6 The tree with a transparent background, superimposed on a dark Web browser background

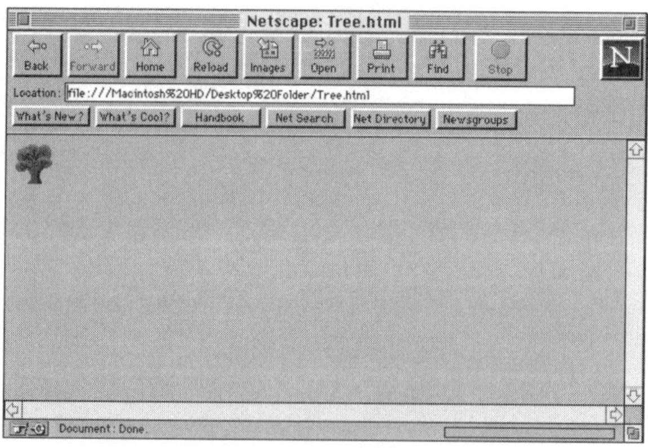

Figure 22.7 The tree with a transparent background, superimposed on a light Web browser background

I made my background transparent—I followed the steps you laid out—but there's still a discolored rectangle around my images when I view them with Netscape Navigator. What's up?

A bug in Netscape, that's what. The portion of Netscape that interprets the transparent "color" code in GIF images doesn't work properly, and you'll often see a "halo" around images you've assigned transparent backgrounds. There's absolutely nothing you can do about this, except hope that future versions of Netscape Navigator interpret transparent backgrounds better.

Graphics Production Hints

Again, this book isn't large enough to include all the information that deserves to be in this section. Since the days of the first cave-dweller who scratched a picture of his dinner on the wall of his home, human beings have tried to understand what makes one picture appealing and another picture repulsive. This book doesn't purport to be a textbook for students of the visual arts.

This section includes a few hints about how to make your graphics look good on the Web, a publication venue that's still foreign to most graphic artists. Between the hints here and the expertise of someone with some artistic skill and design sense, you should be able to generate some good-looking still graphics that take advantage of the Web's unique characteristics.

Keep It Simple

Don't try to dazzle your audience by using hundreds of colors and lots of elaborate shapes, especially when designing icons, rules, and buttons. Often, you can achieve great impact with simple color schemes and basic, unadorned shapes—less is often more on the Web. Also, by sticking to a simple color scheme, you prevent the problem of having a site visitor get some unseemly blob where your beautiful icon is supposed to be, simply because the site visitor's hardware isn't capable of handling the colors you put into the graphic.

Keep It Small

Big graphics require big bandwidth. Small graphics add flavor to your site without placing too much burden on your visitors' connections. If you load your site up with giant, high-resolution images, your pages will take forever to download, especially if lots of other busy sites use the same server. Keep

your graphics small—or, if your subject requires large photographs or other graphics, put them on their own pages and warn visitors about download time before they follow hyperlinks to those pages.

Take Advantage of the Cache: Repeat Images

When a Web browser downloads an image for use in displaying a Web document, it stores it in a cache. It can draw on images in the cache if they're called for again. When designing your site, make sure you repeatedly use the same graphics. Not only does this give your site a consistent look (visitors quickly learn what the various icons mean and what various buttons do), it reduces the load on your visitors' connections to the Web. Their Web browsers need only download the repeated images once, then retrieve them from the cache.

From Here

- Read on for the next portion of your education in preparing multimedia for your Web publication: producing audio.

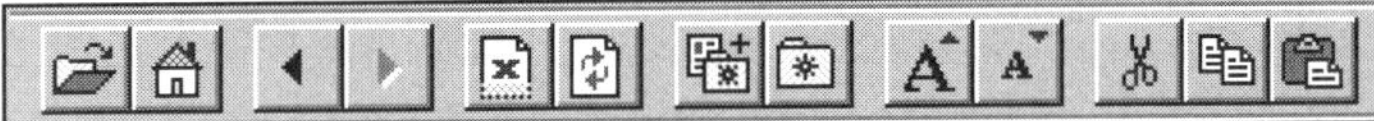

Chapter 23

Producing Audio

You learned about the HTML aspects of embedding sounds in your Web documents when you read Chapter 14, but you're probably still wondering about what those hyperlinks should connect to. You'rc probably not a sound engineer, and the last of your artistic inclination may have perished when you went back to school for that advanced degree. Yet you still need to produce attractive and technically slick sound files for your Web site.

What's the answer? This chapter. While a single chapter of a book can't teach you even the most rudimentary basics of sound production, and certainly can't endow you with creative talent, a chapter of a book can teach you enough to get sounds onto the Web. You learned about capturing audio—recording sounds with a microphone—in Chapter 21. This chapter gives you some idea of what you do after you've collected material. You'll

learn about various sound formats, as well as how to edit sounds and modify them to produce a variety of special effects.

This chapter focuses on Kaboom! Factory, a product of Nova Development of Calabasas, California. I chose to write about Kaboom! Factory because it's a great program that handles all the basic tasks of producing sounds for the Web, and it's not too expensive at around $35. Kaboom! Factory comes with a library of sound files and the Kaboom! Control Panel, which lets you associate sounds with certain system events. Other good Mac sound editors exist, to be sure. Check out DigiTrax and Session Software.

A Guide to Sound File Formats

On the Web, you'll encounter sounds encoded in a variety of ways. Each of these file formats has its advantages and disadvantages. Some of the common sound file formats are listed below:

.AU	The file format generated by Sun and NeXT workstations
.WAV	Windows' favorite file format
.RA	The RealAudio format that allows you to start playing a sound before it downloads entirely
.MID	The MIDI format, designed to simulate musical instruments
.AIFF	A format used mainly by Amiga and Macintosh computers
.VOC	A fairly obscure file format developed by Creative Labs

Put your sounds in a common format. If you don't, you run a serious risk of having your site's visitors download a sound only to find that they don't have the proper helper application for playing it, so they move on to friendlier sites. Generally, .WAV is your best bet, but .AU is widely supported, too. Use RealAudio format when your clips are long—several sites use that format for half-hour recordings of radio broadcasts—but be aware that the sound quality supported by RealAudio files is rather poor.

For the Time-Challenged

- Sounds come in a variety of sound file formats. It's important to use a popular format, such as .WAV or .AU, so visitors to your site won't have to find a helper application before they can play your files.
- Kaboom! Factory is part of a $35 software package called Kaboom!, published by Nova Development. It lets you edit sounds with sufficient flexibility for Web publishing. Most Mac software dealers carry Kaboom!.
- With Kaboom! Factory, you can adjust the sampling rate and resolution with which you record sounds. A sampling rate of 44,100 Hz and a resolution of 16 bits guarantees a high-fidelity file, but at a cost of lots of memory.
- Kaboom! Factory supports cutting and pasting portions of sound, just like a word processing program supports cutting and pasting text.
- Adjust the size of a selection by holding down the Option key and dragging an endpoint of the selection with the mouse.
- Generally, keep your sound files small to save bandwidth.
- Make sure all the files on your pages play at about the same volume, to keep visitors to your site from having to adjust their speaker controls repeatedly.

Sounds in a given file format may have a variety of *resolutions* and *sampling rates*. Essentially, resolution and sampling rates are measures of the quality of a sound—sampling rate describes the number of times a sound was measured each second, and resolution describes the number of bits assigned to record each sample. A sampling rate of 44.1 Hz corresponds to compact-disc quality sound; lower sampling rates indicate correspondingly lower sound quality. 16-bit resolution is superb; 12-bit resolution works for everything but music; you should avoid 8-bit resolution for all but the simplest sounds (such as beeps and whistles). Remember, though, that higher sampling rates and resolutions yield larger sound files, so use the lowest values you can. It may be worthwhile to include poor-quality sound files that site visitors can download and evaluate before deciding to download a better-quality file.

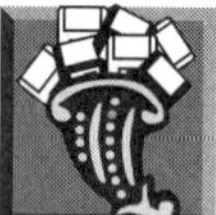

For an in-depth discussion of sound file formats, sampling rates, resolutions, and all the other technical aspects of sound recording and reproduction, look at the Audio File Formats FAQ assembled by Guido van Rossum. Part 1, the body of the document, appears at

http://www.cis.ohio-state.edu/hypertext/faq/usenet/audio-fmts/part1/faq.html

Part 2, the appendices, is at

http://www.cis.ohio-state.edu/hypertext/faq/usenet/audio-fmts/part2/faq.html

Recording Sounds with Kaboom! Factory

This section covers the mechanics of controlling your sound hardware with Kaboom! Factory (Chapter 21 covered sound hardware itself). Figure 23.1 shows the main Kaboom! Factory window.

When you're ready to record a sound with Kaboom! Factory, choose New from the File menu. If you want to use Kaboom! Factory's default sam-

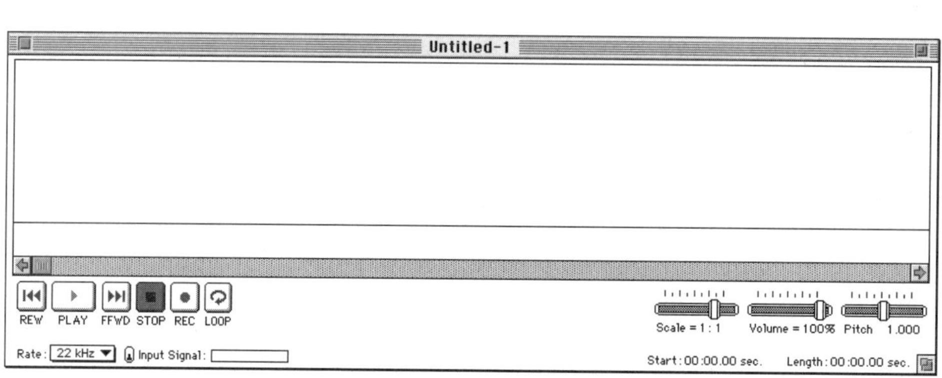

Figure 23.1 Kaboom! Factory

pling rate option (11,000 Hz), move directly to the "Recording a Sound" section. The next section describes how to adjust the sampling rate.

Setting Resolution and Sample Rate

To adjust the sampling rate, use the drop-down list box in the lower-left corner of the Kaboom! Factory window. You can choose between sampling rates of 22,050 Hz (FM radio quality) and 11,000 Hz (telephone quality). Don't forget that by using the higher sampling rate, you'll create a larger sound file and may have trouble getting your computer to record. If you can't record with a sampling rate of 22,050 Hz, try closing other applications to free some memory.

Recording a Sound

Recording a sound with Kaboom! Factory is just like recording a sound on a traditional tape recorder. You click the record button and record the sound you want with your microphone. Click the Stop button to end recording.

If you think you captured the sound you want, click OK to close the Record sound dialog box and return to the main editing window. In the main editing window, you can fine-tune the recorded sound until it meets your needs. The next section covers editing sounds.

Modifying Sounds with Kaboom! Factory

If you found a sound on the Web that has some redeeming portion but is otherwise loaded with useless chaff, you'll need to use Kaboom! Factory to trim out the unwanted portions. Likewise if you recorded a sound yourself and want to, um, cut out the, uh, parts you don't, you know, want.

When you open or record a sound in Kaboom! Factory, you'll see a graphic representation of the sound in the main editing window (Figure 23.2). The graphic representation of the sound isn't terribly useful unless you have a lot of experience with sound editing or your sound is made up of distinct parts with silence between them (such as a series of gunshots), but by placing the cursor at various points in the graphic representation, you can isolate the portion of the sound with which you want to work.

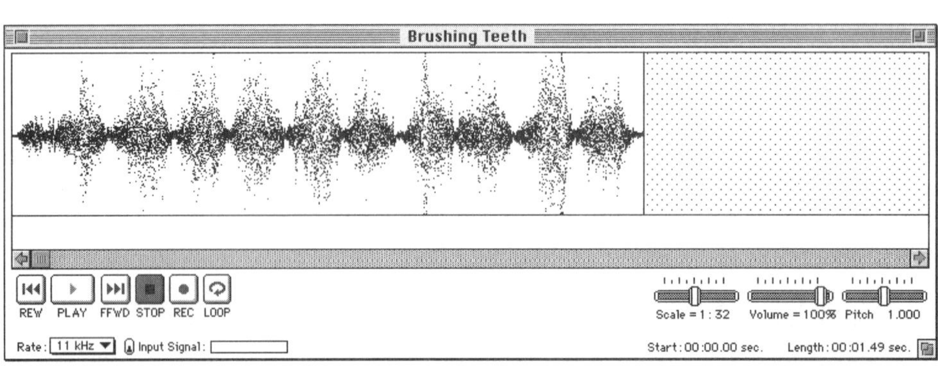

Figure 23.2 A graphical representation of a sound file in Kaboom! Factory

Selecting a Portion of a Sound

To select only part of a sound, drag the mouse pointer across the portion you want to select. You'll see a black highlight over the selected area (Figure 23.3). If you decide, perhaps after using the Play button to examine the selected portion, that the selection is not the right length, you can relocate

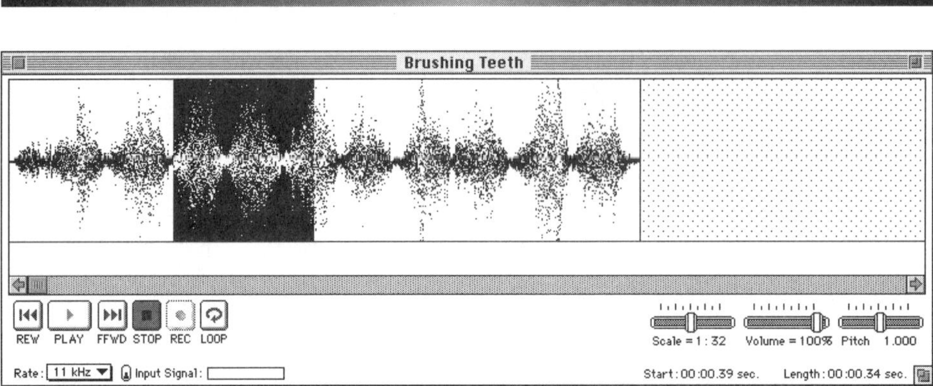

Figure 23.3 A selection in Kaboom! Factory

either end of the selection. Do this by holding down the Option key while dragging the edge of the selection left and right.

Cutting and Pasting

You can cut and paste portions of sounds in Kaboom! Factory just like you can cut and paste passages of text in your word processing program. Just highlight a selection and choose Cut or Copy from the Edit menu (or click the corresponding button on the button bar). Then, to insert the clipped sound into the same (or another) sound file, choose Paste from the File menu or click the Paste button on the button bar.

Kaboom! Factory also supports drag-and-drop editing. To move a highlighted section of the graphical representation of the sound, hold down the Command and Option keys, and drag the selection to another point with the mouse (the vertical line in the middle of the rectangular box shows where Kaboom! Factory will insert the selection when you release the mouse). To use drag-and-drop to copy a selection so it repeats at some other point in the clip (or in another one), hold down only the Option key while dragging the selection.

Using the Mixer Palette

From the menu, choose Window, Show Mixer. You'll see the Mixer Palette (Figure 23.4) appear on your screen. With the Mixer Palette, you can sequence sound files or portions of sound files, adjust the order in which Kaboom! Factory plays them, and save the edited sequence to a sound file. You might find the Mixer Palette useful for inserting sound effects between narration clips—thereby creating an "illustrated" sound narrative.

Organized as a series of "tracks," you should think of the Mixer Palette as a timeline with the beginning at the leftmost edge and the end at the right. When your Mac plays the sounds you arrange in the Mixer Palette, it starts at the left and moves rightward. If you arrange one sound under another, both sounds will play simultaneously—which is useful, for example, if you want the applause at the end of one music track to overlap the initial chords of the following song. To move a sound clip in the Mixer Palette just click on it and drag.

When you're done arranging sounds in the Mixer Palette, choose Window from the Mix To drop-down list box in the lower-left corner of the Mixer Palette, and click the Mix button. Kaboom! Factory will compile your arrangement to a new window, from which you can save it to a file.

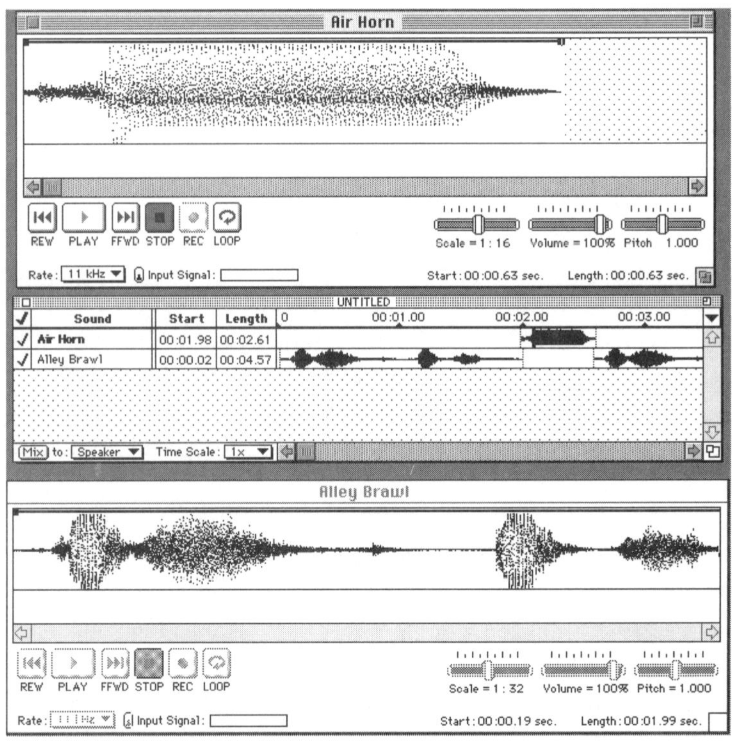

Figure 23.4 The Mixer Palette

Changing the Volume

If you recorded a sound at the wrong volume level or you've found a sound that's much louder or softer than the other sounds on your Web publication, you'll need to adjust the volume. Kaboom! Factory makes it easy to increase or decrease the volume of an entire sound file, or just a portion of one. Be careful about increasing the volume of a sound file, though—too much volume quickly leads to distortion.

Note that the Volume control in the lower-right corner of the Kaboom! Factory window and the Volume control in the Preferences dialog box don't alter the volume of the sound itself—they just increase the volume at which it's played back. To change the volume of the sound, you need to use the Amplify command or the Normalize command.

To use the Amplify command, choose Effects, Amplify from the menu and enter a percentage in the dialog box. One hundred percent represents no change, 120 percent indicates a 20-percent increase, and 80 percent indicates a 20-percent decrease.

The Normalize command makes the volume as loud as possible without introducing distortion. To use it, choose Effects, Normalize. You may find that the Normalize command is a good way to make all the sounds on your Web site play at the same volume.

Other Effects

Kaboom! Factory boasts lots of effects generators—you can waste tons of time applying effects to sounds in different strengths and combinations. You can find all of Kaboom! Factory's special effects under the Effects menu on the menu bar and can apply these effects to the entire sound or just portions of it. Some of the effects are as follows:

- **Echo** Allows you to set the delay time and strength of the echo, and simulates sounds made in a tunnel. If you apply echo to an entire sound, don't forget to add some extra time at the end to allow the echo to fade away naturally.
- **Reverb** Similar to Echo, Reverb simulates specific venues, including concert halls and basements.
- **Flange** A weird, metallic, psychedelic effect. Use Flange sparingly, unless you're up for some really mutant sounds.
- **Reverse** Allows you to reverse files—the same thing as spinning LP records backwards with your finger to hear deviant messages from recording artists.
- **Smooth and Sharpen** Makes waveforms more rounded or more angular, respectively. Choose the criteria you want from the dialog box, and achieve some unusual results.

For weird effects, you can adjust the Pitch slider in the lower-right corner of the Kaboom! Factory window, then choose Effects, Apply Pitch to make the changes to the waveform. Remember that percentages greater than 1 percent represent stretching (sounds are slower), and percentages less than 1 represent shrinking (for Chipmunk-like effects). You can also choose Playback Rate from the Effects menu and adjust the rate at which the program plays back samples to accomplish the same effects.

Saving Sounds in Kaboom

Unless you tell it to do otherwise, Kaboom! Factory saves sounds in a proprietary format. Be sure to use the File, Save As command and save your sounds as either .AIFF or .WAV files. Use .WAV files unless you have a good reason not to do so—many more people have .WAV helper applications than have .AIFF helpers.

Hints for Successful Sound Production

This section attempts to distill some basic wisdom about sound production into a few key points. Obviously, this isn't all there is to sound production, since working with sound is an art and a science that requires years of education and experience to master. Still, this is a start, and if you follow these hints, you'll be ahead of many Web publishers in terms of sound quality.

Keep It Short

Often, you can bring to mind an entire piece of music (or the television show or movie with which it's associated) with just a short clip. All that's necessary to bring to mind all the cultural baggage associated with *Star Trek* is the "These are the voyages of the Starship *Enterprise*" portion of the show's intro. You can suggest either American patriotism or baseball with the first few bars of *The Star-Spangled Banner*—there's no reason to reproduce the whole song.

Keep It Small

This follows from the previous paragraph, but with the added consideration of resolution and sampling rate. There's no need to record simple beeps and buzzes at 16-bit resolution with a 44.1 Hz sampling rate—that creates huge files and wastes bandwidth. Instead, use high resolutions and sampling rates for music and other applications in which sound quality figures prominently and stick with 8-bit resolution and 22,050 Hz sampling rate for less quality-critical situations.

Keep the Volume Consistent

Nothing is more annoying than having one sound on a site be very loud and the next one barely audible. Don't make visitors to your site adjust their volume settings repeatedly—make all your sounds audible but not overpowering at a common speaker-volume setting. You should do volume adjustments in the production phase—your site visitors shouldn't do them while surfing. Try the Normalize command.

Remember the Visitor's Hardware

Don't put CD-quality sounds on your site if members of your audience typically use their computers' internal speakers. Likewise, don't put sounds with 8-bit resolution and 11,000 Hz sampling rates on a site designed for people with direct, high-speed network connections and fancy sound hardware. Pay attention to the planning you did before building your site.

From Here

- Sounds are cool, but by themselves they're so...*1935*. Flip to the next chapter and get into the really cuspy stuff—video production.

Chapter 24

Producing Video

Until relatively inexpensive videocassette recorders became available in the early 1980s, home video involved great expenditure and technical challenge. If you wanted to watch recorded movies at home on demand, you had to invest in what amounted to a small television production studio, complete with a skilled technician—and that enabled you only to tape video from television and play it back later. Those dark ages of home video parallel the state of personal-computer video production today.

It's *possible* to produce video on your personal computer, but only by the same token that it's possible to run all your household utility functions with your computer, too. Video production requires, at minimum, a top-of-the-line Power Mac with a lot of RAM and a good monitor—and that only allows you to edit video. If you want to capture your own material (and you probably do, since stock footage of a caribou grazing or a bicycle whizzing

by probably won't convey your persuasive or artistic message), you'll need a camcorder, a VCR, and a video capture card—an investment that can easily total more than $10,000. Take a look at Chapter 21 for a more complete discussion of videotaping real-world action.

In short, true taping-to-broadcast video production is not within the capabilities of most Web publishers. If it's what you want to do, several fine books on the topic exist—this chapter doesn't pretend to compete with them. Here, you'll find a brief, basics-only introduction to video editing with Adobe Premiere, a program widely considered the finest desktop video editor ever published. After reading this chapter, you'll be able to modify video clips to fit your needs—whether you find the clips on the Web, hire a professional to tape them for you, or tape them yourself.

A Brief Introduction to Video File Formats

Like all information encoded for use by a computer, video clips are translated into digital datastreams that can be stored in RAM or on a hard disk. Several schemes exist for doing this, though, and each scheme requires a particular kind of player. When publishing video clips to the Web, you have to be careful to use the video file format that best suits the needs of you and your audience.

Fortunately (because there's less to get confused about) or unfortunately (because other formats might offer better characteristics than the ones that exist now), there are only a few video file formats in widespread use. These include the following:

- .MOV The QuickTime format supported at the System level of all recent Macintosh computers. A utility called QuickTime for Windows enables Windows machines to play .MOV files—but without the system-level elegance with which Macs play them.
- .AVI The Microsoft Video for Windows format. Microsoft designed this format to work well with Windows machines. Video for Windows files employ a special scheme for synchronizing audio with video—AVI stands for "Audio-Video Interleaved." Windows 95 users can play .AVI files with Media Player, included with Windows 95.

For the Time-Challenged

- Several video file formats exist. The most common formats are .AVI (Video for Windows), .MOV (QuickTime, native to the Macintosh), and MPEG (used for big video files and other large-scale applications, such as satellite television).
- Adobe Premiere is a very powerful video-editing program. If you can't afford professional video editing, Premiere makes it possible (even easy, sometimes) to assemble video presentations on your home computer.
- Premiere uses a timeline analogy in the Construction window to help you understand how various components of your presentations fit together. You drag parts of your presentation onto the timeline from the Project window.
- To bring a clip (audio, video, or still graphic) into the Project window, choose Import, File from the menu bar and select the clip you want.
- You can put transitions between clips by dragging them from the Transitions window to the transitions track between two video tracks. Don't go crazy with transitions, though—too many will spoil the show.
- Create titles (such as credits) by choosing New, Title from the menu bar and using the tools as if they were part of a presentation graphics program. The "T" tool allows you to add text to the title window.
- When you're done editing your presentation, choose Make, Make Movie from the menu bar. Give your movie a filename, then click the Output Options button. In the Project Output Options window, choose Entire Project from the Output drop-down list box in the upper left corner and choose the file format you want from the drop-down list box in the upper right corner. Click OK, then click OK in the Make Movie box. You'll see a bar graph showing Premiere's progress in assembling your movie. When it completes compilation, it will show the first frame of your movie in a window; click the right-pointing arrow at the bottom of the window to view your movie.
- If Premiere overwhelms you or you lack creativity, consider hiring a professional video producer to do editing for you (check the Web search engines for videographers' home pages). If that's beyond your means, see if your local vocational-technical school will do the editing as part of a class project.

- **.MPEG (or .MPG)** A lossy compression scheme used mainly for professional transmissions of video information, such as from a remote camera installation to a studio, or from a communications satellite to a dish antenna on Earth. MPEG employs *lossy compression*—that is, it's a digitization scheme that sacrifices some image quality for a reduction in file size. Several versions of MPEG exist (MPEG 1, MPEG 2, and MPEG 4; there's no MPEG 3). Later versions have better image quality and compression.
- **.FLI or .FLC** A fairly rare animation format designed by AutoDesk and used in their popular Animator software, which performs morphs, distortions, and other special effects.

Which format should you use? If your production is to be five minutes or fewer in length, you'll probably want to use .AVI, since viewers can be had all over the place. Use the .MPEG format for longer clips. Remember, though, that even a "short" video clip can occupy several megabytes of memory, so you can quickly get into download times of 15 minutes or more if you're not careful.

Using Adobe Premiere

Widely acclaimed as a program that simultaneously offers power and ease of use, Adobe Premiere is in the toolkit of nearly every serious producer of personal-computer video. Though it's not as powerful as the Video Toaster software found in television production studios, it's more than adequate for most Web publishers' needs. It handles editing—including insertion of spiffy transitions and picture-in-picture insets—and supports elaborate titling effects and frame-by-frame tweaking. Basically, if you can't learn to do some task with Premiere, the task is probably so complex as to require a professional anyway.

Expert videographers (which I am not) have written entire books about desktop video production and Adobe Premiere—and most of those books enable you to sit three inches taller when you're not reading them. This section offers only a taste of what Premiere can do—read the program's documentation or a book dedicated to Premiere's details if you want a more in-depth look at this powerful program.

Understanding the Timeline Analogy

Think back to grade school. Remember when the teacher gave you a long strip of paper, and told you to write "Fort Sumter—April 12, 1861" at one end, "Appomattox—April 9, 1865" at the other, and a couple of dozen other Civil War dates in between? That was a timeline, and it helped you understand the way historical events fit together in a continuum. Premiere uses the same analogy to help you organize your video presentations.

Instead of having just one timeline, though, Premiere's default configuration has seven. It calls them "tracks": two for video, one for transitions between the two video tracks, one for titles and other overlays, and three for audio. All seven of these tracks appear in the Construction window (Figure 24.1), in which you'll do most of your work in Premiere. If you need more than seven tracks, you can add up to 98 more audio or video tracks. You'll learn how to add clips to the Construction window in the next section.

When Premiere assembles a movie from the various clips you've placed in the Construction window, it starts at the left edge of the window and moves to the right, looking at all the tracks simultaneously and compiling the con-

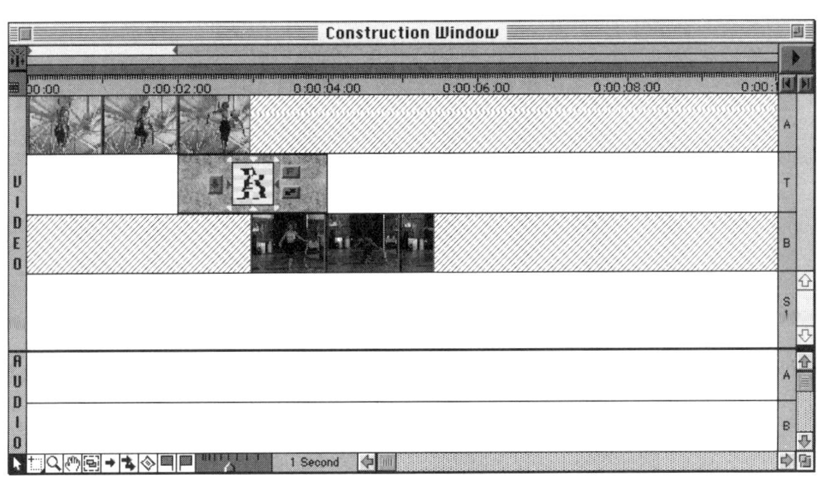

Figure 24.1 Clips and transitions arranged in the Construction window

tents of all of them into a single video file. This way, you can overlay one video image with another, or play a music clip as a nature scene occupies the screen. The timeline analogy makes it easy to keep track of the logical flow of your presentation.

Placing Clips in the Construction Window

The timeline analogy's great, but you need to put clips into it before it's at all useful. Importing clips into Premiere involves another window: the Project window (Figure 24.2). To bring a clip into the Project window, bring the Project window to the foreground by clicking it, then choose File, Import, File from the menu bar. You'll see a mostly standard Macintosh Open dialog box. Find the file you want, highlight it (note that you can see a preview of the clip at the right of the dialog box), and click OK.

When the clip's information block (including the first frame of the clip and some data about the clip) appears in the Project window, you can move it to the Construction window. Click the information block, hold down the mouse button, and drag the block to the appropriate track in the construction window. You can slide the clip back and forth in its track to properly coordinate it with other clips (of all kinds) elsewhere in the Construction window. Refer back to Figure 24.1 to see clips arranged in the Construction window.

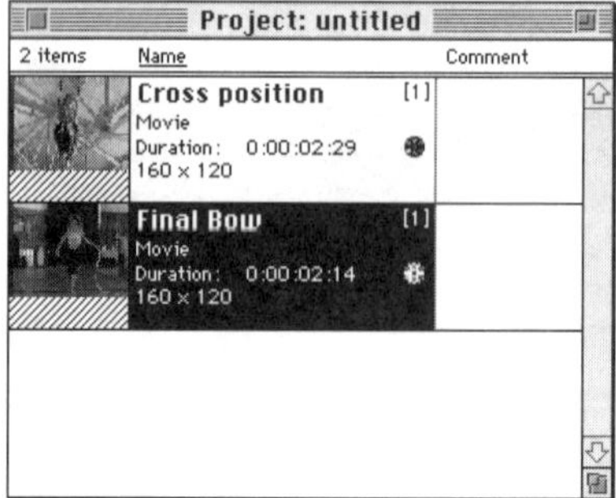

Figure 24.2 The Project window

Using Transitions

Premiere makes it easy to insert a slick effect between two video clips. To put a transition effect (such as a wipe or fade) between two clips, make sure the clips are on different tracks and the transition track is between the two. Then bring the Transitions window (Figure 24.3) to the foreground, select the transition you want (aren't the animated illustrations helpful?) and drag it to the transition track in the Construction window. Now when you tell Premiere to compile your movie (as you'll learn to do later in this section), it won't just cut abruptly from one clip to the next; it will insert the effect you selected between them.

Some common attractive transitions include Additive Dissolve, in which the old clip fades and the new clip appears; Center Merge, in which the old clip shrinks into a tiny box in the center of the new clip and disappears, and Page Peel, in which the old clip "lifts away" from the new clip to simulate turning the pages of a book. Premiere also supports some weird transitions, including Curtain, in which the old image splits in the middle and lifts up like a theater curtain, and Tumble Away, in which the old image shrinks and spins to reveal the new image.

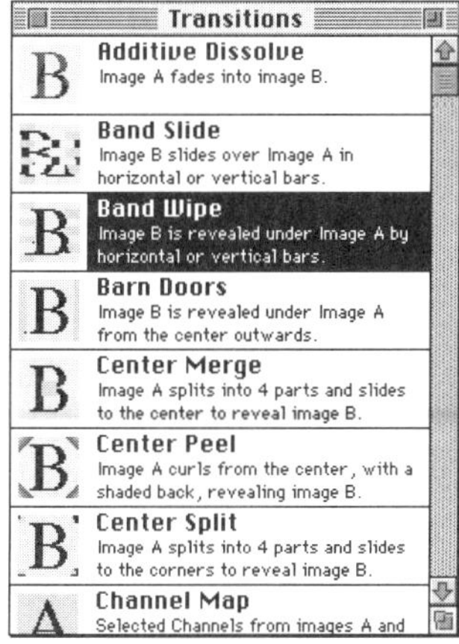

Figure 24.3 The Transitions window

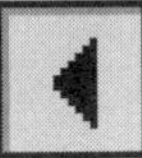

Don't overdo it with fancy transitions—you don't want your editing to draw attention away from your subject. Use simple splices (sometimes called "cuts") and unobtrusive fades instead of bizarre circular wipes and other novelty effects. Just as desktop publishing software and laser printers spawned newsletters with a dozen fonts or more on each page, desktop video-editing software makes everyone think they're an effect-happy Spielberg. Resist the temptation—don't load your videos with unusual effects.

Titling

At the very least, you'll want to give yourself credit for your editing efforts, and that means you'll want to make your printed name part of the video file. Video experts call this *titling*. To create a title for your presentation, choose File, New, Title from the menu bar. You'll see the Title window (Figure 24.4). The Title window looks a lot like a slide-creation window in a presentation graphics program (the Title window and such programs serve the same purpose, after all). You can select the text tool (marked with a "T"), position the cursor on the blank area, and type your title. Then, save your title by choosing File, Save from the menu bar and typing a name for your title in the Save dialog box.

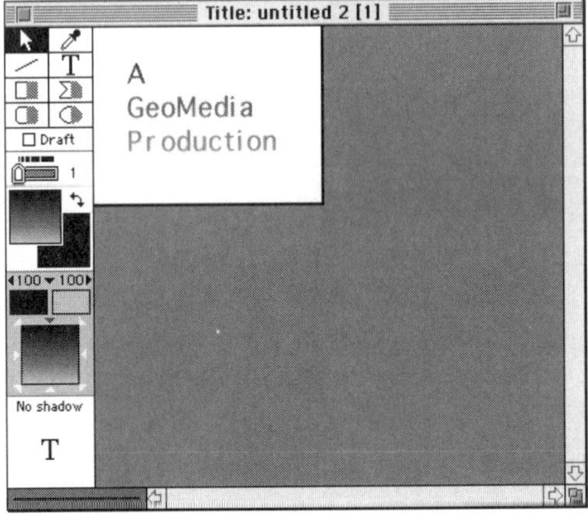

Figure 24.4 The Title window

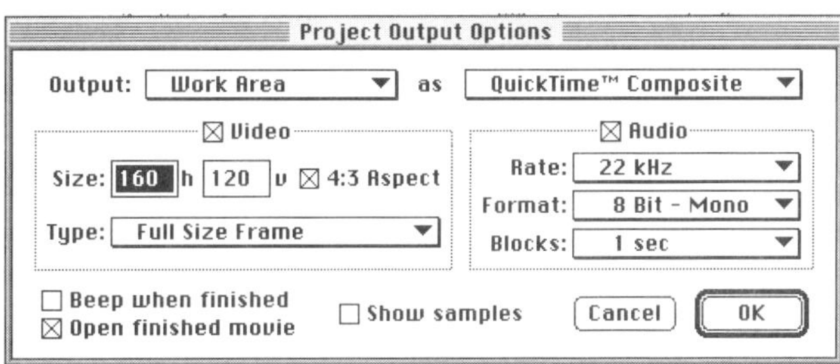

Figure 24.5 Project Output Options dialog box

To bring the newly created title into the editing window, choose Import, File from the Menu bar and pick your title from the files listed in the dialog box. The title will then appear in the Project window, from which you can drag it to the overlays track (labeled S1) in the Construction window.

Compiling Your Presentation

When you're happy with the way you've arranged clips in the Construction window, you're ready to assemble the contents of the various timelines into a movie. To do this, choose Make, Make Movie from the menu bar. You'll see the Make Movie box, in which you type a filename and select the directory in which Premiere should save your movie.

Before clicking OK, click the Output Options button. In the Project Output Options dialog box that appears (Figure 24.5), choose Entire Project from the Output drop-down list box in the upper left corner and choose the file format you want from the drop-down list box in the upper right corner. Click OK, then click OK in the Make Movie box. You'll see a bar graph showing Premiere's progress in assembling your movie. When it completes compilation, it will show the first frame of your movie in a window; click the right-pointing arrow at the bottom of the window to view your movie.

Video Production Hints

You learned a lot about video production in Chapter 21, and the Webmaster tip in the last section is probably the single most important piece of advice

you can heed as you begin working with Premiere and other video-editing tools.

Consider Farming it Out

This doesn't sound like much of a tip, but it's probably good advice. Video production involves such a high degree of specialized skill and so much expensive equipment that, unless you'll be doing enough video production to justify a big investment in equipment and training, you're better off leaving it to the pros. Check the Web search engines for production houses that specialize in clips for Web distribution.

You need not spend a bundle to get good-quality video editing, though. Vocational and technical schools often have complete production studios and will often make your job part of a class exercise if you provide some supplies. Granted, following this route is like stopping by the barber school for a cheap haircut, but the bang-for-buck of student editing often exceeds that of professional producers.

Keep It Short

This tip appears in every multimedia chapter in this book, and that's because it's very important. Especially with video, it's easy to create enormous files that will choke even powerful server computers. Considering that most people access the Web, at least part of the time, via a 14,000 bps connection, you can't ask them to download a giant video clip—it could take hours. With that in mind, use video in small doses, or at least warn site visitors before they commit to downloading a 5 MB video file.

From Here

- Now you know how to produce still graphics, audio, and video. What about text layouts that exceed the capabilities of HTML? The next chapter explains how to use Adobe Acrobat and the Portable Document Format to publish complex documents on the Web.

Chapter 25

Producing Adobe Acrobat Documents

Introducing Adobe Acrobat

Adobe Acrobat 2.0 provides computer users with a means of creating and interpreting *portable documents*—documents that appear the same on different machines running different software. Acrobat isn't one program, but rather a package of several programs designed to work together.

The Need for Adobe Acrobat

Before portable documents came about—and Acrobat is not the first portable-document software package—computer publishers spent hours carefully laying out and formatting documents, but were unsure what their products

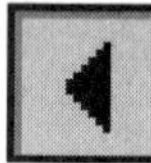

would look like when they were transmitted electronically to a viewer. This uncertainty led publishers to cling to paper, printer, and facsimile technology for applications in which appearance was key, because it enabled them to know exactly what document recipients would see.

For applications in which page layouts, typefaces, and graphics were not important, exchange standards such as ASCII and Microsoft's Rich Text Format (RTF) were (and are) adequate. Such standards support the sharing of alphanumeric characters but cannot support the fancy formatting that is essential to business communication and that word processing program users have grown accustomed to.

With the growth of the World Wide Web and the corresponding growth in businesses' interest in publishing there, the need for a portable document format became apparent. The limited formatting capabilities of HTML and the omnipresent need for a consistent corporate look conflicted, and Web publishers began to look for a way to make their publications appear the same to both their creators and their consumers. Also, faxing documents to every Web user who visited a site would be impractical and would defeat every advantage of the Web.

Although several companies, including WordPerfect, have published portable document solutions, Acrobat seems to have been anointed the standard for Web publishing.

Adobe Acrobat Reader

One of the main reasons for Acrobat's success is Acrobat Reader, a program distributed free of charge on the Internet and many bulletin board systems. Most sites that offer PDF documents, in fact, can also download Acrobat Reader.

Reader is a read-only interpreter—it enables you to look at PDF documents but does not allow you to modify them or create new ones. If you plan to use Reader to view documents downloaded from the Web, you can configure Reader as a helper application that automatically displays any PDF file you download.

Adobe Acrobat

Acrobat is not one program, but rather a package of programs that extend a user's abilities to work with PDF files. The Acrobat package contains Acrobat Reader as well as the following:

Acrobat Exchange	Allows you to modify PDF documents by adding text, annotations, security restrictions, and hyperlinks.

Acrobat PDF Writer	Lets you direct print output from a word processing or page layout program to a PDF file instead of a printer.
Acrobat Search	Enables you to look for words in PDF documents indexed with Adobe Acrobat Catalog software, which is not part of the Acrobat package.

For the Time-Challenged

- The various Adobe Acrobat products enable you to use documents in Portable Document Format (PDF), which ensures that they look the same on all computers equipped with Acrobat software.
- Acrobat Reader—which enables you to look at PDF documents, but not alter them—is distributed free of charge and can be configured to act as a helper application to a Web browser.
- Navigate around an Acrobat document by following hyperlinks, by selecting a particular page from the outline or thumbnails on the left side of your screen, or by choosing to go to a page by clicking the page indicator (the one that says "Page 3 of 34" or something like that) in the lower-left corner of your screen.
- Acrobat Distiller is used to convert Encapsulated PostScript (EPS) files to PDF.
- PDF Writer works just like a printer driver. When you want to make a file (such as a word processing document or desktop publishing layout) into a PDF file, select PDF Writer from the list of printers available, follow your program's print procedure, and respond to the dialog boxes that appear. Your word processing file will be saved as a PDF file.
- You can create a hyperlink from one part of a document to another by clicking the link button on the toolbar (the one with the links of chain on it), adjusting the settings in the Create Link dialog box, moving to the view to which you want the link to lead, and clicking Set Link.
- You can make text items into "articles"—easy-to-follow units of text—by choosing Article from the Tools menu and dragging rectangles around each block of text. When you've surrounded the last piece of text, click the End Article button at the bottom of the screen.
- Axcess Magazine's experimental PDF edition (available for download from http://www.internex.net/axcess/) is the best example of Acrobat use on the Web. Take a look.

Adobe Acrobat Pro

The standard Adobe Acrobat package is fine for most applications, but those Acrobat users with *legacy documents*—documents written and published before Acrobat technology came into being—need a way to convert old files into PDF form. Adobe Acrobat Pro, with its Acrobat Distiller component, is the way to do this.

Acrobat Distiller converts Encapsulated PostScript (EPS) files, word processing files, page layout files, and images to PDF. It enables you to convert an archive of correspondence, documentation, personnel reports, or resumes to a common form. Acrobat Catalog, sold independently and as part of the Adobe Acrobat for Workgroups package (which includes ten licensed copies of all the programs in the Adobe Acrobat package, as well as copies of Acrobat Catalog and Acrobat Distiller), lets you prepare the converted archive for full-text searching with Acrobat Search.

The prospect of keeping business records in a common, searchable format is exciting. Imagine you're a human resources expert. Each day you receive dozens of resumes, even when there are no jobs available. Instead of trashing them or filing them away to be forgotten, you could scan them and convert the resulting word processor files to PDF format. Then, when a job opens, you can search the stored documents for keywords, such as "B.A. in English" or "PageMaker 5.0." Re-engineering opportunities like this exist in many fields, so think about how Acrobat and other technologies can make your work easier.

Reading Adobe Acrobat Documents

Adobe has done all it can to ensure that before long, you'll be faced with the need to read a PDF document. By making the format open and providing Acrobat Reader software free of charge, the company has made PDF an appealing option for those who wish to put formatting-rich documents on the Web.

But how do you read PDF documents? Both Acrobat Reader and Acrobat Exchange enable reading, and both use the same interface. This section walks you through opening and navigating PDF documents—the instructions apply to both applications.

Opening a Document

To open a PDF document for viewing, choose Open from the File menu and, in the Open dialog box, select the file you want to see. Double-click its filename or highlight its filename and click OK.

Modifying the Display

The Reader or Exchange window, after you have opened a document, is divided in two (Figure 25.1). To the left of the vertical dividing bar is a guide—an outline or a set of thumbnail icons (you can choose which, or eliminate the guide portion of the screen altogether by choosing among the buttons in the leftmost cluster of buttons on the toolbar). To the right of the dividing bar is one page of the document itself.

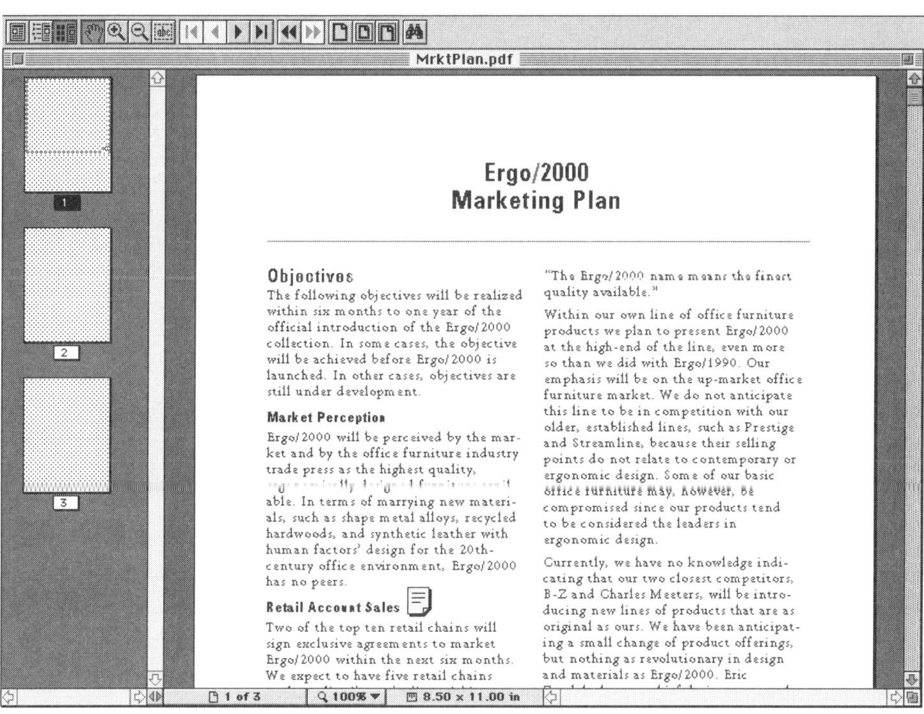

Figure 25.1 Adobe Acrobat Reader or Exchange window

Chances are, you can't see the entire page in the portion of the window Reader or Exchange has allocated for document display. There are three ways to adjust how the document is shown:

1. You can click the Zoom Out button (the magnifying glass with a minus sign in it), then click the document. You can click several times with the Zoom Out tool to make the document appear even smaller, but the on-screen representation quickly becomes too small to use.
2. You can use the grabber hand to move the document around your screen. Use the grabber hand by clicking the hand button on the toolbar, then dragging the document up and down and from side to side with the hand-shaped pointer that results. Note that when you drag the document, the hand pointer turns into a fist that, if you have a strong imagination, looks like it's holding onto the document and pulling it around.
3. You can use the three buttons immediately to the left of the Search button (the one that looks like a pair of binoculars) on the toolbar. These buttons, which contain rectangular icons of various sizes, automatically adjust the document to fit into a space of a specific size. Try clicking each of the buttons to find the size that best suits your needs.

Navigating within a Document

PDF documents support hyperlinks—the same sort of navigation employed on the World Wide Web. Embedded hyperlinks, which are red, allow you to move from one location in a document to another quickly and without losing your train of thought. Acrobat software also supports hyperlinks to URLs on the World Wide Web—it will launch your browser automatically when you click such a hyperlink.

Aside from using hyperlinks, you can move among the pages of a document in several ways. The traditional way is to view the pages of the document sequentially, by using the single-arrow buttons at the top of the display window. Clicking the right-pointing single arrow moves you to the next page of a document; clicking the left-pointing single arrow moves you to the previous page. To move to the last page of a document, click the right-pointing-arrow-and-vertical-bar button; click the left-pointing-arrow-and-vertical-bar button to move back to the first page of a document.

You can also navigate within a document by clicking in the guide area to the left of the vertical dividing bar. Click an outline entry or thumbnail representation of a page to move to that page. Or you can click the page indicator in the lower-left corner of your screen (it says something like "Page 1 of 5") and enter the number of the page to which you want to move.

Creating Adobe Acrobat Documents

Chances are, you won't want simply to read PDF documents. If you're a Web publisher or a member of a workgroup that needs to share documents, you'll need to create PDF documents yourself. The Adobe Acrobat package provides an easy way to create PDF documents, and Adobe Acrobat Pro includes two.

Creating Documents with PDF Writer

The easiest way to create a document to be stored as a PDF file is to use your word processing program. Create a document in that program just as you would for any other purpose, but follow this special printing procedure:

1. Choose PDF Writer from the Chooser menu of printers, then choose Print from the File menu of your application. Click OK.
2. Acrobat Writer will prompt you for the name of the PDF file it will create.

If you want, you can click the View PDF File check box to bring up Acrobat Reader after you print to the file so that you can examine your work. You can also click the Prompt for Document Info check box, which will bring up another dialog box in which you can enter information about the document, such as the author's name and a brief summary of the document's contents (Figure 25.2).

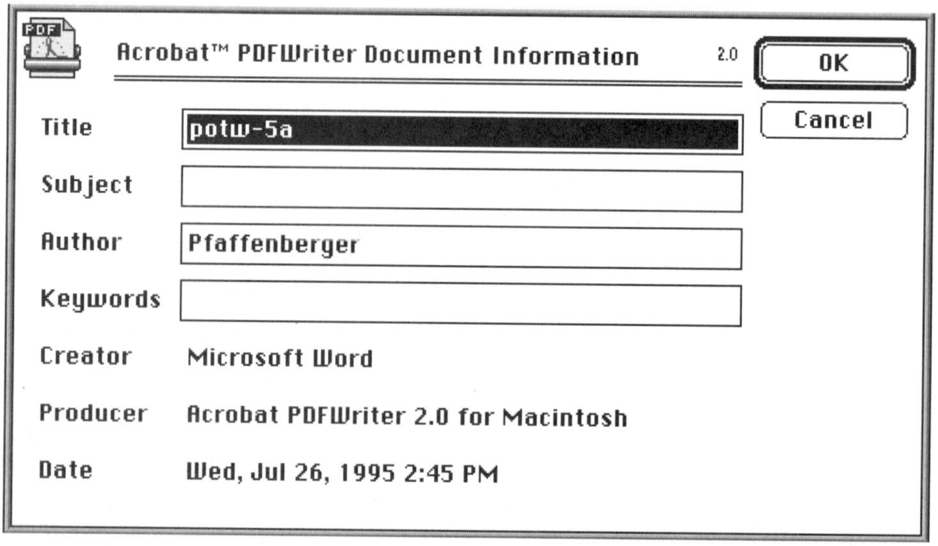

Acrobat™ PDFWriter Document Information 2.0

OK

Cancel

Title potw-5a

Subject

Author Pfaffenberger

Keywords

Creator Microsoft Word

Producer Acrobat PDFWriter 2.0 for Macintosh

Date Wed, Jul 26, 1995 2:45 PM

Figure 25.2 Creating a PDF document in Acrobat Writer

Creating Documents with Acrobat Distiller

Acrobat Distiller converts Encapsulated PostScript (EPS) files to PDF format. You can use Distiller in three ways:

1. The most intuitive way is to choose Open from the Distiller File menu and choose the PostScript file you wish to convert. Double-click the PostScript document's filename, or select it and choose OK. Distiller will prompt you for the name of the PDF file it will generate. Click OK and watch the progress of the bar graph as Distiller does its work.

2. If you don't want to open a file in Distiller, you can put the Encapsulated PostScript file to be converted to PDF into the "In" folder within the folder in which you store Distiller. Distiller monitors that folder (Adobe calls it a "watched folder") and converts any PostScript files stored there. After converting the files, Distiller

places them in the "Out" folder within the folder containing Distiller.

3. Perhaps the easiest way to convert a PostScript document is to place the Distiller icon on the Desktop and drag PostScript file icons to it. Distiller converts the files to PDF and saves them in its "Out" folder.

Adding Internal Hyperlinks in an Adobe Acrobat Document

One of the appealing features of PDF documents is their ability to contain hyperlinks from one piece of data to another. This feature enables you to create documents that are not necessarily linear in flow, as traditional documents, such as books and letters, are. Hypertext documents—as the Web illustrates—can convey the precise information a reader needs without requiring the reader to waste time reading through extraneous information.

Creating a Hyperlink

Adobe Exchange uses a process of mouse-dragging and dialog-box adjustment to establish hyperlinks between portions of a document. To create a hyperlink, make sure the area of the document you want to link *from* is visible, and click the link button—the interlocked links of chain—on the toolbar. The mouse pointer will turn from an arrowhead into crosshairs. Drag the crosshairs around the area you wish to link. The Create Link dialog box (Figure 25.3) will appear as soon as you release the mouse button.

In the Create Link dialog box, set the Appearance options to your liking (unless you have a reason to do otherwise, make all your hyperlinks a consistent style). Choose Go to View from the Type list box, and choose Inherit Zoom from the Magnification list box (if you don't choose Inherit Zoom, you run the risk of confusing your reader with unpredictable variations in zoom).

Using the scroll bars or navigation aids, move to the view to which you want to link. When you have the view you want, click Set Link in the Create Link dialog box. The link is established, and you can test it by clicking in the area you defined at the beginning of the linking process.

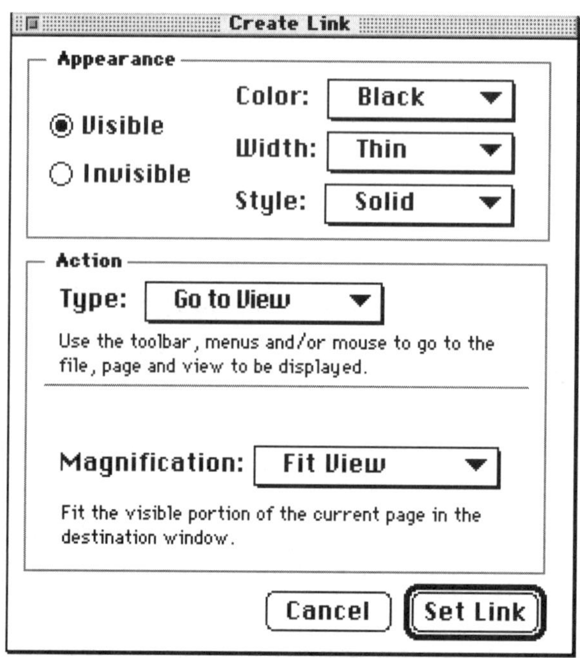

Figure 25.3 Create Link dialog box

Columns and Articles

A real shortcoming of HTML is its inability to handle page layouts that involve columns. Skilled HTML programmers can use the column-creation tags included in the Netscape extensions of HTML, but with only limited flexibility. With Acrobat, you can use the column features of your word processing program, print it to a PDF file, and use Acrobat Exchange's article-creation tools to define the order in which Acrobat Reader will guide viewers through columnar text.

It's important to distinguish between columns and articles. *Columns*, which you create with tools in your word processing program, are a feature of text formatting. You might choose to have two side-by-side columns on a

page, or a single column of text on each page. Creating columns is not a function of any Acrobat product.

Instead, Acrobat Exchange defines *articles*—the way in which related text flows through a document. If you define articles, viewers using Acrobat Reader will be able to follow a piece of writing from its beginning to its end, without having to worry about finding the continuation each time a page ends or the story, for some other reason, ends on one page and continues on another.

Defining Articles in Acrobat

To create an article, first open a PDF document by choosing Open from the File menu and selecting a file. Double-click its filename or select its filename and click OK.

Using the navigation tools in Exchange, find the beginning of the article you wish to define. Choose Article from the Tools menu; the mouse pointer will change from an arrowhead to a set of crosshairs.

Drag the crosshairs from the top-left corner of the first column of the article to the lower-right corner of the same column. Repeat the procedure with each subsequent column. The first column will be labeled (in Article view only) as "X-1," where X is the number of the article. If this is the first article in a document you've identified, the first column will be labeled "1-1."

When you reach the lower-right corner of the last portion of the article, click the End Article button at the bottom of the screen. Exchange will prompt you for information about the article—the author and title, for example. Fill in this information if you want, then click OK.

Now when a reader looks at your document and begins to read some text that's been defined as an article, he or she can simply click on a screenful of text and automatically see the next screenful—even if the text continues on another page. Article definition is a powerful tool that can significantly improve the readability of articles stored in PDF.

An Acrobat Sampler

Acrobat is a fairly new technology and isn't nearly as widespread on the Web as older document types, such as GIF graphics or AU sounds. Still, some site designers have seen the suitability of PDF to the Web and have incorporated it into their products.

Only one implementation of PDF is examined here because it outshines all others by a giant margin. Though many sites make use of PDF's formatting-retention features for a variety of good reasons (the Desktop Publishing Glossary at the University of Pennsylvania's Wharton School of Business is a great example), only one site makes use of Acrobat's capabilities for both technical and aesthetic reasons. Examine this document, and you'll learn a great deal.

Axcess Magazine

The coolest implementation of Acrobat technology on the Web is an experimental issue of Axcess Magazine, available for downloading at http://www.internex.net/axcess/. An electronic variety publication that specializes in alternative music and Internet culture, Axcess' experiment defines the capabilities of Acrobat publishing and sets a standard for others. The magazine's only shortcoming is its size—it's 99 graphics-laden pages long. Once you download the 2.5 megabyte PDF document and start browsing, though, you'll understand the potential of PDF publishing.

My Web browser doesn't know how to handle PDF files! Okay, you need to configure your browser to use Acrobat Reader or Acrobat Exchange as a *helper application*—a program that handles particular kinds of files. In most browsers, the dialog box that tells you the file type is unrecognized offers to let you configure a helper application. Choose that option, and either type the path and filename of the program you want to use (Reader or Exchange) or choose Browse and find it in the graphical representation of your hard disk. Now that application will start automatically whenever you download a PDF document.

If you don't have a copy of Reader or Exchange, the chances are good that any site offering PDF files for download has Reader available too.

Axcess' welcome screen (Figure 25.4) exemplifies the high-quality layout and illustration to be found inside the magazine. The welcome screen makes good, intuitive use of hyperlinks (you click the magazine's logo to proceed to the table of contents), and it takes advantage of the ease with which Acrobat can assign a hyperlink to only part of a graphic—the same task in HTML would be a difficult undertaking.

The magazine's main table of contents (Figure 25.5) exploits the fact that, since hyperlinks in Acrobat are assigned to areas of documents and not to

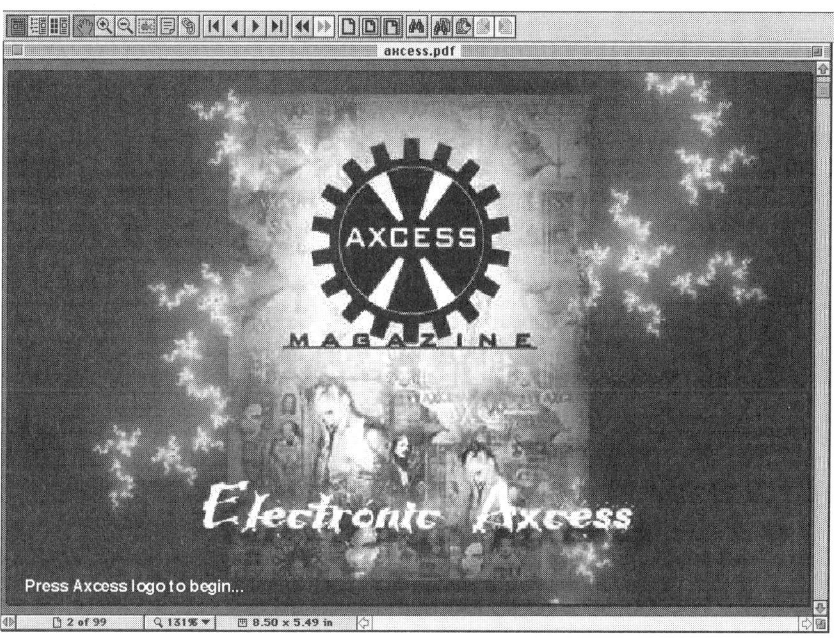

Figure 25.4 Axcess Magazine's welcome screen

passages of text, page designers can make buttons visually appealing—there's no need to use a standard dialog-box button or to slog through tedious imagemap coding procedures.

The table of contents to the Music section (Figure 25.6) is a marvel of attractive design and intuitive functionality. Clicking the Tori Amos button on the Music guide takes you to a story that shows how attractive design can be incorporated with text and stored in the PDF format (Figure 25.7). When combined with good reporting and decent writing, as the Amos layout is, good graphic design can allow a PDF publication to compete with the finest print magazines.

Aside from its large size, Axcess falls short in its failure to use Acrobat's article-definition features. The magazine's designers went to great lengths to include hyperlinked navigation buttons on each page of each article, but they neglected to take advantage of the fact that Acrobat will guide readers through articles automatically. Their means of guiding readers is entirely adequate, but a reader experienced with Acrobat might want to follow an

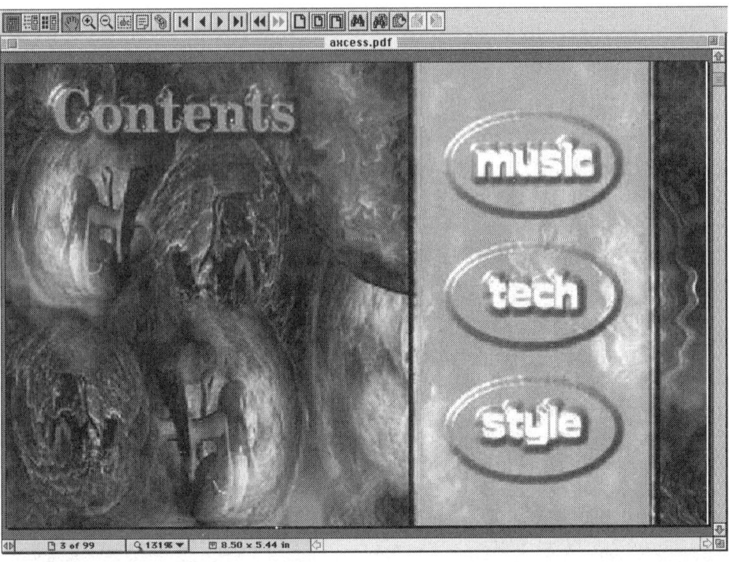

Figure 25.5 Axcess' main table of contents

Figure 25.6 Table of contents for Axcess' Music section

axcess.pdf

Tori Amos

HOLDING HANDS WITH VIOLENCE

by Laura Morgan

"Want a piece of fruit gum?" asks Tori Amos from behind a conference table ten times her size. Amos, a copper-haired, vintage-store bundle of ragamuffin charm, immediately conveys a childlike naiveté. It seems odd that this diminutive woman could be the same Tori Amos who assaults the patriarchy, organized religion, and sexual repression with such brilliant vehemence. The fairy tale references and deceptively pretty melodies of her songs often belie the rage within them. Take "Cornflake Girl" from her new

Illustration by Ken Meyer, Jr.

NIN

Axcess

37 of 99 | 131% | 8.50 x 5.44 in

Figure 25.7 An example of good graphic design in a PDF publication

article without moving his mouse, and be disappointed that none of Axcess' stories are defined as articles.

Overall, though, Axcess' experimental PDF publication—the magazine's publishers are taking mail now to see if there's enough interest in continued PDF publication—is a superb example of the power of PDF. If you're even slightly interested in publishing in this format, visit the Axcess site and examine the experimental issue.

From Here

- By this point, you understand the technical aspects of planning your Web site, coding its HTML, and producing multimedia to add spice. The rest of this book deals with issues affecting Web publishers. Read on to learn about security, copyright, and standardization issues in Part V.

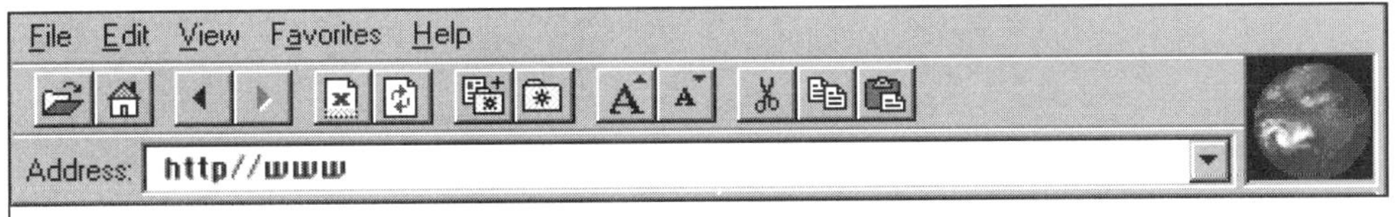

Part V

Web Publishing Issues

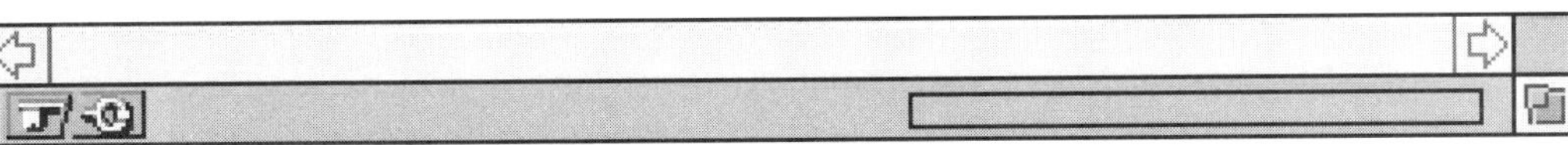

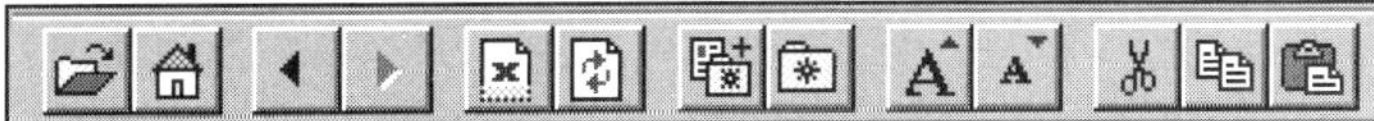

Chapter 26

Security

A revolution in Web commerce is about to happen. The spark for the revolution will not be a riot or an invasion; it will be secure transaction capability for the Internet and the Web. Such capability exists today, but there is no single standard used by all server and browser manufacturers. When a standard is adopted—and one will be adopted within the next year or so, experts say—consumers will be able to send vendors their credit card numbers via the Internet without being concerned about someone intercepting and using them illegally.

This chapter provides you with an introduction to Web security issues and technologies. These subjects are interesting and central to the future expansion of the Web, but this chapter is not an exhaustive treatment of security issues as they apply to Web publishers. Entire books have been written about creating a secure Web site and carrying on secure commerce on the Web.

For the Time-Challenged

- Security actually involves three different aspects: authentication (knowing who's sending you something), confidentiality (knowing that no third party can intercept and read the information you exchange with someone), and integrity (knowing that your message has not been tampered with or altered while en route).
- Public key cryptography, the technology that underlies Netscape's security features, enables any two people to exchange indecipherable messages without needing to exchange decoding keys via a secure channel.
- Netscape's security standard, called Secure Socket Layer (SSL), uses public key cryptography to enable you to establish a secure connection with a Web server.
- There is no single Web security standard yet; in fact, there are several competing standards. In the years to come it is likely that a single standard will emerge.
- Your credit card information cannot be intercepted en route, but you still need to use common sense when ordering via the Web. Order from trusted, well-established firms and make sure you understand their policies.

What Is "Security"?

In the computer world, *security* has three distinct shades of meaning: *authentication, confidentiality,* and *integrity,* as the following sections discuss. Of greatest interest to you, as a potential provider of commercial Web services, are confidentiality and integrity.

Authentication

In brief, *authentication* ensures that you are really who you say you are when you log on to a server.

Most Web servers demand no authentication at all—they just let you in. However, virtually all Web servers support simple protection by password: You must type a login name (user name) and password to access the service.

An example of a Web service that requires password authentication is HotWired, the on-line version of *Wired* magazine.

When you access HotWired for the first time, you're asked to create a login name and password and to supply your e-mail address. You then receive an automatically generated e-mail message that includes an authorization number. You must then supply this authorization number to access the system. What's gained from this? A modicum of assurance that you aren't accessing the site with someone else's name and e-mail address.

Confidentiality

Confidentiality refers to the protection of information while it is en route to its destination. It's not nice to think about, but none of the information you are transmitting via the Web is free from prying eyes. Hackers, criminals, or investigators can easily intercept, record, and print all the information you transmit.

Integrity

Integrity refers to the exact preservation of the transmitted data so that it reaches its destination without any alteration, accidental or deliberate. As with confidentiality, the Web provides absolutely no means of ensuring the integrity of transmitted data. It could be altered while en route, either by chance or deliberate interference, and the receiving computer would have no way of knowing.

The Need for Encryption

The solution to the Web's confidentiality and security problems lies in the use of *encryption.* In essence, encryption is the process of converting a *plaintext* message (a message that could be read by anyone) into an unreadable *ciphertext* by means of a *key* (a method of transforming the message so that it appears to be gibberish). The message can be read only by the intended recipient, who possesses the key and uses it (in a process called *decryption*) to make the text readable again. A simple encryption technique is ROT-13, which "rotates" all letters 13 characters to the right in the alphabet. The ciphertext looks like gibberish, but it is easily decrypted by rotating the letters 13 characters left. Encryption ensures integrity as well as confidentiality; if anyone or

anything has altered the message en route, it won't decode 100% correctly, so you'll know that something has gone wrong.

ROT-13 is a poor encryption technique because its key is so simple. In fact, it's used on Usenet only to keep adult-oriented material away from the eyes of children or those who would rather not see such material. More complicated keys are needed to ensure confidentiality and integrity. With more complicated keys, though, another problem arises: How to transmit the key to the recipient. Traditionally, this has been done by courier, but this is costly and time-consuming. Military strategists in ancient Rome lamented the "messenger problem"—the challenge of getting a key to its intended recipient and running the risk that the messenger carrying it would be captured or, worse, bribed into revealing the key.

A new cryptographic method called *public key cryptography* eliminates the need to deliver the key and raises the possibility that people who have never previously exchanged messages could send encrypted messages to each other, which could not be intercepted by a third party. In public key cryptography, there are two different keys, an encryption key and a decryption key:

- **Public encryption key** You make your encryption key public; people use it to send an encrypted message to you.
- **Decryption key** This key is kept private. You use it to decode the messages sent to you. Nobody else can read the message without this key.

With public key cryptography, there is no need to establish a secure channel to exchange the decryption key; the person who wishes to send an encrypted message to you merely obtains the public encryption key, encrypts the message, and sends it to you. Nobody along the way can decode the message, even if they have intercepted the encryption key; they need the decryption key, and you keep that secret. Rightfully, public key encryption has been described as a revolution in cryptography. It makes cryptography available to ordinary people.

Introducing the Secure Socket Layer (SSL) Security Protocol

To provide secure transactions via the World Wide Web, Netscape Communications Corporation has proposed a standard called the Secure Socket Layer

(SSL) protocol. This proposed Internet standard seeks to provide secure public key encryption capabilities so that people can exchange information securely via any established Internet protocol, including not only the Web but also Gopher, FTP, Telnet, and others. What is more, SSL seeks to do this without placing undue demands on users; much or all of the SSL processing goes on in the background, without requiring any intervention from the user.

An SSL session begins when an SSL-capable client (such as Netscape Navigator) contacts an SSL-capable server (such as Netscape's secure Web servers). A brief exchange of public keys occurs; from that point on, the client and server can exchange secure, encrypted messages and no third party can intercept them. In addition, SSL includes integrity-checking features that assure both parties that the message has not been tampered with or altered during its transmission.

What about Standards?

As of this book's writing, there is no "official" standard for the secure transmission of sensitive data on the World Wide Web. In an effort to gain acceptance for its SSL protocol as the standard security protocol for the Web, Netscape has published SSL's specifications and made the technology widely available. However, competing firms are attempting to do the same. The worst-case scenario is that two or more competing but incompatible security standards will exist. If this happens, the Web's budding commercial ventures could die on the vine; a user of Netscape would be able to access only Netscape-friendly secure sites, while users of Spyglass's Enhanced NSCA Mosaic would be able to access only those sites conforming to Spyglass's protocol.

The most likely outcome of this struggle, in the short run, is that two or three competing security standards will exist and Web servers will have to recognize them all. Netscape has announced its plans to support both its own SSL and S-HTTP, a competing security protocol, in both Netscape Navigator and its server products. In the long run, it seems likely that the Web community will be able to agree on a single standard for secure Web transactions. Most likely, it will include many features from SSL plus additional ones from Netscape's competitors. The *Wall Street Journal* recently reported that Netscape Communications had invested in Terisa Systems, which is developing a Web security standard that would unify all the competing security technologies. A solution to the standardization dilemma may be very near.

Is My Customers' Information Really Safe?

Public key encryption protects information from being intercepted or altered while it is transmitted. Does that mean customers' credit card information is safe? With a secure connection on the Web, you can be assured that nobody can obtain credit card numbers by "tapping" your Internet connection. But sending a credit card number via a secure link is very much like giving it to somebody over the telephone: Customers are still dependent on the honesty and integrity of vendors. In the end, ordering on the Web won't be any safer than any other form of mail order.

If you're thinking about ordering something by credit card on the Web, use all the common-sense rules that you would when ordering by telephone or mail. Order from well-established firms with good reputations. Make sure you fully understand the firm's policies regarding the delivery of ordered goods, returns and exchanges, and refunds. If you're selling things via the Web, handle credit card information with the utmost care, and make sure your customers know they can trust you. You're ahead of the game if your company is well known and has a good reputation. If you're new, you have to establish credibility with customers before others entrust their credit card information to you.

From Here

- Concerned about issues of copyright as well as security? Take a look at the next chapter.

Chapter 27

Copyright

If you've been using the Web and other Internet features, such as mailing lists and Usenet newsgroups, for more than a few weeks, you've probably seen some kind of discussion about copyrights and copyright law. These topics are perennial favorite discussion topics of Internet users, and it makes sense: the Web and the rest of the Internet are designed to make information easy to find and use, while copyright law is supposed to, in one sense, restrict the flow of information. The purposes of information technology and copyright law often conflict, so it follows that users of information technology are concerned about how copyright law applies to them.

This chapter provides a basic introduction to the concepts of copyright. It's not complete: You can go to law school for years and not fully comprehend the vagaries of copyright law, and no one's entirely sure how traditional copyright

ideas apply to relatively new electronic publishing media, anyway. Take a look at this chapter for a general idea of how copyright law applies to your Web publication—but consult a lawyer if you're in copyright trouble or have very specific questions.

What Is Copyright Law?

Copyright law is a collection of laws that protect the expression of those who engage in creative work. Originally put into practice in the time of Queen Elizabeth I of England, copyright law is designed to enable novelists, poets, songwriters, and other artists to profit from their work.

What Does Copyright Law Do?

In the United States, copyright law ensures that the creator of a piece of creative work, such as a play, a painting, a photograph, or a poem, can control what is done with that piece of creative work. Typically, the creator reserves the right to:

- Make and sell copies of the work (this is why book authors get royalties on each copy of their books that publishers sell).
- Perform or display the work publicly.
- Adapt the work to a new medium (to convert a novel into a screenplay, for example).
- Receive recognition as author when the work is used or cited by another creator (this is why students should be careful to attribute quoted material in their papers to its original authors).

It's important to note that copyright law covers only the expression of an idea, not the idea itself. Otherwise, two reporters, each from a different newspaper, would be violating copyright law if they wrote news stories about the same event. For this reason, it's easier to violate a copyright on fictional material than on nonfiction material. Virtually everything a novelist puts into a novel is a product of his or her imagination (the ideas are the novelist's), while an engineer might draw heavily on the decidedly uncopyrighted laws of physics in a professional paper.

For the Time-Challenged

- Copyright law protects the right of those who produce creative work to profit from that work.
- For works created in the United States after 1978, the copyright period ends 50 years after the death of the creator.
- You have a copyright on anything you create. However, you cannot sue for copyright infringement unless you register your copyright with the U.S. Copyright Office.
- Material not protected by copyright is said to be in the public domain and may be used by anyone, for any purpose, including making a profit.
- You can use copyrighted material with permission from the copyright holder or, in small quantities, under the "fair use" rules of copyright law.
- The Web and other new information technologies will probably soon cause an upheaval in copyright law.

Though there have been many changes in the rules regarding how long copyright protection lasts, the general rule for works created after 1978 is that copyright protection of a piece of creative work lasts until 50 years after the creator's death. Earlier laws required copyright holders to renew their copyright claims every few years; that rule is generally obsolete. Talk to a lawyer about the specific duration rules that apply in your case.

How Do I Get a Copyright on Material I've Created?

If you created a piece of work, you automatically have the copyright on that piece of work. You no longer need to register your claim to the work with the U.S. Copyright Office or to include any sort of copyright notice on the work itself in order to have a copyright. There are, however, some good reasons to register your creation and to include a copyright notice on it anyway.

Most important, you cannot sue someone for infringing on your copyright unless your claim is registered with the Copyright Office. You can

register as soon as you see an infringement and want to sue, but it's better to register ahead of time for the following reasons:

- A rush registration, which you would need if you had to complete registration before a court date, costs $200, while a standard registration costs $20.
- You may be eligible for a larger award from the court, including attorney's fees, if you register before an infringement takes place.

You should also include a copyright notice on your work. A copyright notice consists of the © symbol, your name, and the date on which the creative work was completed. By including a copyright notice on your work, you reduce the possibility that someone you sue for infringement will argue ignorance—that he or she didn't know your work was copyrighted—and thereby reduce the penalty.

My computer won't make the © symbol! Is (c) good enough? No. At least, probably not, and you're better off figuring out how to make the © symbol than finding out in court that a substitute wasn't good enough. Copyright law in the United States gives you three options for indicating that a work is copyrighted: the © symbol, the word "copyright," and the abbreviation "Copr." International copyright law recognizes only the © symbol. Avoid trouble: use a circle-c copyright symbol.

Who Enforces Copyright Law?

You may be loathe to comply with copyright regulations, and something along the lines of, "What's going to happen? Are the copyright police going to come get me?" may have passed your lips. The answer to your question is, yes, if you remain in violation of copyright laws long enough, a court can issue an order that law enforcement officers can uphold. Don't panic, though, if your copyright violation is minor or unintentional. If you have copyrighted material on your site and you're not making money from it or detracting from the profits of the copyright's owner, the worst you can reasonably expect is a nasty letter from the copyright owner's lawyer, telling you to take the material off the Web. If you comply with the lawyer's request, you'll be okay.

If you ignore the letter and leave the material up, the copyright holder can sue you for infringing on his or her copyright. The result of such a trial, assuming there is no doubt about the copyright holder's right to the material, could be a court order making you pay damages to the copyright holder or making you stop using the copyrighted material, or both. If you ignore a court order, police can confront you and make you comply with it.

What Does "Public Domain" Mean?

Copyrighted material may only be legally used by the copyright holder; public domain material may be used by anyone in any way they wish. Think of it in terms of the land in a city: Anyone can use the public parks for any purpose they wish, as long as that purpose is within the limits of the city's laws. Private land, in contrast, may only be used by its owners or by people given special permission by its owners. Information is the same. No one can successfully sue for copyright infringement on public domain information.

That's not to say you can't sell public domain information. If you go to the trouble of assembling census data for all the states onto a CD-ROM disc, you can sell it. Likewise, if you print *Hamlet* as a paperback book, you can sell that book. In these cases, though, the product you're selling isn't the information—it's available free of charge to anyone who wishes to compile it—it's the packaging. By putting the census data on CD-ROM or printing *Hamlet* in a readable typeface, you're adding value to the information.

How Does Information Enter the Public Domain?

There are several ways a piece of creative work can enter the public domain. Once it's in the public domain, a work cannot be copyrighted again.

- The most common way is expiration of copyright—the creator's rights to a creative work have been lost because of the passage of time. The rules on copyright terms have changed over the years, but the current rule in the United States is that a copyright expires 50 years after the creator's death. Expired copyrights explain why classical music is used so frequently in advertisements—advertisers need not pay royalties to the creator of a 200-year-old composition.
- Any information created by the U.S. government (such as census data) is automatically public domain, since the government cannot claim copyright on any of its creative products. Before you amble

over to the Pentagon and ask to see the public domain plans for the Seawolf submarine, though, remember that there are lots of other ways the government can protect its creative products.

- Certain creative products, such as brief slogans or words, cannot be copyrighted (though they may be trademarked; trademark law offers similar protection). In a neat example of this rule, General Motors had to use the word "Flxible" (without an e) to describe a line of buses because "flexible" is a common word.
- Copyright holders can abandon or forfeit their copyrights in a variety of legally technical ways.

Can I Use Information That Is Not in the Public Domain?

Yes, you can use copyrighted information in either of two ways: by asking and receiving permission from the copyright holder or by making "fair use" of the material.

Asking permission is straightforward. You go to the holder of a copyright and ask for the right to use the copyrighted material in a particular way. If you're granted permission, you can use the material in a particular way, and if permission is refused, you cannot use the material. It's a good idea to get this permission in writing, as a written document will stand up in court should the copyright holder later claim that permission was not given.

Fair use is a little more complex, but it also makes logical sense. The fair use clauses of copyright laws say that you can use small parts of copyrighted material for certain purposes. These purposes include, among others:

- Including quotes from a speech or presentation in a news article.
- Including quotes from a novel or nonfiction work in a review or critique.
- Reproducing copyrighted material, in small quantities, for instructional purposes.
- Parodying a copyrighted work.

The thing to remember about fair use is that you can't make money from it, and you can only use small portions of a work. Courts recognize that reproducing and sharing copyrighted work is part of the law's purpose.

How Has Information Technology Changed Copyright Law?

In brief, it hasn't. Aside from recognizing that computer programs and other electronic media can be copyrighted since they represent creative work, the ideas behind copyright law haven't changed much in the last 400 years. This is partly due to the inherent conservatism of courts (it took the United States Supreme Court 40 years to conclude that motion pictures are covered by the First Amendment), but it's also due to the totally new nature of many things on the Web. Movies were thought of as a new form of theater, and music recordings were considered a derivative of live concert performance, but there's nothing to which to compare the Web adequately. It will probably be some time before the courts sort out the issues of copyright facing the Web and the Internet. This section lists some of the questions courts will have to deal with as Web publication grows more popular.

What Constitutes a Web Publication?

Does copyright law cover only the HTML code used to create a Web page, or does it cover the way that code appears when interpreted by a browser? Are multimedia clips hyperlinked to a Web page part of that page, or are they separate entities? What about other Web pages, written and maintained by other people?

Who's the Author of a Web Publication?

Is the HTML programmer the sole creator of a Web publication? Or is the person who configures their browser to interpret the HTML code in a certain way an author too? Perhaps the people who developed HTML itself, and therefore made all other Web publications possible, should get some credit for every Web page ever created. If a program, such as a search engine, builds a Web page, is that program an author? Can it receive credit for what it created?

From Here

- This chapter examined the legal issues that govern (or soon will govern) Web publishing. The next chapter describes the technological trends that will change Web publishing in the near future.

Chapter 28

Standardization Issues

In the beginning, there was Standard Generalized Markup Language (SGML), a set of codes used to attach format descriptions to academic papers published on the Internet. When the Web came along, an SGML Document Type Description (DTD) was developed to describe HyperText Markup Language (HTML). The HTML DTDs (one exists for each of the several versions of HTML) describe the function of each HTML tag and give parsers—Web browsers—suggestions about what to do with text attached to each tag.

That's what the DTDs do—they give suggestions about formatting. Browsers can be configured by programmers or even their users to do many different things with text attached to particular tags. Most browsers have a setup dialog box of some sort in which users can specify how big various headers should be, what color text should be, and in what typeface different

types of text appear. This flexibility was cited as one of the big advantages of HTML in its early days. People could make their text extra large if they didn't see well, or could put body text in a sans serif font it that pleased them.

Now, though, as commercial enterprise gains a foothold on the Web, customization has come to be seen by some as more of a liability than an advantage. Commercial site publishers want their efforts to look the same to everyone, no matter what kind of equipment viewers use (just like television). If viewers have the ability to alter the appearance of sites at their will, commercial Web publishers have no way of knowing how their sites will appear—and are afraid they'll look bad.

And so a debate rages about the extent to which the interpretation of HTML should be standardized, if at all. This chapter explains both sides of the debate and leaves it to you to determine which side's points appeal to you the most.

For the Time-Challenged

- There are two camps on the subject of standardizing the way HTML code is interpreted by browsers: the faction that says the interpretation should be standardized, and the faction that says it should not.
- Those who favor standardization say standardization would guarantee an HTML developer the ability to know how his or her code would appear when finally interpreted for the use of a viewer. They also say commercial applications of the Web, in which image is key, demand a standardization of HTML to handle such things as corporate logos and slogans.
- Those who oppose standardization of HTML interpretation say that standardization is contrary to the spirit of the Web—that HTML was designed to give flexibility to producers and consumers of information alike, and that standardizing interpretation makes the Web too much like television or radio. They also say that people will be shut out from the Web community if they can't see the small typefaces publishers using HTML with standard interpretations are sure to use.

The Case for Standardization

Arguments in favor of standardization are put forward mainly by business people who want their site to appear the same to everyone who views it. Among publishers of Web newspapers and magazines, it's primarily those who came to Web publishing after a career in traditional paper-based publishing that want to make HTML into a new desktop publishing tool with strict typographic controls. Their arguments are few but potent.

Better Typographic Control

The appeal of desktop publishing programs like PageMaker and Quark Xpress is that they allow you to place text and graphics in a precise position on a page. They allow you to decide everything from how big a document's margins are to how close to a graphic words and numbers approach. They offer extensive support for color matching and allow you to manipulate the appearance of graphics in dozens of ways.

HTML offers little typographical control. To format a paragraph as body text, you tag it with the <P> tag, instead of defining it as 12-point Times New Roman with 14 points of leading, a 10-pica initial indent, and ragged-right formatting, as you would in a desktop publishing program. The way a particular browser interprets a particular tag is not known to the person coding a document in HTML—and it's possible that a document that looks great on one browser will look terrible on another.

People have devised tricks to circumvent the typographic limitations of HTML. One of the more creative solutions is to use lots of single-pixel transparent GIF files to space text and graphic elements properly—but solutions like these are far from being standard HTML. An HTML standard that is more compatible with traditional ideas of typography and page design is favored by those who want their documents to appear the same to everyone.

Documents Look Good on All Browsers

The truth is, few people actually go into their browsers' configuration dialog box and adjust the way their browsers interpret HTML tags. They assume that the people at the software development house that published the browser knew what they were doing, and unless they have a special need, they don't alter the factory settings (people with special needs are one

of the main arguments against standardizing HTML interpretation—see below). Still, several different software houses publish Web browsers, and they all interpret tags slightly differently. Hyperlinks, for example, are green in NCSA Mosaic and blue in Netscape Navigator.

Standardizing the way HTML is interpreted would eliminate the discrepancies in document appearance among different browsers. It would absolve Web publishers of the need to test their publications on several browsers.

Consistent Corporate Image

It's hard to market a corporation and its products nowadays without a consistent corporate image—and in our society, corporate image rests on visual cues. What would you think if you saw a New York Times whose flag (the words "The New York Times" on the front page) was in Helvetica Light? What if you saw a can of Coca-Cola that was blue, with black Courier lettering on it? You'd probably decide the products were fakes—cheap, illegal Malaysian knockoffs or something. You wouldn't buy them.

That's the problem with putting material that's central to corporate image on the Web. Depending on how viewers have their browsers configured, they can make HTML material appear however they wish. There's no room for corporate consistency in standard HTML. Of course, corporate HTML developers can use graphics or other formatting tricks to get their material to look right all the time, but then they're meddling with issues of reducing flexibility and wasting bandwidth.

The Case Against Standardization

Others, who seem to be in the minority on the Web now, argue that markup languages' flexibility is their appeal. To try to give HTML a standard appearance in every browser, the opponents of appearance standardization say, is to defeat the main point of HTML. Standardization of HTML interpretation makes the Web just another variation on newspapers and television, in which media producers decide how things appear to consumers and the consumers themselves have no real input.

Contrary to Spirit of Markup Language

Markup languages, HTML purists say, are not supposed to be about consistent appearance. They're supposed to be about transmitting basic formatting information from a document creator to a document consumer as efficiently as possible. Creativity and flexibility are due to the consumer of the document as much as they're due to its producer, and the ability to modify the appearance of HTML documents makes the consumer feel more involved in the information-exchange process.

Taking the ability to adjust the appearance of HTML documents away from the consumer is to force them into a passive absorption of data that is contrary to the spirit of the Web. The Web, supporters of this point say, is supposed to promote *exchange*, not just *distribution*, of information.

Less Flexibility for Users

Opponents of the standardization of the way HTML code is interpreted also say that standardizing appearance cuts out people who *need* their information to appear a certain way. Under traditional HTML rules, people who have poor eyesight or who have trouble distinguishing dark text against a dark background can adjust the display of text to their liking. Standardized HTML interpretation puts the power with the producers of information, who, as demonstrated by television and newspapers, will present information in a way that appeals to most, but not all, people. Those with special needs, who don't have to be ignored by the Web (since it's easy to customize Web information, unlike printed or televised information), should not be left out because of a desire for corporate consistency and appearance standardization.

From Here

- This is the last chapter in *Publish it on the Web!* You're well prepared to go to your computer and begin producing Web documents that include formatted text, graphics, sound, and video. You also have a good understanding of the intricacies of HTML code, the coming trends in Web design, and the issues that face Web publishers. If you have questions about particular HTML tags, you can refer to Appendix A, and don't forget to use the icons, sounds, and other elements included on the enclosed CD-ROM disc. Happy publishing!

Part VI

Appendices

Appendix

The Ultimate HTML Cheat Sheet

For reference while coding HTML, here's a list of the most commonly used tags. Look here when you don't remember exactly how a tag is constructed. You'll also find icons that enable you to differentiate between HTML 3.0 tags and the Netscape extensions.

Defining the Document: The Head

Tag	Usage or Example	Notes
Document Type	<!DOCTYPE HTML PUBLIC "-//IETF//DTD HTML 2.0//EN">	
3 Document Type	<!DOCTYPE HTML PUBLIC "-//W3O//DTD W3 HTML 3.0//EN">	

Tag	Usage or Example	Notes
HTML	<HTML>. . .</HTML>	Place these tags at the beginning and end of your document.
Head	<HEAD>. . .</HEAD>	These tags set up the HEAD element.
Title	<TITLE>. . .</TITLE>	Remember that the title appears on the title bar, not in the document. Appears within the HEAD element.
Base URL	<BASE HREF="*URL*">	Gives the current document's URL, which might be useful if somebody downloads or prints the document and wouldn't otherwise know where it came from.

Defining the Document: BODY Tags

Tag	Usage or Example	Notes
Body	<BODY>. . .</BODY>	Adding attributes to this tag can add visual appeal to your document.
Background Color	<BODY BGCOLOR="*color code*">	See Appendix C for a list of color codes.
Background Graphic	<BODY BACKGROUND="*URL*">	You'll find lots of background textures on the CD-ROM disc packaged with this book.
N Text Color	<BODY TEXT="*color code*">	See Appendix C for a list of color codes.
N Link Color	<BODY LINK="*color code*">	See Appendix C for a list of color codes.
N Visited Link	<BODY VLINK="*color code*">	See Appendix C for a list of color codes.
N Active Link	<BODY ALINK="*color code*">	See Appendix C for a list of color codes.
N Base Font Size	<BASEFONT SIZE=*number*>	Type a number from 1 to 7; the default base font size is 3.

Line and Paragraph Breaks

	Tag	Usage or Example	Notes
	Paragraph	<P>	This tag has the same effect as pressing Enter in a word processing program; you get a blank line between two paragraphs.
3	Paragraph	<P>. . .</P>	This is the HTML 3.0 version of the <P> tag.
	Line Break	 	This tag doesn't leave a blank line.
	Preformatted	<PRE>. . .</PRE>	Preserves line breaks and spacing.
N	No Break	<NOBR>	Prevents a line break.
N	Word Break	<WBR>	Shows where to break a word, should the browser need to break a lengthy word or expression.
N	Clear Text Wrap	<BR CLEAR=*option*>	You can clear text wrapping LEFT, RIGHT, or ALL.

Borders

	Tag	Usage or Example	Notes
	Horizontal Rule	<HR>	Adds a horizontal rule. With most browsers, the rule has a three-dimensional look.
N	Alignment	<HR ALIGN=*alignment*>	You can align the rule LEFT, RIGHT, or CENTER.
N	Thickness	<HR SIZE=*pixels*>	Supply a number in pixels.
N	Width	<HR WIDTH=*pixels or percent*>	Supply a number in pixels or type a percentage of page width.
N	Solid Line	<HR NOSHADE>	This option omits the 3-D look.

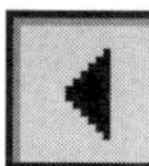

Headings

Tag	Usage or Example	Notes
Heading	<H*number*>. . .</H*number*>	Type a number from 1 to 6.
3 Align Heading	<H*number* ALIGN=*alignment*> </H*number*>	Type a number from 1 to 6 to set up the heading code. Choose one of the following alignments: LEFT, CENTER, or RIGHT.

Emphases and Fonts

Tag	Usage or Example	Notes
Bold	<B>. . .</B>	
Strong	<STRONG>. . .</STRONG>	Usually displayed as bold.
Italic	<I>. . .</I>	
Citation	<CITE>. . .</CITE>	Usually displayed in italics.
Emphasis	<EM>. . .</EM>	Usually displayed as italic.
Underline	<U>. . .</U>	This isn't widely implemented because hyperlinks are underlined.
Strikeout	<S>. . .</S>	Not widely implemented.
Typewriter	<TT>. . .</TT>	Displayed in a monospace font.
Code	<CODE>. . .</CODE>	For computer program listings. Displayed in a monospace font. Not widely implemented; use <TT> instead.
Sample Output	<SAMP>. . .</SAMP>	Not widely implemented. Use <TT> instead.

	Tag	Usage or Example	Notes
	Keyboard Input	<KBD>. . .</KBD>	Displayed in a monospace font. Not widely implemented; use <TT> instead.
N	Blink	<BLINK>. . .</BLINK>	Use sparingly—or avoid altogether.
N	Font Size	<FONT SIZE=*number*></FONT>	Type a number from 1 to 7 (the default font size is 3).
N	Change Font Size	<FONT SIZE=+ *number or – number*></FONT>	Adds or subtracts a number (from 1 to 7) from the current base font size (default is 3).

Building Your Document

	Tag	Usage or Example	Notes
	Author's Address	<ADDRESS>. . .</ADDRESS>	Most browsers display this text in italics
	Block Quote	<BLOCKQUOTE>. . .</BLOCKQUOTE>	Most browsers indent the text from the left.
3	Align Text	<P ALIGN=*alignment*>. . .</P>	Choose LEFT, CENTER, or RIGHT.
N	Center	<CENTER>. . .</CENTER>	This works with in-line images as well as text, but might not be supported by all browsers.
	Unordered List	<UL>. . .</UL>	Put <LI> before each item in the list.
N	Bullet Type	<UL TYPE=*DISC|CIRCLE|SQUARE*>	Choose from DISC, CIRCLE, or SQUARE
	Ordered List	<OL>. . .</OL>	Use <LI> before each list item.

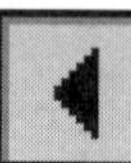

Tag	Usage or Example	Notes
Outline Type	<OL TYPE=*numbering scheme*>	Choose from the following outline numbering schemes for the whole list: A,a; I,i; 1.
Item Type	<LI TYPE=*numbering scheme*>	Choose from the folowing outline numbering schemes for the current item only: A,a; I,i; 1.
Starting Value	<OL VALUE=*number*>	Type a starting value for the list.
Item Value	<LI VALUE=*number*>	Type a value for this and subsequent lines.
Definition List	<DL>. . .</DL>	Use <DT> for terms and <DD> for definition.
Definition Term	<DT>. . .</DT>	Use within a definition list (<DL>).
Definition Text	<DD>. . .</DD>	Use within a definition list (<DL>).
Menu List	<MENU>. . .</MENU>	Use <LI> for each item in the menu.
Directory List	<DIR>. . .</DIR>	Use <LI> for each item in the menu.

Hyperlinks

Tag	Usage or Example	Notes
External Link	<A HREF="*URL*">*text to appear* </A>	Between the tags, type the text you want to appear onscreen.
Define Target	<A NAME="*name*">	Define a name to serve as a target for internal hyperlinks.

Tag	Usage or Example	Notes
Internal Link	<A HREF="#*name*">*text to appear*</A>	Link to an internal target.
External Link with Target	<A HREF="*URL#name*"> *text to appear*</A>	Be sure to type a pound sign (#) between the URL and the target name.

In-line Images

Tag	Usage or Example	Notes
Insert Image	<IMG SRC="*URL*">	Use a relative or absolute URL.
Alternate	<IMG SRC="*URL*" ALT="*text to display*">	Use for the benefit of people who have text-only browsers.
Image Map	<IMG SRC="*URL*" ISMAP>	Requires a CGI script for processing.
Image Alignment	<IMG SRC="*URL*" ALIGN=*alignment* >	Choose from TOP, BOTTOM, or MIDDLE.
N Image Alignment	<IMG SRC="*URL*" ALIGN=*alignment* >	Choose from LEFT, RIGHT, TEXTTOP, ABSMIDDLE, BASELINE, or ABSBOTTOM.
3 Image Size	<IMG SRC="*URL*" WIDTH="*number*" HEIGHT="*number*">	Type a number in pixels.
N Border	<IMG SRC="*URL*" BORDER=*number*>	Type a number in pixels. To hide the border, type 0 (zero).
N Space around Image	<IMG SRC="*URL*" HSPACE=*number* VSPACE=*number*>	Type a number in pixels.
N Start with Low Res.	<IMG SRC="*URL*" LOWSRC="*URL*">	Displays a low-resolution version of the image until the rest of the document is finished loading; then displays the high-resolution version.

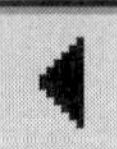

Tables

	Tag	Usage or Example	Notes
3	Create Table	<TABLE>. . .</TABLE>	Create the table rows with <TR>.
3	Table Border	<TABLE BORDER>. . .</TABLE>	To remove the border, take out the BORDER attribute.
N	Table Border	<TABLE BORDER=*number*> . . .</TABLE>	Type a border width in pixels.
N	Cell Spacing	<TABLE CELLSPACING=*number*>	Type a number in pixels.
N	Cell Padding	<TABLE CELLPADDING=*number*>	Type a number in pixels.
N	Width	<TABLE WIDTH=*number or percent*>	Type a number in pixels, or type a percentage width of the available window space.
3	Table Row	<TR>. . .</TR>	Use within <TABLE> tags to set up table rows.
3	Horizontal Alignment	<TR ALIGN=*alignment*>	Choose from LEFT, RIGHT, or CENTER.
3	Vertical Alignment	<TR VALIGN=*alignment*>	Choose from TOP, MIDDLE, or BOTTOM.
3	Table Header	<TH>. . .</TH>	Shown bold and centered in most browsers.
3	Header Horizontal Alignment	<TH ALIGN=*alignment*>	Choose from LEFT, RIGHT, or CENTER.
3	Header Vertical Alignment	<TH VALIGN=*alignment*>	Choose from TOP, MIDDLE, or BOTTOM.
3	Suppress Line Breaks	<TH NOWRAP>	No line breaks in header.
3	Span Columns	<TH COLSPAN=*number*>	Type the number of columns to span.
3	Span Rows	<TH ROWSPAN=*number*>	Type the number of rows to span.

	Tag	Usage or Example	Notes
N	Header Width	<TH WIDTH=*number or percent*>	Type the number in pixels or as a percentage of the available window width.
3	Table Cell	<TD>. . .</TD>	Use within <TR> tags.
3	Cell Horizontal Alignment	<TD ALIGN=*alignment*>	Choose from LEFT, RIGHT, or CENTER.
3	Cell Vertical Alignment	<TD VALIGN=*alignment*>	Choose from TOP, MIDDLE, or BOTTOM.
3	Suppress Line Breaks	<TD NOWRAP>	No line breaks in cell.
3	Span Columns	<TD COLSPAN=*number*>	Type the number of columns to span.
3	Span Rows	<TD ROWSPAN=*number*>	Type the number of rows to span
N	Cell Width	<TD WIDTH=*number or percent*>	Type the number in pixels or as a percentage of the available window width.
3	Table Caption	<CAPTION>. . .</CAPTION>	
3	Alignment	<CAPTION ALIGN=*position*>	Choose from TOP or BOTTOM.

Forms

Tag	Usage or Example	Notes
Create Form	<<FORM ACTION="*URL*" METHOD="*method*">. . . </FORM>	For method, choose GET or POST (POST is preferred for most servers).
Create Input Field	<INPUT TYPE="*type*" NAME="*name*">	Choose from TEXT, PASSWORD, CHECKBOX, RADIO, IMAGE, HIDDEN, SUBMIT, RESET. For name, type a name for the input field.

Tag	Usage or Example	Notes
Checked Radio Button	<INPUT TYPE="radio" CHECKED>	Shows the radio button with a check mark.
Checked Option	<INPUT TYPE="checkbox" CHECKED>	Shows the check box with a check mark.
Size of Text Box	<INPUT TYPE="text" SIZE=*number*>	Type a number in characters.
Max Length	<INPUT TYPE="text" MAXLENGTH=*number*>	Type a number in characters.
List Box	<SELECT NAME="*name*">. . . </SELECT>	Type a name for the list box.
Multiple Choice List	<SELECT MULTIPLE>	You can select more than one of the items in the list box.
Option on List	<OPTION>	Used with <SELECT>. . . </SELECT>.
Default Option	<OPTION SELECTED>	
Text Input Box	<TEXTAREA NAME="*name*" ROWS=*number* COLS=*number*>. . . </TEXTAREA>	Type a name, and type numbers in characters.

Appendix B

ISO Latin-1 Special Characters

Various Useful Symbols

To create this character:		Insert this code in your document:
&	Ampersand	&
<<	Angle quotation mark, left	«
>>	Angle quotation mark, right	»
¦	Broken vertical bar	&brkbar;
¢	Cent sign	¢
®	Circled R registered sign	®
©	Copyright sign	©
¤	Currency sign	¤

To create this character:		Insert this code in your document:
°	Degree sign	°
ª	Feminine ordinal indicator	ª
½	Fraction ½	½
¼	Fraction ¼	¼
¾	Fraction ¾	¾
>	Greater than sign	>
¡	Inverted exclamation mark	¡
<	Less than sign	<
º	Masculine ordinal indicator	º
µ	Micro sign	µ
·	Middle dot	·
¬	Negation sign	¬
	Nonbreaking space	
¶	Paragraph sign	¶
±	Plus-or-minus sign	±
£	Pound sign	£
"	Quotation mark	"
§	Section sign	§
-	Soft hyphen	
´	Spacing acute	´
¸	Spacing cedilla	¸
¨	Spacing dieresis	¨
¯	Spacing macron	&hibar;
^{1}	Superscript 1	¹
^{2}	Superscript 2	²
^{3}	Superscript 3	³
¥	Yen sign	¥

Foreign Language Characters

To create this character:		Insert this code in your document:
Á	Capital A, acute accent	Á
À	Capital A, grave accent	À
Â	Capital A, circumflex accent	Â

To create this character:		Insert this code in your document:
Ã	Capital A, tilde	Ã
Å	Capital A, ring	Å
Ä	Capital A, dieresis or umlaut mark	Ä
Æ	Capital AE dipthong	Æ
Ç	Capital C, cedilla	Ç
É	Capital E, acute accent	É
È	Capital E, grave accent	È
Ê	Capital E, circumflex accent	Ê
Ë	Capital E, dieresis or umlaut mark	Ë
Í	Capital I, acute accent	Í
Ì	Capital I, grave accent	Ì
Î	Capital I, circumflex accent	Î
Ï	Capital I, dieresis or umlaut mark	Ï
	Capital Eth, Icelandic	Ð
Ñ	Capital N, tilde	Ñ
Ó	Capital O, acute accent	Ó
Ò	Capital O, grave accent	Ò
Ô	Capital O, circumflex accent	Ô
Õ	Capital O, tilde	Õ
Ö	Capital O, dieresis or umlaut mark	Ö
Ø	Capital O, slash	Ø
Ú	Capital U, acute accent	Ú
Ù	Capital U, grave accent	Ù
Û	Capital U, circumflex accent	Û
Ü	Capital U, dieresis or umlaut mark	Ü
Y	Capital Y, acute accent	Ý
	Capital Thorn, Icelandic	Þ
ß	Small sharp s, German	ß
á	Small a, acute accent	á
à	Small a, grave accent	à
â	Small a, circumflex accent	â
ã	Small a, tilde	ã
å	Small a, ring	å
ä	Small a, dieresis or umlaut mark	ä

To create this character:		Insert this code in your document:
æ	Small ae dipthong	æ
ç	Small c, cedilla	ç
é	Small e, acute accent	é
è	Small e, grave accent	è
ê	Small e, circumflex accent	ê
ë	Small e, dieresis or umlaut mark	ë
í	Small i, acute accent	í
ì	Small i, grave accent	ì
î	Small i, circumflex accent	î
ï	Small i, dieresis or umlaut mark	ï
	Small eth, Icelandic	ð
ñ	Small n, tilde	ñ
ó	Small o, acute accent	ó
ò	Small o, grave accent	ò
ô	Small o, circumflex accent	ô
õ	Small o, tilde	õ
ö	Small o, dieresis or umlaut mark	ö
ø	Small o, slash	ø
ú	Small u, acute accent	ú
ù	Small u, grave accent	ù
û	Small u, circumflex accent	û
ü	Small u, dieresis or umlaut mark	ü
y	Small y, acute accent	ý
	Small thorn, Icelandic	þ
ÿ	Small y, dieresis or umlaut mark	ÿ

Appendix C

Color Codes for Netscape Backgrounds

Color	RGB Code	Color	RGB Code
Aquamarine	70DB93	Cadet Blue	5F9F9F
Baker's Chocolate	5C3317	Cool Copper	D98719
Black	000000	Copper	B87333
Blue	0000FF	Coral	FF7F00
Blue Violet	9F5F9F	Corn Flower Blue	42426F
Brass	B5A642	Cyan	00FFFF
Bright Gold	D9D919	Dark Brown	5C4033
Bronze	8C7853	Dark Green	2F4F2F
Bronze II	A67D3D	Dark Green Copper	4A766E
Brown	A62A2A	Dark Olive Green	4F4F2F

Color	RGB Code	Color	RGB Code
Dark Orchid	9932CD	Medium Sea Green	426F42
Dark Purple	871F78	Medium Slate Blue	7F00FF
Dark Slate Blue	6B238E	Medium Spring Green	7FFF00
Dark Slate Gray	2F4F4F	Medium Turquoise	70DBDB
Dark Tan	97694F	Medium Violet Red	DB7093
Dark Turquoise	7093DB	Medium Wood	A68064
Dark Wood	855E42	Midnight Blue	2F2F4F
Dim Gray	545454	Navy Blue	23238E
Dusty Rose	856363	Neon Blue	4D4DFF
Feldspar	D19275	Neon Pink	FF6EC7
Firebrick	8E2323	New Midnight Blue	00009C
Forest Green	238E23	New Tan	EBC79E
Gold	CD7F32	Old Gold	CFB53B
Goldenrod	DBDB70	Orange	FF7F00
Green	00FF00	Orange Red	FF2400
Green Copper	527F76	Orchid	DB70DB
Green Yellow	93DB70	Pale Green	8FBC8F
Gray	C0C0C0	Pink	BC8F8F
Hunter Green	215E21	Plum	EAADEA
Indian Red	4E2F2F	Quartz	D9D9F3
Khaki	9F9F5F	Red	FF0000
Light Blue	C0D9D9	Rich Blue	5959AB
Light Grey	A8A8A8	Salmon	6F4242
Light Steel Blue	8F8FBD	Scarlet	8C1717
Light Wood	E9C2A6	Sea Green	238E68
Lime Green	32CD32	Semi-Sweet Chocolate	6B4226
Magenta	FF00FF	Sienna	8E6B23
Mandarin Orange	E47833	Silver	E6E8FA
Maroon	8E236B	Sky Blue	3299CC
Medium Aquamarine	32CD99	Slate Blue	007FFF
Medium Blue	3232CD	Spicy Pink	FF1CAE
Medium Forest Green	6B8E23	Spring Green	00FF7F
Medium Goldenrod	EAEAAE	Steel Blue	236B8E
Medium Orchid	9370DB	Summer Sky	38B0DE

Color	RGB Code	Color	RGB Code
Tan	DB9370	Violet Red	CC3299
Thistle	D8BFD8	Wheat	D8D8BF
Turquoise	ADEAEA	White	FFFFFF
Very Dark Brown	5C4033	Yellow	FFFF00
Very Light Gray	CDCDCD	Yellow Green	99CC32
Violet	4F2F4F		

Index

A

B

D

E

F

G

H

I

J

K

L

M

N

O

P

Q

R

S

T

U

V

W

X

Y

Z

LIMITED WARRANTY AND DISCLAIMER OF LIABILITY

ACADEMIC PRESS, INC. ("AP") AND ANYONE ELSE WHO HAS BEEN INVOLVED IN THE CREATION OR PRODUCTION OF THE ACCOMPANYING CODE ("THE PRODUCT") CANNOT AND DO NOT WARRANT THE PERFORMANCE OR RESULTS THAT MAY BE OBTAINED BY USING THE PRODUCT. THE PRODUCT IS SOLD "AS IS" WITHOUT WARRANTY OF ANY KIND (EXCEPT AS HEREAFTER DESCRIBED), EITHER EXPRESSED OR IMPLIED, INCLUDING, BUT NOT LIMITED TO, ANY WARRANTY OF PERFORMANCE OR ANY IMPLIED WARRANTY OF MERCHANTABILITY OR FITNESS FOR ANY PARTICULAR PURPOSE. AP WARRANTS ONLY THAT THE MAGNETIC DISC(S) ON WHICH THE CODE IS RECORDED IS FREE FROM DEFECTS IN MATERIAL AND FAULTY WORKMANSHIP UNDER THE NORMAL USE AND SERVICE FOR A PERIOD OF NINETY (90) DAYS FROM THE DATE THE PRODUCT IS DELIVERED. THE PURCHASER'S SOLE AND EXCLUSIVE REMEDY IN THE EVENT OF A DEFECT IS EXPRESSLY LIMITED TO EITHER REPLACEMENT OF THE DISC(S) OR REFUND OF THE PURCHASE PRICE, AT AP'S SOLE DISCRETION.

IN NO EVENT, WHETHER AS A RESULT OF BREACH OF CONTRACT, WARRANTY OR TORT (INCLUDING NEGLIGENCE), WILL AP OR ANYONE WHO HAS BEEN INVOLVED IN THE CREATION OR PRODUCTION OF THE PRODUCT BE LIABLE TO PURCHASER FOR ANY DAMAGES, INCLUDING ANY LOST PROFITS, LOST SAVINGS OR OTHER INCIDENTAL OR CONSEQUENTIAL DAMAGES ARISING OUT OF THE USE OR INABILITY TO USE THE PRODUCT OR ANY MODIFICATIONS THEREOF, OR DUE TO THE CONTENTS OF THE CODE, EVEN IF AP HAS BEEN ADVISED OF THE POSSIBILITY OF SUCH DAMAGES, OR FOR ANY CLAIM BY ANY OTHER PARTY.

Any request for replacement of a defective CD-ROM disc must be postage prepaid and must be accompanied by the original defective disc, your mailing address and telephone number, and proof of date of purchase and purchase price. Send such requests, stating the nature of the problem, to Academic Press Customer Service, 6277 Sea Harbor Drive, Orlando, FL 32887, 1-800-321-5068. APP shall have no obligation to refund the purchase price or to replace a disc based on claims of defects in the nature or operation of the Product.

Some states do not allow limitation on how long an implied warranty lasts, nor exclusions or limitations of incidental or consequential damage, so the above limitations and exclusions may not apply to you. This Warranty gives you specific legal rights, and you may also have other rights which vary from jurisdiction to jurisdiction.

THE RE-EXPORT OF UNITED STATES ORIGIN SOFTWARE IS SUBJECT TO THE UNITED STATES LAWS UNDER THE EXPORT ADMINISTRATION ACT OF 1969 AS AMENDED. ANY FURTHER SALE OF THE PRODUCT SHALL BE IN COMPLIANCE WITH THE UNITED STATES DEPARTMENT OF COMMERCE ADMINISTRATION REGULATIONS. COMPLIANCE WITH SUCH REGULATIONS IS YOUR RESPONSIBILITY AND NOT THE RESPONSIBILITY OF AP.

About the CD-ROM

- Includes more than 1000 items of graphical art that you can use in your Web presentations, including rules, icons, clip art, backgrounds, and buttons.

- More than 200 sounds that you can use to make your Web presentations come alive, including beeps, buzzes, witticisms, and audio fluff.

- HTML Editor, an editor that can help you create winning Web presentations in short order.

System Requirements

Macintosh or Power Macintosh with a minimum of 4 MB RAM (8 MB recommended)